Pathways to Heaven

Pathways to Heaven

Contesting Mainline and Fundamentalist
Christianity in Papua New Guinea

Holger Jebens

Berghahn Books
New York • Oxford

First published in 2005 by

Berghahn Books

www.berghahnbooks.com

© 2005 Holger Jebens

Library of Congress Cataloging-in-Publication Data

A catalogue record for this book
is available from the Library of Congress.

British Library Cataloguing in Publication Data

A catalogue record for this book
is available from the British Library.

Printed in the United States on acid-free paper

ISBN 1–84545–005–1 (hardback)
ISBN 1-84545-334-4 (paperback)

Es geht auch anders, doch so geht es auch.

Bertolt Brecht, *Die Zuhälterballade*

Contents

List of Maps and Figures

Maps

Figures

Preface

I

Like most anthropological publications, this book attempts to bridge gaps which are simultaneously cultural, spatial and temporal. From December 1990 to October 1991, I carried out fieldwork in Pairundu, a remote village in the Southern Highlands Province of Papua New Guinea (PNG), documenting the ritual and everyday lives of both Catholic and Seventh-day Adventist villagers. On the basis of this material, I analyse how the adherents of both denominations have been and are actively appropriating and creatively refashioning their particular branches of Christianity. In so doing, I also examine the reasons for the numerical growth and increasing appeal of Seventh-day Adventism, that is, of a particularly 'successful' local form of Christian fundamentalism as a global phenomenon.

Yet in this case the gaps to be bridged do perhaps have an additional dimension, since *Pathways to Heaven* is a translation of an ethnography that was first published in German in 1995. Certainly this ethnography did not receive an overwhelming response: in fact, with the exception of two reviews (Kolig 1997, Reithofer 1997), I have yet to come across any reference to it, reminding me of what, as a graduate student, I had once heard an American guest professor proclaiming: 'If someone publishes something in German, we suppose that he doesn't want it to be noticed'. As a consequence, I was quite surprised when, having been invited to deliver a paper at the University of Western Ontario in January 2002, I saw a copy of the book in Dan Jorgensen's office, although I knew that Dan speaks German fluently. My surprise grew still further when he commented on my reaction by saying that he had actually read it and that, in his view, it should be translated and published in English.

Feeling not only flattered but also prompted at least to have another look at the German text, I was in for an experience that others have also described: what I had written several years earlier, before moving on to do fieldwork in West New Britain (PNG) and expanding my research interests (Jebens 2000, 2003a, 2003b), now looked strangely unfamiliar. It was as if, to paraphrase Karl-Heinz Kohl (1986: 7), the older your own book gets, the more it begins to develop a life of its own. Lorenz Löffler has put it in stronger terms: 'it had already happened to me years ago that

I read, first with interest, then with increasing anger... an old paper, just to wonder in the end, "Who wrote this crap?", only to close the book and to realise with dismay that was none other than myself' (Kapfer et al. 1998: 11, translation H.J.). I hasten to add, however, that my experience was perhaps a bit more ambivalent, because, apart from alienation, I also noted – not without surprise, but with a certain delight – that I had already begun to refer there to some of the issues that had come to interest me since, such as how cultural images of Self and Other are constructed and put to use, particularly in the context of so-called cargo cults (Jebens and Kohl 1999, Jebens 2002, 2004a, 2004b).

II

My experience of alienation and delight showed that I was, in a sense, no longer the same person as the author of the German text. Moreover, the scholarly background against which it had been written had changed as well. While John Barker, almost a decade after deploring the 'anthropological ignorance of Melanesian Christianity' (1992: 145), has recently repeated the view that 'it is still rare for Pacific scholars to view Christianity as a viable subject for study in its own right' (2001: 106), more articles have been published on this topic in the last few years than prior to 1995. Several collections examine local forms of millenarianism (Kocher Schmid 1999, Stewart and Strathern 1997, 2000b) that were particularly prevalent before the beginning of the new century as, in the words of Pamela Stewart and Andrew Strathern (2000a: 4), 'a unique historical moment in which to examine the impact of Christian fundamentalist thinking, as well as other parameters of modernity, on New Guinea communities'. Millenarianism is also one of the elements that Pentecostal and charismatic Christianity, the focus of another collection (Robbins et al. 2001), have in common with Seventh-day Adventism, as is 'an emphasis on self-control', 'support for certain limited forms of gender equality in the religious sphere' and a 'very firm and explicit rejection of indigenous religious traditions' (Robbins 2001a: 8). At the same time, Pentecostal-style, spirit-filled services, practiced in Pairundu by Catholic villagers as part of a charismatic movement in the late 1980s, are strongly opposed by Adventists.

The increasing attention being given to Melanesian Christianity, or at least to some of its aspects, is also reflected in the fact that the literature on this topic has itself become the subject of recent overviews by Barker (1999) and Bronwen Douglas (2001). Barker suggests several questions for future research and advocates 'an ethnographically-grounded approach' (1999: 2). Douglas differentiates between 'converts' and 'cleanskins', including in the first category 'distinguished practitioners' (2001: 619) who only started to write about Pentecostal and charismatic Christianity after encountering it 'on return visits to the field', whereas previously they had published the results of their original fieldwork 'in societies explicitly or tacitly represented as more or less traditional (though not ahistoric)' (2001: 624). By contrast, for Douglas's generally younger '"cleanskin" anthropologists... millennial, charismatic, or pentecostal Christianity has been a normal condition of ethnographic fieldwork' (2001: 626) from the start. This also applies, among others, to Richard Eves, who has examined apocalyptic ideas of New Ireland Methodists in relation to globalisation (2000) and interrelated ideas of money and the nation (2003), claiming that, as people attempt to reconcile local and global knowledge (2000: 74), 'in a two-way process, global events become meaningful locally and local events are globalised' (Eves 2000: 75, cf. Eves 2003).

Douglas's 'major example' (2001: 620) of her category of 'cleanskins' is Joel Robbins. With impressive industry (1995, 1997a, 1997b, 1998a, 1998b, 1998c, 2001a, 2001b, 2001c, 2001d, 2002, 2004a, 2004b), Robbins has analysed the indigenous Christianity of the Urapmin, members of the Min group of cultures (Sandaun Province, PNG), with whom he worked between 1991 and 1993. According to Robbins, the Urapmin live 'between two cultures' (2004a: 327), that is, between their traditional and Christian morality as two distinct, yet coexisting 'cultural logics' (2004a: xxvi). This, of course, results in contradictions which the Urapmin attempt to negotiate by means of their Christian ritual life, but which, in Robbins's view, ultimately cause the Urapmin to suffer and to them 'becoming sinners', as the title of his dissertation (1998a), its published revision (2004a) and one of his articles (1998b) has it. Generally Robbins assumes that the cultural content of Christianity, or of modernity for that matter, is being adopted on Christianity's or modernity's own terms and can therefore unfold a dynamics of change. In his interpretation of a Urapmin charismatic or revival movement, 'Christian meanings... themselves, rather than ones drawn from traditional culture, begin to provide the motive for conversion' (2004a: 115, cf. 1998a: 588).

By emphasising the influence of Christianity on traditional religion, or of modernity on tradition, Robbins seems to me to be writing against the idea that, in having turned Christianity or modernity into something completely their own, the Urapmin may only be Christian or modern 'on the surface'. Particularly in his dissertation, this appears to serve the aim of legitimising Melanesian Christianity as a proper subject of anthropological research. Regardless of whether one considers such legitimation necessary or that the Urapmin require defending, Robbins's concern to take indigenous ideas and practices seriously has, in my view, deservedly been praised, the more so since his description of them proves to be grounded in solid ethnography (cf. Douglas 2001: 628, Jorgensen 2001: 635). Indeed, it is precisely by taking indigenous ideas and practices seriously, as well as by stating a simultaneity of traditional and Christian morality, that Robbins refutes not only any allegation of 'indigenous superficiality', but also the opposite yet equally obsolete claim that Christianity 'spells the dissolution of everything indigenous' (Jorgensen 2001: 635). Thus Douglas's 'major example' of 'cleanskin' anthropologists ultimately tends to go beyond what Barker (1992: 153) has called 'the conventional opposition between Melanesian religion and Christianity... that finds its basis in essentialist distinctions between Them and Us'.

III

The increasing attention given to Melanesian Christianity in the last few years might create the impression that the German edition of *Pathways to Heaven* anticipated subsequent developments (cf. also Jebens 1997). I do believe, however, that, as an ethnography of Catholic and Adventist forms of Christianity and an examination of the latter's 'success', the book can claim to be more than a mere precursor of what was to come.

While, as Robbins states, 'full length monographs focused directly on Christianity and culture in Melanesia are rare' (2004a: 34, cf. 1998b: 4, Barker 2001: 632), the articles published so far largely seem to be preoccupied by indigenous variations of Christian fundamentalism. Douglas speaks of a fascination with Pentecostal and charismatic Christianity, which, in her view, is not unexpected, given 'anthropology's residual (defining) attraction to the exotic', but which may also lead to a kind of blind spot, namely that 'most anthropologists have been – and some still are – bored by or indifferent to mission and even mainline Melanesian Christianity' (2001: 630). Moreover, despite the fact that the characteristic situation in many parts of Melanesia in general or Papua New Guinea in particular is now one of different denominations competing with each other within the same local setting, anthropological assessments of such denominational pluralism are still the exception (cf. Westermark 1998, Goddard and Van Heekeren 2003).

In my view, however, it is precisely the competition between mainline and fundamentalist formations that has the potential to take us further in transcending conventional oppositions and essentialist distinctions. The example of the Catholics and Seventh-day Adventists in Pairundu shows that if men and women – members of different generations as well as Big Men and 'ordinary' men – have been and are struggling for influence and power, they cannot be expected to stop doing this before they adopt some form of Christianity. The aim of legitimising Melanesian Christianity as a proper object of anthropological research should not tempt us to neglect the internal dynamics of religious affiliation, that is, the differences between what the adherents of each denomination say – whether on the formal and 'official' level or the informal and 'unofficial' level – and what they do in the context of their ritual and everyday lives. To respect indigenous statements – for example, about the impending apocalypse, Christian identity or, for that matter, one's own state of sinfulness – and to take them seriously does not necessarily mean that they have to be accepted at their face value.

The example of Catholics and Seventh-days Adventists in Pairundu also shows that inter- and intra-denominational conflicts often become arenas in which people struggle with each other by using 'tradition' and 'Christianity' as resources or rhetorical figures. While the resulting constructions of 'tradition' may be shaped by Christianity, the reverse is also true, and constructions of 'Christianity' may be shaped by tradition. Thus it is perfectly legitimate to see modernity influencing tradition or Christianity influencing Melanesian religion, though here too the reverse is also true: tradition influences modernity, Melanesian religion influences Christianity, to the point where, on the local level, the latter 'has become absorbed into the village's interpretation of its own tradition and is a part of its contemporary identity' (Goddard and Van Heekeren 2003: 146). On the national level, Christianity can be 'installed... as a traditionalized state religion' (Douglas 2001: 618, cf. Barker 1999: 24, Jorgensen 2001: 635) or, as in West Papua, it may become 'a key vehicle for the expression of Papuan identity and indigenous spirituality in opposition to the Indonesian state and Islam' (Douglas 2001: 621, cf. Jorgensen 2001: 635, Hayward 2003). I would therefore argue that the relationship between tradition and modernity in general, like that between Melanesian religion and Christianity in particular, can best be understood as a field of *mutual* influences, not at least because this image increasingly demonstrates that such oppositions and distinctions are artificial.

The recent burgeoning of anthropological articles on millenarian, Pentecostal and charismatic forms of Christianity in Melanesia reflects not only a change in ethnographic awareness, but also the fact that, as such forms continue to expand numerically, they are becoming more and more relevant to Melanesians themselves, regardless of their denominational affiliation (Barker 2001: 632, Douglas 2001: 630). This process proves to be full of ironies: the most anti-modern churches 'seek expressions of identity that transcend culture and place' (Barker 2001: 107). In Pairundu, although the Seventh-day Adventists adopt a decidedly anti-traditional stance, it is precisely their ability to build on pre-existing structures and experiences that helps to endow them with subjective credibility. However, statements about millenarian, Pentecostal and charismatic forms of Christianity becoming more and more relevant, could also be made with reference to Africa, Asia or Latin America. Indeed, the increasing importance of Christian fundamentalism as a global phenomenon has recently led Philip Jenkins (2002: 53) to predict that the resulting fierce and often violent conflicts 'will leave a mark deeper than Islam's on the century ahead'.

The regional, national and international dimensions of Christianity may be hard to see 'from the vantage point of rural villages' (Barker 2001: 632), but, though it would undoubtedly be worth while, any analysis of these dimensions will require detailed ethnographic case studies of the various forms that global Christianity may assume in different local settings. In this sense, *Pathways to Heaven*, while speaking, as it where, from the past, is being offered here with the hope that it may contribute to research in the future.

H.J.

Frankfurt/M., February 2004

Acknowledgements

This publication would not have been possible without the initial impetus and encouragement provided by Dan Jorgensen. I also thank Joel Robbins for fruitful discussions along the way, Robert Parkin for his invaluable help in translating the German manuscript, and Karl-Heinz Kohl for facilitating contact with the publisher, Monika Berghahn. In my acknowledgements in the German edition of *Pathways to Heaven*, I concluded by thanking the inhabitants of Pairundu and by predicting that my gratitude would not soon end. Over the years, this prediction has proved true in more ways that I could have imagined at the time.

References

Barker, J. 1992, 'Christianity in Western Melanesian Ethnography', in *History and Tradition in Melanesian Anthropology*, ed. J. Carrier (Studies in Melanesian Anthropology 10), Berkeley, 144–73.

—— 1999, '"Long God yumi stanap": Repositioning the Anthropology of Oceanic Christianity', MS.

—— 2001, 'Afterword', in Charismatic and Pentecostal Christianity in Oceania, eds J. Robbins, P.J. Stewart and A. Strathern, *Journal of Ritual Studies* 15(2): 105–8.

Douglas, B. 2001, 'From Invisible Christians to Gothic Theatre: the Romance of the Millennial in Melanesian Anthropology', *Current Anthropology* 42(5): 615–30.

Eves, R. 2000, 'Waiting for the Day: Globalization and Apocalypticism in Central New Ireland, Papua New Guinea', *Oceania* 71(2): 73–91.

—— 2003, 'Money, Mayhem and the Beast: Narratives of the World's End from New Ireland (Papua New Guinea)', *Journal of the Royal Anthropological Institute (N.S.)* 9: 527–47.

Goddard, M. and D. Van Heekeren 2003, 'United and Divided: Christianity, Tradition and Identity in Two South Coast Papua New Guinea Villages', *The Australian Journal of Anthropology* 14(2): 144–59.

Hayward, D. 2003, 'Identity Formation and Christianity among the Mulia Dani in Papua, Indonesia', MS.

Jebens, H. 1995, *Wege zum Himmel. Katholiken, Siebenten-Tags-Adventisten und der Einfluß der traditionellen Religion in Pairudu, Southern Highlands Province, Papua New Guinea* (Mundus Reihe Ethnologie 86), Bonn.

—— 1997, 'Catholics, Seventh Day Adventists and the Impact of Tradition in Pairundu (Southern Highlands Province, Papua New Guinea', in *Cultural Dynamics of Religious Change in Oceania*, eds T. Otto and A. Borsboom, Leiden, 33–43.

—— 2000, 'Signs of the Second Coming: on Eschatological Expectation and Disappointment in Highland and Seaboard Papua New Guinea', *Ethnohistory* 47(1): 171–204.

—— 2002, 'Trickery or Secrecy? On Andrew Lattas' Interpretation of "Bush Kaliai Cargo Cults"', *Anthropos* 97: 181–99.

—— 2003a, 'Starting with the Law of the *tumbuan*: Masked Dances in West New Britain (Papua New Guinea) as an Appropriation of One's Own Cultural Self', *Anthropos* 98: 115–26.

—— 2003b, ' Zur Dialektik von Selbst- und Fremdwahrnehmung in West New Britain (Papua-Neuguinea)', *Mitteilungen der Berliner Gesellschaft für Anthropologie, Ethnologie und Urgeschichte* 24 (forthcoming).

—— 2004a, 'Talking about Cargo Cults in Koimumu (West New Britain Province, Papua New Guinea), in *Cargo, Cult, and Culture Critique*, ed. Holger Jebens, Honolulu, 157–69.

—— ed. 2004b, *Cargo, Cult, and Culture Critique*, Honolulu.

—— and K.-H. Kohl 1999, 'Konstruktionen von "Cargo". Zur Dialektik von Fremd- und Selbstwahrnehmung in der Interpretation melanesischer Kultbewegungen', *Anthropos* 94: 3–20.

Jenkins, P. 2002, 'The Next Christianity', *The Atlantic Monthly* 290(3): 53–68.

Jorgensen, D. 2001 [Comment on Douglas], *Current Anthropology* 42(5): 635.

Kapfer, Reinhard, Marie-José van de Loo, Werner Petermann and Margarete Reinhart 1998, 'Vorwort der Herausgeber', in *Wegmarken. Eine Bibliothek der ethnologischen Imagination*, eds Kapfer, Reinhard, Marie-José van de Loo, Werner Petermann and Margarete Reinhart, Wuppertal, 9–12.

Kocher Schmid, C. ed. 1999, *Expecting the Day of Wrath: Versions of the Millennium in Papua New Guinea* (NRI Monographs 36), Boroko.

Kohl, K.-H. 1986, *Exotik als Beruf: Erfahrung und Trauma der Ethnographie*, Frankfurt/Main (orig. 1979).

Kolig, E. 1997, Book Review, 'Jebens, H., Wege zum Himmel, Bonn 1995', *Oceania* 67(3): 262–3.

Reithofer, H. 1997, Book Review, 'Jebens, H., Wege zum Himmel, Bonn 1995', *Anthropos* 92: 614–16.

Robbins, J. 1995, 'Dispossessing the Spirits: Christian Transformations of Desire and Ecology among the Urapmin of Papua New Guinea', *Ethnology* 34(4): 211–24.

—— 1997a, '666, or Why is the Millennium on the Skin? Morality, the State and the Epistemology of Apocalypticism among the Urapmin of Papua New Guinea', in *Millennial Markers in the Pacific*, eds P.J. Stewart and A. Strathern, Townsville, 35–58.

—— 1997b, '"When Do You Think the World Will End?" Globalization, Apocalypticism, and the Moral Perils of Fieldwork in "Last New Guinea"', *Anthropology and Humanism* 22(1): 6–30.

—— 1998a, 'Becoming Sinners: Christian Transformations of Morality and Culture in a Papua New Guinea Society' (Ph.D. diss., University of Virginia).

—— 1998b, 'Becoming Sinners: Christianity and Desire among the Urapmin of Papua New Guinea', *Ethnology* 37(4): 299–316.

————— 1998c, 'On Reading "World News": Apocalyptic Narrative, Negative Nationalism and Transnational Christianity in a Papua New Guinea Society', *Social Analysis* 14(2): 103–30.

————— 2001a, 'Introduction: Global Religions, Pacific Islands Transformations', in Charismatic and Pentecostal Christianity in Oceania, eds J. Robbins, P.J. Stewart and A. Strathern, *Journal of Ritual Studies* 15(2): 7–12.

————— 2001b, 'God is Nothing but Talk: Modernity, Language, and Prayer in a Papua New Guinea Society', *American Anthropologist* 103(4): 901–12.

————— 2001c, 'Secrecy and the Sense of an Ending: Narrative, Time, and Everyday Millenarianism in Papua New Guinea and in Christian Fundamentalism', *Comparative Studies in Society and History* 43(3): 525–51.

————— 2001d, 'Whatever Became of Revival: From Charismatic Movement to Charismatic Church in a Papua New Guinea Society', in Charismatic and Pentecostal Christianity in Oceania, eds J. Robbins, P.J. Stewart and A. Strathern, *Journal of Ritual Studies* 15(2): 79–90.

————— 2002, 'My Wife Can't Break Off Part of Her Belief and Give It To Me: Apocalyptic Interrogations of Christian Individualism among the Urapmin of Papua New Guinea', *Paideuma* 48: 189–206.

————— 2004a, *Becoming Sinners: Christianity and Moral Torment in a Papua New Guinea Society* (Ethnographic Studies in Subjectivity 4), Berkeley.

————— 2004b, 'On the Critique in Cargo and the Cargo in Critique', in *Cargo, Cult, and Culture Critique*, ed. Holger Jebens, Honolulu, 243–59.

Robbins, J., P.J. Stewart and A. Strathern eds 2001, 'Charismatic and Pentecostal Christianity in Oceania', *Journal of Ritual Studies* 15(2).

Stewart, P.J. and A. Strathern 2000a, 'Introduction: Latencies and Realizations in Millennial Practices', in Millennial Countdown in New Guinea, eds P.J. Stewart and A. Strathern, *Ethnohistory* 47(1): 3–27.

Stewart, P.J. and A. Strathern eds 1997, *Millennial markers*, Townsville.

Stewart, P.J. and A. Strathern eds 2000b, Millennial Countdown in New Guinea, *Ethnohistory* 47(1).

Westermark, G. 1998, 'History, Opposition, and Salvation in Agarabi Adventism', *Pacific Studies* 21(3): 51–71.

Acknowledgements

The present work is based on fieldwork, the preparation and carrying out of which was made possible by a postgraduate scholarship from the *Freie Universität Berlin* and by a supplementary grant from the *Deutscher Akademischer Austauschdienst* (DAAD). The *Missionswerk der Evang.-Luth. Kirche in Bayern* supported me with a further supplementary grant while I was evaluating my field data.

I would like to thank the government of the Southern Highlands Province of Papua New Guinea for granting me a research permit, and the employees of the following institutions for their cooperation: the *Archives of the Missionswerk der Evang.-Luth. Kirche in Bayern* (Neuendettelsau), the library of the *Institut für Ethnologie* (Berlin), the library of the *Institut für Ethnologie und Afrika-Studien* (Mainz), the library of the *Museum für Völkerkunde* (Berlin), the *District Archives of Kagua*, the *Institute for Papua New Guinea Studies* (Port Moresby), the *Michael Somare Library*, the *University of Papua New Guinea* (Port Moresby), the *National Archives of Papua New Guinea* (Port Moresby), the *National Museum and Art Gallery* (Port Moresby), and the *Southern Highlands Archives* (Mendi). I also owe a particular debt of gratitude to all those who have helped me in different ways and to different degrees, whether with critical advice, the solution of technical problems, or friendly assistance. I name them in alphabetical order and without titles: Heike Altenhoven, Alex Ari, Pogola Ari, Ripu Ari, Gisela Beyer, Don Debes, Ata Francis, Phillip Hauenstein, Sabine Helmers, Paul Hiepko, Christian Hinrichs, Jos Jacobse, Dunstan Jones, Gerd Koch, Karl-Heinz Kohl, Susanne Lanwerd, Ari Lapua, Ipapula Lapua, Niels Lau, Muya Makoa, Kurt-Dietrich Mrossko, Matthias Olape, Alupa Pondopa, Hillary Pumuye, Wala Rama, Anne Riecke, Kurt Riecke, Monika Schanné, Markus Schindlbeck, Frank Schmitsdorf, Christine Spahlinger, Uland Spahlinger, Scott Strubinger, Hans van Amstel, Robert Wala, Gerald Walter, Kenneth Wama, Katharina Wieker, Otmar Yakasi, Serale Yalanai, Naki Yawa and Hartmut Zinser. (The inhabitants of Pairundu themselves wanted to be mentioned using their own real names. I have respected this desire, especially as I rule out the possibility that the present work could have any sort of disadvantageous impact on the villagers.)

Na nambawan samting i kam las: Mi laik tok tenkyu tru long ol manmeri bilong Pairundu we ol i bin lukautim mi gut na givim gutpela kaikai long mi. Bikpela amamas bilong mi i stap wantaim ol. Dispela amamas i stap yet na bihain tu em bai i no inap lus hariap.

Introduction

The present work is concerned with acculturation in its widest sense, that is, with cultural contact and the cultural change determined by it.[1] Using the example of Pairundu, a village in Southern Highlands Province, Papua New Guinea, in the Kewa language area,[2] I examine how the indigenous people handle Western influences. The data for this research were collected between December 1990 and October 1991 over a total of ten months of stationary fieldwork (Map 1).

I consider it appropriate to view contact between traditional and Western culture in this area primarily from the point of view of the relationship between traditional religion and Christianity.[3] The reasons for this arise equally out of the pre-colonial past and the conditions of cultural contact. For all the heterogeneity of the traditional cultures of Melanesia in general and of Papua New Guinea in particular, religion formed a central aspect (cf. Laubscher 1983: 233) that was interwoven with other aspects by, for example, providing reasons for the economy or social structure (Lawrence and Meggitt 1965a: 12). To that extent, the traditional religion appears as the 'background that provides meaning' (Jebens 1990a: 27) to the traditional culture as a whole. Later, the Western world was represented in many regions initially, and for a long time virtually exclusively, by missionaries, who also directed the building of schools, hospitals and churches (Biskup 1970: 39). Today, a majority of the inhabitants of Papua New Guinea see themselves as Christians, and the preamble to the constitution lays down the goal of handing down to future generations the 'Christian principles' that people claim for themselves today, as well as the 'noble traditions' of their own ancestors.[4] Both the pre-colonial past and the impact of the West upon it therefore suggest that contact between traditional and Western culture should be regarded in the first instance as contact between the traditional religion and Christianity.[5] In the case of Pairundu, from the beginning of missionisation this Christianity was Catholic, then around 1987 some villagers converted to the Church of the Seventh-day Adventists, which is recording increasing numbers of members both in Pairundu and in many other parts of Papua New Guinea.[6] In examining the relationship between the traditional religion and Christianity, I am essentially pursuing two goals. One is to explain how – that is, with what needs and beliefs – the

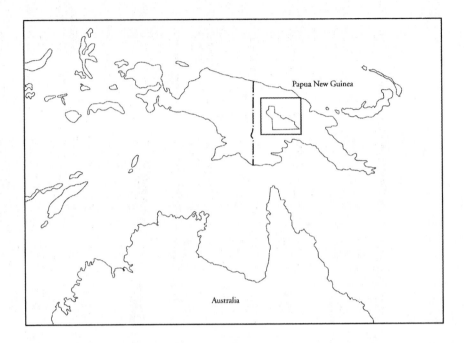

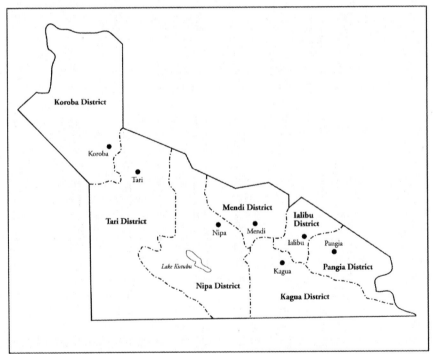

Map 1 Papua New Guinea and the Southern Highlands Province.

villagers adopt the different forms of Christianity, thus providing information on the causes that have led to the 'success' of the Adventists and the rise of the denominational opposition in Pairundu. The other goal is to determine whether, and if so in what form, the traditional religion is still continuing to have an impact today.

In the present work, religions are regarded fundamentally as culturally and historically determined enterprises with which the human species seeks to communicate about itself and about its environment, as well as continually to resolve or balance out individual and social conflicts in a collectively binding manner.[7] Collective liability is created by links to the idea of what from a Western point of view constitutes a transcendent sphere.[8] Through handling individual and social conflicts, religions, in multifarious and often intricate forms, incorporate experiences, ideas and even mutually conflicting needs that arise from confronting a changing social reality. It is precisely these experiences, ideas, needs and conflicts – culturally determined and often unconscious or suppressed – that make religions worthy objects of investigation. In particular, the 'how' of the culturally and historically specific relationship between religion and the respective social reality is of interest, that is, an explanation is required of how, in a historical process, the changing religion incorporates, interprets and constitutes social reality and how, on the other hand, it itself influences that reality.[9] In the present work, the incorporation of social reality is examined through the needs and beliefs with which the inhabitants of Pairundu converted first to Catholic and then to Adventist Christianity.[10] The influencing of social reality is pursued by means of an analysis of the denominational opposition, since this opposition makes manifest the social consequences of adopting Christianity. According to the notion of religion and the epistemological interest just delineated, one can only describe and analyse what people formulate as their ideas and what they express either in their day-to-day lives or in their cult practices. Only this can potentially be perceived by anyone without the precondition of any personal belief – only this is thus open to empirical experience (Zinser 1988: 308). By contrast, the question whether particular ideas or cult practices correspond to the will of God or can be seen as authentically Christian presupposes an essential or substantial definition of God or of the sacred, which can only be provided on the basis of belief.[11] Belief, however, is a precondition of theology[12] but not of the anthropology of religion, which is where I place my own research. Thus I am writing not about the nature, impact and will of God, but about people's empirically perceptible representations – as expressed in statements and actions – that are based on, among other things, references to the nature, impact and will of God.

Examining the relationship between the traditional religion and Christianity by using the example of Pairundu requires taking into account anthropological studies that are available both on this theme and on the Kewa, the language group of the villagers. I will, however, deal later with anthropological research on mission activities in other parts of Papua New Guinea (Chapter 8), concentrating for the present on authors who have published on the Kewa up to now.

Following long stays with the inhabitants of Muli and Usa (Map 2) in the service of the Summer Institute of Linguistics, Karl Franklin translated the Bible into Kewa, so that his work has a mainly linguistic orientation.[13] Social organisation, that is, its reconstruction, is the central theme of John LeRoy, supported by fieldwork in Korapere, Yapi and Koyari.[14] More recently, LeRoy has edited and interpreted a collection of myths (1985a, 1985b), the world-view formulated in them, in his opinion, in no way indicating changes to the traditional culture caused by colonisation and missionisation (1985a: xxii, 1985b: 34). On the basis of fieldwork conducted near Sumbura, Lisette Josephides is concerned above all with the relationship between the genders, while, like Franklin and LeRoy, she more or less excludes the influence of the missions.[15] On the basis of several visits to Mararoko, Mary MacDonald, who is to be seen rather as a representative of mission theology than of anthropology, first infers statements about Melanesian cultures in general from individual aspects of the culture of the southern Kewa, before dealing more particularly with the traditional religion in a longer monograph.[16] The impression here, however, is that the data were not collected through participant observation or systematic interviews but from the 188 stories that, ordered chronologically, make up the second part of MacDonald's monograph and were obviously recorded without any particular thematic restrictions or questions.

In the light of existing anthropological sources, the Wiru are of more interest that the Mendi among the neighbours of the Kewa.[17] Following fieldwork in 1980 and 1985, Jeffrey Clark deals with the Wiru's response to colonisation and missionisation, while concentrating on the question of how contact with the Western world is affecting traditional exchange systems.[18] Unfortunately J. Clark does not provide an exact description of the denominations present in his area of investigation.[19] Also to be mentioned in connection with the Wiru is Andrew Strathern (1968, 1982, 1984), who has repeatedly compared their culture with that of the Medlpa, Western Highlands Province, dealing with processes of transformation, but not taking much account of missionisation. In a later article (1991), however, he compares a Pentecostalist denomination with a traditional Medlpa cult to determine complementary functions in both.

Reviewing the existing anthropological research on the Kewa and their neighbours, it becomes obvious that the adoption of Christianity is often either overlooked or only asserted, but only rarely described and analysed systematically. Traditional religion is not dealt with very much either. While Franklin and MacDonald do provide summary descriptions of particular cult practices, L. Josephides and LeRoy only briefly name individual religious phenomena. Accordingly, overall, anthropological work on the Kewa contains hardly any references to the relationship

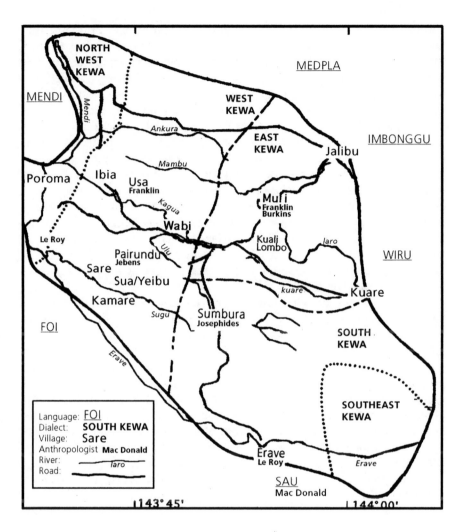

Map 2 Kewa area.

between traditional religion and Christianity. This is not the case with
sources relating to mission theology.[20] However, as opposed to Franklin,
L. Josephides and LeRoy these start out from a basically different
approach. Since the Second Vatican Council at the latest, the mission
theology of the mainline churches (Catholic, Protestant, Anglican,
Methodist) has been striving for inculturation.[21] Starting from the thesis
that in general traditional religions are a kind of preliminary stage or a
'preparation for the Gospel',[22] an attempt is made to convey the Christian
message in a way that is appropriate for the particular cultural

circumstances, so that 'the contents of Christian belief and Christian forms of life are no longer seen as alien and as coming from the outside' (Bus and Landu 1989: 170). Out of this arises the question of the parallels between traditional cultures and Christianity, since these parallels are supposed to provide information about where the message of missionisation can tie in, about where it encounters the already known and familiar. At the same time, these parallels also provide information concerning what in Christianity can be transferred to the particular cultural conditions and what cannot.[23] Thus in contrast to anthropological works on the Kewa, to some extent mission theology pursues a comparative analysis of traditional cultures and Christianity. However, this is not aimed at detecting the experiences, ideas, needs and conflicts that are incorporated by religion or at understanding the changing relationship between religion and social reality. Instead, it is a matter of recognising or constructing cultural parallels in order to prepare or support the process of inculturation, which is ultimately intended to result in the creation of an original Melanesian theology.[24]

If, however, only certain things are transferable from Christianity to the locally specific circumstances that are encountered, if other things prove to be bound to Western culture, to be relevant only there and thus not to be transferable, then for mission theology a problem arises in differentiating between what is significant only in a culturally specific sense and what cannot be dispensed with in missionisation. This ultimately poses the question of what has to be excluded from any relativisation, that is, the substance of the Christian message, the nature, impact and will of God.[25] This becomes obvious in particular in the case of the Holy Spirit movements – also described as 'revivals' (Barr and Trompf 1983: 49) – in which indigenous people, among them those in Pairundu, have sought to enter into direct contact with the Holy Spirit, accompanied by altered states of consciousness.[26] With the exception of the psychologist Robert Robin, the relevant descriptions and interpretations come overwhelmingly from mission theology, in which, when it comes to assessing Holy Spirit movements, the main point of discussion is whether God makes an appearance in them and therefore whether they count as being authentically Christian or not.[27] Accordingly, mission theologists ultimately attempt to do research on the impact of God, perceptible only through beliefs, rather than – as required by the approach of the anthropology of religion evident in the present work – confining themselves to what the indigenous people express in their statements and actions and what is therefore accessible to empirical experience.

If the relationship between traditional religion and Christianity has, on the one hand, hardly been taken into account in anthropological works on the Kewa and if, on the other hand, it is treated by mission theology from the perspective of a different interest and approach, then it can be hoped that the present investigation may help to fill a gap in research. Moreover, in view of the phenomenon of fundamentalism, which is gaining in importance in many areas worldwide, it seems appropriate to examine, using a local example, the adoption of a form of Christianity that is transmitted by a fundamentalist group. This should make it possible to improve our understanding of the numerical growth, that is, the 'success' of the Seventh-day Adventists in Pairundu and other parts of Papua New Guinea.

Today, however, anthropological work must also address the question of its relevance not only for the scientific community, but also for those whose hospitality the anthropologist enjoys. The question of the relevance of my research for the inhabitants of Pairundu, who describe themselves quite definitely as Christians, is expressed in the fact that, even without my influence, they have repeatedly talked about and often intensively discussed, their treatment of Christianity and the relationship between the two denominations. Thus I was often asked for information and advice, since to some extent people doubted that they had properly grasped the Christian message.[28] Still more important, however, may be the fact that the denominational opposition in Pairundu has led to a considerable degree of division within the community and partly to bitter conflicts (Chapter 4). Accordingly Catholics often asked me whether Adventists were correct in their criticisms of them and whether there were also Adventists in Germany.

The questions I am addressing here are the product of a longer development. In studying anthropology and *Religionswissenschaft* (the anthropology of religion), I had already become concerned with change in traditional religions and myths as a consequence of socio-economic and political transformation with reference to New Guinea as a whole. Out of this came an analysis of cargo cults as a religious attempt to cope with the experience of colonialism in the north-east of New Guinea (Jebens 1990a, 1993). This research was then deepened and was actualised through a subsequent examination of Holy Spirit movements, in which I concentrated especially on the Highlands of Papua New Guinea (Jebens 1990b). In my fieldwork, I initially wanted to use the example of a particular village to find out whether any relationships could be recognised between socio-economic differences that have been triggered or strengthened by colonisation and the adoption of Christianity. At the same time, this village should still be relatively little exposed to Western modernisation, so that, I hoped, influences coming from the traditional culture in general and the traditional religion in particular could be detected more easily. In the course of a six-week reconnaissance of the area between Mendi, Ialibu, Kagua and Usa (Map 2), however, I soon noticed that socio-economic differences were in general less marked than I had expected from sources on other Highlands provinces (Brown 1982: 543, A. Strathern 1984: 111). Instead, it emerged that the adoption of Christianity has been determined rather by conflicts between the mainline churches on the one hand and the smaller communities of belief that had intruded subsequently on the other.[29] In conversations with me, Catholic priests and Lutheran pastors especially condemned the fact that the Adventists were increasingly invading existing Catholic or Lutheran areas in greater numbers than any other denomination in order to 'woo away' church members and were thus causing serious problems. These impressions made it appear reasonable not to insist on my preconceived questions but to take the relationship between different denominations more into consideration. Here the Western observer is at first struck by the contrasts between the Catholics and the Adventists in particular, for the Adventists not only place greater stress on well-looked-after Western clothing and frequent washing of the body, unlike many Catholics they also forego the wearing of beards or traditional body decorations, bark belts and head coverings. After modifying my research interest, Pairundu seemed to be particularly suitable for stationary fieldwork. It offered the opportunity to observe the living together of Catholics and Adventists not only from a close distance, but also within a relatively narrow framework, since Pairundu has fewer inhabitants and a more concentrated settlement pattern than neighbouring villages. Moreover, among the different Highlands provinces of Papua New Guinea, Southern Highlands Province is relatively isolated from Western modernisation, as is Kagua District within it and the Wabi-Sumi area, in which Pairundu is situated, within that.

On my first visit in Pairundu on 20 December 1990, I was accompanied by Yano, who was employed at the Lutheran mission station in Wabi as a caretaker. I said that I wanted to live in a local community for a longer period in order to learn something about present-day village life and the customs of the ancestors as part of my education, 'like a pupil'. I reported truthfully that I had heard the name 'Pairundu' for the first time from Fr Dunstan, a priest who had formerly been responsible for the village. Those present on my second visit on 21 December 1990 – which this time was announced in advance – including Yawa, Wala, Ari and Rekepea, that is, the leading men of Pairundu, all agreed in stating that I should pursue my goals among them and that I could live in a house that the Catholic community had already begun to build a few months earlier, originally for the visits of priests and nuns. After this house (no. 32 in Map 3) had been completed in the last week in December with the help of the Adventists, I moved in on 10 January 1991 and lived there until the end of my fieldwork in October 1991. The land on which the house stood belonged to the Rata Kome sub-clan and the family of Ari.

The villagers gave me food, drinking water and firewood on a daily basis, as and when they could or wished. Before leaving, I made payments for this and for the use of the house that had been agreed upon in the corresponding negotiations and that were distributed further by the leaders of the individual sub-clans. At the same time, I also made presents of pieces of clothing and equipment to good informants and friends. Otherwise, however, apart from the daily sharing of meals or tobacco, I did not especially remunerate anyone apart from Alex, who,

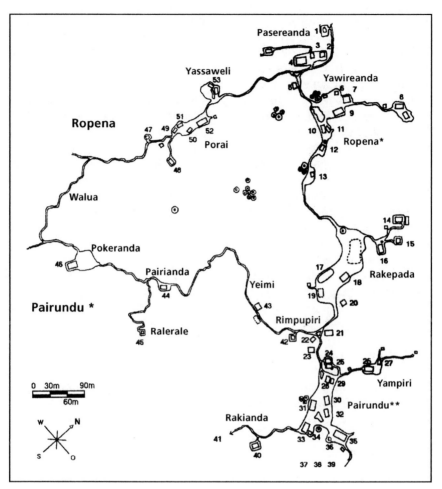

Map 3 Pairundu.

shortly after my moving in, expressed the desire to live with me in order to bring me firewood and water and to cook for me. I agreed and did not have to regret this decision, since my new companion quickly proved to be highly intelligent and a careful translator, who, as a member of the Adventist community, also provided me with pieces of information that were otherwise kept concealed from non-Adventists. At the beginning of my stay in Pairundu, I brought with me a large amount of frozen beef from the provincial capital, to form the basis of a feast for the sake of my making a 'good beginning'. This feast simultaneously gave me an opportunity to introduce myself to a wider public and explain the reasons for my being there. In accordance with the spontaneously expressed agreement with my intentions in general and my staying in Pairundu in particular, the villagers treated me in an entirely friendly and interested fashion.[30] Even those who at first appeared indifferent towards me and did not visit me on their own initiative generally agreed when I wanted to meet them for conversations or interviews. My access to places accorded with my access to people: I never heard that I could not go to particular parts of the bush or to particular gardens or houses. Conversely, my own house was in principle open to anyone at any time. In the first few weeks of my fieldwork I became friendly not only with Alex, but also particularly with his brother Ripu, Coleman Makoa and Amakoa. Later not only did the initially rather reserved Ata Francis, Rekepea and Alupa become involved, but also Otmar, who lived in Anapote.

In the entire region between Mendi, Ialibu, Kagua and Sumi, I proved to be the only white person living in a house of traditional construction, without a corrugated iron roof, without great spatial distance from the other villagers, eating the same food and not possessing a car. Certainly such whites had been heard of from other regions,[31] but nonetheless an anthropologist pursuing stationary fieldwork represented something new for the inhabitants of Pairundu, for which there was no example in the local tradition. Since all the other known whites were missionaries, colonial officers or overseers on coffee plantations in Western Highlands Province, behaviour towards me initially resembled behaviour towards these people. The villagers first addressed me as 'masta', as was usual on the coffee plantations, until I asked them to call me by my first name instead.[32] Otherwise already on my first visit people connected me with 'the Church', especially since I was accompanied by a Lutheran from Wabi and since I myself mentioned the name of Fr Dunstan.[33] This only seemed to be confirmed when I lived in a house that was originally intended for priests and nuns. I soon heard it being assumed that I had been sent to Pairundu by Fr Dunstan, and in interviews on Christianity, even after several months it was still sometimes said that I already knew the answers and was only concerned to test people's general beliefs. Shortly after the start of my fieldwork in Pairundu, the idea that I was connected to a church was expressed especially clearly in the suggestion that a fence be put round my house and that access to it be restricted, since priests and nuns were known to live by themselves too on fenced-off mission stations guarded by dogs. However, the villagers noticed, with not a little astonishment, that I was especially concerned to avoid creating such a distance and to make as many contacts as possible.

From the start, on various occasions I myself repeatedly spoke out against my being connected with any church. Since I basically appeared to be rather reserved, listening more than talking, in course of time many people realised that indeed I could hardly be a missionary.[34] Still more important for the villagers must have been the fact that I took part in both Catholic and Adventist services, so that I could not belong to either denomination. Accordingly, I basically had no problems in either community in conducting conversations and interviews, nor in attending cult practices. My position, that I would first have to know both denominations well before I could opt for one of them for myself, seemed plausible and acceptable to both Catholic and Adventist villagers.

In the first period, people tried to convey to me the impression that living together in the village was generally peaceful and without problems. Here, obviously, an ideal of harmony was at work, which, as I could observe later, tended to be propagated vis-à-vis all visitors who were not from Pairundu. Only after some weeks did some people begin to tell me in individual, whispered conversations about conflicts with members of other families, lineages or sub-clans, who, in these contexts, usually appeared in a bad light. In my view, such reports and rumours, which were often formulated as warnings, indicated a reduction in the initial distance towards me and an emerging relationship of trust. A contributory factor here may well have been the impression that I was not going to leave soon, but obviously actually wanted to go on living in Pairundu for a longer time. The fact that, as a rule, I did not depreciate what was told or described to me – something I avoided, so as not to deter people in advance from telling me something – might also have played a role. Warning me against other villagers also represented an attempt to monopolise me, which accompanied the reduction of the initial distance: members of Ari's family described me as a member of their family, members of the Rata Kome described me as a Rata Kome, and the inhabitants of Pairundu described me as a co-villager.[35] This was connected not only with an admonishment not to spend too much time with members of other families, sub-clans or villages, but also with the accusation that I was doing precisely that. With respect to the inhabitants of other villagers in particular, I was advised to be extremely reserved and not even to give my name. The attempt to monopolise me was also expressed in the desire to get me to settle permanently in Pairundu. Before my departure in particular, I was asked to return later, with the offer of other houses and villages as accommodation. In general I attempted to counter this monopolisation not only by spreading my contacts among different families and sub-clans through interviews or accompanying people on walks through the bush, but also by repeatedly referring to the fact that I had not come to Pairundu in order to stay with just one man or group. I could not see any serious denomination-specific differences in the respective behaviour of Catholics and Adventists with regard either to my being connected with a church or to the attempts to monopolise me.

Describing the relationship between myself and the villagers as having been completely without problems would not be a description of reality as it seemed to me, but would correspond to the very ideal of harmony that had occurred to me at the start of my fieldwork. A strain was placed on the mutual relationship for a time by a conflict with Yawa, the leading man of the Auro Kome sub-clan and, as I was told, of the village as a whole too. After we had already often spoken with one another about various topics, he came into my house on 4 March 1991 and said that he could no longer accept the agreement we had come to earlier, in which the payments I should make at the end of my stay were laid down. If I were not ready to increase these payments many times, I would have to leave Pairundu. He, Yawa, spoke in the name of all the villagers. I indicated that under such circumstances I would indeed leave, simultaneously fearing that my fieldwork would thus come to an early and inglorious end after only a few months. In the days that followed, however, the leaders of other sub-clans, as well as numerous villagers, assured me that Yawa had only voiced his own opinion, which was not shared by anyone else. Altogether this event showed me that, for all the anxieties Yawa had triggered, my presence in Pairundu was welcome to most people, and that, even though he was a leading man, Yawa could not prevail against the majority view.

One restriction on mutual relationships and thus for my fieldwork as a whole, finally, was the fact that, in accordance with the gender antagonism that is typical of the Highlands of Papua New Guinea in general, the women remained very reserved towards me for a long time, not daring, with few exceptions, to come into my house, for example. As a result I was only able to conduct a few interviews with women, and to my regret I must presume that the emic point of view that I am repeatedly trying to describe in the present work is often likely to be a male view.

Permanently living together with the villagers made it possible for me to observe them in their daily lives and during their cult practices, to follow their discussions, to accompany them to trials at court and to visit them while they were at work in their gardens or in their homes. In addition, I was often invited to evening meals and later took part in communal expeditions to other villages for dances or pig-killing festivals.[36] Living together continuously led to informal conversations with differing numbers of participants, initiated sometimes by myself, sometimes by the villagers. The formal conversations can be divided into two groups. On the one hand, I visited all the dwellings of the village in sequence in order to carry out a census, collect genealogies, draw up a plan of the settlement (Map 3) and conduct the only half-standardised interviews of my fieldwork using pre-prepared questionnaires. They included questions about the individual's confession, experience of the world outside the village and district, ownership of land, pigs, objects of value and money, their sources of income and regular expenditure.

The second group of formal conversations consisted of a total of 182 non-standardised interviews with 54 individuals differentiated according to gender, age, sub-clan, confession and social standing. These interviews were less quantitative than qualitative and were open, though nonetheless formal, since they took place at previously arranged times, and I recorded them in whole or in part. Depending on mutual interest, they lasted somewhere between thirty minutes and an hour (with pauses). At first, I conducted mainly narrative interviews (Mayring 1990: 50–53, Lamnek

1993: 70–74) in which informants talked freely about a topic chosen by either themselves or myself. In these cases I exerted no influence over those present and left the degree of detail and course of the account mostly to the knowledge, preferences and imagination of the informants. If the choice of topic was left to me, I asked particularly for people's life histories. Later more structured, problem-focused interviews followed (Mayring 1990: 46–50, Lamnek 1993: 74–78), which remained open in that I still did not exert much influence over the participants but during which I encouraged people to talk about particular areas of the traditional culture in general (pig-killing festivals, warfare) and of the traditional religion in particular (transcendental authorities, magical and cult practices). Within this framework, I also ascertained the emic view of colonisation and missionisation. After some months, when a certain relationship of trust had been created, I began to ask selected villagers about Christianity, that is, about their view of their own and the other denominations. The same people also described the ideas, expectations and anxieties that they linked with the future. Here I sought either to be alone with the actual informant or to keep the number of those present as small as possible. My impression is that the tape recorder was not experienced as disturbing in either the narrative or the problem-focused interviews. Instead, people were pleased to listen to the recording again later, while I sometimes made notes of their ensuing commentaries, including them into the postscripts in which I also documented the basic conditions of the individual interview (place, time, name of those present), as well as my own impressions of the mood, gestures, mimicry and motor activity of the informants.[37] If I did not turn on the tape recorder, people sometimes asked me, with a slightly disappointed undertone, whether I was not finding what they were saying important.

The time available did not permit me to undertake systematic learning of Kewa. By the end of my stay in Pairundu I was only able to master a few words and roughly identify the theme people were talking about in Kewa. However, every serious communication was conducted in the main lingua franca of Papua New Guinea, the Neo-Melanesian Pidgin English, known in the language itself as Tok Pisin, which I had already started to learn in Germany. As a rule, translation from Kewa into Tok Pisin proved necessary in the case of conversations with people older than approximately 35 years, who had only limited competence in Tok Pisin, while younger people mostly spoke it without problems.

In the morning and evening of each day I spent one to two hours at my desk, writing a diary in which I wrote up extensively the notes of observations I had made that day or the previous day.[38] On this occasion I also listened to tape recordings of interviews, informal conversations and cult practices, partly transcribing them and partly summarising them in a combination of German and Tok Pisin.[39] On the whole, my observations and enquiries were not prevented by either sickness or accident, apart from an attack of malaria, which confined me to bed for a week and an inflammation of the ankle ('tropical ulcer'), which restricted my movements for some two weeks.

The ethnographic data that I collected using the methods described above form the basis of the first part of the present work. In the second part I analyse what has been presented, and in the third part I place the example of Pairundu in its regional and theoretical contexts. The separation of presentation and analysis is intended to make it easier to check my interpretation and, if appropriate, come to different conclusions. Admittedly the separation between presentation and analysis cannot be strictly adhered to, since the order of presentation already presupposes some analysis, while analysis without reference to presentation is not plausible.

Presentation of the ethnographic data, consisting of four chapters, begins and ends with a view of the present. In between, on the basis of the relevant interviews, I describe first the traditional religion (Chapter 2) and then the changes brought about by colonisation and missionisation (Chapter 3). In Chapter 1, I sketch the social and economic conditions of present-day Pairundu against the background of, first, the state organisation of Papua New Guinea, and then Kewa culture. In this context, I am focusing particularly on the differences between the genders, the generations and men of different social standing. Here, however, I exclude religion, since dealing with the various forms of Christianity is central to later parts of my account. Chapter 2 follows with a presentation of various elements of the traditional religion, the question of its present-day influence requiring this to be treated in considerable detail. In Chapter 3, the representation of the past concludes with the history of colonisation and missionisation. In reconstructing this history, I contrast the memories of the older villagers with the reports of colonial officers and missionaries. The descriptions of the socio-economic conditions in present-day Pairundu, the traditional religion and the history of colonisation and missionisation form a prerequisite for Chapter 4, in which – again based on both indigenous statements and my own observations – I consider the two denominations represented in Pairundu. First I sketch the composition and structure of the Catholic and Adventist communities, in order thereafter to focus on the beliefs that are specific to each denomination and that in each case refer to the traditional culture, one's own world-view and one's own community.[40] The cult practices described next might to some extent be seen as forms of putting these beliefs into action. Finally, the fourth chapter ends with a presentation of the social consequences of the opposition between Catholics and Adventists, in which I delineate not only the way in which the adherents of the two denominations mutually see each other, but also some of the conflicts in which the antagonists partly come not only from the different communities, but also different villages.

The analysis, Part Two, of the data presented in the first four chapters is aimed at explaining the relationship between Christianity and the traditional religion. In Chapter 5, I examine how the villagers see the significance of the changes that have taken place in connection with colonisation and missionisation for themselves and what hopes they have for the future within the socio-economic domain, that is, in the context of 'development'. In Chapter 6, the view changes from the socio-economic to the religious sphere. Here I focus on the question of the needs and beliefs with which the villagers accept, for example, Catholic and Adventist Christianity. This also gives some indications of the causes that have led to the growth of the Adventists and thus to the emergence of the opposition between the denominations. If the adoption of Christianity incorporates, in a religious idiom, the changes in social reality triggered by colonisation and missionisation, then the inter-denominational opposition itself represents a religiously founded influencing of social reality. In Chapter 7, this interaction between religious and social change is shown to provide information about the present-day influence of traditional religion. Thus the analysis of change leads to an analysis of continuity.

Like Part Two, Part Three of the present work consists of three chapters, in which I seek to explain to what extent Pairundu can be seen as representative in its regional and theoretical context, that is, with respect to missionisation and modernisation. Thus in Chapter 8 I discuss the common features of missionisation throughout Papua New Guinea and in Chapter 9 the phenomenon of fundamentalism as a response to modernity. In Chapter 10 I summarise what is general and what is particular about the example of Pairundu, in order finally, and concerning only Pairundu, to conclude with my own assessment of the Church of the Seventh-day Adventists and its future development.

Notes

1. The term 'acculturation' is used here in Rudolph's sense: 'Acculturation is to be understood as the processes and phenomena that occur in a case of cultural change determined by (direct or indirect) culture contact' (1964: 100, all translations H.J.).
2. The term 'Kewa' describes on the one hand the language and on the other hand speakers of it as a more or less homogenous group culturally distinct from their neighbours (*see* Chapter 1.2).
3. Combining emic and etic perspectives, I describe as 'traditional' on the one hand what is not to be traced back to Western influences etically and on the other hand what the indigenous people themselves attribute to their tradition. Here, the word 'traditional' is not intended to suggest a reality that is still untouched by Western influences. Such an attempt at reconstruction would be problematic for several reasons. First, there is the danger of creating connections from the Western point of view and of projecting them on to the indigenous population when they do not play a role for them, not even unconsciously (*see* Chapter 2). Secondly, the statements in which the indigenous people use the word 'traditional' are always influenced by present-day interests (*see* Chapter 7). Finally, pre-colonial culture was already subject to a constant process of change.
4. 'We, the people of Papua New Guinea, pledge ourselves to guard and pass on to those who come after us our noble traditions and the Christian principles that are ours now'

(Blaustein and Flanz 1985: 25). Rath (1989: 8) cites a statistic from 1980, according to which 96.6 percent of the population of Papua New Guinea are Christian – of which 63.8 percent are Protestant and 32.8 percent Catholic – 2.5 percent 'Animist' (this term, which is not placed in quotation marks in the statistics, presumably here refers to the adherents of 'traditional religions') and 9 percent 'other'.

5. Examining the theme of religion is also demanded from time to time by indigenous people themselves. Thus Aruru Matiabe (1987: 18), a Huli from the Southern Highlands of Papua New Guinea, writes: 'If you want to know the heart of a people, to repeat, you must understand their religion first...'. Cf. also Vicedom and Tischner's view, on the inhabitants of the Mount Hagen area in the 1940s: 'If we wish to understand the indigenous people properly and judge their actions, we must always start from the assessment of their religion, for this is the focus around which everything in their lives moves and from which it radiates' (1943–48, volume 2: 298).

6. The Seventh-day Adventists describe themselves in English as 'Seventh-day Adventist Church' (SDA) and in German as 'Freikirche' (Free Church), while using the term 'Gemeinschaft' (community) in official publications (Gemeinschaft der Siebenten-Tags-Adventisten 1990).

7. This definition is based on, and strongly influenced by, Zinser's definition (1984/85).

8. Vivelo (1988: 254) accordingly refers to the fact that 'belief in a supernatural or superhuman component of reality' is cited in many definitions of religion, though the definition of 'supernatural' depends on each culture.

9. Gladigow (1988a: 33), who understands religion as a 'special type of a culturally specific symbolic system or system of interpretation', counts the question of how religions constitute reality among the tasks of religious studies. The components of incorporating and influencing social reality are also contained in the definition of religion drawn up by Lawrence and Meggitt (1965a: 9) with reference to Melanesia: 'The function of religion within the total cosmic order is: first, to explain and validate through myths the origin and existence of the physical world, its economic resources and the means of exploiting them, and the socio-political structure; and, second, to give man the assurance that he can control the cosmic order by performing ritual'.

10. Following Mohr (1993: 436), I see 'conversion' as 'processes of turning towards or away from belief systems... in the strict sense of joining or leaving religious communities'. Conversion to Catholicism at the start of missionisation in Pairundu thus meant turning towards or joining it, while conversion to the Adventists also assumed for many turning away from Catholicism or leaving the Catholic Church. On the other hand, not all the members of the SDA community had previously been baptised as Catholics.

11. According to Gladigow (1988b: 12), such essential or substantial definitions have also formed the basis of definitions of religion for a long time in religious studies.

12. Zinser (1988: 308) refers to the fact that theology 'is based subjectively on belief or revelation and objectively on the social institution of the Church'.

13. See Franklin (1965, 1967, 1971, 1989) as well as Franklin and Franklin (1978).

14. See LeRoy (1975, 1979a, 1979b, 1981)

15. See L. Josephides (1982, 1983, 1985a, 1985b, 1985c). – The influence of the missions is also excluded by Donald Burkins (1984), who carried out fieldwork in Muli. His work is focused on socio-economic processes of transformation and thus need not be taken into account here. Apart from L. Josephides and Burkins, I shall go later into Simon Apea's theses (1985), which were developed with reference to the area of Ialibu (Chapter 8).

16. MacDonald (1991). Her visits to Mararoko were undertaken during her teaching activities at a catechist training centre in Erave (1973–77) and her employment (1980–83) at the Melanesian Institute for Pastoral and Socio-Economic Service in Goroka (Eastern Highlands Province) (MacDonald 1991: 10). For MacDonald's publications prior to her monograph, see MacDonald (1984a, 1984b, 1984c, 1984d, 1985).

17. The term 'Mendi' describes the language otherwise known as 'Angal', its speakers and the capital of Southern Highlands Province. After field trips in the early 1950s, D'Arcy

Ryan (1955, 1959) attempted to describe the Mendi kinship system, which had still not been very much influenced by the changes introduced by colonialism. Research carried out between 1977 and 1983 north of the provincial capital, however, allowed Rena Lederman to present some investigations into social change, though with the focus on the relationship between individual and collective exchange networks in terms of their significance for gender relations (1980, 1981, 1982, 1986a, 1986b).

18. See J. Clark (1982, 1985, 1988, 1989a, 1989b).

19. *See* the extensive critique of J. Clark in Chapter 8.

20. I am aware here that one cannot always distinguish anthropology and mission theology sharply, in the sense that missionaries have also presented investigations that can be seen as anthropological as far as their object, epistemological interest and research approach are concerned. See, among others, Zöllner (1977) and Triebel (1988) and, on the relationship between anthropology and mission theology, as well as between anthropologists and mission theologists, Forman (1978), D. Hughes (1978), Oosterwal (1978), Whiteman (1983), therein Lutzbetak (1983) and Sutlive (1983), and also Quack (1986).

21. On the notion of inculturation, see Quack (1986: 230). The Second Vatican Council was summoned by Pope John XXIII in 1959 and lasted from October 1962 to December 1965 (Arbuckle 1983).

22. MacDonald (1991: 14). This view also prevailed among the diffusionists of P.W. Schmidt's circle.

23. Alongside this, research by mission theology also has the goal of 'distilling out' basic principles that are common to the various cultures of Melanesia, in the hope of ultimately overcoming the cultural particularism typical of New Guinea as a whole.

24. On the attempt to create a Melanesian theology, see John Barr (1983a: 118), Pokawin (1987: 31), Trompf (1987), Bus and Landu (1989: 172), Fugmann (1989: 229) and Narakobi (1989: 45f).

25. See Tuza (1984: viii), Gesch (1985), Renali (1991: 123) and Pickering (1992: 105).

26. John Barr (1983a: 109) defines Holy Spirit movements as 'collective ecstatic experiences in Christian contexts'.

27. See Flannery (1980, 1983/84), John Barr (1983a, 1983b), Barr and Trompf (1983), Schwarz (1984), Ahrens (1986a) and Opeba (1987). Many of the relevant articles give briefer descriptions, in which it is often not clear whether they are based on authors' own observations or indigenous narratives. These texts can be found especially in the journals *Point* and *Catalyst*, published by the Melanesian Institute for Pastoral and Socio-Economic Service in Goroka (Eastern Highlands Province). On the question of whether Holy Spirit Movements may count as being authentically Christian or not, see Lenturut (1983: 211), Teske (1983: 249) and Flannery (1984: 149). Robin travelled through the present-day Southern Highlands Province in the 1970s on behalf of the government in order to collect information on Holy Spirit movements, basing himself among other things on interviews with participants in these movements who had been admitted to the hospital in Tari (Southern Highlands Province) for psychiatric treatment (1980, 1981a, 1981b, 1981c, 1982). In a personal letter (21 January 1989) to me, Robin expressly referred to the fact that he sees himself as a psychologist, not an anthropologist.

28. For many villagers, my competence arose from the fact that, as a white man, I was from the same country from which Christianity had formerly come. Alongside this, my original identification as a missionary, which I shall go into again later, was also of significance.

29. In the areas I travelled through, these groups included the Apostolic Church, the Assemblies of God, the Christian Life Center, the Church of the Nazarene, the Ialibu Gospel Church and the Seventh-day Adventist Church. See also Renali (1991: 71f).

30. The positive attitude towards me was certainly also fed by the generally prevailing attitude towards white people, to which I shall return later (Chapter 5). At the same time, however, people did differ in their individual ability to understand and communicate – as they do anywhere.

31. After I had been staying for some months in Pairundu, visitors from Sumbura and Korapere told me of other whites who had once also lived with the indigenous people. According to the village names mentioned, these were Lisette Josephides and John LeRoy.

32. I am aware of the fact, however, that it was easier to have the word 'masta' replaced by 'Holger' than to learn that a different attitude could be shown towards me than towards plantation overseers or missionaries.

33. Some people took me for an Adventist, others for a Catholic. In addition, in other villages there had been rumours that I was working for Yako Mano, a member of the Provincial Government, that I had been sent by the Russians, or – quite generally – that I was out to cause trouble.

34. This reserve corresponds to my personality as well as to the fact that I basically agree with the anonymous anthropologist whose words are quoted by Jackson: 'In many ways I see anthropology as the art of listening to the other' (1990: 18).

35. This monopolising also gave rise to an idea, which, however, I only learned about some months later, according to which I was in reality the ghost of Wapi, a deceased brother of Ari. This explained why I should want to live in Pairundu of all places and not, for example, in a village located nearer the district or provincial capital. Ata Francis and Robert reported this idea to me during a formal interview with Yana (95.). '95.' refers to the ninety-fifth entry in the list of 'Interviews and informal conversations'. These entries include the name of the informant, date and place of the interview or informal conversation (numbers in brackets refer to Map 3), the names of the people present and a note on how the interview or informal conversation was recorded.

36. Depending on opportunity, I made notes on the spot of my day-to-day observations, as well as those at cult practices. My impression is that this was not experienced as disturbing even at the cult practices, but was received in a rather amused and well-meaning fashion.

37. I also prepared such postscripts in the case of some of the informal conversations, some of which I recorded as well.

38. I wrote the diary on the right-hand side of DIN A4 pages folded lengthways, leaving the left-hand side for the later entry of comments, associations and ideas. Writing down feelings, hopes, anxieties and dreams was done in a different colour from the description of events and observations, where I switched between German and Tok Pisin. Here usage of Tok Pisin allowed important statements to be retained in the original.

39. The transcriptions and summaries, together with the corresponding postscripts, were systematically arranged according to topic and collected together in different notebooks.

40. It is, however, not an aim of the present work to compare the beliefs of the Catholics and Adventists in Pairundu with those of Catholics and Adventists in Europe. Such a comparison might be the topic of a separate investigation.

PART I:
PAIRUNDU

1

Present-Day Culture

In this chapter I shall concentrate on describing social and economic conditions in present-day Pairundu, which, however, must be viewed against the background of wider contexts. One of these contexts is the political and economic situation of Pairundu within the state of Papua New Guinea. Another is the cultural framework, that is, the cultural parallels and differences that can be recognised between the inhabitants of Pairundu and those of neighbouring communities.

Pairundu within the state of Papua New Guinea

Since 1975, Papua New Guinea has been an independent state and member of the British Commonwealth recognising as the nominal head of state the British Queen, who is represented in the country by a Governor General. It is also a parliamentary democracy of Western type.[1] Papua New Guinea is divided into nineteen provinces plus the National Capital District. The provinces have their own parliaments and administrations.

The question concerning the situation of Pairundu within the state can be answered briefly by saying that Pairundu belongs to Pira Council, Aiya Constituency, Kagua District and Southern Highlands Province (Map 1). To clarify this statement, however, some remarks are required concerning these concepts and thus the political organisation of Papua New Guinea.[2] At the lowest level of administration are the councils, drawn up in accordance with numbers of inhabitants and represented by a councillor, in which, officially, an average of no more than a thousand people live. In Pira Council, as well as the councillor, there are two village court policemen (the so-called 'Peace Officers') and five village court magistrates (*kiaps*). All these officials are initially elected by the people and then appointed by the Provincial Government.[3] Pira Council, together with eleven other councils, make the Aiya Constituency. Constituencies are formed according to area, each sending a representative to the Provincial Government, the so-called 'Provincial Member'. The Aiya,

Erave, Kuare and Alia constituencies all belong to Kagua District, which is named after the district capital and consists of 41 constituencies and about 35,000 inhabitants. The districts also send a representative, the so-called 'National Member', to the National Parliament. Kagua District and six other districts (Koroba, Tari, Nipa, Mendi, Ialibu and Pangia, also named after their respective district capitals) belong to Southern Highlands Province (SHP), which also consists of 27 constituencies. The capital and seat of the Provincial Government is Mendi (Map 2). At 23,800 square kilometres,[4] SHP is the largest province in the Highlands. With 236,100 inhabitants, population density is 9.9 inhabitants per square kilometre, which puts SHP behind all other highland provinces.[5] SHP has nine representatives at provincial level (Puruno 1988: 13). Like all the other provinces, SHP sends a representative to the so-called 'Provincial Seat' in the National Parliament, in addition to the members elected from the individual districts.

Political and economic 'development' in Pairundu and its area has been largely shaped by colonial history up to the present day. The southern part of the eastern half of New Guinea, known as 'Papua', was originally under British rule and then, from the Second World War until 1975, under Australian colonial rule. In the Highlands of New Guinea, which are partly difficult to access, the impacts of colonisation and missionisation were felt considerably later than on the Seaboard. When the first government stations were founded in the Eastern Highlands (at Kainantu in 1930–31) (Berndt 1965: 99) and Western Highlands (at Mount Hagen in 1933) (Biskup 1970: 95), the government and mission stations on many parts of the coast, which had been set up around the turn of the century, already had a good thirty years of history behind them. If we judge 'development' in the sense of Western influence and a resulting convergence with Western culture positively, therefore,[6] the inhabitants of the Highlands were disadvantaged in comparison with the inhabitants of the Seaboard, who had been exposed to historically determined progress to some extent.

However, this relative marginality with regard to the economy, education and health, arising not least from colonial history, characterises not only the Highlands in general compared with the Seaboard, but also SHP within the Highlands, Kagua District within SHP and the area of Pairundu within Kagua District.

SHP was 'opened up' by the Whites later than any other Highland province and thus also later than any other region in Papua New Guinea. The first permanent government station was not founded in the present-day provincial capital of Mendi, until 1950 (Awesa 1988: 1). The 'opening' of the area around Mendi followed in 1965, meaning that the government now allowed people to enter the area without being accompanied by government officials and armed policemen (Lederman 1986a: 5). In the area around Lake Kopiago in Koroba District, this restriction was only lifted in 1974. Better communications with the outside world and thus access to trade beyond the region were provided in 1978, when Mendi was connected to the Highlands Highway linking the Highlands with the coast and the port of Lae via Mount Hagen in Western Highlands Province (Puruno 1988: 7ff.). In 1981, the Highlands Highway was extended to Tari and then to Koroba (Puruno 1988: 25). The lateness of the coming of transport links to SHP has certainly contributed to its present economic situation. Lederman was not wrong in describing SHP as 'the least accessible and least economically developed Highlands province' (1986a: 5). Even in the present-day provincial capital of Mendi, towards the end of the 1970s there were still hardly any locally run shops or other attempts to participate in the monetary economy by, for example, growing coffee or raising cattle (Lederman 1981: 71f). At the start of the 1980s, SHP was producing only one percent of all the coffee sold in the Highlands (J. Clark 1989a: 142 n. 142). Even towards the end of the 1980s, only seven councils had small coffee plantations run by the government (the Southern Highlands Management Unit), though the officially available sources say nothing about their productivity. The few inhabitants of SHP who have found paid positions, for example as administrative officials (public servants), work not in their villages, but in Mendi or towns in other provinces.[7] Whoever wants to be taken on as a contract worker, seasonally on the coffee plantations, for example, must search above all in Western Highlands Province.[8] Altogether, SHP is totally dependent economically on the National Government, since its available labour force is mostly engaged in the subsistence economy.[9] The economic situation in SHP is also found in education and health. According to Awesa (1988: 4), only 18 percent of eligible children go to the existing schools, compared with a province-wide average of 31 percent, a proportion that, according to Weeks (1987: 121f), places SHP last of all provinces in Papua New Guinea.[10] In 1988, there were 30,000 people to each doctor in the available hospitals, health centres and aid posts, compared, for example, to 6,000 per doctor in Manus Province (Awesa 1988: 4).

Like SHP in comparison with other Highland provinces, Kagua District is characterised by a situation of relative marginality with respect to other districts in SHP. However, the reason for this is less that some areas of Kagua District were exposed to colonialism later than others,[11] but rather that these areas are not accessible, or accessible only with difficulty, over existing roads. Thus the only all-weather roads in Kagua District are those from Kagua to Kuare, Erave and Ibia (Map 2). As a result, the prospects of running shops in the villages at a profit are reduced, for the harder it is to reach the wholesalers in Kagua and Ialibu, the more prices rise and turnover falls, given the limited possibilities to earn money locally. Attempts towards the end of the 1970s to grow chilli, vanilla and cardamom proved uneconomic (L. Josephides 1985a: 81). Thus while in both the province and the district most of the available labour is active in the subsistence economy, labour migration represents the only or at any rate best opportunity for young men to earn money.[12] As in SHP as a whole, the economic situation in Kagua District is also reflected in education and health. According to a survey, one admittedly based on the 1980 census, only 18 percent of the estimated seven to twelve year olds go to community schools in Kagua District. This places it fifth after the districts of Nipa (19 percent), Pangia (23 percent), Mendi (29 percent) and Ialibu (32 percent) (Weeks 1987: 122). According to another statistic based on the same census, recording the percentage of the population who have access to an aid post, Kagua District with 88 percent comes last behind the districts of Koroba (89 percent), Tari (91 percent), Nipa (91 percent), Pangia (97 percent), Ialibu and Mendi (each 99 percent) (Weeks 1987: 123).

Within Kagua District, Aiya Constituency is more densely populated than other constituencies, yet is particularly badly equipped with schools, aid posts and government institutions. Those who live in the areas of Ibia, Wabi, Usa, Erave, Kagua and Kuali Lombo are, relatively speaking, least affected by bad transport links which add to economic and social disadvantage. Matters seem worse for the inhabitants of Sumi, since the branch road to Sumi from the road linking Kagua with Wabi, Usa and Ibia is rarely used and bad even by local standards. Nevertheless, Sumi is a centre for its surrounding area, since it already has a health centre and a community school, as well as a number of houses built by the Catholic Church. Pairundu itself is still separated from Sumi by a path which even the local people need two hours to cover and which can only be managed by car with a great deal of effort and only provided it does not rain and all the bridges have been repaired beforehand. As a result, very few inhabitants of Pairundu send their children to the community school in Sumi. Certainly up to now only Ken and Sayna from Pairundu have passed the sixth class, but both then failed to go on to pass the qualification for Kagua High School, so that they had to return to their village.

The relative marginality that ultimately describes the area around Pairundu as accurately as Kagua District and SHP as a whole was articulated by villagers in Pairundu themselves from time to time. Thus they described themselves to me on several occasions as a group stuck in the bush and fairly well trapped there. They complained on many occasions that, in contrast to the district capital, Pairundu had produced no policemen, teachers or doctors, especially given the fact that the salaries provided by such positions would be distributed among relatives. Above all, the villagers criticised the lack of support they received from the government and the economy, in comparison to Western Highlands Province, which is known for its contract labour, or the district capital. People also told me that they had been mocked as a group of opossums (*kapul lain*) by enemy communities because of the isolated situation of the village.[13] In addition, the enemies confirmed their own self-assessment by asking why they hid 'their white man' (the ethnographer) in the bush, instead of letting him live, if not in Kagua, then at least near the road to Sumi, as would have been more appropriate for a white man.

This situation of relative marginality may change in the coming years. The discovery of oil, gas and gold in different parts of the province means that far-reaching economic and social changes can be expected in the future and may increase the importance of the provincial capital, as well as the planned completion of a road from the Lake Kutubu oilfields to Mendi. However, the inhabitants of Pairundu will presumably be affected first by the fact that work on the road leading from Ibia to Mendi is nearly finished. This will make it possible to drive by 'Public Motor Vehicles' (PMV)[14] to Mendi via Sumi, Uma and Ibia more quickly and cheaply than was previously possible via Wabi, Kagua and Ialibu.

Kewa culture

In representing the cultural context, that is, the cultural parallels and differences between the inhabitants of Pairundu and the members of neighbouring communities, I will examine language, habitat and subsistence and social organisation, in that order.

The inhabitants of Pairundu belong to the approximately 40,000 to 50,000 Kewa speakers who mostly live in present-day Kagua District.[15] Franklin divides the Kewa into its western, eastern and southern dialects, also differentiating a northwestern dialect in the west and a southeastern one in the south.[16] According to Franklin (1971: 3), speakers of the three main dialects can understand one another. The eastern and southern dialects are thus related and, taken together, differ somewhat from the western dialect.[17] Pairundu itself is in the western dialect area (Map 2). The term 'Kewa', which is used today for the speakers of the language and their culture as a whole, as well as the language itself, was not originally their self-designation. 'Kewa' or 'Ewa' (a dialect variant also common in Pairundu) was only applied to groups living respectively south, southwest or southeast of one's own settlement. On the southern boundary of the Kewa region, these might also be Foi or Sau.[18] 'Merepa', on the other hand, was in many areas the corresponding term for groups living to the north, northwest or northeast. Within the entire Kewa area, therefore, no group called itself 'Kewa', 'Ewa' or 'Merepa'. Rather, one was 'Merepa' to one's neighbours to the south, whom one called 'Kewa' or 'Ewa', and one was 'Kewa' or 'Ewa' to one's neighbours to the north, whom one called 'Merepa' (cf. LeRoy 1979a: 182). The fact that Western ethnographers describe a group of people as 'Kewa', with or without their agreement, count this group and draw the boundaries of their speech area on maps does not mean that the term 'Kewa' actually corresponds to an absolutely coherent and distinct group. As far as the language is concerned, Franklin and LeRoy clearly indicate a limited degree of coherence or distinctiveness. According to Franklin (1971: 1), people belonging to different dialect groups even dispute whether they share the same language at all, and it almost never happens that different clans speak exactly the same as their neighbours. According to LeRoy (1979a: 180), Kewa living on the edge of the boundaries drawn for the Kewa area on the whole have fewer similarities with other Kewa than with nearby communities, even when these are no longer counted as Kewa. Elsewhere, LeRoy (1985a: 28) goes even further by claiming that there are not only no linguistic features, but also no cultural ones that define the Kewa as a closed group and differentiate them from their neighbours.[19]

The Kewa live in an area of between about 1,500 (L. Josephides 1985a: 2) and 1,750 (MacDonald 1984a: 1) square kilometres, bounded by the foothills of Mount Giluwe to the north, Mount Ialibu to the northeast and Mount Murray to the south. From the northwest to the south, the boundary of the Kewa country is marked by the Erave river (Map 2). The bed of the area is sedimentary and consists of chalk, with sandstone also appearing in the north.[20] From the northwest to the south a number of chains of hills run more or less parallel to one another, as do the large rivers Kagua, Sugu and Erave. One of these chains of hills is the Vakalu Range, which runs from Mount Kagua in the northwest to the southeast via the district capital Kagua, thus cutting the western dialect area approximately in the middle. South of the Vakalu Range stretches an extended valley in which, inter alia, lie Uma, Sumi, Kagua and Pairundu. The Kewa region as a whole falls gradually from a height of about 2,000 metres in the north to 1,000 metres in the south. However, the hills and valleys in the north are generally rather extended and wide, whereas the land in the south is rather more faulted and, as it were, more densely pushed together. A grassy steppe consisting mainly of sword-grass (*Miscanthus foridulus*,[21] or *kunai*) characterises the wide valleys and therefore also the area under the Vakalu Range. The hills and mountains are covered with secondary mixed forest, with primary mixed forest the higher one climbs. Thus the north of the Kewa area is characterised by rather flat grassland, the south by contrast by a rather rough, impassable, partly karstified, partly thickly wooded territory.[22] After trips undertaken together to the south, to Sare, Sua/Yeibu, Roka and Sumbura, inhabitants of Pairundu have occasionally pointed out how pleasant it is to live in a comparatively flat and widely extended region, in which one can walk without effort and enjoy a wide view. The climate in the Kewa area appears temperate. Average daytime temperatures are between 17 and 27°C, night-time temperatures between 9 and 17°C (cf. L. Josephides 1985a: 6). According to L. Josephides (1985a: 6), annual rainfall in Kagua is 3,100 mm. MacDonald (1991: 27) gives 4,000 mm for the area south of the Erave river. When I was in Pairundu, February and March – called the 'time of the sun' (*taim bilong san*) by the indigenous population – were the driest and hottest months. From the middle of July to the end of August, on the other hand, it rains almost every day, with a somewhat reduced average temperature, if not from morning to evening, then into the late afternoon. Here people speak of the 'time of the rains' (*taim bilong ren*).[23] Apart from these long dry and rainy periods, the changes in temperature do not allow clearly different seasons to be distinguished.

Like other inhabitants of the Highlands, the Kewa pursue horticulture and raise pigs (*Sus scrofa*[24]). Nowadays, this is occasionally supplemented by raising chickens and, very rarely, cattle. In contrast to groups from Sare or Sua/Yeibu, for example, the inhabitants of Pairundu claim to have very fertile land available to them. Using slash-and-burn or shifting cultivation, sweet potatoes (*Ipomoea batatas*) and sugarcane (*Saccharum officinarum*) are mainly grown, followed by taro (*Colocasia esculenta*), bananas (*Musa paradisiaca*), different types of *pitpit* (*Saccharum edule*), different spinach-type leaf vegetables, which cannot be identified more exactly (the general term is *kumu*), yams (*Dioscorea spp.*) and pandanus (*Pandanus brosmios*). Pumpkins, (probably *Cucurbita pepo*), gherkin-type fruits (probably *Cucumis sativus*), tomatoes (*Lycopersicon esculentum*), cabbage (probably *Brassica oleracea*), peanuts (*Arachis hypogaea*) and coffee (probably *Coffea arabica*) are other useful plants introduced through Western influence. Since nothing is stored, planting and harvesting goes on in principle the whole year round. Sweet potato mounds, together with the rows of sugarcane planted between them, make up the so-called 'sweet potato gardens' (*kaukau gaden*), which are to be found especially around the settlements, on the more or less gently rising slopes. While these 'sweet potato gardens' represent an essential part of the subsistence economy, not all men are ready to take on the work of clearing, which they find strenuous and laborious, and which is required to lay out bush gardens (*bus gaden*). Here, in addition to the other plants that are exploited, one grows leaf vegetables, taro and pandanus. Bush gardens are located at a greater distance from the settlements and within the hilly secondary forest.[25]

According to L. Josephides (1983: 296) and MacDonald (1984a: 15, 1991: 15, 69), activities connected with horticulture are, like individual plants, gender-specific. Men clear the land on which new gardens are to be laid out and later fence in the gardens to protect them from pigs wandering around. Taro, bananas, sugarcane, pandanus and yams are considered male and are therefore usually only planted and harvested by men. Women, on the other hand, lay out sweet potato mounds, fix the stem supports and take over especially the weeding and daily harvesting. As well as the sweet potato – always the principal basis of sustenance – different types of leaf vegetable are also classified as female. If one observes horticulture over a long period, one is compelled to realise that on the whole women bear the greatest burden of the labour required. Hunting plays virtually no role in the day-to-day life of the Kewa. Some men make traps or search for birds, opossums, cassowaries (*Casuarius sp.*), tree kangaroos (*Dendrolagus sp.*) and pythons (different types) in the forest with bows and arrows, though these attempts usually have little success. If an animal is trapped or killed, its meat is less the basis of food as a welcome change and supplement to the daily diet (cf. L. Josephides 1985a: 7, MacDonald 1985: 4).

The social organisation of the Kewa can be explained with reference to the model of segmentary societies. According to this model, which was used by Stagl (1974) for the Highlands of New Guinea as a whole, people act within groups which come together as larger groups on particular occasions, out of which are formed still larger groups with more inclusive segments. Thus several levels of segmentation accumulate on top of one another.[26] Particular functions are characteristic of each level. On the same level, these functions are fulfilled in the same way by all groups. To this extent, the groups on the same level are of the same type and are usually autonomous in relation to one another. The idea of an egalitarian society refers to the lack of a central ruling authority. The occasion for action determines which level or group will be activated. In opposition to a member of an alien sub-clan, one is a representative of one's own sub-clan. In opposition to a member of an alien clan, one joins together with all those belonging to one's own clan, even when they come from other sub-clans. If an antagonist comes from another clan, all the sub-clans of one's own clan join together. In this way, the segmentary organisation is characterised by a dualism between 'we groups' and 'they groups', between 'inside' and 'outside'. The same action, such as a theft, can be judged quite differently with respect to a member of the 'they group' than one of the 'we group' (cf. Read 1955: 263).

Although there is no terminological agreement in the literature, one can arrange the social units that Franklin, L. Josephides, LeRoy and MacDonald identify for the Kewa into at least four different levels of segmentation,[27] for which I shall use the terms 'phratry', 'clan', 'sub-clan' and 'lineage'.

The phratry is the most inclusive social unit of the Kewa.[28] Despite their using different names, the different authors agree that its members see themselves as linked to particular territorial boundaries and as belonging together. They share a common name and believe that they are descended from a common ancestor, without, however, being able to specify the genealogical links exactly. Phratries are primarily political units, most of whose members formerly fought on the same side in warfare.[29] Phratries consist of several clans,[30] whose members refer to a common name, a common territory and – without having exact genealogical knowledge – a common ancestor. At the same time, clans have greater significance, since people come together with members of other clans rather than members of other phratries, so that clan identity is activated more frequently. Accordingly, clans are important social groups in, for example, the context of disputes over territory, trials, the burials of prominent men, or cult and exchange institutions. Clans consist of several sub-clans.[31] Although, according to L. Josephides (1983: 292) and LeRoy (1981: 26), not even the members of the sub-clans can specify genealogical connections with their common ancestors exactly, the sub-clans play a still greater role comparatively speaking. In contrast to the clans, which are distributed over several settlements, they represent local units.[32] According to Franklin (1965: 414), use rights to land are inherited through them.[33] The members of a sub-clan can, for example, appear as guests at pig-killing festivals. Altogether, therefore, I see the level of the sub-clan as the functionally strongest level of segmentation in Kewa social organisation.[34] Another level of segmentation, to come under the sub-clans, might be the lineages.[35] The only difference between the lineage and the sub-clan is that the members of a lineage can trace genealogical connections with their common ancestors exactly. Apart from that, however, the functions fulfilled by the lineages are the same as those of the sub-clans.[36]

Patrilineal descent prevails among the Kewa, as all over the Papua New Guinea Highlands. The male members of phratries, clans, sub-clans and lineages see themselves as being linked in the male line, that is agnatically, and thus as the sons of the same fathers. Within the clan these 'sons' describe one another as 'brothers' (*ame*) when they descend from siblings and belong to the same generation.[37] The agnatic idiom therefore also involves both the idea and thus also the ideal of an '*ame* relationship'. According to L. Josephides (1985b: 293), the groups are held together by 'a powerful and pervasive ideology of co-operation along agnatic lines'. LeRoy (1985a: 49) speaks of 'the centrality of male siblingship in Kewa social structure'. In their different ways, both statements apply to the social units of all segmentation levels. The fact that the Kewa themselves foreground descent and brotherhood should not deceive one as to the actual composition of the groups that are present. Associated non-members, especially if, for example, they have helped at pig-killing festivals, can also be accepted into the clan individually or collectively, or be described henceforward as 'brothers'.[38] Accordingly, the agnatic idiom creates, as it were, the form in which the indigenous people speak of group composition or relations with other group members, though co-residence and cooperation are also important as principles of social organisation.[39] The comparatively limited significance that descent actually has for group composition may reflect the fact that Kewa genealogies are usually not traced back beyond four generations.[40]

The Kewa social units that have been mentioned up to now are usually regarded as exogamous. According to L. Josephides (1985a: 53) and MacDonald (1991: 180), a man may not marry a woman from his own phratry, clan, sub-clan or lineage. Also prohibited are the lineages of one's father and mother. However, marriage is allowed into groups from which the wives of one's siblings and the siblings of one's own father come (MacDonald 1984a: 3, 1991: 180f). According to LeRoy (1979a: 181), a man marries by preference his brother's wife's sister. Generally speaking, however, the Kewa have no prescriptive marriage rules, that is, the rules state whom one may not marry, rather than whom one must marry.[41] Traditionally, polygyny is not only allowed, but even preferred, though only a few men can assemble the value items to be able to finance several marriages.[42] Although among the Kewa – unlike, for example, the Enga or the Medlpa – marriage does not entail any formal or surviving exchange relationships between different clans,[43] after a marriage prestations and counter-prestations are made between the husband and his affines, his wife's close relatives. For example, affines expect payments from the husband when a child is born, when the latter arrives at different stages in his lifecycle or when he becomes seriously ill.[44] These payments, which, according to LeRoy (1985a: 125), the child continues when it is older, are compensation for his flesh and blood. In Kewa belief, both come from the mother and the affines, the child acquiring his bone structure from the paternal, male line.[45] The fact that, according to Franklin (1967: 79), a husband's name may not be said out loud in the presence of his affines may indicate a tense relationship between 'wife-givers' and 'wife-takers'. LeRoy (1985b: xxiii) reports that brothers-in-law also avoid mentioning one another by name.

Residence among the Kewa is patrivirilocal, that is, the wife moves to her husband on marriage to live on the land handed down to him by his father. Here too, however, there are exceptions. Thus it is usually accepted that individual men prefer to move into the settlement community of their wives.[46] The nuclear family often coincides with the household, but need not necessarily be identical with it, since, by mutual agreement, in principle anyone can attach himself to another household. The household – that is the nuclear family extended around relatives and acquaintances – constitutes, as Stagl (1974: 215) concludes for the Highlands, as a whole the unit of production, consumption and distribution. The daily garden work is thus usually carried out by members of the household. Only in the case of large-scale tasks, such as clearing extensive areas, does one ask members of other sub-clans for help. In return, a meal is provided for the helpers, usually that same evening. However, for the most part whole settlements only assemble together on the occasions already mentioned, which also unite clans and sub-clans.

The Kewa are not isolated from their neighbours. The fact that, as already mentioned, the Kewa originally probably spread from the north towards the south and east indicates connections between the culture of the Kewa, which I have just sketched in its fundamentals, and the cultures of the neighbouring regions. Thus Franklin identifies parallels between the Kewa and the Enga (Franklin and Franklin 1978: 423), Medlpa (Franklin and Franklin 1978: 465 n. 1), Mendi (Franklin 1971: 43f) and Wiru (Franklin 1971: 42). In addition, according to LeRoy (1985a: 32), the Kewa live in an area of 'major pre-contact trade routes for mother-of-pearl shells', meaning that in the pre-colonial period, being in contact with their respective neighbours, they traded pearlshells from the coastal regions in the south to the north and pigs in the opposite direction.

For A. Strathern (1984: 113), the Erave river – that is, the southern edge of the Kewa area – marks a boundary separating the Highlands cultures from the so-called 'fringe cultures' to the south, to which the Etoro, Kaluli, Foi and Daribi belong. According to A. Strathern, the further one moves away from the Highlands in the direction of these 'fringe cultures', the more the influence of Big Men diminishes, the more the intensity of agriculture declines, the more dependence on sweet potatoes and pigs falls and the more the importance of forest products and game increases.[47] The 'fringe cultures', which accordingly seem to be shaped more by the Seaboard than the Highlands, still correspond best on the whole to the south of the Kewa area, which LeRoy describes as 'forest', but less to that wide zone of transition in which the inhabitants of Pairundu also live and less still to the north that LeRoy calls 'grassland'. For LeRoy (1979a: 180), the southern Kewa share with the Daribi 'similar social and mythic systems' Nevertheless even among the southern Kewa sago is not grown, nor do people live in longhouses, as is typical of the 'fringe cultures'. Thus I consider MacDonald's (1991: 30) view that the southern Kewa are an 'in-between people' uniting characteristics of the Seaboard and Highlands cultures, corresponding to their position in the pre-colonial bartering between the two regions, as exaggerated. Instead in my view, one should agree with LeRoy's (1985a: 29) thesis irrespective of cultural heterogeneity and gradations in a north-south direction: 'Culturally, the Kewa are a highland people…'.

Society and economy in Pairundu

The male inhabitants of Pairundu are mostly members of one clan that traces itself back to a common ancestor called Kata and his first-born son. This son's name, Kome, is also the name of the clan. The Mamarepa, who link themselves to Mama, Kata's second-born son, are regarded as a 'brother clan' (*bratalain*) of the Kome. Thus Kome and Mamarepa together form a phratry, the most inclusive unit in Pairundu and the surrounding area.[48] However, although elsewhere Kewa phratries represent exogamous groups, the Kome and the Mamarepa do intermarry, though they claim that this was still prohibited in the pre-colonial period. While the Kome live in Pairundu, the Mamarepa are distributed among the villages of Sua/Yeibu,[49] Ruri and Anapote.

The Kome consist of the three sub-clans of Auro Kome, Rata Kome and Rundu Kome, which themselves consist of different lineages.[50] In the western Kewa dialect, the names of the three sub-clans each refer to sites of possible settlement: *Auro* means 'below' (in the valley; *tambolo*), *rundu* means 'on top of the mountain' (*antap long maunten*), and *rata* means 'in the middle' (on the slope; *namel*). For the clan and the sub-clans the term 'ruru' is also used in Pairundu. The term 'repa', on the other hand, appears both as the last syllable in clan names and as a description of lineages. Like the sub-clan and the clan, therefore, the *repa* is a corporate group that survives its individual members.[51] In January

1991, I carried out a census, according to which 601 individuals altogether belong to the Kome. The Mamarepa[52] living in Pairundu are included here, as well as those who are living permanently outside Pairundu. This means contract workers and their families, as well as Kome women who have left Pairundu after marrying. The husbands and children of these women were also counted, since the Kome can also lay claim to them. When one breaks this census down into clans, so that the Mamarepa living in Pairundu appear as a sub-clan of their own,[53] we see that the Rundu Kome have the highest proportion of the total population (42.76%), followed by the Rata Kome (29.45%), the Auro Kome (25.46%) and the Mamarepa (2.33%). Of the total population, altogether 183 individuals, less than a third (30.45%), live permanently in Pairundu. As many Rundu Kome as Rata Kome (34.97% each) belong to this group. Then come the Auro Kome (22.4%) and the Mamarepa (7.65%). As regards gender distribution, among those who live permanently in Pairundu there is a surplus of men (52.46% as against 47.54%).[54] Statements concerning the numerical proportion of the different generations cannot be provided, since in individual cases age can only be estimated very roughly. The Kome themselves do not keep a count of their ages and are therefore not in a position to give them exactly. With this reservation, the group that lives permanently in Pairundu consists mostly of under ten year olds (42.62%), the smallest number being over forty-five (10.93%). In between come first those between twenty-five and forty-five (25.14%), then those between ten and twenty-five (21.31%).

Pairundu basically consists of a circular path linking the apparently scattered individual houses and smaller spaces with one another (Map 3). The houses range from simple wooden shacks to large men's houses of traditional construction (rectangular houses with gabled roofs and mostly on stilts). While these men's houses often accommodate several families, the smaller houses belong to nuclear families, married couples or individuals. Pairundu consists of two parts called 'Pairundu*' and 'Ropena', which themselves consist of several smaller units.[55] Certainly those living in Pairundu* are mainly Rata Kome and in Ropena Auro Kome and Rundu Kome, but the members of the individual sub-clans do not necessarily settle in close proximity. Similarly, for example, the Auro Kome are distributed among Pasereanda (Ropena), Rimbupiri (Pairundu*) and Pairanda (Pairundu*). In addition, individuals may associate with other sub-clans and lineages. For example, one Rata Kome (Yapua Repa) joined the Rundu Kome (Alia Kome) with Pala in Ropena, while one Auro Kome (Sapu Repa) lived with Ruapo in Yampiri in the men's house of Ari, a Rata Kome (Yapua Repa). Whereas, according to LeRoy (1979a: 181, 1981: 26, 1985a: 40) and MacDonald (1984a: 1f, 1985: 4, 1991: 28), among the southern Kewa clans may be distributed among several settlements – as is the case with the Mamarepa – the Kome are concentrated in Pairundu, so that here their clan represents a local unit. However, the size of Pairundu, with 183 permanent residents, corresponds to LeRoy's 'average'.[56]

In general, individual Kome claim to know how they are related to one another genealogically within their own lineages. Thus one rarely encounters a lack of knowledge or interest, nor does one find many contradictions, between statements from different informants in collecting genealogies. The genealogies reveal that in two cases men have taken over the wives of their deceased 'brothers',[57] and also that in two cases there has been a marriage between a Rata Kome and a Rundu Kome, thus breaching the requirement of clan exogamy.[58] From the etic point of view, such marriages are supposedly refused not least because only a comparatively modest counter-prestation can be claimed for a woman marrying within the clan. However, this in itself represents an economic advantage for the groom, provided he can prevail against the opposition of his clan brothers and accepts the loss of prestige that is linked with such a marriage. Whereas individual Kome are usually able to provide a genealogical connection with their own lineage without further ado, most would be hard put to describe exactly how the different lineages are connected with one another within their sub-clan. Even the question of how their own sub-clan is linked with the mythical ancestor Kata – that is, how the three sub-clans originated from Kata's or Kome's children – usually exceeds their genealogical knowledge. Only Yawa (97.), who was described by those belonging to several sub-clans as a suitable specialist, as well as the leading man of the Auro Kome and the Kome as a whole, was able to formulate a version of the genealogical connections of the lineages of the different sub-clans. In this genealogy, Yawa claimed that a connection existed between Kata, the Sapu Repa,[59] the Raki Repa (both Auro Kome), the Yapua Repa (Rata Kome) and the Aiya Kome (Rundu Kome). Thus Yawa described the members of Sapu Repa, Raki Repa and Yapua Repa as the sons of brothers and – together with the Aiya Kome – as the sons of parallel cousins. However, according to Yawa, no connection existed between Kata and the Yakema Repa, the Kane Repa (both Rata Kome),[60] the Kapia Repa or the Alia Kome (both Rundu Kome). In contrast, Wala (90.), the leading man of the Rundu Kome – who was competing with Yawa for the leading position in the Kome as a whole – created a link between Kata and Yamu, an ancestor of Kapia Repa, as well as between Kata and Keler, which according to Rekepea (73.), however, actually concerned an ancestor of the Alia Kome.

The differences in the genealogies told to me thus give expression, among other things, to a dispute over whether the Alia Kome – as the accounts given by Wala emphasise – ultimately count as the children of Kata and therefore belong to Kome through their ancestor Keler, or whether, as Yawa thinks, their origin is obscure and therefore they are basically not related to the Kome at all. This kinship is also disputed by Ipapula (34.) as a Rata Kome (Yapua Repa). According to his account, he had brought the Alia Kome to Pairundu in the pre-colonial period in order to increase the Kome's numbers and therefore fighting power. In doing so, he had certainly described them as his brothers, although in fact they were not Kata's children. Yawa (98.) denied the link between the Alia Kome and Kata in an even more drastic fashion by claiming that Kaku and Keler were two of Rama's (Aiya Kome) dogs, whose names the Alia Kome had only taken over because they knew nothing about their own ancestors.[61] The keenness of the question whether the Alia Kome actually belong to the Kome by descent or not is due to a permanently smouldering conflict between the Alia Kome and Sapu Repa (Auro Kome) over land use rights. If Yawa's position were to prevail, the Alia Kome would be defeated. The discussion concerning the genealogical location of ancestors and the competition between the different versions of the past in a genealogical idiom are thus partly controlled by opposed present-day political interests. The Kome agree that they were not divided into three sub-clans to begin with. According to the two Auro Kome, Coleman Komea (Sapu Repa) and Coleman Makoa (Raki Repa), this division was originally made by Rena, Yawa's father.[62] The separation of Sapu Repa and Raki Repa is also traced back to Rena. According to Ipapula, Rena had formerly also derived the Yapua Repa from the Auro Kome, to whom they belonged originally, in order to allocate them to the Rata Kome, who already consisted of the Kane Repa and the Yakema Repa.[63]

If the composition of the sub-clans in the accounts of many Kome seems to be the result of a historical process of development in which sub-clans are divided up and lineages newly allocated, this provides a flexibility to social units, which is also manifested in the acceptance of basically non-agnatically related individuals that is also reported for the Kewa as a whole. Both individuals[64] and, in the case of the Alia Kome, whole groups – at least according to Ipapula – have been integrated as 'brothers'. This integration indicates the numerical growth of the Kome in the course of history, as well as the fact that the former rule of exogamy between Kome and Mamarepa not longer exists today. Supposedly Kome and Mamarepa were just one clan earlier, until, after reaching an appropriate size, they separated and became a pair of clans. Through further growth, the separation then probably increased, until the exogamic rule came to be seen as obsolete.[65]

The fact that the Kome are no less organised in a segmentary fashion than other Kewa groups and that the term 'egalitarian society' is therefore as appropriate for them, does not mean that all Kome see one another as equal or as having equal rights. Instead, there exist differences of prestige and power between both the genders and the separate generations, just as much as between men with great and limited political influence.

The relationship between the genders among the Kome is generally characterised by the antagonism that is known throughout the Highlands of Papua New Guinea (see Stagl 1971). As already described, plants that are exploited and particular types of work count as either male or female, and it is claimed that pigs' and humans' bodies both consist of male and female parts. A social separation also goes along with this distinction. Thus in the pre-colonial period women lived separately with their daughters and small sons, according to family, while the men mostly slept in the men's house.[66] The idea that too great a proximity between the sexes is damaging for men still seems widespread today, even though, according to L. Josephides (1985a: 8) and MacDonald (1991: 61), it is less sharply expressed among the Kewa compared to other Highlands cultures. After I sat down opposite Ata (I) by the fire in his house, he suddenly asked me not to stay on that side, because that was usually his wife's side and instead to move next to him. Ripu once told me, in a conversation held far from the village, that he always knew when his wife was menstruating because, in accordance with the corresponding prohibition, she would not bring him any food at this time. If one accepted food from a menstruating woman, one would soon fall ill with tuberculosis or lose one's strength.[67]

Differences of prestige and power go along with the dualism between 'male' and 'female' and the antagonism between men and women, as is already shown by the fact that women have the greatest share of daily subsistence work.[68] L. Josephides (1985a: 8) describes the social position of women as 'clearly politically subordinated to men and economically dependent on them', and she connects this inequality with the fact that the Kewa allocate the private sphere to the women and the public sphere to the men.[69] While on the one hand the men monopolise appearances in public, for example, pig-killing festivals, which are concerned with well-being, power and group identity (L. Josephides 1985a: 214), on the other hand they simultaneously influence the private sphere which actually counts as 'female', in that they make decisions involving the family and the household (L. Josephides 1985a: 130, 217). In addition, according to L. Josephides (1985a: 66), a woman cannot inherit any land of her own according to the patrivirilocal rule of residence. Instead, after marriage she becomes economically dependent on her husband and his relatives on his land. On the other hand, it would certainly be an exaggeration to deny women any political influence. Thus Puku, Ipalula's older daughter, claimed that men had to obey women, otherwise they would not provide them with any food. In addition, in some discussions in Pairundu, I was able to observe that some women, mostly older ones, now and then spoke in public, though this was still rare on the whole.

From the Western point of view, relations between the generations seem just as unequal as relations between the sexes. Stagl (1974: 256ff.) has indicated for the New Guinea Highlands as a whole that the relatively greater power of the elders derives from the fact that they control prestige goods more than their juniors.[70] Accordingly, in Pairundu too, relations between the generations on the level of norms are characterised by obedience to the elders. When your first-born brother undertakes something, Kevin (45.) assured me, you usually join him.[71] While a father still has strength, Kenneth (39.) explained, his son must support him. Ripu (76.) even thought that the son should take second place to his father. For example, it would not be right if he owned as many pigs as his father Ari.

The inequality between the generations is also expressed in conflict. Without my bringing up the issue with him, Robert (83.) complained that the elders, who in the pre-colonial period had themselves murdered, raped and burnt, were now always reminding their juniors to obey and not violate the laws. On the other hand, independently of one another, Otmar and Yapanu criticised the fact that, in contrast to the pre-colonial period, people no longer listened to their parents. Simultaneously, however, young people were sometimes conceded greater competence in dealing with the problems of the present.[72]

The difference between the generations partly coincides with the difference between the 'ordinary' and the leading men, who mainly belong to the older generation. These leading men are described as 'Big Men' by the Kome, the Kewa as a whole and other Highlands peoples. Basically, the differentiation of men among the Kewa and other Highlands cultures is determined equally by the values of strength and equivalence.[73] The value of equivalence requires that for all prestations a counter-prestation of at least the same value must be paid sooner or later, in order to express equivalence with one's exchange partner. If the counter-prestation is not made, the creditor gains in prestige with respect to the debtor. It is precisely this that individuals and groups strive for, in accordance with the value of strength. At the same time, however, anyone striving for prestige must settle all gifts owed. Just as differences in prestige develop from the value of strength, so their growth is balanced by the value of equivalence. In any case, therefore, Big Men are those who have succeeded best in exploiting the tension between equivalence and strength for themselves, in order to create extra prestige for themselves with respect to others. In the pre-colonial period, conducting warfare (*yanda*) and pig-killing festivals (*yawe*) provided opportunities for both the individual and collective demonstration of strength.[74] However, while warfare was already prohibited at the start of colonisation, pig-killing festivals still take place today (Figure 1.1). In principle, they consist of a bundle of exchange activities carried out on different occasions, at which prestations, mostly of pig meat, settle debts, seal marriages and satisfy demands for compensation, for example. Thus they are simultaneously building up or reducing differences in prestige between individuals and groups.[75] Decisive for the success of a *yawe* is the participation of Ewa or Merepa whom one provides with pearlshells and pig meat, when they decorate themselves in the manner typical of them and dance the dances of their region. In this way, the reputation not only of the host group but also the Big Men who represent these host groups to the visitors is increased. Accordingly, to the question, what was the most important thing about a *yawe*, Ari named the attempt to trump others and the efforts of the leading men to increase their own prestige.[76] In fact, as LeRoy (1979a: 200) stresses, compared to 'ordinary' men, Big Men usually carry out more exchange activities and have more exchange partners and in remoter settlements. In order to be able to play a leading

Figure 1.1 Cooking pig meat (Kamare, 2 August 1991; photo: Holger Jebens).

role in exchange activities, it is necessary to develop a particular level of productivity, that is, to produce greater harvests out of the garden and keep more pigs than others.

In Pairundu, Yawa counts as a Big Man for the Auro Kome, Wala (Figure 1.2) for the Rundu Kome,[77] and Ari for the Rata Kome. With respect to the Kome as a whole, Yawa is ascribed the first rank, Wala the second. Their respective influence is expressed on different occasions. As I was told, both led the discussions when the Kome and the Mamarepa demanded compensation together in another village for a man descended from a Kome woman who had supposedly been murdered. When Yawa asked me to increase the payments I was to make later or leave the village, Ari and Rekepea, who were also present and who did not share Yawa's view, looked at the ground without saying anything, not daring to contradict him openly.

The example of Yawa shows that rhetorical skills also belong to the properties of a Big Man, since, in the Kome's overall view, Yawa can 'talk the best'. As a result, for preference he is trusted to represent the clan's affairs to the outside world. Coleman Komea praised him as a politician who is able to take in others.[78] At the same time, however, the respect shown to a Big Man is not necessarily connected with personal sympathy. Thus the members of some sub-clans reckoned Yawa to be a 'bad man' (*man nogut*), whom they accused especially of spending more time in Wasuma than in Pairundu. In contrast to Yawa, the reputation of Wala, who participates less in public discussions, is due rather to the fact that he frequently shares food with other Kome. As his 'foster-son' Serale (87.)

Figure 1.2 Wala talks to the ethnographer (Yawireanda, 18 March 1991; photo: Katherina Wieker).

told me, Wala always instructed him that it was necessary 'to eat quickly' (*kaikai hariap*), that is, to provide food often for as many people as possible, so that the esteem of one's name remains high. The example of Wala shows that it is less a matter of having great possessions than of passing them on in quantity. One therefore becomes a Big Man not by accumulating goods or consuming them oneself, but, as it were, by allowing many goods to pass through one's own hands by distributing a lot of them. The requirement not to accumulate or consume too many goods, which corresponds to the value of equivalence and, to that extent, is immanent in the culture, might sometimes seem like an 'obligation to share' from the Western point of view.

Given that the value of equivalence balances the value of strength, the difference in power between leading men and 'ordinary' men should not be overestimated. In accordance with the segmentary social organisation of the Kewa in general and the Kome in particular, what is involved in the position of the Big Man is not an office that is inherited[79] or allocated by a central authority, but a collectively more or less recognised status in which, as it were, the individual element gradually increases on the basis of personal characteristics and merits. To that extent, this status depends on the support of the group. Mostly one loses it as gradually as one acquires it, since in old age at the latest, social prestige declines along with one's bodily performance. The village community will certainly continue to respect a former Big Man because of his past merits, but no longer approach him in connection with actual decisions. A limitation in Yawa's power, for example, is indicated by the fact that he was not able to persuade other Kome to accept his demand that I should leave Pairundu. After it had become clear that most of the inhabitants of the village were on my side, Wala, Ari and Rekepea also came over to me. To that extent, they were leading men because they articulated the majority opinion. This shows that Big Men generally try to coordinate their own positions with the group's interests. The differences between 'ordinary men' and Big Men are limited by the fact that in principle they must both carry out the same subsistence work. In principle too, all men become economically independent at marriage at the latest. Even the Kome themselves make a clear reference to this independence. According to Wala (91.): 'We have not contracted anyone else to till our land or fetch water and firewood. Everyone has his own stomach. Equally, everyone has his own house and thus his own thoughts and way of behaving'. In my opinion, this emphasis on independence and the structural equality of all individuals articulates an egalitarian ethos corresponding to the value of equivalence, which is simultaneously the expression of an individualism which, I assume, is characteristic not just of the Kewa, but also of the Highlands peoples as a whole.[80]

In accordance with their egalitarian ethos, the Kome claim that there are hardly any economic distinctions in Pairundu. Thus Ripu (76.) expressed the view that anyone who secretly claimed that he possessed a lot a money and pigs would be lying. Nonetheless, in separate conversations I asked a selected group of informants to provide a list of who were, in their opinion, the richest villagers. According to this, Wala, Rekepea and Yawa occupy the leading positions, followed by Naki and Ari, the latter being named third or fourth more frequently that the others.

In order to find out what this 'wealth' consists of and how one acquires it, I asked the same group of informants to provide details of their average income and expenditure, as well as their property, which I describe metaphorically as 'capital'.[81] Basically today, one receives money for assisting with clearing work, building a men's house or preparing a pig-killing festival, whereas earlier one obtained only food, pearlshells or pig meat for these activities. Money has also become a part of the brideprice. For most Kome, one important possibility to earn money, used mainly by women, is selling food in the markets in Sumi, Rake or Kagua, which are usually open on Wednesdays and Saturdays,[82] where those asked earn roughly equivalent weekly amounts ranging from 1.5 to 3.5 K and above. In January and again between the end of June and the beginning of July, the inhabitants of Pairundu sell the coffee they have grown.[83] The profit targeted here usually amounts to between 30 and 80 K per year. Only Naki, Coleman Komea and Robert have been active up to now as middlemen, buying coffee in the area at a low price, transporting it to Ialibu or even Mount Hagen and selling it there for a profit of between about 160 K (Robert) and 200 K (Naki, Coleman Komea) per year. In general, the period of coffee-selling in Pairundu counts as a 'time of money' (*taim bilong moni*), which many villagers spend playing cards for hours or days. Young men in particular also find a few months' work from time to time as contract workers on the coffee plantations of Western Highlands Province, where they earn between 20 and 50 K on average per year. A final source of income to be mentioned are the shops owned by Naki, Rekepea, Ari and Simon. Coleman Komea has a share in Naki's shop, while Robert has a share in a shop owned by his brother-in-law in Rake. These individuals have the following monthly earnings: 7 K (Simon), under 8 K (Ari and Rekepea), 13 K (Robert) and 32 K (Naki).[84] In the 'good' time following the selling of coffee, those I asked spent on average less than 2 K in the markets, but up to 5 K in the shops.[85]

Apart from money, the capital available in Pairundu consists of pigs, pearlshells, coffee plots, gardens and bush gardens.[86] The value of individually owned pigs exceeds 2,500 K only in the case of a few villagers, all of whom belong to the Rundu Kome: Serale (4,500 K), Nosope (4,580 K) and Wala (5,540 K). The largest group of informants assured me that they had no money. Otherwise the assets available to most of them amount to up to 50 K. Only Yapa (480 K), Rekepea (530 K), Robert (680 K) and Naki (700 K) said they had more than 250 K. Those with a share in one of the shops valued the total worth of their stock at the time of the interview at between 50 and 100 K (Ari), 80 K (Robert), 90 K (Simon), 200 K (Rekepea) and 250 K (Naki). Only eight people possessed pearlshells. Most of those I asked had laid out up to five coffee plots, from two to ten gardens and up to three bush gardens.

If one compares Pairundu with more centrally located villages like Kuali Lombo (Map 2), for example, where people generally have shoes and often a radio or even a walkman, the economic situation among the Kome corresponds in general to the situation already described of relative marginality, which characterises the area around Pairundu no less that Kagua District and Southern Highlands Province as a whole. The further growth of economic differentiation has been limited up to now by the continuing importance of the subsistence economy as well as the fact that villagers usually hardly save money[87] or reinvest it, but spend it on 'luxury goods' like rice, tinned fish and clothes, or gamble it away. To that extent, from the etic perspective too, the picture drawn up by the Kome themselves in accordance with their egalitarian ethos, according to which people compare one another in economic terms, is confirmed. On the other hand, this picture should not tempt one to overlook personal differences between the villagers, since the quite different personal motivations that lead one to decide whether it is sufficient to obtain just enough food for survival from one's garden, or whether one should attempt to increase income and capital through a greater use of labour, are matters for the individual. Thus Naki, who due to the higher income he obtains from growing coffee and from his shop, had the largest sum of money in Pairundu, seemed to me precisely the 'ambitious entrepreneur' type. Accordingly, his companion Coleman Komea (29.) said that he too regarded him as the richest man in the village and that when they were all sitting round together talking, Naki would not take part but instead be thinking about his shop. As well as Coleman Komea, Robert, with his work as a coffee middleman and shares in shops, also corresponds to the Naki model to a lesser extent.

On the whole the economically leading positions are held by the Big Men in Pairundu, who own more pigs, coffee plots, gardens and bush gardens overall than most of the other villagers. If Yawa, Wala and Rekepea have a relatively higher income from selling food or coffee, they owe this not least to the fact that as individuals they have more wives, who simultaneously represent more labour power. Ultimately, therefore, the list of the richest villagers obtained from the information given by my informants mostly reflects the actual situation. However, I think Naki is about to catch up with Yawa, Wala and Rekepea. After them come Serale, Robert and Coleman Komea, whereas many Rata Kome might overestimate their Big Man Ari in economic terms. While both the Big Men and Serale owe their economic position overwhelmingly to their gardens and pigs, thus representing, as it were, the traditional sector, Naki, Robert and Coleman Komea represent rather the changes brought by colonialism, because of the incomes they obtain from coffee-growing and shops.

Like the Kewa in general, the Kome in particular are not at all isolated from their neighbours. Rather, influences were already present in the pre-colonial period through the adoption of particular practices. According to Wala, for example, the usual custom in Pairundu of giving guests at a pig-killing festival a gift of sugarcane beforehand, to indicate to them how much meat they would receive later, came originally from the Wiru of Pangia. The style of construction of Ari's, Rekepea's and Alupa's men's houses, on the other hand, was adopted from the Erave area, according to Wala. A myth I recorded, in which Kata learned how to mow grass, make fire, construct an earth oven and defecate from a member of the Eno, indicates a connection between the Kome and the Eno.[88] In addition, contacts arose out of relationships of friendship and enmity, the historical development of which Ari (17.) summarised for me in a brief sketch. Originally the Kome lived in Pairundu*, Ropena* and Sua, the Mamarepa in Yeibu and Anapote. The first battles took place between the Kome and the Uma (Uma).[89] Finally the Uma came to Pairundu to destroy their houses and gardens. So the Rundu Kome fled to Sua/Yeibu and the Rata Kome, together with the Auro Kome, to Sare, where affines of theirs were already living. They only returned later. The Rata Kome and Auro Kome built new houses in Walua, while the Rundu Kome did so northwest of Yassaweli. Afterwards the Kome and Mamarepa fought against the Akuna of Rulupare. These linked up with the Mirupa (Porane, Yame, Pira) living northwest of Kagua, the Ramirepa (Mapata) and the Ape (Ondere). Although the Kome and Mamarepa had joined up with the Akuna-Rola (Yakoa), Anerepa (Kira) and Auerepa (Wabi), they were put to flight again. The Rundu Kome and Mamarepa went to Sua/Yeibu, the Rata Kome and Auro Kome to Sare. It was still some time before they could return in order to lay out new gardens and erect new houses in Pairundu* and Ropena. In the next set of battles too, the Kome, Mamarepa, Anerepa and Akuna-Rola stood on one side, opposite the Rulupare-Akuna and Mirupa on the other. On this occasion too, the Rundu Kome had to retire to Sua/Yeibu and the Rata Kome and Auro Kome to Sare. This time, however, it was not long before the Kome and Mamarepa united with the Anerepa, Auerepa, Pamenderepa (Kanoa) and their former enemies, the Rulupare-Akuna, against the Mirupa. The whites made their initial appearance at the time of these battles. There was further defeat and flight to Sua/Yeibu or Sare. Only afterwards did the Kome return to Pairundu, for the last time up to now, where they settled first in Walua and Yassaweli. In Kira, Wabi, Yakoa and Rulupare too, most of the houses had been destroyed by their enemies. This report is notable in that Ari makes the Kome and Mamarepa seem like passive victims always having to flee from warlike attacks. To some extent enemies turned into allies,[90] but most of the old rivals are still classified as enemies today.[91]

Concluding remarks

Altogether, at first sight social and economic conditions in present-day Pairundu create the impression that the lives of the villagers are still mainly shaped by the traditional culture. Kinship, co-residence and co-operation still represent the essential principles of group composition. These groups continue to distinguish themselves above all according to the differences in power that exist between the genders, the generations and the 'ordinary' and leading men. Since the subsistence economy has retained its basic significance for the most part, as in the pre-colonial period the Kome must visit their gardens daily, in order to harvest enough food for the day there. At the same time, economic differentiation is relatively little developed in comparison with centrally located villages. The relatively limited extent not only of this economic differentiation, but also of Western influences of any sort, is certainly due in the first instance to the situation of marginality outlined here, which is just as characteristic of Kagua District and Southern Highlands Province as a whole as for the area around Pairundu. To that extent, from an etic perspective, I would agree with the Kome when they describe themselves as a group stuck or trapped in the bush.

Drawing attention to the continuing significance of the traditional culture does not at all mean that this should be understood as static or unchangeable. The flexibility of the traditional culture is demonstrated by the relationships that the Kewa in general and the Kome in particular have with their neighbours. Such relationships, and certainly mutual influences too, manifest themselves on the one hand in linguistic parallels and trade contacts and on the other hand in elements of the pig-killing festivals and the manner of building men's houses. With respect to the social units of the Kome, flexibility is shown in the integration of originally non-agnatically related individuals and groups, as well as the fact that new sub-clans have been divided up and new lineages classified. Finally and not least, the mobility forced on people by pre-colonial warfare may have required a considerable degree of adaptability of villagers. Corresponding to the picture of a changing traditional culture is the fact that, from time to time, the Kome articulate different and mutually contradictory versions of the past. Thus in disputes over the origin of the Alia Kome in particular, to some extent attempts are made to advance present-day political interests through the genealogical manipulation of the past.

Notes

1. The National Parliament consists of a House of Assembly whose members are elected for a five-year legislative period. The members of the cabinet, the so-called National Executive Council, led by the Prime Minister, are responsible to Parliament as the highest legislative organ. Members of the cabinet must simultaneously be members of parliament. According to the constitution, however, not more than a quarter of members of parliament may belong to the cabinet.
2. Unless otherwise stated, I have drawn the information in the following paragraphs from conversations with the following individuals: Yaungtime Koromba (former Prime Minister of Southern Highlands Province), Henry Koyu (First Assistant Secretary for Economic Services, Southern Highlands Province), Wane (Councillor for Pira Council), Ralia (Peace Officer for Pira Council) and various other officials of the Provincial Government in 1990.
3. The role of the Peace Officers is to report criminal offences to the police and to send conflicts that cannot be settled informally to the village courts. These village courts, which are usually held once a week, are presided over by the village court magistrates, who decide the cases brought before them.
4. Rath (1989: 51). Awesa (1988: 2) gives a figure of about 26,000 square kilometres.
5. The other Highland provinces are Enga (12.9 inhabitants per square kilometre), Eastern Highlands (24.7), Chimbu (29.2) and Western Highlands (31.3). Source: Statistik des Auslandes. Länderbericht Papua-Neuguinea 1984 (after Rath 1989: 51).
6. In this sense, the notion of 'development' is normative, Western culture as a goal being the basis on which the process of change labelled 'development' is to proceed. To me, this idea is highly problematic. Instead, we should basically grant the inhabitants of Papua New Guinea the possibility to change in other directions too, without negatively judging these trends a priori. An additional consideration is that 'development' in the sense of change had already occurred before contact with Western culture. My scepticism concerning the ideas that are often connected with the notion of 'development' is reflected in my putting the term in single inverted commas.
7. The only exceptions are the health workers or Aid Post Orderlies (APOs).
8. Writing of labour migration, L. Josephides (1985a: 9) points out that the Southern Highlands has the same position with respect to the Central Highlands that the latter once had with respect to the coastal region.
9. In 1988, 98 percent of the expenditure in the provincial budget (19,505,524 Kina) was assumed by the National Government, only 2 percent (457,000 Kina) coming from its own income (Puruno 1988: 3). The Kina is the official currency of Papua New Guinea. One Kina (abbreviated to 'K') is divided into 100 Toea (abbreviated to 't') and was worth USD 1.34 in November 1989.
10. Further data on education, though for the end of the 1970s, can be found in Hecht (1981).

11. In general, the 'state of development' of a region cannot be explained solely by its colonial history. Certainly Kagua District was crossed by patrols of the colonial government and provided with government stations earlier than, for example, parts of Nipa District (on the Nembi Plateau, see Crittenden 1987) or Pangia District. However, the latter quickly became 'most developed' and in the mid-1980s was already exporting more coffee than all the other districts in SHP put together (J. Clark 1988: 45).

12. Cf. L. Josephides (1985a: 88) on the Sugu river region.

13. The allusion in this description is to the isolated location, since opossums live in the bush and not in settlements like humans.

14. PMV are usually small buses run as public transport by a few private individuals.

15. On the basis of a census carried out between July/August 1965 and December 1966, Franklin (1971: 9) gives an initial figure of 39,453. Later he estimated this speech group at about 40,000 (Franklin and Franklin 1978: 74). LeRoy (1979a: 179) shares this view, though MacDonald (1984a: 1) gives a figure of 50,000.

16. On the basis of the census carried out between July/August 1965 and December 1966, Franklin (1971: 9) gives the following numbers of speakers for the different dialects: 17,921 for the western dialect (including 684 for the northwest subdialect); 17,758 for the eastern dialect; and 3,774 for the southern dialect (including 404 for the southeast dialect). According to MacDonald (1991: 91), the southeast subdialect is also called *Pole*.

17. Franklin (1971: 43). According to Wurm (1982: 117, 126) the Kewa as a whole belongs to the Angal (Mendi)-Kewa subfamily of the West Central family of the East New Guinea Highlands stock of the Papuan (non-Austronesian) languages. Franklin suggests that Kewa derives from the Proto-Enga of the present-day Enga linguistic area and that, from there, it moved south about 2000 years ago (Franklin and Franklin 1978: 72).

18. See also LeRoy (1985a: 29) and L. Josephides (1985a: 2, 200 n. 3).

19. This statement, which means that the term 'Kewa' must be given up, even by LeRoy, seems exaggerated to me. Although the material published up to now on the Kewa certainly gives an impression of heterogeneity, the common features presented below allow the general characteristics of a 'Kewa culture' to be recognised.

20. For a description of the habitat of the Kewa region, see Franklin (1971: 7), L. Josephides (1983: 292), LeRoy (1979b: 10, 1985a: 29, 1985b: xxf) and MacDonald (1984a: 1).

21. Unless otherwise stated, all Latin terms for plants have been provided by Paul Hiepko (personal communication).

22. LeRoy (1979a: 179f, 1985a: 29, 292 n. 13) employs a distinction between 'grasslands' and 'forest' adopted from MacDonald (1984a: 1). These appear to me to be ideal types, between which stretches a broad transitional zone. In Pairundu and its area, for example, the type of settlement recalls what LeRoy describes as 'forest', while the topography corresponds to the 'grasslands'. On the other hand, on the hills to the south, southwest and southeast of Pairundu, especially on the paths to Sare and Sua/Yeibu, both topography and vegetation resemble 'forest' rather than 'grassland'. According to L. Josephides, south of Pairundu too, between Sugu and Erave, elements from both regions are still in evidence (1985a: 6).

23. These observations contradict the findings of MacDonald (1984a: 1), who describes February as the wettest month and August as the hottest. Franklin also sees February as usually the wettest month (Franklin and Franklin 1978: 445).

24. All Latin terms for animals have been provided by G. Heidemann (letter of 25 May 1993).

25. According to MacDonald (1984a: 2), the sweet potato mounds together with drainage ditches are particularly characteristic of the area in the north described as 'grassland' by LeRoy, and horticulture here follows the general pattern of the Papua New Guinea Highlands. Lederman (1986a: 11f) says the same for the Mendi. However, according to MacDonald, in the south of the Kewa region, which is labelled 'forest' by LeRoy, the comparatively short periods of cultivation and long fallow periods remind one rather of the horticulture that is otherwise usual on the Seaboard (MacDonald 1984a: 2, 1985: 4).

26. Stagl (1974: 180) also points out that segmentation can be seen as both structure and process. When segments shrink, they fall to lower levels of segmentation. When

segments grow, they rise to higher levels of segmentation. Then they divide, these parts taking over the functions that formerly the whole group had.

27. According to Stagl (1974: 172), on the other hand, in the Eastern Highlands there are between four and eight levels of segmentation, with an average of six.

28. Franklin speaks here only of 'a group with some sort of common ancestor myth' (Franklin and Franklin 1978: 446). L. Josephides (1985a: 17) uses the term 'tribe'. LeRoy (1979a: 11) and MacDonald (1984a: 4) mention respectively a pair or a group of clans.

29. See Franklin and Franklin (1978: 446), as well as L. Josephides (1983: 292, 1985a: 17f). Only LeRoy disputes the idea that the members of a phratry believe that they are linked to a common ancestor (1981: 30).

30. The term 'clan' is used in the same way by Franklin (Franklin and Franklin 1978: 385), L. Josephides (1985a: 17), LeRoy (1979a: 181) and MacDonald (1985: 4). Franklin (1965: 416) associates 'clan' with the Kewa word *ruru*. For L. Josephides (1985a: 16) and LeRoy (1979a: 10), by contrast, *ruru* is a general term used by Kewa for all social groups. Instead of *ruru*, MacDonald uses exclusively the Kewa word *repa*, which according to L. Josephides (1983: 292) is a dialect variant of *ruru* that only appears in the Sumbura area as a suffix for group names. Franklin (1965: 416) says the same for the Muli region, though one searches LeRoy in vain for the term *repa*.

31. Franklin also uses the term 'sub-clan' (Franklin and Franklin 1978: 385). L. Josephides (1985a: 292) speaks of a 'clan section', LeRoy (1981: 26) of 'clan sections or segments' and MacDonald (1984a: 3) of a 'repa section'.

32. LeRoy (1981: 26) says clearly: 'Clans themselves are thus not local and coresidential units, though clan segments are'. Cf. Franklin (1965: 414): 'the sub-clan among the Kewa is a definite territorial unit'.

33. Given that the individual takes over these use rights and also his group membership from his forefathers, then transfers them, as it were, to his descendants, the sub-clan survives its individual members to some extent. In this sense, the sub-clan is a corporate group or corporation, like the clan (cf. L. Josephides 1985b: 293).

34. The general conclusion that there are functionally weak and functionally strong levels of segmentation is Stagl's (1974: 174).

35. At this level, the group is described as a 'family' by Franklin (Franklin and Franklin 1978: 384) and MacDonald (1984a: 1), as a 'patrilineage' by L. Josephides (1983: 292) and as a 'sub-section' by LeRoy (1979a: 181).

36. According to Stagl (1974: 173), however, distinctive functions are required precisely to identify autonomous levels in segmentary systems. This would mean that one must combine the lineages with the sub-clans, so that they remain the lowest level of segmentation. If, however, one sees distinctive functions as the sole criteria determining some levels of segmentation, one can also dispute the separation of the levels of phratry and clan. This separation nonetheless appears sensible to me because, in contrast to phratries, clans are activated unequally but with greater frequency and because they are therefore given far more significance.

37. According to Franklin (1965: 416), 'Within the clan all collateral males are called ame, "brother"'. From the Western point of view, one can speak of an 'extension' or classificatory use of the term 'brother'. This is the 'Iroquois' type of kinship terminology: siblings have the same terms as parallel cousins and cross cousins are distinguished from them, though they themselves all share the same term. See Franklin and Franklin (1978: 445), as well as LeRoy (1979b: 11).

38. See LeRoy (1979a: 11, 1979b: 11, 1981: 31) and L. Josephides (1983: 292).

39. Thus LeRoy writes: 'It may be that "descent" is just a way Highlanders have of talking about social units constituted by non-kinship forces such as residence or co-operation' (1981: 35 n. 2, cf. MacDonald 1984a: 3). Stagl (1974: 39) describes kinship, neighbourhood and association (which I call 'cooperation') as the 'basic principles of socialization'.

40. See L. Josephides (1985a: 19), LeRoy (1981: 26) and MacDonald (1991: 36).

41. L. Josephides concludes: 'The Kewa have no positive marriage rule and marriages are contracted randomly. No pattern emerges and concentration exists...' (1985a: 62, cf. MacDonald 1984a: 4, 1991: 181).
42. See Franklin (1965: 416). L. Josephides (1985a: 2) writes that the brideprices she recorded had each been provided by different numbers of people. Sometimes only the groom had 'paid', sometimes a large number of his agnatic relatives.
43. See L. Josephides (1985a: 62, 216) and Marilyn Strathern (1972).
44. See L. Josephides (1985a: 142), LeRoy (1985a: 124) and MacDonald (1991: 187).
45. MacDonald (1984a: 16). According to the Kewa, the bodies of pigs also consist of male and female parts.
46. L. Josephides (1983: 292) concludes: 'present cases of uxorilocality and matrilocality are few'.
47. A. Strathern (1988: 207f) adds that the numbers and density of the population becomes less and that ceremonial exchanges become less significant. See Weiner (1988) regarding other factors that differentiate the 'fringe cultures' from their northern neighbours.
48. Some Kome can also enumerate other groups with a similar name from other villages, most of them further away, though there is general agreement that they do not have common origins. The names of these groups are Wapia Kome, Puti Kome, Amala Kome, Ewalu Kome, Wabi Kome, Amburepa Kome, Eta Kome, Sumi Kome and Papenda Kome.
49. Sua and Yeibu are basically two villages. However, they are so close to one another that their names are, as it were, spoken in the same breath.
50. The Mamarepa are similarly organised.
51. This was expressed to me once by Ripu as follows: 'The repa must continue' ('Repa mas i go yet').
52. These Mamarepa are in the first instance affines who have followed their Kome wives or mothers to Pairundu, that is, to their home village.
53. The Kome did this themselves, when they divided the meat I had brought for the feast held at the beginning of my fieldwork and allocated it to the three sub-clans and to the Mamarepa.
54. 'Men' and 'women' here means all those of the respective gender, regardless of their age.
55. To Pairundu* belong Pairundu**, Yampiri, Rimbupiri, Rakepanda, Rakianda, Yeimi, Pairanda, Ralerale and Pokaranda. To Ropena belong Ropena*, Yawireanda, Pasereanda, Yassaweli, Porai and Walua. The term 'Pairundu' thus has three meanings: the whole village (when this meaning is intended, I write 'Pairundu'), one half of the village ('Pairundu*') and a unit within this half ('Pairundu**'). Similarly, the term 'Ropena' refers to one half of the village ('Ropena') as well as a unit of this half ('Ropena*').
56. According to LeRoy (1985a: 291 n. 1), in the south of the Kewa area between 60 and 450 people live in each village, usually, however, about 200. Elsewhere LeRoy (1981: 26) gives an average figure of 150.
57. Thus after his brother Yalanai died, Wala married his brother's wife. Ata (I) (Raki Repa, Auro Kome) married the wife of his deceased parallel cousin Usa. I write 'Ata (I)' to distinguish him from another Ata (Yapua Repa, Rata Kome), whom I list as 'Ata (II)'. The Kome themselves describe Ata as the 'first Ata' (*nambawan Ata*) and Ata (II) as the 'second Ata' (*nambatu Ata*). A third Ata in the village is known as 'Ata Francis', a reference to his Catholic name.
58. These marriages link Ata (II) (Yapua Repa, Rata Kome) with Renu (Alia Kome, Rundu Kome) and Ruben (Yapua Repa, Rata Kome) with Ruri (Aiya Kome, Rundu Kome).
59. On an earlier occasion, the line of descent from Kubuta to Ibaka to Sapu had also been described by Ari, the leading man of the Rata Kome.
60. Thus along with Ipapula (Yapua Repa), Kapu (Kane Repa), Nosupinai and Yapa (both Yakema Repa), members of all three lineages within the Rata Kome, claimed that Kane and Yakema were brothers and therefore that Yakema Repa and Kane Repa belong together.

61. Yawa provided this information in response to a specific question of mine (Alex had told me beforehand that Yawa had expressed this view).
62. In an earlier interview, Yawa claimed that Auro, Rata and Rundu had been Kata's three children. Many Kome see this as possible, others doubt it, but most say they do not know. However, I am sceptical of this statement of Yawa's, since he never repeated or confirmed it in later conversations on the same theme, whether by himself or in replying to specific questions.
63. Yawa told me the same on another occasion, independently of Ipapula. Accordingly the genealogy drawn up by Yawa also emphasises a close connection between Yapua Repa, Sapu Repa and Raki Repa.
64. Including, for example, Ata Francis, a Nakurepa from Sare, who joined Rekepea and who is now regarded as Alia Kome. Another example is Kande, an Akuna Rola from Yakoa who lives with his family in Yassaweli, today as Raki Repa.
65. This development confirms Stagl's (1974: 180) thesis, already mentioned, according to which segmentation involves both a structure and a process.
66. See Franklin (1965: 414). MacDonald (1984a: 14) even claims that, in the pre-colonial period, women of child-bearing age could only enter the men's house on particular ritual occasions.
67. Ruben (85.) expressed himself similarly on another occasion. The prohibition on taking food from menstruating women is also mentioned by MacDonald (1984a: 11) and LeRoy (1985a: 66). In addition, MacDonald (1991: 68) reports the idea that too great a frequency of sexual relations leads men to lose power and vitality and to age prematurely.
68. When I told a large circle of men that in Germany some married couples tend to share domestic work with one another, they reacted immediately with horror and confirmed unanimously that things were arranged better in Papua New Guinea, where women have to subordinate themselves to the men.
69. On the separation and sex-specific allocation of the private and public spheres, see also LeRoy (1985a: 141).
70. One searches Franklin, L. Josephides, LeRoy and MacDonald in vain for indications concerning relations between generations.
71. '...nambawan brata ya... sapos em i mekim wanpela samting, mipela save bihainim'.
72. A remark of Wala's (92.) indicated this: 'We old men don't know our way around so well, but the young ones who are growing up today... they have more ideas and know a bit more...' ('Nau mipela ol lapun man, dispela tingting bilong mipela, em sotpela tru, na ol boi long nau, ol kamap nupela long en... i gat moa idea na moa save liklik...'.
73. Read (1955) uses the terms 'strength' and 'equivalence' with reference to the Gahuku, Eastern Highlands Province, and Stagl (1974: 85ff.) adopts them for the Highlands as a whole. In my understanding, 'equivalence' is more all-embracing than, for example, 'reciprocity' and is more meaningful in the present context.
74. However, 'great warriors' were not necessarily identical to Big Men.
75. Cf. Franklin and Franklin (1978: 458), L. Josephides (1985a: 198) and, for the Highlands in general, Stagl (1974: 272–285).
76. Ari (20.) speaks of the 'humiliation of the name of another man' ('daunim nem bilong narapela man') and that 'the leading men raise their own names' ('ol hetman liftimapim nem bilong ol').
77. After Wala comes Rekepea, though his influence is restricted to the Alia Kome.
78. However, one must take into account here the fact that Coleman Komea belongs not only to the same sub-clan (Auro Kome) as Yawa, but also to the same lineage (Sapu Repa).
79. However, the first-born sons of Big Men especially are more subject than other representatives of their generation to the general expectation that they should follow the model of their fathers, an expectation that they also fulfil in many cases.
80. Stagl (1974: 79) sees the individualism of the Highland peoples as a consequence of their 'ideals of strength'.

81. In these interviews, which were carried out using standardised questionnaires, it proved necessary to call on informants alone or only with a translator they trusted, so as to exclude their concern that the information could create envy in others. With respect to average incomes and expenditures, one difficulty that arose was that villagers do not keep accounts themselves. Moreover, neither income nor expenditure is constant throughout the year but instead often rise rapidly after the harvest or sale of coffee beans, only to sink back towards zero again.

82. However, the market in Kagua is visited only rarely, due to it being a greater distance away.

83. Coffee is not planted in the usual gardens, but in separate plots, called 'blocks'.

84. However, Naki derived this sum from the income of the first one and a half months after his shop was opened, a period in which a lot of money was circulating in the village following the sale of coffee. I therefore do not think that this level of income could be maintained.

85. The following goods were bought at the markets in Sumi or Rake: sugarcane (10 t each), cucumbers (3 for 20 t), peanuts (20 t a bundle), betel nuts with lime and bunches of pepper (3 for 50 t to 1 K) and sweet potatoes (ca. 500 gm for 70 t). Many of these prices are considerably higher in the markets in Kagua or even Mendi. The following were offered in the shops in Pairundu: kerosene (ca. 0.35 l for 1 K), tuna fish (small tin for 1.20 K, large tin for 1.80 K) and rice (ca. 250 gm for 2.50 K). Many of these prices are considerably lower in the shops in Kagua or even Mendi. Thus whereas prices in the markets fall with distance from the main roads, in the shops they rise.

86. In recording the various data, I have not taken outstanding debts into account, since whether, when and at what rates of interest counter-prestations are provided can never be predicted. Information concerning coffee plots, gardens and bush gardens cannot be entirely accurate since individual units do not always balance: for example, many gardens cover more square metres than others.

87. Only those who can call a comparatively high level of assets their own bury or hide their money.

88. In another myth that I recorded, Kata learned from Rolasi, an Eno from Apuma, how to mow grass, teaching Rolasi how to defecate in return. Cf. here MacDonald, myths no. 49, 'Biene and Rau' (1991: 312f) and 183, 'Lusala: A Man without an Anus' (1991: 514f). See also the collection of Kewa myths published by Beier (1977).

89. In each case I give here the name of the clan (*ruru*) and then in brackets the name of the village or villages in which the clan lived (in the Uma case, the two names are identical).

90. This goes for the Akuna (Rulupare) and should also apply to the Ariarepa (Yapaia, Payande) and Urupa (Rakere, Sukere).

91. These are the Ape (Ondere, Apote), Mirupa (Mokere, Pira, Asuataba, Porame, Yame, Rurili, Wambu), Ramirepa (Mapata, Walidamu) and Uma (Uma). Other groups that also count as enemies must be added: Alarepa (Yakure), Alopa (Maka), Birirepa (Yari), Eno (Apuma, Kimbupi), Kamarepa (Roka, Ora), Koyari (Wassabibi, Omai), Mui (Ruri, Walere), Mumukurepa (Alawia, Ambore), Oropa (Mendo), Pamerepa (Pagure, Malare), Polosi (Suki, Amasa), Rekerepa (Kelemapi), Yamu (Yalu, Maita) and Yaporepa (Rokoma, Marili). However, the allies in Ari's account also retain their former estimation so that they are still regarded as friends today. As already mentioned, they include the Akuna-Rola (Yakoa), Anerepa (Kira), Auerepa (Wabi) and Pamenderepa (Kanoa). To be added to them are merely the Kapiarepa (Sare), Kome from Sumi, Rairepa (Yaware), Wasuma (Wasuma) and Yamala (Imuya).

2

Traditional Religion

From the culture of the present, the view now changes to the pre-colonial past and especially to the traditional religion.[1] Given that many of the practices belonging to the traditional religion are no longer carried out, the present description of it is based, in the first instance not on observation, but on the particular memories of the Kome, that is, on emic reconstructions. These reconstructions mostly derive from specialists, that is, mostly old men who had either learned the knowledge involved from their fathers or 'bought' it with particular gifts. The analysis of emic reconstructions makes it necessary to identify those points at which emic representation apparently merges with emic evaluation. Today, such merging may go back especially to the influence of Christianity.

In describing the traditional religion, I shall deal with transcendent authorities, magical practices and cult practices, in that order.[2] By 'transcendent authorities', I mean figures that, at least from the Western point of view, cannot be perceived in the context of the ordinary experiences of day-to-day life. For me, these figures exist to the extent that they are accessible to the experience of the anthropology of religion, because they prove to be socially effective, as is the case when people explain particular modes of behaviour by referring, for example, to ancestral or bush spirits.[3] By 'magical practices' and 'cult practices', I mean more or less fixed bodily or linguistic actions whereby the villagers seek to exploit contexts of effectiveness which are overwhelmingly non-existent from the point of view of either natural science or, in general, day-to-day experience in the West.[4] Magical practices tend to be carried out individually, cult practices collectively.[5] From the Western point of view, in what follows one might miss the representation of ideas – for example, in myths of the origin of the world – that embed transcendental authorities, magical practices and cult practices in an all-embracing context of meaning. However, such ideas cannot be elicited from the statements of my informants. There may be various reasons for this. The particular ideas may have been forgotten, or the Kome did not want to tell me about them. However, I think forgetfulness is unlikely, given the relatively short period of colonisation and missionisation overall. I would also rule out silence, since, after a mutual relationship of trust had developed, I was told things belonging to the traditional religion that were normally kept secret from the outsider. On the whole, therefore, I incline to the view that, even in the pre-colonial period, the Kome themselves were not interested in making connections between transcendental authorities, magical practices and cult practices. Accordingly their myths only explain, for example, the origin of individual mountains, plants and cultural practices, not the world as a whole.[6]

Transcendent authorities

An essential element of the traditional religion consists in collective belief in the existence and effectiveness of transcendental authorities, to which the bush and ancestral spirits belong, as well as a separate figure called Yaki.

The word 'remo' is used for ancestral spirits and also today for bad men (*man nogut*), as well as being a sort of collective term for the different religious practices of the past, which are sometimes summed up as 'this whole remo stuff' (*ol dispela remo nambaut*).[7] In general, villagers continue to be convinced that every person, upon changing into a *remo* after his death, retires to a distant place in the direction of the Erave, which is not specified further. However, before this he or she remains in the vicinity of the living for some time. Although one cannot see the *remo*, or only in dreams, this nearness is sometimes clearly discernible, as when, walking at night in the bush, the trees snap and rustle. In the different stories, the *remo* mostly appear as the originators of sickness and death. According to Ipapula (37.), formerly missing people were sometimes found in rock caves or at the foot of tree trunks, cowering, completely tensed up and lacking consciousness and with their ears, eyes and nasal passages blocked up with saliva. After being warmed by a fire and returning to consciousness, these people claimed that they had been taken by the *remo*.[8] Moreover, if, for example, anyone fails to settle his debts over a long period and his creditor dies, the latter's *remo* might kill him. Even close relatives of the creditor may sometimes haunt the debtor or his family as *remo*. One may also ask a *remo* to act against debtors or thieves. According to Ipapula (37.), ten people have already fallen victim to the *remo* of his father in this way. Otmar (62.) said that the *remo* would spit at, hit and kill especially those who usually inflicted bad thoughts or deeds. However, the effectiveness of the *remo* is not limited to the pre-colonial period. Thus Ripu and Serale told me independently of one another that once, coming back together at night from contract work at Mount Hagen and approaching Pasereanda while eating some lamb flabs, a *remo* grabbed hold of them and flung them into a ditch. On the other hand, the living sometimes enjoy the help of the *remo*, as when they receive protection from them or advice, for example in a dream. However, according to Ipapula (37.), for this it is necessary to keep their names secret. On the whole, it seems that there is a prevalent fear of injury in the case of those who have died only a short while ago, whereas the chance of a positive influence is increased when a long time has passed since the corresponding death.[9] Accordingly, today the Kome still avoid referring to the recently dead by name (cf. Franklin and Franklin 1978: 464), and it can be some months before this precaution lapses. Basically, then, it is obvious that the *remo* limit their impact, whether positive or negative, to their own close relatives.[10]

The traditional term for 'bush spirit' is 'kalando', but the Tok Pisin term 'masalai' is gradually being introduced too.[11] The same is said of the *kalando* as of the *remo*, namely that they seek to be near people, though no more than the *remo* are they linked with known sites in the topography. In the Pairundu area, therefore, there are no particular 'holy sites'. It is merely assumed that the *kalando* are present especially on the river banks or in water, or else in holes in trees and in rocks in the forest and not so much in human settlements. In general, the *kalando* are not visible, even in dreams, though I occasionally heard the view that the colour of their skin is white.[12] Compared to the *remo*, people only ascribe injurious effects to the *kalando*. Even in the daytime, but especially at night, they will trigger off an illness that manifests itself in shaking attacks and a loss of consciousness and, if no counter-measures are taken, leads to death. Small children and menstruating or pregnant women are frequent victims.[13] According to the prevailing opinion, a special danger arises for anyone leaving the house at night or going into the bush after eating 'something good', that is, rice, meat or tinned fish. The *kalando* are attracted by the smell of these foods, as well as the smell of coffee beans and are thus stimulated to cause illness.[14] Such ideas proved still to be effective even during my presence in Pairundu. When, on one occasion, I wanted to remove food leftovers from my house in the late evening, my visitors remarked that it was not actually usual to do this and that I might as well wait until the next morning. Obviously it was thought possible that the *kalando* might be attracted by the thrown-out leftovers. Moreover, during my fieldwork, numerous mild sicknesses, as well as the death of a child, were put down to the *kalando*.

Whereas the terms *remo* and *kalando* refer to several different figures, Yaki is a single male being who is equally invisible, but who lives in heaven.[15] The Kome say that formerly they believed thunder and lightning to be signs with which Yaki indicated that he would soon be coming to fetch people who had been stealing or killing. Generally, however, Yaki is almost exclusively seen as an authority who is well-disposed towards people, giving them advice, helping them in the hunt and granting them fertility. According to Ipapula (37.), Yaki formerly left behind particular marks in trees in order to show whether, for example, one should proceed with the preparations for building a house or a pig-killing festival, or whether one should put off such undertakings because of an imminent battle. Various villagers related that they had formerly thanked Yaki when they had managed to catch a cassowary or tree kangaroo in the hunt. Yaki's most important function, however, was most probably to care for the fertility of the gardens and of women. According to Ari (18.), in the pre-colonial period it was usual to ask Yaki for productive plantings, numerous pigs and pearlshells and many children. Especially after the completion of a men's house, or at dawn on the day on which a feast was held to celebrate the new house with guests from other villages, a man would climb on to the roof to appeal to Yaki – who in this context was called 'father' (*apa*) – with the appropriate wishes. Also at dawn, in front of the house, the firewood for the preparation of the planned feast was struck, the assumption being, according to Ari, that Yaki would hear this noise with pleasure. It is generally the case with ideas linked to transcendental authorities within the traditional religion that these authorities are thought of less as part of a separate, other-worldly sphere than as being able to demonstrate effectiveness in this world.[16] This effectiveness cannot be either positively compelled or negatively obstructed. To that extent, the Kome ascribe themselves a passive role in their respective memories. In addition, belief in transcendental authorities, at least with respect to the *remo* and *kalando*, proves to be still effective today.

Magical practices

Magical practices can be differentiated according to the results that are being aimed at. If these results are negatively assessed by those to whom they are addressed, then black magic or witchcraft is involved, in the case of magic causing injury or death, for example. A positive assessment, on the other hand, is made in the case of white magic, to which procedures of healing and divination belong, as well as love, fertility and rain magic. Only the appropriate specialists have the knowledge required to carry out any magical practices, since only they know which rules to follow in any particular case, which words one recites in the case of witchcraft, for example and which plant materials a patient must consume in treatments for sickness. This knowledge creates capital to some extent, since the application of magical practices is usually remunerated with counter-prestations. Accordingly specialists keep their knowledge secret, except, for example, when they transfer it to their sons or 'sell' it to an interested person, also for counter-prestations.[17]

The witchcraft practices known in Pairundu are called 'Neambu', 'Romo', 'Sanguma' and 'Malu'.[18] Serale and Nosope count as experts in Neambu, which originally came from the area of Erave, though both claim only to be able to cure illnesses caused by Neambu, not to be able to carry out Neambu themselves.[19] In order to use Neambu, one needs material belonging to the designated victim, such as hair cuttings or nail parings, scraps of clothing or excrement. According to Serale, these substances are picked up without being touched, secret words are said over them,[20] and they are thrown into a pond, or into a hole in a rock or tree that is occupied by insects. Nosope said that the substances must be placed in a bamboo tube and this held over a tree hole, whereupon the insects in the tree will emerge and eat up the substances.[21] While this leads to the victim's death, according to Nosope, if the substances are placed in water, only sickness is the consequence. Typical symptoms are large ulcers, emaciation, shivering, fever, headaches and pains in the joints. The Kome still avoid leaving food leftovers or excrement on the land of traditional enemy groups out of fear of Neambu. When I told Alex that someone had stolen some clothing from Serale during a pig-killing festival in Kamare, his spontaneous answer was that now witchcraft would be practiced against him (*ol bai poisenim em*).

Of Yawa and Nosope, the specialists in Romo, it is also said that they could only cure the particular sickness, not cause it themselves.[22] Romo, which, according to Nosope (59.), is given to the victim as a powder secretly mixed into his food, is supposedly as dangerous as Neambu. Thus, on the way to a night-time dancing event (*singsing*) at Yapapia, Ata Francis insistently pointed out to me that enemies also lived there and that I should therefore not consume any food that was given to me without the prior approval of the Kome present there. The fear of Romo obviously makes the acceptance of food an indication of trust.[23]

'Sanguma' is the Tok Pisin term for a process that is supposed to have originated in both the Mendi and Erave regions and which, in Pairundu, only Ondasa knew about, saying that he could only cure the associated illness.[24] According to Ondasa (61.), after Sanguma has been used, a so-called 'Sanguma dog' approaches the house of the victim, changes into a fly or flea, forces itself first into the house and then into the anus of the victim, moves up into his heart and finally drinks his blood. Before the victim dies, he suffers back pains and blood drips out of his mouth and nose. As in the case of Neambu and Romo, belief in the effectiveness of Sanguma can influence behaviour. When the daughter of Rekepea left her husband and the latter demanded the brideprice back, Rekepea was quickly ready to pay. He himself openly gave as his reason the danger that otherwise he might fall victim to Sanguma, since the deserted husband came from the Erave area, which was generally known for witchcraft practices.

Unlike Neambu, Romo and Sanguma, hardly any information could be obtained concerning Malu, since no specialist in it was still living in Pairundu. All I learned was that with Malu a specially decorated stone was directed towards the victim while certain words were secretly said.[25] Although he is too young to have firsthand knowledge, Robert (83.) said that the stone was first smeared with menstrual blood or, if this was not available, the blood of a red or white pig.

The magical practices with which sicknesses caused by witchcraft were to be cured consist basically in the preparation of food consisting of different plant materials and pig's blood. The respective specialists did not pretend to know how these foods worked or whether, for example, transcendent authorities aided in the recovery or not.[26] Serale (86.) enjoys the reputation of having cured numerous Neambu illnesses. According to his own description, he first gives the patient a mixture of ginger, salt and some pieces of tree bark. If the patient thinks this tastes good, he is rubbed with red earth and a special leaf. The next morning, Serale will slaughter a pig and prepare a meal from the kidneys, ears and fat of the pig and also ginger, different types of bark and small animals like ants and bees. Only the patient and Serale himself may eat this. Simultaneously the area is closed off: no outsider and no one who has had sexual relations with a woman during the night, may come near in this period. However, the therapy only counts as having ended when the sick person finally consumes a special leaf, which Serale only provides him with when he is satisfied with his remuneration. During my fieldwork, Serale was summoned, among other places, to Wapuanda, Usa and Wabi to apply this process. As he told me, he had acquired the appropriate knowledge through gifts of pig meat, pearlshells and money. Although he does not enjoy a comparable reputation, Nosope (59.) also tries to cure Neambu illnesses. The mixture he uses consists of four different sorts of tree bark, ginger and an insect of the same type as used by the author of Neambu. If the patient reacts to this food, the therapy is continued using another dish consisting of another insect, other types of tree bark, pig's kidneys and pig fat. Nosope (59.) enjoys a comparatively higher reputation as an expert in healing Romo illnesses. Here the appropriate meal consists of a particular leaf that causes the vomiting of the last meal and with it the Romo powder. Then a pig is slaughtered and the patient consumes the kidneys. Part of the therapy to heal the consequences of Sanguma involves a leaf that is given the generic term 'rara', which Ondasa, the specialist in this, stretches over the patient while whispering secret words.[27] If the patient's condition then improves, a pig is slaughtered, which the patient must eat from. Ondasa (61.) related that he had formerly inherited the *rara* leaf he uses from his father.

Illnesses caused not by witchcraft but by the impact of bush spirits are also treated with food, especially by Pogola and Ondasa. Whereas Pogola (72.) usually prescribes a mixture of tree bark, leaves, fruits, ginger, salt and pig's blood, Ondasa (61.) first makes the patient drink water in which different pieces of bark, salt and ginger have been placed. Only when recovery begins can one be sure that the sickness was caused by *kalando*. Then Ondasa mixes several different types of bark, ginger he has previously been chewing, small pieces of pig meat, vegetables, salt and pig's blood. After enjoying this meal, the patient finally drinks more water over which Ondasa has previously spoken a secret formula. I myself was able to follow how, in the context of such a procedure, Ondasa prepared a pig obtained from Nosope for the cure of the latter's daughter. Like Pogola, Ondasa said that he had 'bought' the necessary knowledge.

As well as witchcraft techniques and *kalando*, thoughts and feelings that arise in connection with social conflicts and that are viewed negatively, are also regarded as dangerous causes of sickness.[28] From time to time, these negative thoughts and feelings may, as it were, be taken up by *remo* and activated. The death of a small child of Rekepea's was explained by the fact that Rekepea's creditors had become angry, because they thought that they would never be repaid. If only Rekepea had taken his savings out of their hiding place, held the money high and called out the name of the recipient it was meant for, then, as Ata Francis (22.) told me afterwards, he would have calmed his creditors and his child would still be alive. For the Kome, moreover, a cure is effected the moment the negative thoughts and feelings lose their power to injure because they have been expressed in public. Thus when someone is made ill through the anger or disgruntlement of an adversary, he should persuade this adversary to express his anger or disgruntlement clearly by giving him a present as quickly as possible.[29]

Basically, in Pairundu people are prepared to try out a whole series of therapies in the absence of a recovery. Thus Marcus dragged his dangerously ill child, as it seemed at first, to the health centre in Sumi on 8 May 1991. However, once there he was told that nothing could be done for the child, since the sickness had been caused by negative feelings and thoughts and therefore he should go back to the village for an *autim tingting*. First, however, the child was taken to Wasuma, where members of the Catholic community laid hands on the sick child in a night-time service and prayed for its recovery. On the 10th Marcus's parents appeared and expressed their anger (single and in the context of a public *autim tingting*) that their son spent more time in Pairundu than in his home village of Sua/Yeibu. Then, that same day, a small pig was killed, in order to feed pig's blood to the child. Finally, by the 15th, the sickness had been almost completely cured. Here the different procedures of Western medicine, prayers with the laying on of hands, *autim tingting* and drinking pig's blood do not seem to be mutually exclusive. Instead, in principle they are applied one after another until the sickness either ends in death or is cured.[30]

In choosing a therapy that promises success, it may be considered necessary to know the exact cause of the illness concerned or the *remo* that has caused it (cf. MacDonald 1985: 11). In order to discover this and to grasp the causes of past events or be able to predict future ones, the Kome turn to divination. This involves magical practices enabling one to come into the possession of otherwise inaccessible knowledge, for example, trying to make contact with a *remo* in order to obtain the desired information from it. Still during my fieldwork, dreams represented an important form of divination for the Kome. Atasi (26.), who lives in Wasuma and is the father of the former catechist Kenneth, claimed that two of his deceased relatives appeared to him in his sleep both in his own house and also in a purposely built hut on Mount Sumi, in order to answer his various questions.[31] In this way, he is allegedly able to explain how a sickness arose and also to find the hiding place of stolen property, as well predict fighting, deaths and the outcome of elections. However, according to Atasi, his contact with the *remo* would be broken off for good if he revealed their names.[32] Those interested, however, can themselves experience such dreams of divination. To do so, they must visit the 'dream hut' on Mount Sumi together with Atasi and contribute pig meat or beef for a meal to be eaten there. Then Atasi ties one end of a long piece of string to the head of his client, ties a leaf on the other end and throws it down the valley. In the night, the two *remo* follow this string and give both Atasi and his clients dreams with the desired information. However, this requires the observance of specific rules, which, according to Atasi, the two *remo* themselves originally laid down. Thus one can only enter the area around the 'dream hut' if one has not had sexual relations beforehand. Moreover, the Kewa terms for water, sugarcane and bamboo tube are replaced by other words. In addition, only Atasi himself may raise his voice on Mount Sumi, that is, when he calls out the name of his client and thus bids the two *remo* to come near. According to Ata Francis, through a dream Atasi was able to find one of Rekepea's pigs that had long been missing. Ripu reported that he had once visited the 'dream hut' on Mount Sumi in order to discover the reason for a large number of sicknesses and deaths in Ari's family.[33]

Before the start of colonisation and missionisation, however, a combination of two practices, called 'Pulu' and 'Ayaka', were mainly used to discover the cause of a death or the identity of a murderer. In Ari's memory of this, with Pulu, the appropriate specialist – who, however, had to come from another sub-clan – tied the deceased to a stick of wood called an 'eno repena'.[34] He then fixed this piece of wood to two upright posts so that the corpse could swing from side to side. Then he stood near the deceased, laid a spear across his breast, moved the spear back and forth, blew along it and quietly whispered the names of different witchcraft practitioners and murderers. If, Ari told me, the witchcraft practitioner who caused the death was named or the name of the murderer uttered, blood ran out of the dead person's nose, his skin split open at the shoulders and breast, and he began to rock to and fro. According to Ari, this could be repeated several times for up to three days, after which one was sure that the name really was that of the murderer.[35] Nevertheless, the result of the Pulu was checked to some extent using Ayaka. Here, the appropriate expert fixed the lower jaw of the deceased to a bamboo tube in which he had previously placed the deceased's hair or one of his teeth. This bamboo tube was carried by one man at each end. According to Ari, the *remo* of the deceased now began to act by jerking the bamboo tube back and forth until, in this way, the men came to the house of the murderer.[36] Today there is general agreement in Pairundu that the causes of deaths and the identity of murderers could always be determined through Pulu as well as Ayaka, and that they never failed. Today both practices are prohibited. Nevertheless, on 16 January 1991, while visiting Yakoa, by chance I met a man with torn hands, who told me that his injuries had been caused by carrying a bamboo tube which had been used for an Ayaka a few days before.[37]

As well as the procedures just described concerning witchcraft, cures for sickness and divination, the magical practices of the Kome also include techniques which can be described respectively by the terms 'love magic', 'fertility magic' and 'rain magic'. 'Love magic', which is practiced by both men and women, serves to initiate or increase an attraction for the opposite sex. In their youth, Yawa and Ipapula had the reputation of having had such 'love magic', supposedly because of their success. Coleman Makoa, who assumed that even whites had such means, once asked me to give him some. Given the reserve that women usually showed me, it is not surprising but yet unfortunate that I could not learn anything precise about the practices with which many women occasionally sought, according to some of the men, to increase the yields of the gardens and the growth of the pigs (cf. MacDonald 1991: 176). The goal of 'rain magic', finally, is to bring forth heavy rainfall, in order, for example, to disturb rival Big Men in the preparation of a pig-killing festival. In Pairundu, only Yawa of the Kome was said to be able to do this. Often, when it was raining heavily over several days, I heard the view expressed that a human was behind it (*man i mekim*).

As with the emic ideas that are linked to transcendent authorities, the emic accounts of magical practices also convey the impression that the Kome regard themselves as passive to some extent. Certainly they can cure some illnesses and discover their cause, but they do not have the knowledge required to trigger these illnesses themselves through particular witchcraft practices. The fear of such practices therefore does not seem to belong to the past any more than carrying out different procedures for curing illnesses and divination do.

Cult practices

For the Kome themselves, it is not so much transcendent authorities or magical practices that are central to the traditional religion as the cult practices of the pre-colonial period. Even in response to the general, undifferentiated question concerning the traditional religion, most informants first mention what they did in their traditional cult houses. On the whole, therefore, comparatively more information can be collected on this topic today. Like particular magical practices, traditional cult practices also provide a procedure for curing sickness, though they are conducted collectively and in houses especially erected for the purpose. Both participation in the cult practices and their leadership require the appropriate knowledge, especially of the rules to be observed. As with magical practices, on the whole this knowledge is secret and also represents capital: participation in cult practices permits the consumption of, for example, pig meat, and for appropriate counter-prestations individual cult practices can also be passed on to other groups.

The Kome classify a large part of their traditional cult practices under the term 'rimbu'.[38] First the so-called Aga-palaa Rimbu was held in Sua/Yeibu and Anapote, though not in Pairundu itself.[39] When the Aga-palaa Rimbu was already in use, the Kamarepa from Roka brought the Alamu-palaa Rimbu to Yeibu,[40] from where it spread to Pairundu and Sare. According to Mindu (51.), as well as the Kome and Mamarepa, the Akuna, Pamenderepa, Anerepa and Wasuma also adopted it. In Yeibu, Otmar served as cult leader and in Sare and Pairundu, Yawa, Ipapula and – succeeding the latter – Ari.[41] The cult house used for the Alamu-palaa Rimbu is called *rimbu rekeanda*, as is the case for other types of Rimbu. This *rimbu rekeanda* is divided into two halves by a long fireplace, each half having its own entrance door. The cult community, including the cult leaders, are allocated to one half and may only step through the corresponding door.[42] At the back is a false ceiling called *reke*, which gives the house its name.[43] Even while the *rimbu rekeanda* is being built, the cult leaders place different leaves, small red stones, frog's eggs, different sorts of vegetable and dry wood in the ashes in the fireplace while uttering secret words. According to my informants, the term 'rimbu' originally referred to these things, which normally no one had any knowledge of apart from the cult leaders.[44] In the case of each of the different Rimbu processes, the desire was to cure precisely that sickness which had been caused by that particular type of Rimbu (cf. Franklin and Franklin 1978: 443). In the case of the Alamu-palaa Rimbu, for example, one of its leaders visits the sick person in order to stretch a *rara* leaf over his body and to ask him, whispering words that are kept secret, whether the Alamu-palaa Rimbu is responsible for the corresponding illness. If the patient then feels better, the question counts as a yes. Only then is the Alamu-palaa Rimbu carried out, since the general conviction is that only then can it bring the illness to an end.

At the start of an Alamu-palaa Rimbu, the cult leaders, as the appropriate specialists, enter the cult house in order to kindle the fire while uttering secret words. The 'ordinary' members of the cult community first fetch bananas, sugarcane and vegetables and then run around the *rimbu rekeanda* while blowing on bamboo flutes. The latter action is frequently repeated subsequently, according to another Ari (Mamarepa) (64.), to make the women and children afraid and keep them away.[45] After the cult community, including the patient, has assembled in the house, the cult leaders go outside and look for a concealed site where they can kill a pig provided by the patient or his family with a specially painted stone.[46] This stone is then buried in a secret place until the next Alamu-palaa Rimbu is carried out. While they are killing the pig, the cult leaders whisper secret words, the content of which Otmar did not want to reveal to me.[47] He simply said that particular *remo*, mostly close relatives of the patient, were asked to bring the illness to an end.[48] Apart from the Alamu-palaa Rimbu itself, some informants also describe these *remo* and the stone used to kill the pig as the cause of the particular treated sickness. When the pig is killed, the cult leaders carry it into the cult house, where it is butchered and cooked in an earth oven, above which is the fireplace. It is also the task of the cult leaders to carve up the pig and distribute it to the two halves of the cult community, who consume it immediately. After the meal, the banana skins and chewed-up sugar canes are burned, most of the pig's bones are shoved into the ashes and the vegetable leftovers, the leaves of the banana plant that were used for the earth oven and the pig's lower jaw are thrown on to the false ceiling or *reke*. The rules to be observed in the case of a Alamu-palaa Rimbu include first of all the strict exclusion of women and children, who must stay away from the *rimbu rekeanda* even when it is empty. The members of the cult community may not enter the other half of the *rimbu rekeanda*, nor use its door. It is also strictly prohibited to leave the cult house with any of the food consumed there. Among the requirements regarding the Alamu-palaa Rimbu is the observance of its own secret language, which consists especially in substituting substantives.[49] Whoever unwittingly uses a word from everyday speech or violates one of the other rules is obliged to give up a valuable object, which apparently becomes a possession of the cult leaders. People in Pairundu are still generally convinced today that the correct carrying out of a Alamu-palaa Rimbu in accordance with all the rules cured all sicknesses within three days, even when these sicknesses had first seemed fatal. If, however, the Alamu-palaa Rimbu failed, then the sickness could not be traced back to it and another Rimbu had to be tried.[50]

In the case of both the Alamu-palaa Rimbu and the Aga-palaa Rimbu introduced earlier, after a few years a set of cult practices called 'Rimbu Eta' began to be held in both cases, of which it was said that it would 'end' the respective type of Rimbu.[51] If ashes had piled up in the fireplaces of the different cult houses, the posts had already been provided with many pig bones from Aga-palaa Rimbu and the false ceiling was already filled to overflowing with pig's jaws, vegetable leftovers and leaves of banana plants from Alamu-palaa Rimbu, for both types of Rimbu this meant that the time had come to hold a Rimbu Eta, though here too the immediate occasion was a particular sickness. If a particular sickness occurred after such a Rimbu Eta, that is, after the 'ending' of the corresponding Rimbu, this counted as a sign that a new beginning should be made with the Aga-palaa Rimbu or Alamu-palaa Rimbu, as the case may be. The cult members would therefore re-erect the *rimbu rekeanda* on the same site where the old cult house had formerly stood but had in the meantime fallen down and become overgrown with grass.[52] Altogether, therefore, Aga-palaa Rimbu and Alamu-palaa Rimbu both occur in cycles, each of which is closed by a Rimbu Eta. In comparison with an individual Alamu-palaa Rimbu, for example, a Rimbu Eta is of greater dimensions, because more people take part, including those from other villages, and more pigs are slaughtered.[53] In addition, a Rimbu Eta must have extra buildings erected for it. A house called a *maeanda* is put up opposite the actual *rimbu rekeanda*. This is divided by an internal wall into two halves, each of which is provided with its own fireplace. One is called a *yapanda* (opossum house or *haus kapul*), the other a *pimakusanda* (pig house or *haus pik*). While most of the cult members circle the *maeanda* while singing and doing a sort of stamping dance, some men sit in the *yapanda* consuming opossum. However, only the cult leaders may enter the *pimakusanda* and prepare and eat the head of a pig there. As soon as the food in both halves of the *maeanda* has been cooked, a round disc is hung on the outside wall of the *maeanda*, which the cult members paint, fix a mushroom to the centre and call *pakuinia*.[54] After the meals in the *maeanda* have finished, a start is made on building the *pokalanda* (*wan saide haus*). These are shelters that provide protection from the rain, in which visitors from other villages spend the night and in which food is stored. Anyone wishing to slaughter pigs on the occasion of a Rimbu Eta may erect a *pokalanda* and may attach it to someone else's or not. Thus, at different Rimbu Eta, a lot of *pokalanda* are set up around the *rimbu rekeanda* and *maeanda* for different lengths of time. On a path leading to the *rimbu rekeanda*, finally, the cult participants put up two tree trunks together in the form of an upright triangle, called a *rimbukete*.[55] As a sign that the Rimbu Eta is coming to a conclusion, the *rimbukete* is decorated with, among other things, the *pakuinia* taken from the *maeanda*. Then all the pigs that are to be slaughtered are driven through the *rimbukete* and killed by the men standing behind it. In comparison with an individual Alamu-palaa Rimbu, for example, not only is the number of participants and of pigs killed greater, but the basic rules also seem to be less strict. Even women and children may take part. Earth ovens are created, not only in the *rimbu rekeanda*, but also in front of the individual *pokalanda* and thus at different places. Nor is the consumption of pig meat linked to particular places, for the cult members can even take it with them to their own houses or villages and distribute it further there.

After the Kome saw the first aeroplane and heard of the coming of the whites – Aga-palaa Rimbu and Alamu-palaa Rimbu were still in use then – groups from Sumi and the Sare region brought the so-called 'Salu Rimbu' to Sua/Yeibu. There the Kome and Mamarepa adopted it, in order to carry it out under the joint leadership of Yawa and Otmar.[56] However, this did not develop up to the point of holding a Rimbu Eta. In the case of Salu Rimbu too, particular *remo* were summoned with a request to end the particular sickness. After killing the pig, the cult leaders rub the stone used for this purpose with pig's blood, wrap it in a palm leaf (*limbum*),[57] and hide it in a hole in a tree or in a rock.[58] Unlike an Alamu-palaa Rimbu, however, with a Salu Rimbu no *rara* leaf is used in the diagnosis, there are no bamboo flutes, no words uttered secretly while the pig is killed,[59] and no secret language is to be generally observed. If the carrying out of a Salu Rimbu seems comparatively little regulated, the reason for this may lie in the fact that, as Mindu (51.) disparagingly remarked, 'it had no origin' ('no gat wanpela as') and arose 'just like that' ('em kamap nating'). Actually no origin myth seemed to exist for the Salu Rimbu, whereas for the Aga-palaa Rimbu and Alamu-palaa Rimbu it was even possible to record different versions of such myths.[60]

Besides the different types of Rimbu, the procedures known as Rombake, Akera and Opayo also belong to the traditional cult practices.[61] In these cases too, in principle, sicknesses are cured in special houses from which women and children are excluded, again using stones and pig's blood and the consumption of particular foods. Exactly as with the different Rimbu procedures, one uses Rombake, Akera or Opayo to respond to the very sicknesses that are supposed to be caused by Rombake, Akera or Opayo respectively. As with Rimbu Eta, moreover, after a period of time somewhat 'enlarged versions' of the otherwise usual procedure take place which are intended to 'end' the particular practice, so that here too there is a cycle instead of a conclusion. In contrast to Rimbu, however, there is only one form of Rombake, Akera and Opayo respectively.

The Kome and the Mamarepa have neither adopted Rombake from, nor transferred it to, other groups. According to Otmar, rather like Aga-palaa Rimbu, Rombake was 'always just there'.[62] The name 'Rombake' originally describes two or three round stones that are placed in the fireplace at the building of the corresponding cult house, the *rombakeanda*, without decoration, though accompanied by the recitation of secret words.[63] Unlike the *rimbu rekeanda*, the *rombakeanda* is not divided into two halves and has only one entrance door. Ari (20.) reported that an earth oven would first be set up with small rats, sweet potatoes and some earth placed over it and this earth then rubbed onto the sick person. If there was an improvement, it was considered certain that the sickness had been caused by Rombake.[64] Then the cult participants prepare the meat of pigs, birds and opossums in the *rombakeanda*, asking Rombake to end the illness it has caused. The killing of a pig in the *rombakeanda* occurs without any secret words being spoken. Moreover, Rombake as a whole is not carried out under the control of particular specialists. In principle, any man may not only prepare food in the *rombakeanda*, but also consume it outside or distribute it further to other men. If, in the course of time, the ashes in the *rombakeanda* have piled up, following a renewed outbreak of a corresponding illness a cult event took place to 'end' the Rombake. However, this event did not have its own name, in comparison to the Rimbu Eta fewer guests turned up to it and only some *pokalanda*, but neither *maeanda* nor a *rimbu kete*, were erected for it. As soon as a sickness occurred that appeared to have been caused by Rombake, the Rombake cycle began again.

As with Rombake, the Kome and Mamarepa have neither taken Akera from, nor passed it on to, other groups.[65] At the beginning of an Akera, the cult leaders enter the *akeranda* or cult house, which is sited in a hidden location, before the other men, in order secretly to place particular leaves in the fireplace and to coat the Akera stone, which gives its name to the cult practice as a whole, with oil, a red colour and earth. Then the Akera stone is placed with some large pearlshells laid out in a semicircle. The general conviction is that finding one of these highly dangerous stones in the bush, stepping over them or touching them unwittingly leads to serious illness, which is said to be caused by 'an Akera woman' (*Akera meri mekim*). The cult leaders make a diagnosis with the aid of a *rara* leaf, as also used in the Alamu-palaa Rimbu. In carrying out Akera, it is rather small pigs that are killed, though unlike the Alamu-palaa Rimbu, this is not a privilege of the cult leaders. Young men can also kill a pig and carry it at night into the house, where the cult leaders cook it in the earth oven and divide it up. Then, as with Rombake, in principle the cult participants can consume the meat anywhere, including their own houses. The Akera stone, however, remains in the *akeranda*. In contrast to the Alamu-palaa Rimbu, carrying out Akera requires neither the uttering of secret words nor the observance of an exclusive secret language.[66]

According to Otmar, the cult practices named 'Opayo' were first adopted by the Mamarepa from the Mendi region and passed on to the Kome as well as groups from Roka and Sumbura.[67] According to Ari (20.), out of fear the Kome were only able to make up their mind to 'acquire' Opayo from the Mamarepa and the Ariarepa after a brother of Lapua (Yapua Repa, Rata Kome) became ill. Ultimately, however, the cult practices were held in Sare and Yeibu, as well as elsewhere, but not in Anapote, Sua or Pairundu. In order to determine whether an illness really is caused by Opayo, one of the cult leaders first rubs a *rara* leaf over the skin of the sick person. Then he folds a banana leaf into a funnel-shape, puts ginger inside it and crushes the ginger with the bone of a cassowary while whispering secret words. Only when an improvement can be traced in the patient after he has consumed this ginger is Opayo seen as having been 'responsible', as it were, for the cure too.[68] In conducting the corresponding cult event, three buildings are needed, called respectively *yapanda* (opossum house; *haus kapul*), *tapanda* (men's house; *haus man*) and *onanda* (women's house; *haus meri*), which are sited somewhat away from the settlement, in a concealed location. All cult members, including the cult leaders, are allocated to either *tapanda* or *onanda*. It is forbidden to change from one house to the other.[69] At the beginning of Opayo, the cult leaders enter the *tapanda* or *onanda*, as the case may be. There they put small insects in the ashes while reciting secret words and place several pearlshells in a semicircle on skins and leaves. Small, flat stones, which they have coloured red and black, are added to these. The name 'Opayo' also refers to these stones, which are permanently kept safe in the *tapanda* or *onanda*.[70] Finally, a pig is killed in full daylight and in the open air, though with a wooden cudgel and not, as with Rimbu, a stone. Cutting up the pig is a task for the cult leaders.[71] They divide the meat into two halves and prepare the head, bones and some of the innards for later distribution to the women and children. After the slaughter, the cult participants, their faces painted and bodies oiled and blackened, carry the two halves of the pig into the *tapanda* or *onanda* under the guidance of the cult leaders. There the two halves are cooked in an earth oven, taking care to separate the kidneys from the rest of the meat. Then, as with the Rombake and Akera, the cult participants may take their shares back to their own houses and consume them there. From time to time in the *yapanda* that stand near the *tapanda* and *onanda*, opossums and tree kangaroos are prepared, eaten or hung up to smoke. When, after some years, the *yapanda* has obviously become blackened from doing this, a feast takes place from which women are excluded and which is accompanied by dancing and singing, as well as the assembling of all the immediately available opossums and tree kangaroos. Thus the time for the 'ending' of the Opayo is said to have come. As a sign of this, a large pile of firewood is burned. The 'ending' of the Opayo, which, as in the case of the Rombake, has no name of its own, requires the building of some *pokalanda* and a *reke* platform, on which the cult participants spread out the meat to be distributed. In addition, the *tapanda* and *onanda* are fenced in with thick tree trunks, so that, as Ari (20.) said, 'the Opayo doesn't get out'. As with the Rimbu Eta, numerous pigs are slaughtered, prepared and also given to guests from other villages. After these guests have departed, the following day, the cult participants again make earth ovens in the *tapanda* and *onanda*, this time distributing the meat prepared there just among themselves.[72]

One common feature of the various traditional cult practices is certainly that, rather like particular magical practices, they were not necessarily restricted to individual settlement communities. Just like the Neambu and Sanguma practices, Alamu-palaa Rimbu, Salu Rimbu and Opayo, at least, were also adopted from other groups. These could even be traditional enemies, such the Kamarepa, the 'teachers' of the Alamu-palaa Rimbu. The Kome and Mamarepa have then themselves later passed the Alamu-palaa Rimbu and Opayo on to others who were interested in them.[73] To do this, it was necessary to instruct the 'recipients' over the rules to be followed and, where appropriate, the secret words to be recited and the secret language. This instruction was always paid for with counter-prestations, so that many informants mention 'sale' or 'purchase' when talking about the spread of cult practices today. Basically, the Kome have conducted their different sorts of cult practices simultaneously from the period of their respective introduction to the arrival of the whites. In Pairundu, Sua/Yeibu, Anapote and Sare, the different cult houses stood within reach of one another. Provided one had enough pigs available, therefore, one could practice not only different magical practices to cure illnesses, but also different cult practices, one after the other, until the patient either recovered or died. A further common feature between particular magical and cult practices was the attempt to cure a particular illness through precisely those same factors that seemed to have caused it. Thus to treat a victim of Neambu, Nosope uses the same leaf that whoever caused the Neambu has used. The same thoughts and feelings are supposed to call up the sickness and then, in the moment of speaking out loud, cure them again. In the case of most traditional cult practices, however, several factors are simultaneously involved with respect to causes and cures. First, from among Aga-palaa Rimbu, Alamu-palaa Rimbu, Salu Rimbu, Rombake, Akera and Opayo, villagers always choose whatever also counts as the cause of the sickness. As the first step in the treatment, the diagnosis thus already specifies the therapy to be used. However, it still remains unclear whether, and to what extent, people link the names 'Aga-palaa Rimbu', 'Alamu-palaa Rimbu', 'Salu Rimbu', 'Rombake', 'Akera' and 'Opayo' with transcendent authorities represented personally, or rather with formless energies.[74] In addition, the cult leaders – when killing a pig, for example – sometimes make an appeal for a cure to the same *remo* as that to which they ascribe the cause of the sickness.[75] Finally, in the context of individual cult events, the same stones are placed in the ashes (Alamu-palaa Rimbu, Rombake) or arranged in a particular way (Akera, Opayo) and are believed to make people ill.[76]

In view of the parallels between magical practices and cult practices, the differences that the view on the present reveals may be surprising. While the fear of witchcraft practices and the belief in specific transcendent authorities are as widespread as ever and while different procedures for the treatment of illness and divination continue to be practiced, the different sorts of Rimbu, like Rombake, Akera and Opayo, today only take place in memories of the pre-colonial period, which has since come to an end. The bush has long since grown over the sites where the cult houses once stood.

Concluding remarks

If, following the approach of the present study, religions on the one hand both incorporate reality and constitute it, yet on the other hand simultaneously influence it themselves, then, with respect to the traditional religion of the Kome, one must pose the question of the 'how' of the process of constituting and influencing.

Regarding the constitution or contemplation of reality within the traditional religion, what stands out first is the passivity that people ascribe to themselves. The Kome claim that although they certainly have techniques of divination as well as both individual and collective procedures for curing sickness available to them, they are still not in a position to apply witchcraft techniques against others themselves. With respect to pre-colonial warfare too, the Kome represent themselves almost exclusively as the victims of attacking groups. To this passivity corresponds the feeling of a basic uncertainty regarding one's own existence. In principle, there is a permanent threat arising from the possibility that particular transcendent authorities, magical practices or attacking enemies may cause sickness or death. Out of the idea that, in such a situation, one may not have sufficient options for one's own active defence may arise a feeling of fear, which perhaps characterises the fundamental situation of the Kome and the Kewa as a whole.[77] The only protection from the dangers that threaten comes from following orally laid down rules. In general, these rules state first of all that one should not draw the anger of others on to oneself, in order not to call forth negative thoughts or feelings, or give any occasion for the application of witchcraft techniques. Because of such techniques, one should not leave any food leftovers or excrement with hostile groups (Neambu), nor accept food from aliens or enemies (Romo). With respect to transcendent authorities, it is forbidden to mention the name of anyone who has recently died, or to go into the bush at night after eating valuable food. However, following the rules laid down not only offers oneself protection against the dangers that threaten, it also guarantees that the results being aimed at through magical or cult practices will be attained. The idea that attaining these results depends on following the rules rather than on the individual beliefs of the participants can be described as legalistic.[78]

Thus just as, for the Kome, with their magical and cult practices, following the rules is more important than individual belief, in my view traditional religion as a whole is less about belief or spiritual development targeted at redemption, than about individual and collective actions or the concrete results thus aimed for.[79] Accordingly, in response to the general question concerning the traditional religion, to begin with many informants do not talk about their former ideas, but instead describe what, for example, they did in the cult houses. Here I see a primacy of action over belief that points to the villagers' basically pragmatic attitude – especially in view of the fact that in general they judge individual actions on the basis of their concrete consequences rather than ethical categories.[80] This pragmatism, which is in harmony with the flexibility noted for the traditional culture as a whole (Chapter 1), certainly made the introduction of Neambu and Sanguma practices, as well as of Alamupalaa Rimbu, Salu Rimbu and Opayo, easier. This importation of new practices therefore does not represent a substitution but a supplement, since the new magical and cult practices are not mutually exclusive with the old ones. Instead, they are to some extent simultaneously available for selection and are applied in parallel or, if necessary, one after the other. It is in accordance with this primacy of action over belief that the introduction of new processes was made dependent on their practical effectiveness in particular. On the other hand, whether the introduction of new processes gave rise to contradictions on the level of beliefs was of secondary importance. The pragmatism of the villagers therefore not only eased the importation and duality of different practices, it is also expressed in a relatively limited need, from the Western point of view, for systematisation and coherence. As already mentioned, there is no all-embracing myth of creation explaining the origin of the world as a whole and creating a connection between the different elements of the traditional religion. Individual transcendent authorities are not, for example, connected to one another through kinship or power relationships. The different cult practices are not classified in accordance with their greater or lesser effectiveness.[81] With respect to the stones used in the cult houses, the *remo* and the Aga-palaa Rimbu, Alamu-palaa Rimbu, Salu Rimbu, Rombake, Akera and Opayo, the individual factors that are supposed to cause as well as cure particular illnesses stand disparately alongside one another.[82] Just as the Kome do not really attempt to connect up the different elements of their traditional religion, so the ideas linked to the different elements do not appear particularly differentiated from the Western point of view.[83]

The possibility of a relatively limited emic need for systematisation and coherence must, I believe, also be taken into account in examining other religions in Papua New Guinea and in Melanesia as a whole. It is precisely when the need for systematisation and coherence is weakly expressed that there is a danger that the Western observer – who is involved in recognising connections – assumes that his opposite number, whom he is observing, is also making these connections, even when that is apparently not the case. Out of this, an attempt can be made to make whatever might appear contradictory, inaccurate or incomplete in the collected data disappear. If the observer formulates what are conclusive statements from his point of view in order to put them into the mouths of the observed, then there is a projection in which the observer is for his part creating connections which, however, work neither consciously nor unconsciously for the observed himself. Thus the describing and analysing anthropologist becomes a donator of meaning, a theologian constructing the religion being treated.[84]

With respect to the question, how the traditional religion has itself influenced the reality constituted within it, in general it can be said that it gives expression to the values of strength and equivalence that are important for the traditional culture as a whole and strengthens these values. First of all, the Kome try to guarantee health and fertility as preconditions for the demonstration of strength by invoking Yaki and conducting magical and cult practices. A gain in prestige for the respective participants or specialists results from the fact that magical and cult practices not only permit the consumption of pig meat, they are also remunerated with counter-prestations. In addition, specialists in magical practices and cult leaders have the option of passing on their knowledge to other groups, in order to obtain counter-prestations from them too. On the whole, the prestige that is fed by magical and cult practices is based not least on their being bounded off from those who are excluded from participation and, even more so, from taking over the functions of leadership. This delimitation and exclusiveness is created through the secrecy of the knowledge that is required in each case.[85] Accordingly a breach of secrecy is essentially equivalent to a loss of power. Naming a helpful *remo* means losing its support. If negative thoughts and feelings are expressed, their effectiveness is dissolved. Apart from the value of strength, the traditional religion also confirms the value of equivalence. This occurs mainly though the threat of sanctions. For example, whoever keeps desirable food to himself, delays giving a counter-prestation as a fee or steals must reckon on witchcraft techniques being used against him or negative feelings and thoughts being created, which, perhaps supported by a *remo*, bring with them sickness and death.[86] Even Yaki, who is otherwise held to be a well-intentioned figure, can kill thieves or murderers. If a *kalando* grasps someone, especially after he has consumed an especially valuable foodstuff, this can be interpreted as retaliation for the fact that the victim did not share his food with others. If the sanctions that are threatened within the traditional religion concern, above all, cases in which exchange activities and relationships do not correspond to the appropriate equivalence, this gives rise to support of what, from the Western point of view, can be described as an 'obligation to share'. Simultaneously, the threatened sanctions strengthen the feeling of a basic danger to human existence, since all exchange activities and relationships in principle include the possibility of acting contrary to the value of equivalence. Finally, the value of equivalence is also expressed where magical practices and cults are addressed, as it were, to a transcendent authority and where there is a prevailing expectation that the desired result will occur as a counter-presentation for, so to speak, following all the rules.

By expressing and strengthening the values of strength and equivalence, which are important for the traditional culture as a whole, the traditional religion is fulfilling an integrating function. Thus, for example, in the case of the participants in the different Rimbu events, some male clan members are always being brought together.[87] They simultaneously represent a part of the male village population, since the clan, at least in Pairundu, forms a local group (Chapter 1). Consequently, to some extent the traditional religion is restricted to the members of the same settlement community. This goes along with the fact that the *remo* – at least of the recently deceased – are said to stay in the immediate vicinity of Pairundu only, like the bush spirits. On the whole, therefore, in the case of the Kome's traditional religion, the integrative function coincides with that particularism which, according to Kohl (1986: 194f), represents a characteristic of tribal religions in general. A particularism of this sort corresponds in principle to the segmentary social organisation of the Kewa as a whole, with their dualism of 'we groups' and 'they groups', of 'inside' and 'outside' (Chapter 1).

The thesis that the traditional religion contributes to group integration does not mean that these groups must be homogenous. Rather, the traditional religion strengthens the difference in power between the genders, between the generations and between 'ordinary' men and Big Men. The very possibility of obtaining prestige by carrying out or leading magical and cult practices was exclusively reserved to men. Certainly today, this is the impression gained from interviews with men. However, it would appear that the role of women in the traditional religion has been restricted to conducting 'love magic' and 'fertility magic', to participating in Rimbu Eta and to consuming pig meat in the context of the Opayo. At the same time, out of the exclusiveness of cult participants and specialists in magical and cult practices, a division emerges between the generations, since young men could still not take over any functions of leadership, even when they had become old enough to enter the men's house.[88] Since both the specialists in magical practices and the cult leaders were frequently not only older men but also simultaneously Big Men, the traditional religion also confirms the division between them and 'ordinary' men.[89] If the members of the older generation in general and the Big Men in particular have easier access to religious leadership functions, this has less to do with their having a better relationship with transcendent authorities than with the fact that they can produce the gifts that are necessary to 'acquire' the knowledge that is needed for the appropriate functions.[90]

Notes

1. Franklin signals some scepticism with respect to this theme, though in general this seems exaggerated to me: 'Perhaps the Kewa religion can never be adequately described by an outsider' (Franklin and Franklin 1978: 471).
2. A certain level of detail, especially with respect to traditional cult practices, is justified by the fact that the traditional religion has hardly been dealt with in the ethnographies that have up to now become available on either the Highlands in general or the Kewa in particular. In addition, for the most part it is only the old men who still have the appropriate information in Pairundu today. Thus unless it is recorded in writing, this information will be lost after their deaths.
3. Naturally social effectiveness goes along with psychical effectiveness, expressed especially in the form of the anxiety that is linked to these particular ideas.
4. I am aware that I am here defining magical and cult practices by exclusion, i.e., negatively. However, this should not in any way create the impression that magical practices, for example, are not used in the West too in a different form.
5. However, I agree with Lawrence and Meggitt (1965a: 6) that a division between magic on the one hand and religion on the other is not sensible (cf. Vivelo 1988: 260).
6. At the same time, naturally I cannot rule out the possibility that, in a longer or second period of fieldwork, connections between the different elements of the traditional religion that I had not previously realised might have emerged.
7. In my judgement, this terminological usage cannot have been usual in the pre-colonial period. Instead the influence of a negative evaluation conveyed through missionisation may be at work here. The term 'remo' is given by Franklin (Franklin and Franklin 1978: 432), LeRoy (1985a: 104) and MacDonald (1985: 5). In Pairundu and its area, *remo* have also been referred to as 'waya' since the start of missionisation.

8. According to Ipapula, many people were mistreated by bush spirits in the way described. However, other informants did not confirm this information.
9. According to Lawrence and Meggitt (1965a: 14), this view is widespread in the Highlands.
10. According to Ari (18.), for example, the *remo* only kill members of their own sub-clan.
11. In the literature, bush spirits are also called 'kapo kalado' (Franklin and Franklin 1978: 463), 'kolapu', 'tapo' (MacDonald 1985: 5), 'kolapu ali', 'pado ali' and 'lepe' (MacDonald 1991: 33). However, none of these terms were usual in Pairundu. According to Ondasa (61.), the bush spirits are subordinate to the ancestral spirits, though other informants did not confirm this.
12. The visibility of the *kalando* was decisively disputed by Ari (18.). On the other hand, Ipapula (37.) told me that, long before the whites appeared, he had seen a large man with a white skin and long hair in a river in the bush, which must have been a *kalando*. As well as Ipapula, Ondasa also mentioned the white skin colour of the *kalando*.
13. Pogola (69.) told me that the *kalando* would only kill people of the same gender and would befriend members of the other gender. For example, a female *kalando* might help a man win at cards all the time. However, other informants did not confirm this.
14. In the pre-colonial period, people told me, the *kalando* would smell the meat of pigs and opossums especially.
15. The term 'Yaki' only appears in L. Josephides (1985a: 77). Franklin (Franklin and Franklin 1978: 465) and MacDonald (1985: 4, 1991: 43) write 'Yakili', which, according to MacDonald (1991: 43), is regarded as the father of the 'sky people' – also mentioned by LeRoy (1985a: 112) – though they were unknown in Pairundu.
16. Accordingly, Lawrence and Meggitt (1965a: 9) write on Melanesian belief systems as a whole that 'the realm of the non-empirical is always closely associated with, in most cases part of, the ordinary physical world'.
17. Because of this secrecy the specialists did not want to name for me the plant materials they used, nor hand them over for botanical classification.
18. L. Josephides also lists a practice that she calls 'nu yapara' (1983: 301, 1985a: 121). However, this term is unknown in Pairundu and is not mentioned by Franklin, Leroy or MacDonald.
19. Serale (86.) and Nosope (59.) are my most important informants for Neambu.
20. Nosope disputed Serale's information here.
21. This description of Nosope's is also found in MacDonald (1985: 13f, 1991: 157f, 388f, 539). The term 'big wasp', with which MacDonald (1985: 13) translates Neambu, is a reference to the insects in the tree.
22. The term 'Romo' also occurs in Franklin (Franklin and Franklin 1978: 470), L. Josephides (1985a: 121) and MacDonald (1985: 13f, 1991: 158, 386).
23. Accordingly, people reacted in astonishment when I told them that in Europe one would accept food without knowing the people who had prepared it.
24. However, Amakoa (11.) contradicted this, concluding that Ondasa would occasionally use Sanguma for payment to kill people over long distances by saying their names. Yali too contradicted Ondasa by expressing the view that nothing could counter Sanguma illnesses. – The term 'Sanguma' is not mentioned by Franklin, L. Josephides, LeRoy or MacDonald.
25. MacDonald describes a similar process with the term 'kaipi ali', which she translates as 'stone man' (1985: 13ff., 1991: 158f, 387f, 476f).
26. The fact that, in the following I describe certain practices of curing sickness as magical practices does not mean that I deny either physiological or psychical effects to the substances used, when seen from the Western point of view.
27. *Rara* leaves have a rough surface, and 'ordinary' men often rub them on their temples when they have a headache.
28. Cf. LeRoy (1985b: xxv) and MacDonald (1985: 9). Negative thoughts and feelings are directed equally against adversaries and against one's own person. If someone has stolen something or has lied, is jealous, angry or suspicious, harbours excessive desires regarding property or power, or has unfulfilled sexual needs, in the belief of the Kewa all

of these things may make him ill, according to MacDonald (1991: 154, cf. LeRoy 1985a: 163, 166).

29. Such a statement is called *autim tingting* in Tok Pisin. For the Kome, the injurious power of feelings and thoughts is also expressed in those illnesses whose cause is called *daunim spet* (swallowing saliva) in Tok Pisin. For example, if one consumes a meal that is generally desired without offering any to anybody else, the latter swallow their saliva out of frustration, which can lead to sickness for themselves or for the person eating. One effect of this idea is that, for example, tinned fish and rice are often consumed in secret.

30. Accordingly, MacDonald (1991: 156) reports that in Mararoko the Western-trained employees at the aid posts and the traditionally oriented healers do not see one another as rivals but rather as colleagues.

31. According to MacDonald (1991: 107), such huts are called *raleanda*.

32. After the end of the interview, Atasi immediately left the house in a great hurry out of fear (as Ata Francis told me later) that he had unwittingly spoken the secret names in the course of answering my many questions.

33. According to how Ripu's dream was interpreted, the cause was determined to be the *remo* of a former wife of Ari, who had beaten her to death in the pre-colonial period. However, not even compensation payments to her relatives had satisfied the *remo*.

34. Ari's (20.) explanations were supplemented by another Ari, a Mamarepa from Yeibu (12.).

35. In addition, according to Ari the deceased's stomach was then examined, to see if there was any Romo in it.

36. Franklin (Franklin and Franklin 1978: 467), L. Josephides (1985a: 171 n. 16) and MacDonald (1991: 161, 477) briefly describe a similar technique, though without using the term 'ayaka'.

37. Apart from this, experiments still seem to be made using other divination techniques. Thus Ari (20.) said that after Usa had been buried, a bamboo tube had been inserted into the earth up to his mouth, in order to ask in a whisper for the name of the murderer, whereupon a loud hissing noise was heard, so that everyone fled in fear. Pogola (72.), who had been present as a small child at the same event, said that, instead of a hissing sound, a message from a *remo* was heard, saying that Usa had not been dead long enough and therefore could not answer. However, Pogola also described the flight of all those present.

38. According to Franklin, the procedures thus described come originally from the Mendi region (Franklin and Franklin 1978: 424).

39. However, the respective cult leaders have all died in the meantime, so that no one is still able today to describe this Rimbu exactly. According to Franklin, 'aga-palaa' means literally 'pandanus branch spirit' (Franklin and Franklin 1978: 256).

40. According to Otmar (64.), the Kamarepa instructed his father in how to carry out the Alamu-palaa Rimbu. According to Franklin, 'alamu' means 'sugarcane' and 'palaa' 'branch' (Franklin and Franklin 1978: 442).

41. Accordingly, the following account of the Alamu-palaa Rimbu is based on descriptions provided by Otmar (64.), Ipapula (36.) and Ari (14.). However, the name 'Alamu-palaa Rimbu' is only used by Otmar today. Ari and Yawa speak of 'Eno Rimbu' or 'Kamarepa Rimbu', Ipapula of 'Oranu Rimbu'. However, analysis of the contents of the respective interviews permits the conclusion that ultimately 'Eno Rimbu', 'Kamarepa Rimbu' and 'Oranu Rimbu ' refer to nothing other than Alamu-palaa Rimbu. Some informants confirmed this by expressing the view that the different terms basically described the same thing. Thus Alupa (7.) said that Eno Rimbu and Kamarepa Rimbu resembled one another and were both actually Alamu-palaa Rimbu. According to Mindu (51.), Oranu Rimbu and Alamu-palaa Rimbu, which were also identical to one another, were formerly brought together by the Kamarepa and Oranu Rimbu, Kamarepa Rimbu and Eno Rimbu also all have the same origin. Finally, Otmar (64.) explained that just as, with the Catholics, Lutherans and Adventists, there were several churches ('kainkain nem

bilong lotu i kamap') but still only one God, so Oranu Rimbu, Kamarepa Rimbu, Eno Rimbu and Alamu-palaa Rimbu were ultimately just different descriptions for the same thing. In addition, some terms appear in the literature that were not known at all in Pairundu and the surrounding area, namely 'rudu ribu' (Franklin and Franklin 1978: 256, LeRoy 1979b: 29), 'koi ribu' (L. Josephides 1985a: 77) and 'adalu ribu' (Franklin and Franklin 1978: 256, L. Josephides 1985a: 77, MacDonald 1991: 316f).

42. According to Franklin, the cult community as a whole is usually recruited from the same sub-clan (Franklin and Franklin 1978: 434).

43. 'Anda' means 'house'. According to Otmar (64.) the *rimbu rekeanda* is also called *rimbu noianda*, since 'reke' and 'noi' have the same meaning.

44. According to Franklin, however, 'ribu' means 'feared' and 'sacred' (Franklin and Franklin 1978: 443). MacDonald (1991: 135) translates 'ribu' as 'poor' and 'rich'. For her, 'rimbu' is not an umbrella term for different cult practices.

45. Cf. MacDonald (1991: 137). I shall go into the question of whether the sounds of the bamboo flutes are regarded as the voice of a transcendent authority later.

46. According to MacDonald (1991: 136), on corresponding occasions in the Mararoko region, the pig is killed by being stabbed with a sharpened bone.

47. Otmar, who has since joined the committee of the Catholic Church in Anapote, justified his refusal by saying that, being a member of the church today, he feels ashamed to admit having taken part in such customs. In my view, he wanted to emphasise in this way how he had broken with tradition and how much he belonged to the church. At the same time, however, it becomes clear that even today he is not entirely indifferent to the practices just described.

48. At this point differences emerge in the accounts of Otmar and Ari on the one hand and Ipapula on the other. In contrast to Otmar and Ari, Ipapula (36.) said that the cult leaders would kill the pig with an unpainted, not a painted stone and do so inside, not outside the *rimbu rekeanda*. And in the secret address made simultaneously, the pig was called different names (*utakiapimena, auramumomena, meleparandalumena, irandalumena*, 'mena' meaning 'pig') and the sun and moon were invoked. Moreover, again in contrast to Otmar and Ari, Ipapula reported that the cult leaders would then send the other men out of the house briefly, in order to wrap a small frog and pig fat in a particular leaf and place it in the ashes. This was allegedly destined to remain in the ashes.

49. Thus for 'pig', for example, one says not 'mena' but 'kuki', for 'sugar cane' not 'wa' but 'yadolu', for 'banana' not 'ai' but 'ekeadula' and for 'stone' not 'ana' but 'rakola' (cf. Franklin and Franklin 1978: 435).

50. With reference to the older Aga-palaa Rimbu, the best informant in Pairundu today proved to be Ipapula, who, although he was not a cult leader, had himself taken part in it (35., 38.). According to Ipapula, the Aga-palaa Rimbu was distinguished from the Alamu-palaa Rimbu that has been described up to now by the fact that in the case of the former, the cult members fixed the pig bones to a post erected in the *rimbu rekeanda*. Moreover, there were more rules to be observed. Thus Ipapula complained that one could not even drink water in the *rimbu rekeanda* during an Aga-palaa Rimbu.

51. The following description of the Rimbu Eta is based on accounts by Otmar (64.), Ipapula (36.) and Ari (20.). Of these informants, Ari was the only one who expressed the view that the set of cult practices the others called 'Rimbu Eta' did not have a name of its own and that 'Rimbu Eta' was just the term for the head-dress worn on this occasion. On the Rimbu Eta, cf. Franklin and Franklin (1978: 433).

52. According to Otmar (64.), when such illnesses broke out, it was said that the Rimbu that had been ended had come back again and was going to make people sick again, so it was necessary to begin again and hold the corresponding Rimbu.

53. In contrast to the pig-killing festivals (*yawe*), however, no group classified as 'Ewa' or 'Merepa' appears.

54. 'Paku' means 'sun', 'ini' means 'eye'.

55. The term *rimbukete* may also be of recent origin. To my ear, the word 'kete' sounds like the English word 'gate' spoken in a Kewa accent.

56. The following information on the Salu Rimbu comes mainly from Otmar (64.) and also from Nosupinai (60.). According to L. Josephides (1985a: 77), the Salu Rimbu is also called Mae Rimbu.
57. Mihailic (1971: 122) gives the Latin designation *Kentiopsis archontophoenix*, though this is disputed by Paul Hiepko (personal communication).
58. In contrast to Otmar, Alupa (7.) claimed that the stone was buried between the two doors of the *rimbu rekeanda*.
59. Here too, Alupa (7.) contradicted Otmar by saying that the cult leaders spoke secret words as the pig was killed.
60. I am reserving the presentation and interpretation of these myths for a later publication, since the relevant material would exceed the limits of the present work.
61. The fact that in Pairundu and the surrounding area the names of various cult practices given in the literature were totally unknown, namely 'kerekaiada' (L. Josephides 1985a: 200 n. 2), 'savada', 'makalawai' and 'keveta pamo' (MacDonald 1991: 138f), might serve as an expression of the cultural heterogeneity that prevails in the Kewa area as a whole.
62. The following description of Rombake is based mainly on Otmar's (64.) and also on Nosupinai's (60.) descriptions of it.
63. In contrast to Otmar, Ipapula (38.) claims that the stones were rubbed with oil and the skin of an opossum. The term 'rombake' is also mentioned by Franklin and MacDonald. Franklin translates 'robaa' as 'stomach' and 'ke' as 'thigh' (Franklin and Franklin 1978: 442). MacDonald adopts this (1991: 138), though her description of Rombake differs at many points from the accounts given to me.
64. However, I am sceptical of Ari's account, since neither Otmar nor Ipapula confirmed it.
65. The term 'akera' is also used by Franklin and Franklin (1978: 256). Otmar (66.) and Ipapula (38.) agreed in their view that Akera had probably arisen later than Rombake but earlier than Alamu-palaa Rimbu. These two were my most important informants for the following account.
66. According to Otmar (66.), at the next outbreak of the corresponding sickness, the old *akeranda* was replaced by a new one. According to Ipapula (38.), on the other hand, the same house served for several cult events one after the other. Another source of contention is whether, in the context of Akera, there was ever periodically a 'concluding event' comparable to the Rimbu Eta. Ipapula (20.) claimed that there was, whereas Otmar (66.) disputed it.
67. Otmar (65.) said that this transfer occurred 'in order to get back the purchase cost'. The following description of Opayo is based on Ari (20.), Ipapula (38.) and Otmar (66.). The adoption and handing on of the Opayo apparently occurred after the importation of the Alamu-palaa Rimbu but still before the first Salu Rimbu was carried out.
68. Contrary to this account, given similarly by Otmar and Ari, Ipapula (20.) claimed that a *rara* leaf was not used, nor was a secret utterance recited.
69. To that extent, *tapanda* and *onanda*, which together fall under the umbrella term *opayoanda*, correspond to the two halves of the *rimbu rekeanda*.
70. According to Franklin, on the other hand, 'opayo' is translated as 'leaves which come up' (Franklin and Franklin 1978: 257).
71. Contrary to this account, provided similarly by Otmar and Ipapula, Ari (20.) claimed that the former owner of the pig would cut it up.
72. This account, which comes from Otmar and Ari, contradicts Ipapula, who claimed that there were no further earth ovens to 'end' the Opayo after the departure of the guests.
73. On the whole, therefore, Franklin's thesis is to be accepted: 'There has... been a pragmatic approach to all cults and members are willing to borrow new rituals to supplement the old' (Franklin and Franklin 1978: 444). The spreading of cult practices is also mentioned by L. Josephides (1985a: 77). According to Crittenden and Schiefflin (1991: 135), this follows the trade routes.
74. Even with the same informants, the corresponding information was contradictory. For example, I could not obtain any more or less uniform version when I asked former participants in the Alamu-palaa Rimbu whether they connected the noises created by the

bamboo flutes with the voices of the Rimbu. However, different indications point to ideas of personification at other cult events. Rombake was involved with the request to end sicknesses caused by him, particular sicknesses were believed to be caused by the Akera woman and at the 'conclusion' of Opayo the different cult houses had been fenced in 'so that the Opayo can't get out'. Generally, however, to the question whether personal transcendent authorities or formless energies were involved, the villagers were not only not of the same opinion, they ultimately seemed to find this question unimportant.

75. As Otmar (62.) expressly emphasised, however, the killing of a pig to accompany such a request does not on its own constitute a Rimbu. The fact that, according to Otmar, the cult participants said, with reference to Rimbu, that they would carry out a *remo* (*mipela i wokim remo*) indicates a close connection between Rimbu and *remo*. However, it is possible that this connection had only emerged during missionisation.

76. The fact that the term for these stones is often identical with the term for the corresponding set of cult practices as a whole points to the significance that is attached to the stones.

77. In this respect, the region of the Erave river is clearly especially dangerous, since *remo* are said to go there and Neambu and Sanguma to come from there. Sr Marie (48.), who has lived in Kagua District for twenty years as a nun, has described fear as a basic characteristic of the indigenous people in general: 'The element of fear is very great... whatever they do, it comes from fear, not love...' However, this view seems to me to have been shaped by the efforts of Christian missionisation and to be exaggerated.

78. When the belief of the individual is left as his 'private business', as it were – so long as he adheres to the necessary actions – then this can be seen as a sign of individualism, which, in accordance with their egalitarian ethos, is characteristic not only of the Kewa, but the inhabitants of the Highlands as a whole (Chapter 1).

79. Accordingly, Trompf (1991: 20) writes that Melanesian religion generally stresses the material results of rituals and relations with the transcendent rather than, for example, the internal peace of the soul.

80. Forman (1982: 89), writing about the peoples of the Pacific in general, also notes a primacy of action over belief: 'Traditional religion never had sharply defined beliefs, it conveyed its benefits not through believing certain things but doing certain things'. The primacy of action over belief on the one hand explains that, in my representation of the traditional religion, practices rather than the contents of belief are placed in the foreground. On the other hand, it might lead one to assume that the people themselves did not necessarily share my interest in the beliefs that have developed out of the confrontation with Christianity. According to Lawrence and Meggitt (1965a: 18), the fundamentally practical attitude that arises out of the primacy of action over belief exists all over Melanesia: '...the prevailing attitude towards religion is essentially pragmatic and materialistic. Religion is a technology rather than a spiritual force for human salvation'.

81. According to Otmar (66.) and Ipapula (38.), the procedures used were all equally successful.

82. A connection between these factors might be made by means of the thesis that the Aga-palaa Rimbu, Alamu-palaa Rimbu, Salu Rimbu, Rombake, Akera and Opayo – whether personified authorities or formless energies – possess the stones and either cause the *remo* to trigger off illnesses, or are caused to do so themselves by the *remo*. This thesis, which arises out of the perspective of the Western observer, draws its attraction from the fact that it ascribes a certain coherence to the ideas of the villagers. However, it must be clearly stated that the former cult participants themselves, at least according to their statements, do not create any such coherence. Thus, for example, the view was never expressed to me that the Aga-palaa Rimbu, Alamu-palaa Rimbu, Salu Rimbu, Rombake, Akera and Opayo were embodied in the cult stones. This, however, is precisely what Franklin is convinced of: 'In a sense the spirit is somehow thought to be embodied in the stone' (Franklin and Franklin 1978: 439).

83. With respect to life after death, for example, there is merely the view that one is taken by the *remo* in the direction of the Erave. The specialists in the magical treatment of

illnesses claimed not to know how the food they prescribed worked or whether transcendent authorities helped with recovery or not. In the case of the cult practices, whether the Aga-palaa Rimbu, Alamu-palaa Rimbu, Salu Rimbu, Rombake, Akera and Opayo count as personalised beings or whether they were identical with the respective *remo* that were invoked, remains an open question.

84. Keesing (1989: 15) in particular has pointed out the problem here: '...there are grave dangers of the anthropologist becoming the theologian of a system which may be less global and systematically coherent than our assumptions and theories lead us to expect'. Keesing (1989: 18) is writing with reference to Oceania in general: 'Anthropological discourse on tribal religion has been prone to over-exoticize, over-theologize, over-systematize'. On this, cf. Brunton (1980) and Juillerat (1980).

85. Accordingly Franklin writes: 'The esoteric nature of cult activities assumes that outsiders maintain an appropriate distance' (Franklin and Franklin 1978: 435, cf. LeRoy 1985a: 165, 240). In Pairundu, the secret knowledge of the cult leaders is a matter of which substances to place in the ashes of the cult house (Alamu-palaa Rimbu, Akera and Opayo) and which words they must recite when making a diagnosis (Alamu-palaa Rimbu, Rombake and Opayo), kindling a fire there (Alamu-palaa Rimbu) or killing a pig (Alamu-palaa Rimbu and, according to Alupa, Salu Rimbu). However, in creating exclusiveness, what is decisive is that something is kept a secret, rather than its actual content. Nor does the effectiveness of a magical or a cult practice depend, for the Kome, on the complexity of the respective secret knowledge that lies at its basis.

86. Accordingly MacDonald (1985: 9) was not wrong when she described an emic link between illnesses and disturbed social relations: 'The South Kewa believe that sickness is a symptom of damaged relationship in the world of land, people, and spirits'.

87. Although the traditional religion fulfils an integrative function and brings together cult participants, according to my information it does not include initiation rites. L. Josephides also concludes, with respect to the Sumbura area, that: 'No formalized puberty or initiation rites for either sex seem to have existed in the area' (1983: 295, see also L. Josephides 1985a: 77, 120). Nor do Franklin, LeRoy or MacDonald mention any initiation rites. This 'lack' of initiation rites among the Kewa is surprising, since they have certainly been described in other regions of Papua New Guinea (M.R. Allen 1967, A. Strathern 1970, Herdt 1982).

88. The thesis put forward by LeRoy (1985a: 66) and MacDonald (1991: 135, 140), that unmarried young men in particular are among the cult leaders, was not confirmed by the informants I asked.

89. Thus, as already described, among the Kome, Ari and Yawa presided over the Alamu-palaa Rimbu and Yawa also counted among the cult leaders of the Salu Rimbu. Among the Mamarepa, a former Big Man, Otmar, belonged to the leading functionaries of Alamu-palaa Rimbu and Salu Rimbu.

90. If the conduct of magical and cult practices confirms differences in power, then the particular secret knowledge simultaneously represents knowledge connected with rule. In addition, it was obviously open to those who were economically in a position to do so, like Yawa and Otmar, to accumulate several functions by learning different magical practices or taking over leadership positions in different cult practices.

3

Colonisation and Missionisation

The traditional religion, like the traditional culture in general, was subjected to the influences of colonisation and missionisation. The Kome themselves could not at first distinguish between the representatives of the colonial government and of the different churches. In describing colonisation, I shall contrast the views of the colonial officers as manifested in their patrol reports with the memories of the villagers themselves.[1] The term 'missionisation' means, very generally, the process of the acceptance of Christianity, triggered first by white, then by indigenous religious functionaries. This process consisted of various stages. It began with the spread of Catholicism, followed first by conversion to the Church of the Seventh-day Adventists and then the introduction of a Holy Spirit movement. In describing missionisation too, etic and emic perspectives will be confronted with one another.[2] However, I shall only go into the emic assessment of the consequences of colonisation and missionisation in a later Chapter (5), since this evaluation is shaped by Catholic and Adventist beliefs, which have yet to be described (Chapter 4).

Colonisation

The Kome apparently received hardly any information concerning the first patrols with which the 'opening up' of the Highlands began.[3] Rather, people learned about the Leahys, who stayed in the area of Mount Ialibu between 1933 and 1934 (Schiefflin and Crittenden 1991a: 34f map 2), and especially about Hides and O'Malley, who at least visited the South Kewa, living between the Erave and Sugu rivers, in 1935 on their Strickland-Purari patrol.[4] However, while not even the following patrols entered the Pairundu area, both Champion and Timperley (1938–39) and Adamson and Atkinson (1938–39) were able to come into contact with the Kome themselves and their neighbours respectively.[5] On all these excursions, the colonial officers were accompanied by porters and policemen whom they had recruited from among the coastal population of New Guinea. Direct contact with the first whites was usually preceded by indirect contact, which took the form of rumours as well as, for example, the steel axes that reached the Highlands, apparently along the traditional trade routes.[6] According to Josephides and Schiltz (1991a: 224), the next encounter with the Western world was the sight of military aircraft in the Second World War flying from Australia to the northern coast of New Guinea, where the allied troops were fighting the Japanese. However, the inhabitants of the Southern Highlands were not affected by the war. Only in the late 1940s and early 1950s were regular patrols carried out in the area of Kagua. Permanent government stations were set up in Erave in 1950,[7] in Ialibu in 1955 (Franklin and Franklin 1978: 75) and in Kagua in 1957 (KPR 1971/72–18).

To begin with, the colonial officers sought to contain the traditional warfare and to carry out censuses. Then the indigenous people were made to erect rest houses (*haus kiap*) for later patrols, dig latrines and clean and make up the paths between the different villages. To supervise such work, individual villagers were appointed Village Constables, who had to ensure that their villages took part in the various building projects of the colonial government. These included an airstrip at Kagua[8] and the road from Kagua to Ibia and Erave.[9] From the start of the 1960s, the colonial officers promoted markets and shops, opened aid posts and schools, introduced new species of plants and recruited contract workers for other provinces. Elections were also organised. The first one, which was held from 20 April to 14 May 1964 in Pairundu and the surrounding area, was for the then Local Government Council (KPR 1963/64–18). In this period, the whole area of what was to become Papua New Guinea was still under Australian colonial rule. In their patrol reports, the colonial officers called Sua/Yeibu 'Sui'aibu' (KPR 1959/60–8) and Pairundu 'Akuna'.[10] The first visits mentioned date from 14 November 1958 to Sua/Yeibu (EPR 1958/59–5) and 9 December 1958 to Pairundu (KPR 1958/59–4). At this time, being a 'restricted area', the region could only be entered with official permission and accompanied by armed police. The routine tasks of the patrols are frequently listed in the patrol reports and consisted of carrying out censuses, treating sicknesses, resolving conflicts and supervising work on the roads. Less frequently mentioned are the penalties with which they reacted to the non-observance of their various orders.[11] The colonial officers usually made speeches in Tok Pisin, which those accompanying them translated. In them, the local population was called upon not only to give up their traditional warfare, but also to send their children to school, to make use of the medical care provided by the colonial government and to obtain an income for themselves by growing coffee.[12]

From the outset, reports mention in particular the difficulties with which colonial officers initially saw themselves confronted. The local people attacked them,[13] fled from them and were not prepared to let themselves be counted in a census.[14] Particular problems seem to have been caused by the inhabitants of Sua/Yeibu.[15] With respect to the whole Wabi-Sumi region, it was stated at the end of 1959: 'All groups patrolled are openly uncooperative and most are given to intolerance and arrogance. Generally it appears that they have no other desire than to be let alone to live as they were before the advent of the Administration'.[16] However, this picture quickly changes and after a brief period a 'good degree of equilibrium among the people' (KPR 1960/61–9: 5) is noted with satisfaction, as well as their readiness to provide services for the patrols.[17] According to the accounts, the local population especially welcomed pacification, which allowed them to return to their home villages again, after expulsions and flights caused by war.[18] Accordingly, the colonial officers assessed the attitude being shown towards them at the start of the 1960s as overwhelmingly positive: 'Generally the attitude of all groups reflected a clear responsiveness to what was being said. To this end the various projects such as inter-village tracks, rest houses etc. well indicate that the people do indeed look forward to the arrival [of the patrol] in their region' (KPR 1962/63–18: 5). Although, therefore, the initial resistance, especially from members of the younger generation,[19] seems to have softened into a readiness for obedience and cooperation, at the end of the 1960s some patrol reports still contain complaints that the goals of the colonial government are not being supported sufficiently: 'There are, however, many of these people who show no interest in any aspect of government, they are quite content to sit in their gardens and live as their forebears have'.[20]

When the villagers who were thus subject to different assessments by colonial officers recall the start of colonisation themselves, they relate how they heard, even before the first direct contact, of the imminent arrival of beings called at that time 'kapena' or 'nokerepa'.[21] Already in this period – according to Ari (17.), young men like Serale, Ripu, Yali, Naki, Ondasa and Amakoa had just been born[22] – some Ewa showed a steel axe and a scrap of red cloth to their astonished hosts at a pig-killing festival in Sare.[23] Apart from this, seeing the first aircraft has become a fixed theme in people's different memories. Thus the Kome willingly relate that at first they thought the noise of the aircraft to come from a particularly large opossum, until they looked up into the sky and saw an alien-looking bird flying fast. As in other parts of Papua New Guinea, the whites in Pairundu and its area were initially regarded as ancestral spirits or *remo*.[24] It was simply unclear whether they came out of the air, from under the earth or out of the water. In favour of the latter view was their white skin colour, as well as the fact that the patrols frequently marched along the courses of rivers and camped there.[25] In any case, there was a unanimous fear that alien beings had arrived to kill people. This fear determined people's initial reactions in fleeing, trying to conceal the paths leading to their villages with bushes, branches and tree trunks and hiding pearlshells, pigs, women and children.[26] Ipapula (38.) claimed that people only ate at night, so that smoke from their fireplaces did not attract the intruders. At the same time, however, individual young men, like Rekepea or Wapa (93.), sought to attach themselves to the foreigners, in order to serve them as guides, for example. All in all, according to Ari (14.), the general fear only decreased when it became clear that the whites wanted to exchange glass beads, salt, matches and razor blades for vegetables, bananas and sugarcane. For whole sweet potato mounds, according to Wala (92.), the Kome received some salt and razor blades. Although this established that it was not *remo* who were involved, but beings who consumed food, at least, the idea still remained – for example, with Otmar (63.) and Yana (95.) – that the whites must be immortal and that they could transfer this immortality on to the villagers themselves.[27] However, such hopes were rapidly disappointed by experience, since, simultaneously with the arrival of the first patrols, an illness spread which created many victims and, in the opinion of Wapa (93.), had been brought by the whites and could not be cured by the different types of Rimbu.[28]

Many older Kome report that one of the first measures taken by the colonial government was to bring a war between the Yame and the Mirupa to an end by imprisoning numerous villagers in the area of Kagua. This was followed by the building of the first government station and an airstrip in Kagua. In Pairundu a *haus kiap*, a house for the accompanying policemen, a cooking hut (*haus kuk*) and one toilet hut (*haus toilet*)[29] each for the colonial officers and the policemen were put up. In addition, people had to make up the bush paths with tree trunks and make themselves available for patrols. The wages for this consisted of matches and glass beads. In order to have their instructions carried out, the colonial officers named Makoa, Yawa, Otmar and Wapa, among others, as Village Constables. Those who were selected had their hair cut, learned to salute and received a steel axe and a rubber truncheon. For clothing, they had to wear a black cloth called a 'pomberenu'. The villagers called the officials appointed by the whites 'luluai' or 'bossboi'.[30] Accepting such offices was obviously linked not only with acquiring prestige, but also with the hope of remuneration from the colonial government. As I was told unanimously, the colonial officers demonstrated their power right from the first patrols by, for example, shooting at birds and pigs.[31] Using razor blades and scissors, the policemen cut through some banana leaves and threatened to do exactly the same to the throats of local people if they were not obeyed.[32] In their memories, the Kome emphasise especially the penalties they were threatened with if they failed to obey the colonial officers' instructions. Thus many of the older villagers described frequently and insistently how they were beaten, kicked and dragged off to prison in Kagua by the whites, or by the police and Village Constables acting as their representatives.[33] According to Ari (14.), the police and the Village Constables pursued those who sought to disappear through flight, until, out of anger, they beat them to force them to eat rotten food and mistreat their own wives and children. Ari (13.) also mentioned the shooting of two local people. Yana (95.) reported that punitive expeditions slaughtered pigs belonging to those who had fled and killed a man named Koyari Mendo. According to Otmar (63.), when, on one occasion, the Mamarepa refused to go to Yakoa, to where a patrol had summoned the inhabitants of the surrounding villages, some policemen came to Yeibu to burn down houses and rape the women. Altogether, therefore, the Kome and Mamarepa soon realised that the whites and their representatives not only demanded obedience, but could enforce it at any time with superior power. However, according to Ari (14.), direct contacts between the villagers and the whites were mainly restricted to the first years of colonisation. In the following period, the colonial officers transferred to their police the task of visiting individual villages, they themselves mostly staying in Kagua.

The confrontation of patrol reports and indigenous memories explains the different attitudes of the two sides that colonisation brought together. While the colonial officers first condemned the villagers for their lack of cooperation, lies and flight, only arriving at positive assessments after obtaining a greater degree of acceptance, the villagers for their part stress throughout their respect for and fear of the colonial officers and their punitive measures. Even at the start of the 1960s, that is, at a time when an increasing number of former colonies were being granted independence worldwide, the Australian patrol officers were still articulating an unquestioned colonial mentality, believing themselves not only entitled, but even obliged to bring the local population what they understood to be, and valued as, Western civilisation. In line with this attitude, when the villagers reacted first with active and then passive resistance to foreigners intruding uninvited into their country, giving instructions and having them carried out by means of the violence of superior weapons, the colonial officers appear to have seen this as ingratitude and reacted with a certain feeling of disappointment. Moreover, each of the two parties that colonisation caused to be confronted with one another leaves unmentioned especially those points that are of particular importance to the other side.[34] Thus the colonial officers mention neither the epidemics which spread upon their arrival, nor the exchanges conducted or the demonstrations of their weapons. Of the sanctions imposed, only prison and forced labour are noted. For their part, the Kome describe neither the treatment of diseases by the whites, nor their speeches. The fact that these speeches, which were held regularly by all patrols, left no apparent traces in the collective memory shows, in my view, that they obviously had hardly any relevance for the villagers. In both the patrol reports and indigenous memories, the only common aspects to be mentioned are the ending of warfare, the building of houses and roads, the various attempts to flee and the prison sentences. A lack of intercultural understanding is also indicated by the fact that, although the colonial officers criticised the behaviour of the villagers to begin with, they did not recognise the causes of this behaviour. The fact that they created fear by being seen as *remo* remained concealed from them. Conversely, at first the Kome might have failed to see why they should, for example, build a *haus kiap* or reinforce their bush paths.

Missionisation

The spread of Catholic Christianity began when, on 31 March 1958, Catholic priests stationed in Ialibu learned that the colonial government had lifted access restrictions for parts of the Kagua valley a few days earlier.[35] Following this, on 15 April 1958 Fr Stanley Miltenberger arrived with two indigenous catechists from Muli in Kagua, where – according to Burkey (n.d., without pagination), in his history of the Mendi diocese – thirty villages already had Lutheran mission helpers. Lutheran Pastor Merrill Clark (1958), on the other hand, who that same month had founded a mission station near a *haus kiap* in Wabi,[36] claimed that the Catholics came a week before him. According to Bergmann (n.d.: 34), at this time the Pairundu region still came within the restricted area and the road from Ialibu to Kagua was still being built, though the first Cessna aircraft had already been able to land on the airstrip at Kagua. Accordingly, the Kome and the Mamarepa say that they only encountered missionaries after they had already seen aircraft and government patrols.[37] Those who were staying in Sare at that time claim today that the Catholics and Lutherans appeared there simultaneously.[38] In Sua/Yeibu, on the other hand, according to Rekepea and Wala, first the Catholics arrived and then Norman Imbrock, a Lutheran pastor, who relieved Merrill Clark in Wabi in 1960.[39] After people had learned first to distinguish them from the colonial officers and then from one another, they called the Catholics 'pasere' and the Lutherans 'misi'.[40]

In the initial period of missionisation, both denominations aimed to open up as large a mission field as possible in relation to the other group, in other words, to set up as many outstations as quickly as possible and to provide them with catechists (Catholics) or evangelists (Lutherans), as the case may be. Thus while in Sua a Lutheran church was built, the rest of the Kome and Mamarepa area fell entirely under Catholic influence. Between 1959 and 1988, a total of six priests lived at the Catholic mission station in Sumi, relieving one another every two to six years, with an average stay of five years.[41] These priests held regular Bible classes, like their catechists in the separate villages.[42] Because of their mutual competition, the relationship between the Catholic and Lutheran functionaries was obviously very tense. In their annual reports, M. Clark and Imbrock do not mention the names of the Catholic priests, nor do they report any personal conversations at all. In 1961 Imbrock writes:

The catholic priests have acted very much according to pattern: 'Let's co-operate and avoid friction' to your face; 'Don't follow that bad mission or we'll put you in purgatory' when you're not around. Our evangelists have comported themselves creditably even though the R.C.'s [Roman Catholics] approach in the new areas got rather disgusting. In addition to slander and threats they surpassed the Wise Men in effort (instead of 3 gifts, as many as 6 to 8 were given at the first contact).[43]

In the memories of the Kome, on the other hand, there is no mention of conflicts between the denominations. Instead, missionisation is described as if the friendly relations that can be observed today have always prevailed between Catholics and Lutherans. The first building of the Catholic Church in Pairundu stood in Pasereanda, where the priests bought land with pearlshells. Here young catechists from Wasuma held religious services and taught reading and writing.[44] As Ari (15.) told me, however, these catechists were soon sent back to Wasuma because of some cases of pre- or extra-marital relations with women from the village.[45] Then, after the Kome had been going to the services in Wasuma and Sumi for some time, they asked the priest there to send them a new catechist. The priest carried out this wish and thus in the mid-1970s a dwelling block and a new church building was put up – though this time in Pairundu** – upon pressure from Ari.[46] From the mid-1980s, Kenneth from Wasuma officiated as catechist. Ruben replaced him, Augustin followed him apparently at the end of 1987, though, since he also came from Wasuma, he only visited Pairundu on Sundays. In January 1990 Coleman Makoa took over the office from Augustin.

Very different answers were given to my question concerning the content of the teaching and religious services provided by the catechists and evangelists at the start of missionisation. In particular, there was a division between the leading representatives of the Church leadership on the one hand and the 'simple' villagers on the other. The catechists and evangelists sometimes deviated considerably from the respective 'official line', which may be due to the fact that since their villages were far away from Kagua, Wabi or Sumi, in practice there was little control over them by their superiors. According to Fr Dunstan, the life, words and actions of Jesus Christ were central to the teaching and religious services. Through both prayers and the sacraments, the aim was to allow the villages to enter directly into contact with Christ, his father and the Holy Spirit. After two or three years and following an examination of one's personal way of life, there followed 'the invitation to join the Church through baptism'. In harmony with the attempts at inculturation already mentioned (Introduction), Fr Dunstan (undated letter) also claimed that the very first missionaries had emphasised their conviction that God had been with the local people even before contact with the whites and that therefore 'Christianity had to be built on their traditional forms of expression of their faith in "God"'. Thus the term 'Yaki' was used for 'God'. With respect to the beginnings of missionisation, Ari said that God was discussed: 'I heard a rumour that God made food, heaven, the earth, the moon, the sun, the stars, and everything that is in heaven and on the earth. We were told that, when someone is ill, we should no longer kill pigs or make Rimbu, but pray and then the sickness would come to an end'.[47] The Kome unanimously interpreted the requirement to cease the traditional cult practices as a prohibition, which also extended to traditional magical practices, except for particular healing procedures. Thus, according to present-day memories, the catechists and evangelists claimed that cult and magical practices constituted devil worship and that it was wrong, for example, to exclude women from the consumption of pig meat at the different types of Rimbu. Instead of engaging ritually with *remo* and *kalando*, one should from now on worship the Christian God. This rejection affected other aspects of traditional culture, apart from the different elements of the traditional religion, such as the pig-killing festivals,[48] and the warfare that was also prohibited by the colonial government. Accordingly the Kome often claim that it was demanded of them that they 'give up everything' (*lusim olgeta samting*). To this extent, in peoples memories concerning the start of missionisation, Christianity appears primarily as a comprehensive structure of prohibition. Thus right from the start, the Catholic and Lutheran functionaries apparently linked their demands with the claim that obedience meant that one would go to heaven, disobedience that one would go to hell.[49] Many informants told me that, right from their first sermons and speeches, the catechists and evangelists had described heaven as a future reward and hell as a future punishment. Ari (15.) reported:

> I heard it thus, they said, the missionaries said, if we stop fighting or cease the earlier Rimbu and Rombake customs, and if we obey God's word, so, they said, this word of God's will bring us to heaven. If we do not obey but continue fighting, arguing and making Rimbu, we shall go into a great fire that burns in heaven... they said that... to begin with.[50]

Confirmation of the promise of reward, the threat of punishment and the demands linked to them came from the announcement that the Last Day of Judgement, on which Jesus Christ shall decide who shall go to heaven and who to hell, was immediately imminent. According to Wala (92.), the very first catechists and evangelists announced the Last Day of Judgement as coming in the near future. This is disputed by other informants, though it is confirmed by relevant indications in the patrol reports, as well as by the annual reports of the Lutheran Church.[51] The statements of leading representatives of the Church leadership on the one hand and the 'simple' villagers on the other differ with respect not only to the message announced at the start of missionisation, but also to how it was conveyed. This affects Catholics and Lutherans equally. Functionaries like Kenneth (39.) speak of a cautious and patient way of proceeding (*isi isi*). Fr Dunstan wrote to me that, for example, the priests did not move directly against traditional methods of treating sickness and that they did not burn down any cult houses.[52] However, precisely this was claimed by Pogola (72.), among others. According to Mindu (51.), 'the missionaries', together with the colonial officials, removed the stones kept in the cult houses in order to throw them into the water, hide them or bury them. All in all, the memories of the beginning of missionisation articulated by 'simple' villagers imply that, right from the start, the aim was first to obliterate the traditional religion by prohibiting the traditional magical and cult practices and discrediting the old transcendent authorities and then to replace it with Christianity. Just such a replacement seems actually to have taken place, judging from the first impression that the members of the Catholic community in Pairundu give one today. They claim that they had fulfilled the demands of the priests and catechists and 'given up everything'. The traditional magical and cult practices, they say, are no longer carried out and the transcendent authorities are no longer effective, so that the traditional religion now belongs entirely to the past.[53] By emphasising their breach with the traditional religion, villagers are seeking to stress that they have become convinced Christians.[54] In a similar vein, Otmar (63.) pointed out to me, with a certain pride, that the Kome and Mamarepa together have as many as five church buildings, three of them Catholic (Anapote, Yeibu and Pairundu), one Lutheran (Sua) and one Seventh-day Adventist (Pairundu).

The history of the Seventh-day Adventists (SDA) in Papua New Guinea can only be reconstructed with difficulty, especially as the relevant functionaries have generally not written anything down. Apart from the various memories of the villagers, therefore, replies in letters from Adventist functionaries are often the only sources available.[55] According to these sources, Adventist mission work in the Kagua valley only began in 1963, when Ron and Gladys Timewell arrived in the district capital. There they worked as employees of the colonial government in the health centre and ran a branch Sabbath school on the side, until they were replaced by an indigenous mission assistant from Ialibu.[56] According to Litster, emissaries from remote villages frequently appeared in Kagua to ask for Adventist missionaries to be sent to them, so that the SDA communities gradually grew.[57] Membership clearly grew dramatically all over Papua New Guinea around the end of the 1960s and the beginning of the 1970s. In this period, according to Forman (1982: 200), there were already more Adventists in the Pacific than in Australia and New Zealand combined, from where the first SDA missionaries originally came. With reference to the end of the 1980s, Renali (1991: 17) describes the Seventh-day Adventists as 'the fastest-growing denomination in the country'.

Members of both the Adventist and Catholic communities trace the appearance of the Adventists in Pairundu back to the fact that, while gardening on one occasion, Muya heard a voice he took to be the voice of God telling him to go to Kagua to fetch something. Following this 'divine inspiration' he met Peter, an Adventist mission assistant, with whom he attended the Sabbath service henceforward in Kagua.[58] Then he brought Peter to Pairundu to build up the SDA community and lead it for one to two years. Peter was followed by Inok for about a year.[59] The Sabbath services took place in Muya's house in Rimbupiri (no. 12 in Map 3), where he had several benches for sitting made. Of the Kome, however, apart from Muya only his two brothers Kevin and Wabi took part. After these three first Adventists from Pairundu had been baptised in Kagua, Kevin built the SDA church building in Rakepanda. In the meantime, Muya was constantly seeking to persuade as many of the local population as possible to take part in the Saturday service. Thus visitors frequently appeared who, according to Coleman Makoa (30.), also came from neighbouring villages, as well as from the Western Highlands or even from the coast on occasion. All this happened around the mid-1980s. At that time, first Kenneth, then Ruben lived in Pairundu as catechists. In Sumi first Fr Dunstan officiated, then Fr Jim. In present-day memories, the central statement of the Adventist functionaries was that one should hold the major cult practices on Saturdays instead of Sundays, in order to be among those whom Jesus Christ shall take with him to heaven on the Last Day of Judgement, which was drawing near. This necessarily involved people leaving the Catholic Church, joining the SDA community and having themselves baptised into it. In the beginning, Muya met with bitter resistance to his attempted missionising. In frequent though purely verbal arguments, the members of the Catholic community demanded that he leave 'his new church in Kagua', since they had already been baptised. At the same time, however, as Alupa (7.) among others regretted, it was not possible to prevent Muya from proceeding, especially as he was, after all, moving about his own home village and land. Muya himself (55.) said that, out of anger, the Catholics stopped sharing food with him. According to Robert (53.), the Adventists were disturbed and mocked by heckling during their services.

The highpoint of the conflicts between the members of the two denominations appears to have been the only direct meeting until now between leading representatives of the leaderships of the two churches, which was arranged by Muya. He had heard that Fr Dunstan, Kenneth and a candidate for the priesthood wanted to come to Pairundu for a Sunday service and had therefore recruited an SDA pastor from Papua New Guinea called Wilson and an Adventist policeman for that day. According to Kenneth (40.), Fr Dunstan asked the policeman to take off his trousers, in order to show him whether had been circumcised. Only then could he correctly claim to be following all the prescriptions of the Old Testament, as Adventists claimed to be doing. At this, the policeman took to flight. This same event was also described by Coleman Makoa (30.), though at that time he was staying at Mount Hagen. Kenneth (40.) went on to explain that generally the Catholics usually avoided long conversations, which mostly led to conflict and wars of words (*tokpait*). Accordingly, said Pogola (72.), Fr Dunstan and the Adventists parted company without much discussion. Fr Dunstan himself wrote to me as follows: 'I did refuse to argue or fight verbally with them'. In addition, he claimed that he had merely contradicted the threat, circulated by the Adventists in Pairundu, that the police would arrest all those villagers who did not want to convert to the Adventists.[60] The memories of present-day Adventists contradict those of the Catholics at many points, even though many of the former were still members of the Catholic community at the time of the controversial event. First, SDA informants like Coleman Komea strongly disputed the story of Fr Dunstan demanding that the policeman's trousers be removed.[61] The Adventists also did not mention the threat that those who did not want to convert would be sent to prison.[62] The most important difference from the memories of the Catholics, however, is that, in the Adventist's view, a long argument resulted between the leading representatives of the two denominations. Thus, according to Robert (82.) and Muya (55.), Pastor Wilson first read out some of the passages in the Bible that justified the Sabbath and asked Fr Dunstan which texts in the Bible documented the holding of a Sunday service. Lacking an answer to this, Fr Dunstan fled. Kevin (45.) and Naki (56.), who, like Coleman Makoa, were themselves not in Pairundu at this time, said that others had told them about this flight too. Apart from this, Robert (82.) and Coleman Komea claimed that, as Catholics at that time, they planned to give the Adventists a beating, although Ripu and Pogola, for example, who had not been converted, dispute this.

On the whole, it is clear that the members of the two communities represented in Pairundu are each handing down their own, as it were, denomination-specific version of the events of that time, which differ from one another in essential points. In my view, the concern today is less to determine what, on that Sunday, 'really happened', as how the Adventists and Catholics orchestrate their different versions. With the agreement of the other Adventists, Robert (53.) said: '...this Father Dunstan is a white, yet he didn't answer the blacks' questions. Apart from this, among the Adventists there is not a single white, yet he did not answer the Adventists' questions and afterwards ran away. Everyone thought about this and went to the church of the Adventists'.[63] Similarly on the Catholic side, Pogola (72.) among others assured me that people would have converted uniformly had there been arguments and had Fr Dunstan really fled as a result. Although, therefore, they formulate quite different memories, the members of the two churches agree in seeing the debate between their respective leading representatives as a power struggle. The outcome of this decides which denomination one should belong to, since there is a general readiness to join the group of the victor, that is, of the more powerful. For the Adventists, their leading functionaries had won this struggle for power, while for the Catholics there had never been such a struggle, meaning that Fr Dunstan could not have lost the superiority ascribed to him either. Thus each set of denomination-specific memories is used to justify each respective decision as to whether to remain with the Catholics or join the Adventists.

If Muya's missionisation attempts in the initial years were hardly crowned with any success beyond his brothers Kevin and Wabi, the meeting between Fr Dunstan and leading SDA representatives seems to have brought about a change. First Robert and Kandipia took part in a Saturday service, then, after their baptism in Kagua, they were joined by Naki, Coleman Komea and Simon. In making this move, Kandipia and Simon certainly followed Robert, while Coleman Komea was oriented rather towards Naki. To that extent, the growth of the Adventist community in Pairundu is due not least to the influence of Robert and Naki, who, like Muya, are the sons of Big Men.[64] Like their fathers, these sons convince other men to follow them. The growth of the SDA community, which continued undiminished during my fieldwork, began around 1987, when Inok's successor Ralia, who came from Kuali Lombo, was replaced by the returning Peter.[65] In this period, first Ruben and then Augustin lived as catechists in Pairundu. Fr Jim officiated in Sumi.

After the spread of Catholicism and after the first Kome were converted to Adventists, a Holy Spirit movement, described as a 'prayer group' (*prea grup*) or a 'custom to receive the Spirit' (*pasin bilong kisim spirit*), was active in Pairundu between 1987 and 1989. Among its members were mostly old women, and no Adventists participated.[66] Kenneth, the former catechist, assumed the leading role.[67] Similar phenomena took place and are taking place in other parts of Papua New Guinea, both in the form of charismatic movements of renewal within the larger churches and in the context of smaller Evangelical or Pentecostalist communities of belief, influenced by North American Protestantism, which have flooded into the country in increasing numbers since the Second World War.[68] In general, Holy Spirit movements consist of a series of meetings, mostly lasting several hours and held in the evenings or at night, at which the participants attempt to enter into direct contact with the Holy Spirit through Bible readings, prayers, rhythmic hand-clapping and hymns. Indications of such contact are attacks of shaking and trembling, spasms of crying and shouting, trances and attacks of fainting and glossolalia or speaking in tongues. Sometimes, however, such symptoms are interpreted as an indication of links with the devil, which then leads to exorcism practices being applied.[69] The impact of the Holy Spirit, on the other hand, is supposed to enable people to cure the sick, to recognise the sins of others and to predict future events in visions. Like the traditional magical and cult practices, the Holy Spirit movements are also imported and passed on, the respective 'teachers' again receiving counter-prestations. The Kome, for example, had themselves been taught in Wasuma and Sare, in order to impart their knowledge to Mamarepa living in Sua/Yeibu.[70] According to the literature, similar phenomena occurred in other parts of Southern Highlands Province as early as the mid-1960s.[71]

The Holy Spirit movement in Pairundu mostly corresponded to a generally occurring pattern.[72] Those taking part met together for several hours throughout the night until Sunday morning in different houses, which, like themselves, were decorated beforehand with flowers. After several church hymns had been sung first to the rhythmical clapping of hands, the Bible was opened with eyes closed, the text thus found at random was read out and its significance for the community as a whole, as well as for individual villagers, discussed. After further hymns, some people began to dance, shake and speak incomprehensibly. This meant that contact with the Holy Spirit seemed to have been made, allowing the sins or negative thoughts of individuals who were present to be recognised and voiced, the hiding places of stolen property to be discovered and future deaths, as well as the Last Day of Judgement, to be predicted.[73] Participants also sought to cure illnesses through administering light blows or the laying on of hands. Certainly, as with many Holy Spirit movements, in Pairundu too there was a general conviction of the danger of entering into contact with an evil spirit (*spirit nogut*) sent by the Devil instead of the Holy Spirit. To keep such evil spirits away, people prayed while touching the skin of the person affected. This also occurred with those whose day-to-day life generally appeared bad and therefore influenced by the Devil.[74] A majority of those present would decide whether someone had been possessed by the Holy Spirit or by an evil spirit.[75] At the time of my fieldwork, Holy Spirit movements continued to be held in the Ialibu, Kagua and Roka area, as well as in Sumi and Wasuma.[76] In Pairundu, however, no such meetings had been held since 1989. According to my informants, Big Men like Yawa and Rekepea in particular, but also Catholic priests and nuns, had spoken in favour of ending them. Afterwards, the Big Men claimed that the women were using the night-time meetings to seduce men into pre- or extra-marital sexual relationships,[77] while the priests and nuns pointed out the danger of coming into contact with evil spirits and thus losing one's spiritual health.[78]

The ending of the Holy Spirit movement clearly shows that, just as with conversions to the Adventists, it had led to conflicts among the Kome, especially when those who, in their own view, were possessed by the Holy Spirit accused others of stimulating bad thoughts or of committing sins like theft, for example. This resulted, according to Ata Francis and Pogola (24.), in serious quarrels in which people argued over whether the accusations had really been inspired by the Holy Spirit or by an evil spirit, that is, whether they were true or not. Such conflicts between mostly female participants and mostly male non-participants constitute a disintegrating effect of the Holy Spirit movement in Pairundu.[79]

Concluding remarks

A comparison of the mutually implicated processes of colonisation and missionisation shows that the colonial officials had the relatively greater power. They were the first to 'open up' the 'restricted' areas and decided when the missions could follow them. The first Lutheran pastor in the region, M. Clark (1959), reported that he was warned expressly by a district officer against missionising in the Kagua valley too soon and not co-operating with the Catholics. While, on the one hand, colonial officers certainly believed that the local population should be protected from church representatives acting too fast, on the other hand they judged the indigenous attitude towards the missionaries as sceptically as the 'success' of missionisation as a whole.[80] At the same time, however, mutual support by colonial officers and missionaries, extending to the personal level, is to be noted.[81] Points of contact arose not least from the fact that, as with pacification, they were partly pursuing the same goals. The first patrols of the colonial officers to some extent paved the way for the arrival of the church representatives, who for their part contributed to the common aim of 'development' by providing teaching in government schools and later supervising the building of aid posts and educational institutions.[82] Today, almost twenty years after Papua New Guinea attained independence, the initial tensions that arose between the government and the churches belong to the past. Since Article 45 of the Papua New Guinea constitution makes provision for religious freedom, it is open to anyone to convert to any community of belief, even when a majority of the members of his or her own village already belong to another denomination. At the same time, however, it is expressly forbidden to fight other communities of belief, even though in practice this cannot be supervised by the state at the village level.[83]

The changes introduced to some extent by colonisation and then reinforced through missionisation can, in the first instance, be explained with respect to the traditional values of strength and equivalence (Chapter 1). Traditional ways of demonstrating strength disappeared because war was suppressed and pig-killing festivals discredited. Also to be mentioned is the prohibition of magical and cult practices through missionisation, since these had provided the respective participants and specialists with opportunities to gain prestige (Chapter 2). In place of the old ways of demonstrating strength, however, new ones have emerged in the form of the offices bestowed on people by the colonial government and the churches, as well as the sources of income that have opened up. A tendency towards economic differentiation has arisen, in particular through selling in the markets, cultivating cash crops and contract work.[84] After all, money received as income is easier to conceal than pigs, thus allowing one to withdraw oneself from the 'obligation to share' (Chapter 1). At the same time, increasing pig herds is easier for those who forego traditional methods of cure and no longer resort to slaughter in cases of sickness. Although the tendency towards economic differentiation is certainly noticeable, it should not be exaggerated, since, as already described, it is restricted by various factors and appears quite limited compared to other regions (Chapter 1). If the leading economic positions in Pairundu today are occupied by younger men (Naki, Serale, Robert, Coleman Komea) as well as traditionally legitimised Big Men (Yawa, Wala,

Rekepea), then colonisation and missionisation have contributed to an increase in already existing economic differences in the case of the latter and to the rise of new economic differences in the case of the former. Further increase in economic differentiation would be possible, if the Kome were justified in stating the decline of their traditional religion, since in this case not only would magical practices and possible attacks by *remo* or *kalando* disappear, so would the threats which compelled the maintenance of equivalence (Chapter 2). According to my observations, however, individuals still regard themselves as obliged in principle to share and to accommodate the various requests of those to whom they feel obliged or whom they want to place under an obligation.[85] Such sharing certainly increases one's prestige, but it simultaneously hinders capital accumulation and thus the enhancement of an economic advantage.

To the extent that new ways of demonstrating strength arise in place of, for example, wars, pig-killing festivals and magical or cult practices, traditional differences in power between the genders, between the generations and between 'ordinary' men and Big Men diminish at the same time. The status of women in respect to men is increased by the fact that they are acquiring a source of income for themselves by selling food in the markets and that, with Christianity, they are no longer excluded from participating in cult practices as in the traditional religion. Even the separation of the genders is beginning to change, since, in the context of missionisation, the close living together of married couples is being promoted. In addition, in driving out traditional possibilities to obtain prestige, I see a loss of power for the elders, including the Big Men, since it was precisely they who exploited these opportunities. At the same time, it is the 'ordinary' men, including the young men, who were taking over the offices appointed by the colonial government and the churches and trying to help themselves to new sources of income like, for example, contract work, even though Big Men also sell food in the markets and grow coffee.[86] Members of the younger generation also frequently deny their fathers and grandfathers any competence when it comes to managing the issues and problems of a rapidly changing present, one that is very different from the pre-colonial period.

If the traditional religion exercised an integrative function by expressing the values of strength and equivalence (Chapter 2), then the replacement of the traditional religion by Christianity that the Kome claim has happened ought to create a tendency towards the dissolution of social cohesion and a greater degree of individuality. This arises from the fact that villagers need to co-operate less than in the pre-colonial period in respect of the joint holding of pig-killing festivals and that they no longer see themselves as subject to the joint threat of enemy attacks.[87] However, the dissolution of social cohesion as a consequence of colonisation and missionisation can also be viewed positively, namely as a 'widening of horizons', the overcoming of the traditional particularism. Thus, for example, compared with the pre-colonial period, pacification has allowed travel further afield and, together with contract work, direct contact with previously unknown groups or individuals.

The inhabitants of Pairundu did not, to begin with, ask the different representatives of Western civilisation to enter their land. In the beginning, they could apparently neither understand, nor consciously influence, the actions or statements of the colonial officers and missionaries (cf. Crittenden and Schiefflin 1991: 124). Instead the latter, as the representatives of a superior power, appropriated all control and exercised it thoroughly themselves by making demands and compelling their fulfilment, whether through the power of weapons or the threat of the Last Judgement. Thus the experience of colonisation and missionisation includes a loss of autonomy, so that the Kome seem to be justified when they also ascribe the passivity they articulate with respect to traditional warfare and religion (Chapter 2) to their relations with the first colonial officers and missionaries.

In summarising the changes that can be traced back to the processes of colonisation and missionisation, it has to be noted that, at first sight, the consequences of colonisation and missionisation differ, at least gradually. Although their contact with the first colonial officers was certainly traumatic for the Kome and although the attacks of the latter or their representatives are certainly to be condemned, these attacks were comparatively less blatant in Pairundu than in other regions.[88] In addition, according to Ari, the whites only met the villagers at the start and then mostly got native policemen to represent them. One factor here was that Pairundu lay away from the usual routes, which took the patrols via Kira to Sare or via Wabi to Sumi or Usa instead. Even if a patrol did actually arrive in Pairundu on some occasion or other, it usually only remained for a short time. If the colonial 'opening up' of the region – which, corresponding to the situation of relative marginality, was quite limited right from the start – leads to life still being determined to a large extent by the traditional culture (Chapter 1), then the consequences of colonisation as a whole cannot have run too deep. While the composition of social groups continues to depend on kinship, co-residence and co-operation and the subsistence economy is still of central importance, most changes might have taken place in the area of material or materialised culture. Thus today the Kome use steel rather than their traditional stone tools, and they have not only partly exchanged their traditional dress for Western clothing, they have also given up traditional ornaments like bangles, ribbons and belts. Although warfare is no longer conducted in Pairundu and although people help themselves to new sources of income or European medicines from time to time, this has the appearance of elements of tradition being partly supplemented by Western influences rather than replaced by them. Thus, for example, rice is valued as an additional food, but it cannot force out the sweet potato as the staple.

While, therefore, the impact of colonisation remains on the surface to some extent, at first sight the impact of missionisation seems to go much deeper, since, in the present-day statements of many villagers, the traditional religion has not merely been changed but completely eradicated and replaced by Christianity. I shall go later (Chapter 7) into the question of whether the respective consequences of colonisation and missionisation also diverge this strongly from the etic point of view.[89] Here, however, we should recall the observation that, contrary to the emic claim of the demise of the traditional religion, belief in *remo* and *kalando* still continues into the present (Chapter 2), like the fear of witchcraft techniques and the carrying out of specific magical practices for treating illnesses and divination (Chapter 2). In addition, contradictions occur even within the emic view. Thus among the Catholics in particular, the statements of the leading representatives of the Church leadership differ from those of the 'simple' villagers in respect to the message preached at the start of missionisation and how it was imparted.

Notes

1. Extensive quotations from the patrol reports are intended to convey their generally prevailing tone and also to give information on the attitude of the colonial officers to the indigenous people. A confrontation between etic and emic perspectives, such as Schiefflin and Crittenden (1991a) have undertaken in their reconstruction of the 'Strickland-Purari patrol', seems particularly instructive to me. Franklin, L. Josephides, LeRoy and MacDonald, on the other hand, restrict themselves in their accounts to colonisation as seen mainly from the etic perspective.

2. Especially in the case of Holy Spirit movements, in my view the emic perspective has not been taken account of sufficiently up to now. This is perhaps due to the fact that the relevant sources come overwhelmingly from authors oriented towards missiology, who usually do not base themselves on stationary fieldwork. The latter applies to the work of Robin (1980, 1981a, 1981b, 1981c, 1982) (cf. Introduction). In contrast, my stay in Pairundu gave me an opportunity to ask numerous villagers about the Holy Spirit movement conducted there in a systematic way. In Sumi, in addition, I was even able to observe the relevant phenomena myself.

3. These first patrols were carried out by Staniford-Smith in 1911, Beaver in 1911, Flint and Saunders in 1922 and Rentoul in 1925. In 1929, Faithorn and C. Champion reached the Samberigi valley, south of the Erave river, from the south coast of New Guinea.

4. On the stay of Hides and O'Malley in the Kewa area, see also Franklin (1989).

5. The Strickland-Purari patrol was followed in 1936 by the Bamu–Purari patrol (I. Champion and Adamson) and in 1937 by the Kutubu patrol (C. Champion and Andersen) (Schiefflin and Crittenden 1991a: 258f map 13).

6. According to Schiefflin and Crittenden (1991a: 133), steel axes were seen by Beaver as early as 1911 and according to Josephides and Schiltz (1991a: 210) by Hides and O'Malley in 1935.

7. That is, according to the Kagua Patrol Report 1971/72–18. Henceforward I abbreviate 'Kagua Patrol Report' to 'KPR' and 'Erave Patrol Report' to 'EPR'. Unfortunately, in the National Archives (Port Moresby), Southern Highlands Archives (Mendi) and District Archives (Kagua), not all the patrol reports from before 1975 were available in 1991.

8. According to Bergmann (n.d.: 40), the colonial government took three hundred hectares of land into its possession and assembled the inhabitants of the nearby villages one after the other to work on the airstrip without payment. In a letter to J. Kuder dated 14 October 1958, Bergmann reports that, for over a year, some five hundred locals had

been occupied with this work in shifts lasting three weeks each. Bergmann visited the Kagua valley from 11 to 18 April 1958.

9. (Map 2). According to L. Josephides (1985a: 72), in the case of the road from Kagua to Erave – which, according to MacDonald (1991: 48) was begun in 1968 and finished in 1976 – every two months the neighbouring villages had to supply workers for two weeks.

10. In both Pairundu and Yakoa, I was unanimously told that the colonial officers had inaccurately called Pairundu first 'Akuna' and then 'Yakoa'. Accordingly, in one patrol report (KPR 1965/66–1) it is claimed that the locals call their area 'Yakoa', not 'Akuna'. Today, the Kome are still entered in the district administration's list of inhabitants, together with the Akuna-Rola, under the village name of 'Yakoa'.

11. See, for example, the report of a patrol to Wabi (12–21 December 1960): 'However, four men who had removed pegs and built gardens on the road site were sentenced to three months gaol with hard labour and fifty-eight other men were gaoled for two weeks by the Court for Native Matters for failing to work on the roads as ordered' (KPR 1960/61–8: 4).

12. The colonial officers would usually point out the following in connection with such speeches, which were made, for example, before taking a census: '(a) The importance, usefulness and necessity for census-taking; (b) The importance of, and the responsibility for, obtaining medical attention in the early stages of sickness or injury with special reference to children and infants; (c) The advantages of economic advancement and the material benefits therefrom, with special reference to coffee; (d) The advantages of Education and where warranted the introduction of the idea that parents should take an interest in the school which their children attend; (e) The position of Village Constables and the obligation of the populace to them, etc' (KPR 1961/62–13: 1).

13. With reference to a patrol in the Wabi-Sumi region, for example, one of the officers reports: 'On that visit the patrol personnel were attacked on a number of occasions and the general impression given was that the people didn't want the administration in their area interfering in their lives and customs' (KPR 1956/57–7: 1).

14. See, for example, the following reference to Sua/Yeibu: 'Census taking is something which these people can't quite fathom, despite detailed explanations, and while they have trouble understanding the reasons for our actions, they appear bent on clothing our activities with sinister interpretations... During most census checks, it was found that the majority of absentees had not come because they were frightened that we might use the fact that we have their names against them. Long and careful questioning could elicit nothing more than their fears arose after a great deal of speculation on why we should be collecting names and the resulting conviction that no good could come from it' (KPR 1958/59–5: 17).

15. Thus the following claim is made: 'The SUI'AIBU people were full of lies, evasion and deceit... No particular reason could be found for their unco-operative behaviour' (KPR 1959/60–8: 5). A year later, a colonial officer complained: 'SUI'AIBU again took a lot of persuasion to appear. Lies and evasion were still encountered... General co-operation was still not good, and few men appeared to carry the patrol onwards' (KPR 1960/61–no number: 6; capitals in the original).

16. (KPR 1959/60–6: 2). Accordingly, with respect to the southern Kewa, Josephides and Schiltz (1991b: 279) write: 'The Kewa tried many strategies, including avoidance and non-compliance, to evade government control'.

17. Thus it is claimed for the Wabi-Sumi region: 'The people throughout the area are now accustomed to group carrying for patrols and no trouble except for some delays is normally encountered in this regard' (KPR 1960/61–11: 6).

18. See, for example, the following reference to Pairundu and its area: 'The advantages of British Law and Justice are being realised by the people. No longer do they fear attacks by enemy groups, and they can now devote their time and labour to beneficial activities, instead of preparing to defend themselves' (KPR 1960/61–9: 9). A year later it is stated, also regarding Pairundu and its area: 'The people appear to appreciate the aims and intentions of the Government and the resultant freedom from fear' (KPR 1961/62–13: 2;

cf. also KPR 1962/63–7). Here the indigenous claim that, in pre-colonial warfare expulsions were frequent, is confirmed by the government side (Chapter 1).

19. See, for example, the conclusion that: 'One can notice now a core of youth who are oriented towards the Government' (KPR 1965/66–1).

20. (KPR 1969/70–7). In this report, the whole area of the Sugu river is described as 'the most isolated and primitive in the Administrative Area'.

21. J. Clark, Josephides and Schiltz, MacDonald and Schieffin and Crittenden all mention the term 'kapena', giving slightly different spellings and also explaining it differently. J. Clark (1992: 17) writes that the term 'kapona' was connected simultaneously with Europeans, steel and witchcraft. According to Josephides and Schiltz (1991a: 222), 'kapona' is a type of grass that grew in the southern Kewa area for the first time when the Strickland-Purari patrol appeared. MacDonald (Kamale 1982: 194) translates 'kapana' as 'weeds, useless grass which destroys the garden'. According to Schieffin and Crittenden (1991c: 300), 'kapona' is the name of a policeman who had accompanied several patrols from Lake Kutubu to the southern Kewa before the Second World War. To my ear, the word 'kapena' results when the English word 'governor' is said in a Kewa accent. 'Nokerepa' is the name of a man who, in a myth I collected, sits on Mount Sumi, his extraordinarily long penis ('longer than a snake') clearing a way for itself underground to women busy working in the gardens, in order to penetrate them.

22. In my judgement, those mentioned by Ari were around twenty-five to forty years old at the time of my fieldwork.

23. This was reported independently by Ari (15.) and Yana (95.).

24. The whites were also seen as ancestral spirits by the Onabasulu, Etoro, Bosavi (Schieffin 1991: 84), Huli (Allen and Frankel 1991: 104), Wola (Sillitoe 1991: 147, 149), Nembi (Josephides and Schiltz 1991a: 209, 222), Wiru (J. Clark 1988: 47) and Kewa in the areas of Sumbura (Josephides and Schiltz 1991a: 209, 222) and Usa (Franklin and Franklin 1978: 490–503). Many of the accounts provided by MacDonald (1991: 107, 263, 325, 490, 509) also contain this identification.

25. The *kalando* also live in this manner, in the general view, at or in the water (Chapter 2). J. Clark (1992: 19) writes concerning the Wiru that they 'associated white men with river spirits and watercourses'.

26. Wala (92.) gave exactly this order. According to MacDonald (1991: 264), women and pigs were also hidden in caves in the Mararoko region.

27. In addition, Ipapula (38.) told me that people believed in the immortality of the whites.

28. According to Schieffin (1991: 68), an epidemic, which can no longer be identified, broke out in January or February 1935 in the southwest of the Papuan plateau and spread east among the Bosavi communities, though not among the Onabasulu or Etoro.

29. These were small huts with a trench inside.

30. The term 'bossboi' does not appear in the patrol reports I have examined. L. Josephides (1985a: 71) reports that, although the colonial government certainly did not appoint any *bossboi*, individual locals would call themselves 'bossboi' in order to be able to act with the appropriate prestige. According to J. Clark (1989a: 127), the same happened among the neighbouring Wiru.

31. Otmar (63.), for example, said this.

32. Information from Ata Francis in the context of an interview with Wapa (93.). Ari (14.) said the same.

33. Ari especially pointed out the fear of prison.

34. However, in their patrol reports, colonial officers seem to have striven to make themselves appear in a positive light to their superiors. This may have led to them not mentioning incursions and stressing especially, for example, treating illnesses or making speeches.

35. These priests belonged to the Franciscan order, Ordinis Fratum Minorum (OFM), which had already sent the first missionaries into the Southern Highlands of Papua New Guinea in 1954 from the Province of St. Augustine in Pennsylvania (U.S.A.) (letter Fr Stanley Miltenberger, 28 May 1993).

36. Merrill Clark arrived in the Southern Highlands with forty evangelists, who came from the coast (personal communication, N. Imbrock, 13 May 1994).

37. For example, Ipapula (36.) and Otmar (63.) both said this.

38. Among these are Nosupinai (60.) and Ipapula (38.).

39. In contrast to Rekepea and Wala, Yana (95.) claimed that Imbrock came first.

40. The term 'pasere' originally referred to the area to the northwest of Pasereanda, from which the first Catholic missionaries arrived in Pairundu. 'Misi' is a Kewa version of the Tok Pisin term 'misin' (mission).

41. In an undated letter (which I received at the beginning of June 1992), Fr Dunstan Jones gave me a list of priests who lived in Sumi permanently, with a rough estimate of the years of their stays: Fr August Rebel (1959–65), Fr Victor Kriley (1966–72), Fr Otmar Gallagher (1972–78), Fr Matthew Gross (1978–81), Fr Dunstan Jones (1982–86) and Fr Jim Durken (1986–88). Sumi has not been permanently occupied by a priest since 1988. Instead, Fr Matthias Olape, a Huli from Tari, visits the region, and he also looks after the southern part of Kagua parish. In contrast to the Lutheran pastors, M. Clark and Imbrock, the Catholic priests have not drawn up annual reports.

42. According to a patrol report, the teaching took place twice daily and three times on Sundays (KPR 1963/64–19). According to MacDonald (1991: 53), all the catechists appointed by the Catholic Church throughout the Southern Highlands came from Chimbu Province.

43. To my written question concerning the relationship between the denominations, Fr Dunstan (undated letter) also hints at tensions in retrospect: 'It is true there was a less harmonious relationship between the Catholic Church and other Christian denominations at the very beginning'.

44. Among others, Ripu (15.) and Robert, (53.) told me this. The young men from Wasuma were trained by the first Chimbu catechists as their successors.

45. According to MacDonald (1991: 53), similar problems arose with the first Chimbu catechists among the southern Kewa. On the missionisation of the Highlands of Papua New Guinea in general, cf. Mrossko (1986: 212).

46. Ripu (15.) reported this. He said that at this time Alex, whose age I estimated to be about fifteen, had not yet been born or only just.

47. A rather compressed rendition of a statement by Ari (15.).

48. Councillor Wane, for example, claimed that, according to the Bible and the words of Imbrock, *yawe* must not be carried out so as to trump others. From this it follows, according to Wane, that the Bible also prohibits men's houses and the shelters (*pokaranda*) erected for the pig-killing festivals.

49. According to Walaya (63.), Imbrock, for example, said: 'If you give everything up... you shall go to heaven' ('Sapos yu lusim dispela olgeta samting... yupela bai i go antap long heven'). According to Yana (95.), Imbrock said: 'If you don't come to church once... you will go into the fire' ('Wan days yu no kam lotu... bai yu go long paia').

50. 'Mi harim olsem, ol tok, misin em i ol tok olsem, yumi stopim pait o yumi stopim Rimbu na dispela Rombake pasin bilong bipo na yumi harim tok bilong God, ol tok olsem, dispela tok bilong God bai kisim yumi i go long heven. Sapos yumi no harim na yumi wok long pait na kros, na wokim Rimbu i stap, em tok, yumi bai go long bikpela paia, em i lait i stap long heven... ol tok olsem... festaim'.

51. According to Ipapula (38.), nothing was said about the immediate coming of the Last Day of Judgement. Conversely, a patrol officer says that most of the indigenous people 'seem to be living in fear of the fiery furnace of which they are being told so much' (KPR 1963/64–19). In 1959, M. Clark (1959) described his reply to the complaints of colonial officers that the mission had occupied the Kagua valley so completely and so soon after 'de-restriction': 'The first point was explained, though I'm not sure appreciated, by our belief in the imminent return of our Lord Jesus Christ'. Fr Dunstan (letter dated 17 October 1992) did not believe that the priests had predicted that the world was nearing its end, though he thought this was possible of the catechists.

52. (Undated letter). In a later letter (17 October 1992), however, he considered it possible that the first Chimbu catechists had burnt down cult houses.
53. Some informants even assured me that people had already ceased their traditional cult practices before the initial contact with priests, catechists, pastors and evangelists, simply because of the report of their arrival. On the other hand, the Salu Rimbu, at least, was only introduced after people had already heard of the arrival of the whites (Chapter 2). Nevertheless, the readiness to adopt Christianity relatively early must have been widespread. Thus according to Burkey (n.d., without pagination), even shortly after the founding of the mission station in Kagua, representatives arrived from various villages to ask for a catechist to be sent to them.
54. What exactly the villagers understand by a 'convinced Christian' will emerge in the description of denomination-specific belief systems (Chapter 4).
55. In accordance with this, SDA Pastor Glynn Litster (letter dated 10 May 1992) wrote to me that 'no written records of the development of our work exist.' As a reason for this, Steley (1988: 105) concluded, concerning the Adventists: 'Their introverted nature does not extend to self-analysis or self-evaluation except in rare cases'. Patrick (1987) gives a list of Adventist sources on the origins of SDA churches in the United States, a brief description of the bases of Adventist belief and church organisations and a general overview of Adventist journals and monographs. Apart from Glynn Litster, the replies in letters used in what follows are from SDA Pastors Ed Parker (1 July 1992), Len Barnard (3 July 1992) and Louis T. Greive (19 July 1992). Among the memories of villagers themselves that I have used, in the first place is a formal interview that I carried out with Muya on 13 March 1991 in Rimbupiri (53.). Before this interview, at my request, Muya had prepared his life history in order to give it to me. Further memories are from Kevin (45.) and Naki (56.).
56. Personal letter from Ed Parker (1 July 1992). According to Imbrock (1967), the first indigenous and English-speaking Adventists arrived in Kagua in 1967. With respect to Papua New Guinea as a whole, however, it must be said that SDA mission work got under way in the Gulf of Papua in 1908 and in the Eastern Highlands in 1934. After the Second World War came the founding of the first stations in the Western Highlands (Forman 1982: 20) and then the Southern Highlands. Litster (letter dated 10 May 1992) writes: 'During the 1950s and early 1960s the Adventist work was spreading like a kunai fire in all directions'. Pastor Koya (46.) provided the following dates for the first foundations of the respective mission stations: Kainantu, Eastern Highlands Province, 1932, Wabag, Enga Province, and Mount Hagen, Western Highlands Province, 1952, Ialibu 1965 and Kagua 1971.
57. Letter dated 10 May 1992.
58. Ata (I) (25.) told me that, shortly before, some Kome had killed a rising Big Man, a close friend of Muya called Usa (and like him, Raki Repa, Auro Kome), with the help of witchcraft. However, Ruapo disputed this claim.
59. According to Coleman Makoa (30.), Inok was the brother of an SDA pastor from Kagua.
60. For this reason, wrote Fr Dunstan, he also reported the policemen who took part in this in Mendi: 'I reported this SDA policeman to Mendi Police Commander for intimidating our people and disturbing the Catholic Community on Sunday at their worship time' (letter dated 17 October 1992).
61. Fr Dunstan himself never mentioned this, incidentally.
62. However, not even the 'simple' members of the Catholic community mentioned such a threat.
63. '...dispela Fata Dunstan, em wanpela waitman, tasol em i no bekim ansa bilong ol blak skin ya. Sevende tu, em i no wanpela waitman tasol em i no bekim kwestin bilong ol SDA bihain em ranawe. Olgeta man i kisim dispela kain tingting nau, ol pulimapim church Sevende'. On another occasion, Robert (82.) claimed: 'If Dunstan had been able to answer these questions, I would not have gone to this church, I would still be with the Catholics, but he did not answer the questions of the SDA, and so the SDA won, they won, and I joined them' ('Bikos Dunstan inap long bekim dispela kwestin, em, mi no

inap long i go long dispela lotu, bai mi stap yet long Katolik misin, tasol em i no bekim kwestin bilong SDA, olsem na SDA win, win nau, mi go insait').

64. Makoa, the former Big Man who has since died, was Muya's father. Yawa is Naki's father, and Wala the father of Robert.

65. Peter was followed by Kevin in March 1990.

66. At the meeting I attended in Sumi too, those present were almost entirely old women.

67. Only in later years did he become a decided opponent of the Holy Spirit movement.

68. On these communities of believers, see Renali (1991: 71f). In the Wabi-Sumi region, on the other hand, Holy Spirit movements are only maintained by Catholics, not by Lutherans.

69. Robin (1981a: 160) refers especially to this.

70. Phillip (68.), who still takes part in such meetings in other villages, reported that the Holy Spirit movement had been taken over from Wasuma. Yapanu (96.), who belonged to the first participants in Pairundu, named Sare as the 'place of origin'. The particular practices had originally come from Ialibu and then moved to Wasuma, Sare and many other villages in the Kagua valley. Ata Francis (24.) mentioned the further transfer to the Mamarepa.

71. Those named are Tari, Nipa, Margarima (John Barr 1983b), Pangia (J. Clark 1989a: 124) and, among the Kewa, Erave (Robin 1981c), Kataloma (MacDonald 1991: 80 n. 19) and Kuali Lombo (L. Josephides 1985a: 75).

72. Information on the Holy Spirit Movement in Pairundu comes mainly from interviews with Ata Francis (24.), Yapanu (96.), Phillip (68.) and Kenneth (39.).

73. Yapanu (96.) claimed that they could predict whether, and when, someone would die. Ata Francis (24.) and Augustin (27.) mentioned the announcement of the Last Day of Judgement. Kenneth (39.), on the other hand, disputes such announcements having been made.

74. In Tok Pisin, one spoke and speaks of 'rausim spirit nogut'. During an interview with Ata Francis (24.), Pogola said that people had attempted, in the course of the same meeting, among other things to remove an evil spirit from Yawa, only to withdraw without having achieved anything after Yawa explained that he did not wish to change. The attempt to remove a *spirit nogut* from Yawa corresponds to the assessment of him as a *man nogut* (Chapter 1).

75. In Wasuma, however, according to Kenneth (39.), this was the role of a generally recognised specialist chosen by the community for the purpose.

76. This conclusion is based on several sources. On Ialibu, information comes from Daniel, a Lutheran pastor, whom I met on 25 November 1990, in his house in Ialibu; on Kagua, from several informal conversations with local catechists, who assembled for a further education course in the Catholic mission station in Karia in December 1990. On Roka, it comes from a formal interview with Sr Marie (48.). In Sumi, I was able to be present myself in the Catholic church building on 24 August 1991 at a corresponding meeting. However, I was told, this was only held as a demonstration on the occasion of my visit, though the participants emphasised that they also held these meetings in the same way without Western observers. On Wasuma, information is from a formal interview with Kenneth (39.).

77. (96.). According to Augustin (27.), the Big Men had said: 'You women are dancing around and outdoing us men' ('Yupela meri kalap kalap na yupela winim mipela man'). The accusation that pre- or extra-marital sexual relationships were going on in the course of meetings of the Holy Spirit movement appeared to have been confirmed by the death of one of Yapa's wives, which was generally traced back to the fact that she had previously slept with some of the men of the village. According to Alupa (7.), at least, had the woman not died, the Holy Spirit movement would not have ended.

78. Phillip (68.), Ata Francis (24.), Coleman Makoa (30.) and Councillor Wane claimed this.

79. Accordingly, Kenneth (39.) concluded: 'With respect to this spiritual movement, we have two groups' ('Mipela i gat tupela lain long dispela spiritual movement'). The division between participating women and non-participating men is also observed in

other regions. Thus in Pundia (a Kewa village situated between Mendi and Ialibu), the Lutheran Pastor Tane (89.) told me that the women took part in such a meeting because they were weary of the hard physical work demanded of them. According to the Lutheran Pastor Uland Spahlinger (89.), a German who occasionally visits the village, the women demanded that they manifest their corporeality on a larger scale, since in the end Jesus had also been born of a woman.

80. Thus a patrol report states (on the inhabitants of the Sumi region): 'The people have little idea of the functions or aims of the Missions, and are suspicious when buildings are erected and gardens made at the evangelist stations... at the present stage the natives are only interested in his [the missionary's or evangelist's] activities to the extent to which they can gain by them' (KPR 1957/58–4: 3). Robin (1980: 275) writes that, in reading the patrol reports of the Mendi area, he gained the impression that, in the past twenty years, the colonial officers had generally been of the view that the inhabitants of the Southern Highlands had only accepted Christianity superficially.

81. For example, according to a number of patrol reports, some colonial officers rested on Imbrock's mission station in Wabi during their patrols.

82. According to Imbrock (1961), in 1961 half an hour of religious instruction was provided twice weekly by Lutheran evangelists at the government school in Kagua. However, according to the written sources available to me and the indigenous memories I recorded, unlike the colonial officers the church representatives did not press for the cultivation of cash crops.

83. Article 45, sentence three runs: 'No person is entitled to intervene unsolicited into the religious affairs of a person of a different belief or to attempt to force his or any religion (or irreligion) on another, by harassment or otherwise' (Blaustein and Flanz 1985: 59f).

84. The significance of contract work is indicated by the high numbers of those who live permanently away from Pairundu (Chapter 1).

85. Lederman (1982: 10) concludes for the Mendi region too that the money earned there flows into social networks rather than being either reinvested or saved.

86. With respect to the posts of Village Constable created by the colonial government, it should be noted that, at the time of their appointment, Makoa, Yawa, Otmar and Wapa did not yet count as Big Men. I therefore cannot confirm J. Clark's conclusion (1982: 8) concerning the Wiru that the Big Men were striving for the positions provided by the government and missions. Josephides and Schiltz (1991b: 280) also point out the increasing independence of the young, based especially on contract work. Cf. LeRoy (1979a: 203) and, for the Mendi area, Lederman (1982: 7). A. Strathern (1969: 46, 1971b: 108f) also describes a reduction in traditional power differences for the Western Highlands in noting the 'inflation' of pearlshells and thus of exchange activities as a consequence of colonisation.

87. According to J. Clark (1985: 151), the colonial experience therefore contributed to 'a breakdown in the spirit of community and group co-operation'. A tendency towards the dissolution of social cohesion and an increase in individuality have also been described for various other regions of Melanesia (cf. Keck 1993: 88).

88. Whereas in Pairundu 'only' Ari and Yana report the shooting of local people, according to MacDonald such events were more frequent among the southern Kewa (1991: 263ff., 288, 325, 491, 508f). According to Schiefflin and Crittenden (1991a: 232), in the context of the Strickland-Purari patrol alone, at least fifty-four local people were shot. In addition, the Kome did not see themselves compelled to alter their mode of settlement. An example of one such change, introduced on the part of the church, is described by Fischer (1992: 77) for the Watut, Morobe Province.

89. For a start, the fact that the Catholic Church, with its priests living in Sumi and the catechists distributed among the villages – and despite their comparatively lesser power – has been able to develop a larger presence than the colonial government, with its officers concentrated in Kagua, argues in favour of such a divergence.

4

Catholics and Adventists

Turning away from the traditional religion (Chapter 2) and the processes of colonisation and missionisation (Chapter 3), the view now shifts more fully back to the present. Now, however, I am are no longer concerned with general social and cultural circumstances, but particularly with religion, that is, the Christianity that is represented today in the form of the Catholic Church and the Seventh-day Adventist Church (SDA) in Pairundu. First, I describe the structure of the two communities by discussing their personal composition and present officials, together with the emic evaluation of the different functionaries. In the case of both Catholics and Adventists, there follows an analysis of the beliefs that people expressed to me in formal interviews, informal conversations and sermons that I recorded, which refer to the traditional culture, their own world-view and their assessment of their own denominations. Then I describe the behaviour of the two groups as I observed this in their respective cult practices. The conclusion of this chapter deals with the relationships of Catholics and Adventists with one another. Here I describe first the ways in which Catholics and Adventists judge one another, in order afterwards to go into the conflicts in which the members of the two denominations oppose one another and in which they jointly encounter representatives of other clans.

Community structure

In principle, members of the Catholic community are the baptised permanent inhabitants of Pairundu who have not yet converted to the Adventists. Only through baptism does one become entitled to take communion distributed at the major cult practices, or to act as a church official. However, those who, after baptism, go to services in other villages or do not go at all do not count as members of the community.[1] On the other hand, the unbaptised, who, like the Big Man Rekepea, regularly take part in services without taking communion, are counted as wholly belonging to the community. As a whole, over half the permanent inhabitants of Pairundu are baptised Catholics (55.74%). The greatest proportion of them are apparently Rata Kome (65.62%), since it was Ari, one of their leading men, who had pressed for the Catholic Church to be represented in Pairundu** by a building and a catechist (Chapter 3). After the Rata Kome come the Rundu Kome (55.25%), while the Auro Kome have the lowest proportion of baptised (41.46%). On the whole, more men than women have been baptised, both in absolute terms and also in relation to the whole group of male villagers, since the proportion of baptised women is relatively small in relation to the whole group of female villagers.[2] Information concerning the age structure can be obtained by dividing the baptised Catholics into four roughly demarcated age groups. The youngest (up to ten years) and second-youngest (ten to twenty-five years) emerge as under-represented, while those between twenty-five and forty-five and to a considerable extent those over forty-five, are over-represented. Of the baptised Catholics, on the whole 74 percent take part in services regularly, with on average twenty-seven men and fifty women. Inhabitants of neighbouring villages also go to services sporadically.[3]

As with the Catholics, among the Adventists only baptised members of the community (*church memba*) are entitled to take communion or take over church offices. Somewhat less than half of all Adventist *church memba* (46.15%) were previously baptised Catholics. For a good half of the present-day members, the Adventist baptism took place in July 1991, meaning that their numbers more than doubled during my fieldwork. Only thirteen permanent inhabitants of Pairundu are *church memba*, mostly Auro Kome (seven), then Rundu Kome (five) and Rata Kome (one). The relatively high proportion of Auro Kome corresponds to the fact that they have fewer baptised Catholics compared to other sub-clans, as well as to the fact that the missionisation attempts of Muya, the initiator of the SDA Church in Pairundu (Chapter 3), have so far had the greatest success within his own sub-clan. No Alia Kome belong to the Adventist Rundu Kome. Presumably because of their tensions with the Auro Kome (Chapter 1), they have refrained from attaching themselves to Muya as an Auro Kome. The minimal number of Rata Kome corresponds to the fact that, in comparison with other sub-clans, they have the most baptised Catholics. Here the influence of Ari, already mentioned, may have been decisive. Among the Adventists as among the Catholics, more men than women, both absolutely and relatively, belong to the baptised members of the community. As regards the age structure of the *church memba*, there are no under-tens. The second-youngest age group, however, is doubly over-represented and thus almost as strong as the twenty-five to forty-five year-olds. The proportion of over-forty-fives corresponds roughly to their proportion in the total group of permanent inhabitants in Pairundu. Also counted as *church memba* are those people in the SDA community who have not been baptised as Adventists, but who regularly participate in the major cult practices, the Saturday services in the so-called *klas baptais* or *klas redi*. Accordingly these individuals must also be taken into account in describing the SDA community. As candidates for baptism, the members of the *klas baptais* have committed themselves to the obligatory rules, while the members of the *klas redi* are awaiting acceptance into the group of candidates. Together, the members of the *klas baptais* and *klas redi* form a majority in respect of the *church memba*, the *klas redi* being larger than the *klas baptais*. If the Adventist community lived permanently in Pairundu with all three sub-groups, they would make up just under a quarter (24.59%) of the village population. Among the entire SDA community, the proportion of women is just greater. This means that they are clearly over-represented, since, with respect to the whole group of permanent inhabitants of Pairundu, they are a minority (47.54%) in comparison with the men (52.46%).

On average fifty-seven participants (twenty-five men and thirty-two women) go to the Saturday service, more than belong to the Adventist community. Among these participants are always numerous visitors from other villages.[4] The SDA's weekday evening services, on the other hand, are on average visited by twenty-nine people (fifteen men and fourteen women). To them belong almost all the community members living in Pairundu and a proportion of community members from outside, otherwise there are no outside visitors. However, from time to time I was able to observe mainly younger people, who otherwise neither came to the Saturday services nor had been converted.[5]

The contrast between the two denominations directly affects most of the permanent inhabitants of Pairundu, around two-thirds of whom have joined either the Adventists or the Catholics. The group of baptised Catholics, who include 55.74 percent of the permanent inhabitants of Pairundu, is more than double that of the SDA community, who have partly been recruited from the inhabitants of other villages. The kin composition of the two communities shows that the boundaries between the denominations cross-cuts the clan, sub-clans, lineages and families. In the case of Coleman Makoa and Kevin, indeed, two sons of the same father have become office-holders in different churches. However, the boundary between the denominations has not divided any married couples, since married women belong to the community of their husbands. With respect to the situation regarding the genders, it emerges that among the Adventists and even more so among the Catholics, the women are more regular visitors to the services than the men,[6] although they represent a minority in respect to the men as baptised members of the community in both denominations. The average age of the baptised Catholics is higher than that of the baptised Adventists. Among the Catholics, the over-forty-fives are considerably over-represented, among the Adventists the ten to twenty-five year-olds. When the respective age groups between ten and forty-five are added together, 47.06 percent of the baptised Catholics prove to come from this group and 90.48 percent of the baptised Adventists. Accordingly, in the first instance it is younger people who feel themselves drawn to the Adventists and moved to convert. To that extent, the contrast between the denominations tends also to be a contrast between the generations. Corresponding to the age structure, one also finds among the Catholics the Big Men of Pairundu and therefore the leading men economically as regards possession of gardens and pigs.[7] The baptised Adventists, on the other hand, rather include younger people who, like Naki, Robert and Coleman Komea, take part more in the money economy than the exchange economy. They are catching up economically through the innovations brought about by colonisation such as shops or coffee-growing.[8]

Although the Adventists are, as it were, inferior to the Catholics in numbers, they outdo them when it comes to growth, the ability to attract the inhabitants of other villages and participation in cult practices. While the number of baptised Catholics was generally stable in 1991, the number of baptised Adventists more than doubled in the same year. The fact that, as a whole, more members belong to the *klas redi* and *klas baptais*, that is, to the circle of future and present candidates for SDA baptism, than to the present-day *church memba* also indicates continuing future growth. While people who do not come from Pairundu only participate sporadically in the Catholic Sunday services, such individuals appear relatively frequently at the Adventist Saturday services. Indeed, about two-thirds of the Adventist community as a whole consist of the inhabitants of other villages, which even integrates traditional enemies in the case of the Mui from Ruri.[9] Finally, a readiness to participate in cult practices seems relatively more marked among the Adventists. While only barely three-quarters of the baptised Catholics take part regularly, the number of participants among the Adventists even exceeds the number of community members, thanks to the extra visitors. This is also true of the SDA weekday services, though to a lesser extent.

The Catholic inhabitants of Pairundu invoke a historical connection with Jesus as the founder of their church. According to the generally expressed view, formulated to me by, among others, Ripu (77.), Alupa (7.) and Phillip (68.), on one occasion Jesus charged Peter to take over his position. From Peter, the governorship was transferred to the first Pope and from him to his various successors, up to the present office-holder, Pope John Paul II. As was further explained to me, the latter tells the bishops, including Bishop Firmin Schmidt, living in Mendi, which passages in the Bible to treat within the different Sunday services. Then the Bishop gives instructions to the priests, and finally the priests convey them to the catechists.[10] The hierarchical structure that can be recognised here was frequently emphasised. Thus, to unanimous agreement, Phillip (68.) told me:

> Pope John Paul is in Rome... he hears what the angels in heaven are saying and writes it down on paper. Bishop Firmin, who is in Mendi, goes there and fetches it. The other priests cannot go to Rome, only the Bishop can, so he goes

and fetches it, he fetches it and he keeps it. The priests fetch it from Mendi, they fetch it and give it to the catechists. Then the catechists have it and they give it to the people.

The office-holders of the church function as representatives of the church leadership with respect to the 'ordinary' members of the community. Among them, the priests have the leading position, since in Pairundu one never sees the Bishop, let alone the Pope himself. However, because of a lack of personnel, the priest is responsible for a larger area, so that often he only visits the individual villages very rarely. For example, Fr Matthias, who has been responsible for the area between Kagua and Sumi and the southern part of Kagua Parish since 1989, only appeared twice in Pairundu during my fieldwork.[11] At the village level, in reality the office-holders who are subordinate to the priests represent the church leadership. The members of the church committee, who are chosen by the community, control the catechists to some extent. They can ask the priests to remove them and can also suggest candidates for appointment to him.[12] Ari, Alupa and Mayanu belong to the church committee in Pairundu. Since these members of the church committee do not exercise basic functions during the cult practices and since the priests visit Pairundu only rarely, the catechist – who leads the Sunday service and is charged with giving instructions on how to conduct one's life in a Christian manner to those about to be baptised, people wishing to marry and parents – becomes the most important transmitter of belief at the village level. Education as a catechist includes schooling, which is mostly provided in Sumi by the Catholic sisters on different numbers of days. More rarely, one- or two-week seminars take place in Sumi or Kagua.[13] The office of catechist is remunerated at 4 K a month. In addition, the community is obliged to help the catechist with garden work or, if required, house-building. He also receives donations of food given at the Sunday service. Since 1990, the office of catechist in Pairundu has been filled by Coleman Makoa (Figure 4.1). Other office-holders are subordinate to him, their role, however, generally being restricted to taking over particular functions in the context of major cult practices. As 'Eucharist minister' (*komunio lida*) chosen by the community, instructed by the sisters and blessed by the priest, Kande distributes the communion at the Sunday service. As 'prayer leaders' (*prayer lida*), Sayna and Neambunu read out the prescribed Bible passages.[14] In addition, they lead the Catholic weekday evening services in Pairundu**, Porai and Walua.[15]

The office-holders need not present themselves for rotational re-election, though in principle, apart from the priest, they can be relieved of their functions at any time with the agreement of the community. From the emic point of view, there is a close connection between the offices and those who exercise them. It is therefore important how communities judge individual office-holders. Fr Matthias enjoys greater popularity in contrast to his predecessor, Fr Jim, who, during the two years he spent in

Figure 4.1 Catechist Coleman Makoa (centre) explains a Bible passage (Pairundu**, 30 June 1991; photo: Holger Jebens).

Sumi, only came once to Anapote and never to Pairundu and indeed ultimately left Sumi early. People appreciate that Fr Matthias is always on the move, that he visits many villages, that he benefits the church by selling food, that he takes care of the health centre in Sumi and that he supports the building of a new community school between Pairundu and Anapote.[16] With respect to the church committee, the members of the community recognise the role that Ari played in establishing the Catholic Church, but at the same time they accuse him of using this to claim a leading role and of thus treating the church as his own private property. When it comes to assessing the different catechists who have replaced one another, Kenneth still enjoys a high reputation. Thus when he came to visit me in Pairundu, members of the Catholic community greeted him in a friendly fashion while simultaneously plying him with gifts of food. His successors, however, have overwhelmingly been criticised. For example, even during his period of office, Ruben is reputed to have 'stolen' (*stilim*), as the Tok Pisin has it, numerous women of the village, that is, seduced them into extra-marital sexual relations. Ultimately, his marriage to Renu not only offended against the requirement of clan exogamy, it also led to him being relieved of his office, since Renu was already married to another man at this time. Today he no longer attends the church. Against Augustin, Ruben's successor, Coleman Makoa (30.) in particular claimed that he only ever came to Pairundu from Wasuma for the Sunday cult practices and that he hardly cared at all for the affairs of the community. Coleman Makoa himself, however, is also subjected to massive criticism. Leading representatives of the church leadership such as Fr Matthias (50.) and Sr Marie (47.) stressed that they did not know how he could have become a catechist. After hearing a recording of a Sunday service that Coleman Makoa conducted on 24 August 1991, Kenneth (42.) criticised it, saying that many parts went on too long, others appeared in the wrong order, the prescribed text of the Gospel had been omitted from the sermon, even though it was supposed to be the heart of it and in general Coleman Makoa seemed to be more concerned to make a name for himself by talking a lot than to worship God.[17] In contrast to this, the 'ordinary' members of the community testify that their catechist leads the service well, though they criticise other aspects of his way of life and accuse him in particular of laziness.[18] Thus, for example, Ripu held it against him that, up to now, he had neither cleared bush gardens nor paid the brideprice for his wife. In addition, Ripu (79.) reported to me that Coleman Makoa had only been appointed catechist because of the pressure he had exerted himself. One sign of his widespread rejection is the fact that, as he himself complained in numerous sermons and in some conversations with me, people hardly ever supported him with food donations or labour.[19]

The Catholic community in Pairundu draws its income from the collections taken at the Sunday cult practices and the community work sessions (*wok sol*), which usually take place once a week, generally on a Tuesday. For two Kina, anyone can engage the community to have sweet potato mounds laid out, for instance. If there are no such tasks for the church committee to accept, improvements are made to the church building, among other things. Members of the community who stay away from work assignments must, according to Coleman Makoa (30.), pay a fine of 20 Toea. If they refuse even to pay this, they are excluded from taking part in communion until they have undergone a confession with Fr Matthias. Nevertheless, the *wok sol* are often not particularly popular. Sometimes they simply do not happen, and sometimes only Ari and Alupa turn up. In any case, the church committee brings the incomes from the monthly collections to the priest in Sumi, who pays it into a savings account kept in the community's name. It is hoped that one day the money can be used to obtain a corrugated iron roof for the church building.

Those Adventists who do not exercise an office and therefore belong to the 'ordinary' members of the community are usually not able to describe the upper levels of their church's organisation. People merely say that from Pairundu as a kind of 'sub church' (*han church*), reports about, for example, the size of the community are sent to the 'main church' (*mama church*) in Kagua and from there to Ialibu, Mount Hagen, Goroka, Lae and Port Moresby.[20] From there they are sent first to Australia and then to America, where the headquarters of the world SDA Church is located.[21] Only office-holders like Kevin (43.) and especially Koya (46.), who officiates in Kagua and its area as a pastor, have more exact knowledge. According to what they say, Kagua belongs to Ialibu District. Together with other districts in the Highlands, this constitutes the local mission, led by a president and with its headquarters at Mount Hagen. Papua New Guinea as a whole has ten different local missions, which are linked to the Papua New Guinea Union Mission, whose president officiates in Lae.[22] Alongside other union missions,[23] the Papua New Guinea Union Mission belongs to the South Pacific Division. Twelve divisions world wide form the General Conference as the highest forum of the SDA Church.[24] The General Conference has its headquarters in Washington DC and is led by an American, Neil Wilson, a man who, in Pastor Koya's (46.) words, referring to his leading role, is 'like the Pope'.[25]

Like the Catholic priest, the Adventist pastor assumes a leading position among the office-holders. His period of office is similarly fixed at between three and six years and his responsibility also extends over a wide area. On the whole, however, Pastor Koya spent more time in Pairundu than Fr Matthias, not only during an Adventist evangelism week (30 June to 6 July 1991), but also on the occasion of three Saturday services held from Friday evening to Saturday midday.[26] As he told me, he had had three years of education, finishing in Lae, in order to be ordained in Mount Hagen. Only this entitles him to baptise or marry members of the community, for example.[27] Like the catechist among the Catholics, the so-called layman among the Adventists is the most important purveyor of beliefs at village level. He leads most of the services, carries out conversations on spiritual welfare with members of the community and supervises the finances. Training as a layman includes attending a six-week course held twice a year in Mount Hagen and Tari. Although Kevin, the serving layman in Pairundu, was allowed on to this course even though he had no previous school education, usually passing through the fifth or sixth class in the community school is a precondition. As in the case of the pastor, there is an ordination at the end of the training. Apart from the food donations of the community[28] and their help in building houses or making gardens, according to Pastor Koya (46.), the layman receives no regular payment except for a contribution of 10 to 20

Kina now and then from the *mama church* in Kagua.[29] The church deacon is subject to the layman and is responsible for taking care of the church building and the church property. In addition, he should visit sick members of the community, look after discipline during services and among other things assist at baptisms. The deacon is elected by the *church memba* for a year and, like the pastor and layman, is ordained. Also for a year, he is assisted by a deaconess who is also elected, but not ordained and whose responsibility is restricted to the female members of the community. In Pairundu, Robert and his wife Wareame serve as deacon and deaconess. Endowed with even fewer powers is the office of church clerk, occupied by Don. As well as the lists of *church memba*, *klas baptais* and *klas redi*, he supervises the list of reports drawn up for each Saturday service.[30]

Among the Adventists as among the Catholics, any office-holder, apart from the pastor, can in principle at any time be relieved of his office.[31] Moreover, from the etic point of view, there is again a close connection between office and person, so that, for the Adventists too, it is important how the community judges each office-holder personally. In general, Pastor Koya enjoys a high reputation. A contributory factor here may be that, as a Kewa from Kuali Lombo and therefore from Kagua District, he shares the same mother tongue with those belonging to the communities he has been entrusted with. Among the layman, Peter, Kevin's predecessor, is basically regarded more negatively than Pastor Koya. Like Coleman Makoa, he is accused of laziness. Alex said that Peter had always just waited to be provided with food by the community, until, at the request of the community, the Pastor transferred him as a punishment, as it were. By contrast, Kevin's personality and the way he carries out his office receive a rather positive response, as is shown by the fact that the members of the community help him with house-building and garden work and that they provide him with food now and then. Against Robert, on the other hand, Adventists complain that he speaks too much in public, simply to raise his own prestige.[32] Muya, finally, although he exercises no office himself, does have a special significance as the person who contributed decisively to the setting up of the SDA church. With Muya as with Ari, who assumes a similar position among the Catholics, people honour his past services, while at the same time accusing him of treating the church as his private property in cultivating his personal image.[33] Unlike Ari, however, Muya is also criticised for often being too irascible and thoughtless – as I will show, hardly the behaviour expected of an Adventist.

The Adventists share with the Catholics the claim that they finance themselves. Sources of income consist of the money donated during services and a tenth of the income of each member of the church (*tait*). Before being baptised, each Adventist promises to give this tenth to his church. In addition, the Adventists plan to sell food grown jointly on a piece of land that Muya has donated to the church. In the future, paid work assignments are also to take place, on the model of the Catholics. The Adventists want to obtain uniforms with their income, in order to give themselves a better image when they come into contact with the inhabitants of other villages.[34] Unlike the community work of the Catholics, however, the SDA *wok sol*, usually held by Kevin on a Sunday and often on an additional weekday too, is mainly intended not to earn money, but above all to missionise. Accordingly, other villages are visited in order to bear witness, sing, or prepare the building of a new church. On 27 August 1991, SDA women brought food to Yapa's disabled wife Mane, washed her, cleaned her house and lectured her. During my fieldwork, assistance in building a house for Kevin and preparation for an evangelism week was added to missionisation. Even though the Adventists' community work may in general be more comprehensive than that of the Catholics, it seems to me that, relative to the size of the congregation, it receives a comparatively greater response from Adventists.

The two denominations present in Pairundu have certain structural similarities. These include not only the attempt to be self-financing, among other things through work assignments, but also the offices present in both. At the top is the priest or pastor, a leading representative of the church leadership on the supra-regional level, who admittedly only comes to Pairundu rarely in the case of the Catholics and somewhat less rarely in the case of the Adventists. One office-holder who is subordinate to the priest or pastor is the catechist or layman, who has the task of, as it were, representing the church leadership at the village level. The offices of catechist and layman differ structurally only in the sense that the layman has a comparatively longer and rather more formal education and a supposedly higher remuneration.[35] Despite the basically hierarchical order, among both Catholics and Adventists, the possibility of forcing people to resign from their office, which was actually used in the case of both Ruben and Peter, in reality creates an element of community autonomy. This possibility of removal from office seems relatively more actual among the Adventists, because of their more frequently expressed threats to one another. In addition, both communities have the figure of a 'church father' in the form of Ari and Muya, though both are equally subject to the internal critique of being too concerned about their own prestige.

Beliefs

After having described the framework, i.e., the structure of the two communities, in what follows I shall discuss the beliefs that exist within this framework, describing for Catholics and Adventists equally the respective attitudes they have adopted towards their own tradition, their own view of Christianity and their assessment of their own community. If, according to the 'ordinary' members of the community, the first catechists and evangelists decisively rejected the traditional religion

(Chapter 3), it is not surprising that the traditional religion is still linked with the devil, negatively valued and ascribed to a past that is sealed. Accordingly, Ari (21.) claimed: 'Satan's different customs and practices, all those have been removed by the Word of God and no longer exist here. We believe only in the Word of God, and only God made everything, that we believe'.[36] This picture begins to differ, however, when one examines the individual elements of the traditional religion separately. Although, for example, in accordance with the officially propagated view of their church leadership (Smits 1981: 123), the Catholics outwardly claim that the *remo* no longer exist today, Ripu and Serale reported to me in confidence an attack by a *remo*, and in general it is considered dangerous to mention the names of the recently deceased (Chapter 2). Usually the *remo* are ascribed to the devil and condemned, while in the pre-colonial period opinion about them depended on whether they had helped people or caused them harm. As with the *remo*, the church leadership also denies the existence of the *kalando* (Smits 1981: 123), though this does not prevent the members of the community from continuing to fear the sicknesses that they ascribe to the *kalando*, though they do not make any link with the devil.[37] Yaki too, who is regarded as equivalent to the Christian God and therefore has retained his positive assessment, is ascribed an equally undiminished effectiveness. Otmar (62.) said:

> If you climbed on to the roof of the men's house and invoked Yaki, he gave you whatever you asked him for... today we still believe that earlier, we invoked our god and he gave us food to eat... now God gives us food, it's true, God exists... the priest said: 'We name this same man "God". Before, you said to Yaki, he should give you everything; if you say that to God now, he'll give you everything'. We think that God exists. Yaki, he is, quite simply, this God... it's true, today we do the same as before and everyone says: 'This man Yaki, he is the same man whom everyone calls "God" today, he is just the same man'.

Traditional magical practices in general and injurious thoughts and feelings in particular, have lost their effectiveness even less than the traditional transcendent authorities have for the Catholic villagers, although outwardly they are mostly valued negatively.[38] Only traditional methods of curing sickness are viewed positively. Obviously no role is played here by the fact that Sr Marie (48.), as a prominent representative of the church leadership, came out against one of its central elements by criticising the practice of slaughtering a pig to effect a cure. However, traditional divination procedures are subjected to a negative reassessment. Accordingly, Atasi told me that, following a ban imposed by Fr Dunstan, dreams are no longer deployed in divination. Indeed, Sr Marie (48.) referred to such dreams as 'ancestor worship', while Fr Matthias (46.) claimed that he was not acquainted with Atasi. Only after some time and some discussion, during which those who knew me better assured others in the Kewa language that I was not a representative of any church, did it emerge that dreams connected with divination had not actually been prohibited that strictly and still took place.

On the whole, a tension emerges between official and unofficial views of how the Catholics assess their traditional religion. The official view is mostly expressed by office-holding villagers who outwardly describe an ideal situation that corresponds to their own norms. They say: 'It is as it should be'. The unofficial view, on the other hand, only became accessible to me after I had lived together with the villagers for a longer time and built up a relationship of mutual trust with them. Here, mostly 'ordinary' members of the community, when among themselves, describe their own version of reality. They say: 'It really is like this'. If on the whole the traditional religion is, as already described, linked with the devil, valued negatively and ascribed to a sealed past, in the first instance this occurs in the official view. The office-holding villagers thus express an attitude that the 'ordinary' members of the community say was propagated by the very first catechists and evangelists and also corresponds to the version of the present-day priests and nuns. Officially, therefore, people claim that they have adapted to Christianity, which in principle, as at the start of missionisation, they still see as a ban on the traditional culture in general and the traditional religion in particular. Accordingly Coleman Makoa (30.), for example, assured me that the main representatives of the church leadership prohibited pig-killing festivals as a 'custom of Satan'.[39] If, on the other hand, transcendent authorities and magical practices continue to be regarded as effective and differentiated, that is, valued partly negatively and partly positively, then this is mainly an unofficial view. Here 'ordinary' members of the community in particular confess that they have not got as far as they desire, as it were, with the obliteration of their traditional religion and its replacement by Christianity. One of the rare statements in which, so to speak, the continuation of tradition is explicitly articulated was provided by Kenneth (39.): 'Today, we are split down the middle, our old customs are still there, and the customs of the whites have arrived, and we are split down the middle. We have not yet ceased the old customs, they are all still there, and we mix them up and mix them up and make something of them'.[40] Certainly the example of the pig-killing festivals shows that the main representatives of the Catholic Church leadership actually often do not propagate the decisive rejection ascribed to them by the 'ordinary' members of the community. Fr Matthias claimed that he had nothing against pig-killing festivals, and Kenneth also said that holding them should be allowed.[41] As already described (Introduction), the Catholic leadership has regarded traditional religion in particular as a kind of early version of Christianity since the Second Vatican Council. Accordingly, Fr Dunstan and Fr Matthias (46.), among others, expressed the view that the villagers had already been praying to God, in the form of Yaki, in the pre-colonial period. Certainly this version was only communicated to the Kome some time after the start of missionisation. When it comes to the equivalence between Yaki and the Christian God, at any rate, which is also expressed at the village level, it has not been entirely without influence. However, in my view it could not alter anything concerning the basic conviction that Christianity and the traditional religion as a whole are basically confronted with one another as incompatible and mutually exclusive contrasts.

In their official view of tradition, the members of the Catholic community express the idea that acceptance of Christianity is only possible through the prior rejection and overcoming of tradition. Thus to the question of what one must do in order to be a good Christian, first place is usually given to maintaining prohibitions and commandments.[42] These prohibitions and commandments are directed not only against traditional magical and cult practices, but also against activities and types of behaviour in general which are seen as typical of the pre-colonial period. Equally forbidden, according to Coleman Makoa, are gossiping, defamation of character, lies, envy, theft, quarrelling, fighting and murder. Ata Francis added consuming beer and playing cards.[43] Coleman Makoa's demand to the community in general and the Big Men in particular to understand the importance of 'removing the old customs' (*rausim pasin bilong bipo*) and not to think so much about their own prestige – that is, business, pigs and pearlshells – also represents a distancing from tradition.[44] With respect to the emphasis on obedience, the idea that as a Christian one must help others is usually in the background. At only one Sunday service I visited did Coleman Makoa urge that one should like one's fellow humans and, for example, take in alien people for the night and feed them.[45] Even the significance of one's own belief is seldom articulated in interviews and sermons. Instead, following all prohibitions and commandments is seen as a precondition for baptism, which is achieved through aspersion, that is, being sprinkled with water.[46] In addition, in the Catholic community participation in weekly community work and the regular *lotu* is expected. As a verb this Tok Pisin term is used to describe participating in Christian cult practices, including saying prayers and taking communion, while as a noun it refers to the Church as an organisation and Christianity as a whole (cf. Mihailic 1971: 124). However, less importance seems to be placed on going to church than on the prohibitions and commandments, since, in answer to my question, Coleman Makoa, Ata Francis and Ripu all said independently of one another that one could go to heaven without *lotu* if one followed all the prohibitions and commandments.

This idea of 'going to heaven' is, in my judgement, the decisive goal for the members of the Catholic community. One way of attaining this goal and thus a 'pathway to heaven', for Catholics is the 'hard work' (*hatwok*), which consists equally of following all prescriptions, community work and regular *lotu*. In the Catholic version, carrying out this work had already been anticipated by Jesus. Thus the phrases 'obey Jesus' and 'follow Jesus', which are frequently heard in sermons and interviews, mean that one should, as it were, belatedly tread the path laid down by Jesus in the Bible and thus to an extent re-enact a primordial mythical event. Ripu (77.) clearly articulated the motive of imitation, together with the desire to go to heaven: 'We go to the service, we go to the service. Jesus went to the service, he was buried, and he got up from the cemetery and went to heaven, and we want to follow that'.[47]

The idea that the Last Day of Judgement (*las de*) is imminent, with the decision between heaven and hell, has lasted from the announcements of the first catechists and evangelists through appropriate statements in the context of the Holy Spirit movement into the present. Eschatological beliefs may assume different forms. When I first visited the region between Kagua and Sumi in November 1990, in many villages I was first told, with an anxious expression, that Australian scientists had looked into telescopes and written to the Provincial Government of Southern Highlands Province that in 1994 seven stars would fall down and destroy the earth.[48] In Pairundu too, the Kome reported similar rumours on their own initiative right at the start of my fieldwork, in order to obtain my opinion. When, on one occasion, I explained to them that there was fire in the earth's core, Pogola (70.) spontaneously asked me whether this fire was getting any bigger and would kill everybody. Before 15 January 1991 in particular, when, as could be learned from the radio, the US government's ultimatum delivered before the first Gulf War had expired, the sudden outbreak of a major war and the end of the world that would accompany it was the focus of many anxious conversations.[49] Eschatological ideas can certainly be concretised in various ways,[50] though for most of the Catholic community the Last Day of Judgement is fixed for 2000. As Ata Francis and Nosupinai (60.), among others, told me, all the communities of believers they were acquainted with were announcing the *las de* for that year. Otherwise no one could imagine how further years were to be counted. Accordingly, in numerous conversations, as well as one of Coleman Makoa's sermons, I heard the phrase 'only nine years are left'.[51] Even on my first visit to Pairundu, as well as in the months to come, people asked me what would happen after 2000, without my being able to recognise the reason for this to begin with. Ari (17.) asked me explicitly to reveal the exact date of the *las de*, since the villagers themselves were in general greatly concerned. This conclusion is far from being an exaggeration, since my impression was that the eschatological ideas were linked in part with evident fear.

The example of the expected end of the world certainly shows that the differences between the unofficial and the official view may be congruent with the differences between what 'ordinary' members of the community and church office-holders say. In contrast to the rather unofficially expressed and approximate expectation that prevailed at village level, Fr Matthias (46.) and Kenneth (42.) affirmed that the date the world would end was not known at all. Kenneth explained that, according to the teachings of the Catholic Church, it is merely that everyone has his or her own *las de*, that is, the day of death. Moreover, the omens for the return of Jesus described in the Bible have not yet occurred. Among these signs are the government taking action against the Catholic Church and fights breaking out between villages and within families.[52] With Ripu, Ata Francis and Coleman Makoa, the same people occasionally outwardly adhered to this 'official attitude' who were otherwise convinced, in confidential conversations, of an, as it were, collective *las de* in 2000. To some extent, therefore, the different positions are expressed by the same villagers, depending on the context of the conversation.

If the members of the Catholic community see, in the first instance, a 'pathway to heaven' in their form of Christianity, the question then arises how they see life in heaven after the Last Day of Judgement. From the etic point of view, the corresponding ideas do not appear to be very coherent, since people imagine both the satisfaction of all needs and their absence. Coleman Makoa said that in heaven there was no darkness, no rain, no trouble, no work and no death. Ata Francis added to this list sickness and age. Most informants stress the possibility of obtaining food in heaven without working for it. While an all-embracing wish fulfilment arises out of the absence of everything that makes one's real life arduous or full of sorrow, at the same time, Ata Francis (23., 30.) thought and Ripu (77.) affirmed, that in heaven, as in the womb, there were no longer any needs.[53] Apart from the satisfaction or absence of all needs, the Catholics' idea of heaven involves the disappearance of all differences in respect of gender, body size, age, skin colour, language, thoughts, actions and property. Ata Francis (23.) told me: 'When we are both together with God, we will have the same skin, the same language and the same thoughts. That's what it will be like'.[54] Simultaneously, along with the disappearance of personal differences, kin ties and obligations would also vanish. A comment of Ripu's (77.) hints at this point: 'And there is no marriage... You have parents, but actually you don't have parents, it is as if you are an, as if you are an independent man...'.[55] Thus the members of the Catholic community ultimately imagine heaven as a place of comprehensive equality, where social equality is, as it were, transposed into the natural environment, meaning that heaven has an entirely flat landscape, without mountains, caves or valleys. Ripu (77.) said, about Jesus: 'He will completely flatten this sort of earth and if we stay here, we will be able to see as far as Port Moresby, or even America or Australia'.[56] On the whole, the concept of heaven constructed by the Catholics appears to be an inverted image of reality, a description of reality with inverted characteristics.

Since Christianity, and especially the traditional religion, are basically seen as mutually exclusive opposites, the claim that the traditional religion has been dissolved does imply claiming an identity as a Christian, as it were. Just as the villagers in general see themselves as convinced Christians, so the Catholics in particular affirm that they know the Word of God exactly, have strong beliefs and are in harmony with God's will.[57] By this is meant mainly keeping all appropriate prescriptions and regularly carrying out *lotu* and community labour. To this corresponds simultaneously the idea that the equality imagined in the concept of heaven has been partly realised already in the present. Ari (21.) justified the ban on traditional pig-killing events in the following words: 'Now, among us, the men are equal and the women are equal and the children also, and no one can outdo anyone else... We must follow the words of the Bible and be comrades. That is good'.[58] In addition, the members of the Catholic community show conviction that as good Christians they are participating in the power of God. According to Otmar (62.), for example, prayers provide protection against the damaging influence of ancestral spirits, while according to Ari they cure illnesses.[59] Coleman Makoa (30.) advised me to donate money to the church, so that in future God would help me obtain success.[60]

However, the more access I obtained to unofficially formulated views and ideas in the course of time, the less remained of the initially articulated self-certainty. In conversations within a small circle, doubts were mainly expressed in the form of accusations that Christian prescriptions were not being followed sufficiently. Such accusations certainly do not occasion surprise when coming from an 'outsider' like Ruben (84.). He pointed out that only a few Catholics really believe: while most certainly go to services, afterwards they indulge in defamation, among other things. Alongside him, however, Ari (21.), Nosupinai (60.) and Ata Francis (74.) complained about breaches of prohibitions and commandments as well. Moreover, Ata Francis concluded that people usually did not just profane Sunday as the day of God's service, but also continued to steal and lie. During an evening service in Porai, he said, although people washed their arms and legs all right, they did not cleanse themselves inside. On the same occasion, some women complained that even members of the Catholic community who had neither washed or taken part in community work were allowed to take communion on Sundays.[61] This unofficial self-criticism was supported in numerous sermons by Coleman Makoa, in which he accused the members of the community, among other things, of observing the day of the holy service too little, thinking too much of quarrels or court cases, supporting the catechist – that is, himself – too little and staying away from community work too often. Yali drew a link between breaking rules and the idea of a secret connected with Catholic Christianity by saying, concerning a text from the Bible, that people could not understand it because their own bad customs were preventing them from doing so. Yet it was also necessary, he continued, to find the 'secret words' (*tok hait*) and unravel them in order to go to heaven.[62] Accordingly, at the beginning of my stay in Pairundu, I was often asked how the teachings of the Church should be understood. During an interview with Ata Francis (23.), Rekepea regretted that with Christianity one never knew what lay behind it, how it all hangs together, or how it originated.[63] In my view, by means of the motif of a secret that has not yet been revealed, the members of the Catholic community are expressing the idea that they had not got as far as they actually wished in accepting Christianity. As already described, this idea is otherwise articulated in the belief that many of the old transcendent authorities and magical practices remain effective and that the traditional religion has therefore not entirely retreated before the advance of Christianity. All in all, the self-assessment of the Catholic community, with its tension between certainty and doubt, is a topic in which official and unofficial views diverge particularly strongly and clearly.

Like the Catholics, the Adventists basically regard their own form of Christianity and the traditional culture as a whole as incompatible and mutually exclusive opposites. Moreover, the members of the SDA community also believe that acceptance of Christianity requires the prior rejection and overcoming of tradition. The distancing from tradition is expressed most clearly in the prohibition, which is different with the Adventists compared to the Catholics, on keeping pigs, let alone consuming them. In this sense, the Adventists to some extent see pigs as emblematic of tradition. Pastor Koya justified the ban on pigs by claiming that, according to the Bible, the Devil stayed in the belly of the pig.[64] The Adventist villagers seem to have internalised this view straight away, since they always stayed away whenever a pig-killing festival took place in Pairundu. Moreover, they often expressed the view that pigs smelt as badly as the men who ate them. Thus the Adventists did not participate when, on 20 September 1991, two pigs were killed at a goodbye feast held for me in Pairundu**. Whereas, therefore, the Catholics partly criticise the pig-killing festivals, partly approve of them and partly continue to hold them in a modified form, the Adventist ban on pigs leads to a decisive rejection of pig-killing festivals. According to Muya (55.), the Bible says that no one can enter heaven who takes part in *yawe*.[65] In addition, Adventists articulate the rejection of tradition in the idea that the Bible prohibits not only decoration, but also traditional clothing like the bark belt.[66] Owning pearlshells is also forbidden.

While on the one hand pigs are valued differently by the two denominations represented in Pairundu, on the other hand members of both communities agree in linking the whole traditional religion with the Devil, valuing it negatively and ascribing it to a sealed past. However, in contrast to the Catholics, the Adventists themselves claim, even in the context of the unofficial view, that the traditional transcendent authorities do not exist and that the traditional magical practices have no effect. For Robert (83.), the Bible proves that there are no ancestral spirits on the earth. According to Muya (55.), the sicknesses that were earlier ascribed to the *kalando* were actually caused by God, in order to punish breaches of prohibitions. As different Adventists explained to me, the only people who believed in the existence of the traditional transcendent authorities are those the Devil has led astray. Thus, according to the SDA church leadership (Robertson 1990: 211), the Devil sometimes assumes the form of ancestors in order to deceive people. Robert (83.) said that belief in the *kalando* is traceable to the effect of evil spirits. For Adventists, it follows that *remo* and *kalando* cannot harm anyone who partakes in God's superior power. Accordingly, Naki (57.) pointed out to me that, in contrast to the Catholics, he can go into the bush at night after eating a good meal without any problems, for example, whereas earlier, while he was still a member of the Catholic community, this would have made him ill.[67] Exactly like the traditional transcendent authorities, according to the Adventist version, the traditional magical practices are only of significance to those whom the Devil has led astray. In principle, this also applies to witchcraft practices, negative thoughts and feelings, procedures to cure sickness and divination practices. With respect to witchcraft techniques, the SDA Pastor Epawa, who comes from the Erave region, claimed that their power is subject to the power of Jesus.[68] Muya (55.) expressed himself similarly: 'If we do not follow God's law, then this [witchcraft techniques] has power [over us] and if we follow God's law, then, I say, it [witchcraft techniques] has no power [over us]'.[69] According to a remark of Alex (5.), in respect of God's power, even negative thoughts and feelings lose their significance. According to Kevin (45.), they only damage those who have them.[70] The members of the SDA community regard the traditional magical practices not only as ineffective for believing Christians, but also as negative and forbidden, because of their connection with the Devil. According to this prohibition – which is formulated in interviews, sermons and publications of the church leadership (cf. also Robertson 1990: 212) – in contrast to the Catholics, the Adventists are neither ready to take part in, for example, traditional divination practices, nor to submit to traditional methods of treatment in cases of sickness. Because of the ban on pig meat – and because Adventists deny all existence and effectiveness to traditional transcendent authorities and magical practices, even informally – their distancing from tradition appears more rigid when compared to the Catholics. Accordingly, even in confidential conversations, the members of the SDA community claim that they have 'given up everything' and that the traditional religion has been completely dissolved and replaced by Christianity.

Adventist Christianity, like Catholic Christianity, is for its adherents a 'pathway to heaven'. This 'Adventist pathway' also involves 'hard work', which, in the biblical image of Jesus, consists in following all prescriptions, community work and regular *lotu*.[71] However, just as the Adventists distance themselves from tradition more rigidly, so simultaneously they stress to a relatively greater degree the prohibitions and commandments which they think it necessary to follow, in order to change, as it were, from adherents of the traditional religion into Christians. Acceptance into the SDA community requires not only giving up gossiping, defamation of character, lies, envy, stealing, quarrelling, fighting and murder, but also the observance of food rules which prohibit the consumption of pigs, cassowaries, tree kangaroos, rats and flying foxes, as well as the enjoyment of tea, coffee, beer, betel nuts and tobacco.[72] However, Robert (83.) and Naki (57.), for example, listed to begin with the Biblical ten commandments, which are hardly mentioned among the Catholics. In contrast to the Catholics, the Adventists understand the fourth commandment as a demand to hold their major cult practices not on Sunday, but on the seventh day of the week, that is, on Saturday, which in general they call the 'Sabbath'. Thus, also in contrast to the Catholics, the Adventists rule out the possibility of going to heaven without regular *lotu*.[73] To my direct question, Muya (55.) answered that if he did not plant anything he would not harvest anything and in exactly the same way, God would not let anyone into heaven for nothing. The significance of the prohibitions and commandments, which is also emphasised in official SDA publications (Robertson 1990: 202ff.), arises mainly from the fact that, according to the Adventist conviction, only those who have completely followed the rules go to heaven. Even a small error, on the other hand, a small breach of the rules – a stepping out of the footsteps of Jesus, a deviation from the proper path, as it were – is sufficient to make access to heaven impossible, or to bring about God's punishment in the form of sickness or death.[74] In this sense, the Adventists see themselves as compelled to obedience even more than the Catholics. For the Adventists, the Bible is a compendium of all prohibitions and commandments. According to Robert (83.), it is the teacher that tells you what you may and may not eat. According to Muya (55.), God demands from his adherents the following: 'You must follow the Bible, from Genesis to Revelation, you must follow it, you must not neglect the Bible... What the Bible will say, this you must follow, the Bible will save you'.[75]

Through this repeated mention, in numerous interviews and sermons, of 'from Genesis to Revelation', Adventists frequently claim to have a thorough knowledge of the Bible. Accordingly, Adventist office-holders, as well as the 'ordinary' members of the community, cite different passages in the Bible much more frequently than the Catholics, in order to support their ideas. For preference, people cite from the Book of Daniel and the Revelation, though generally the Old Testament has priority over the New Testament. Kevin (44.), the layman, explained to me that the Old Testament was related to the New as a father to his son, since the father surpasses the son in knowledge and power. Apart from the stress on being faithful to the Bible and obedience, Adventists also regard praying regularly as indispensable, in contrast to the Catholics. Thus Kevin said, during a sermon: 'Friends, what will bring us to heaven? Our prayers will bring us to heaven, God will fetch us on the basis of our prayers... Later, on the Last Day of Judgement, God will judge us individually from our prayers'.[76]

In the Adventist understanding, carrying out the different elements that 'hard work' consists of will only bring to heaven those who are also baptised members of the SDA community. Before baptism, one must belong to the *klas baptais* for about a year. In this period, the novices must follow the appropriate prescriptions and take part in the Bible teaching that is mostly provided by the layman within the framework of the Saturday service and which concludes with an examination by the Pastor.[77] At the same time, this supports the Adventist claim to a thorough knowledge of the Bible. Unlike the Catholics, baptism itself occurs not through aspersion but immersion, that is, the full submersion of the novice while standing in the water. According to Pastor Koya, this is understood to be repeating the baptism of Jesus as described in the Bible and also, symbolically, his three-day sojourn in the realm of the dead. In that the novice dies with Jesus like this through baptism, according to Pastor Koya (46.) all his bad thoughts, characteristics and habits simultaneously die with him and are no longer evident after he re-emerges.[78] For the Adventists, the necessity for a social withdrawal arises from their concept of baptism. Dying with Jesus in the baptism means, in Naki's (57.) words, 'giving up everything and being like a dead person'.[79] According to Naki, this means that Adventists expect members of their community not to go about in large numbers, to stay away from big discussions or quarrels and not to speak loudly or shout. According to Kevin, as a member of the community one should also not wander about at night[80] and basically keep away from the following people: 'Heathens, people who never pray, people who never study the Bible, people who do not have Jesus in their lives...'.[81] Here, clearly, is the idea of purity, obtained through baptism and then maintained by, for example, food rules, which can be lost, among other things, by remaining too close to non-Adventists. This purity of humans, who are to be understood as in a sense the temple of God, is thus not the outcome of a gradual process of change, but the consequence of the sudden 'ending', so to speak, of negative thoughts, feeling and habits in the immersion. In my view, such an ending is basically only possible if one sees humans not as ambivalent, as capable, in and of themselves, sometimes of good and sometimes of evil. Indeed, Adventists trace the negative exclusively back to the influence of Satan.[82]

The adherents of the two denominations represented in Pairundu share the conviction that the *las de*, the Last Day of Judgement, with its decision between heaven and hell, is imminent. As with attitudes to tradition and the stress on prohibitions and commandments, I see differences in this respect as gradual, that is, in the relatively greater rigidity of the Adventists. They talk more often of the end of the world, the expectation of nearness is more strongly marked, and they have a more exact idea of what will happen on the *las de*. According to Pastor Koya, Jesus will appear one Sabbath, that is, on the seventh day of the week, with heaven opening around him and to the sounds of angels blowing on trumpets, to take to him his chosen ones, while bad people go down below, together with their bad thoughts, characteristics and habits.[83] However, before that, according to Muya (55.), the Devil will pose as Jesus, thus deceiving those who do not trust sufficiently in Jesus. Finally, after a stay in heaven lasting one thousand years, there will be another decisive struggle between the powers of good and evil. Only when, as a result, the Devil and all his followers have been destroyed forever will Jesus and his chosen people live forever on a newly created earth.[84] Like the Catholics, the Adventists linked their eschatological expectations with, among other things, rumours of falling stars and news of the first Gulf War. In addition, the members of the SDA community mention comparatively more signs of the *las de*, claiming furthermore, again in contrast to the Catholic church leadership, that these have all occurred already in different countries.[85] While Catholics officially say that the date of the end of the world has not yet been determined, among the Adventists there is great unanimity that it would take place in 2000.[86] Accordingly Robert (80.), for example, told me that although he had planted pandanus palms, he did not want to look after them, since the earth might not last until they could be harvested in ten years time. However, if the Last Day of Judgement is more immediately imminent for Adventists than for Catholics, then the hope of heaven increases, as does the fear of hell. This fear strengthens the compulsion to obey, since in principle all breaches of the rules have consequences and, as Pastor Koya stated clearly in a sermon, whoever does not obey will go straight in the fire.[87] Consequently, in the Adventist interpretation, humans are basically permanently threatened by the possibility of incurring punishment for bad thoughts or deeds on the *las de* at the latest. All in all, the relatively detailed and general expectation of Jesus' arrival in the near future in connection with the end of the world represents a basic characteristic of Adventist Christianity. Not for nothing is the day of the week named in the self-designation 'Seventh-day Adventist Church' also the day on which the Last Judgement shall take place. The statement that Jesus will soon come and that one must then belong to his chosen ones forms an integral element of many remarks and sermons within the SDA community. The decision between heaven and hell, which is represented as being imminent, gives rise to a dualism which in general determines the beliefs of the Adventists more than the Catholics. Heaven and hell, God and the Devil, appear as antagonistic poles between which there are no mediations, transitions or ambivalences. Thus in the Adventist view, basically humans are not ambivalent beings either.[88]

Since Adventists also see a 'pathway to heaven' in their type of Christianity, the question of how they imagine life in heaven arises no less than with the Catholics. To begin with, unlike the Catholics they conceive heaven as a city they call the 'New Jerusalem', where there is not the absence of one's needs, but their complete satisfaction. According to Naki (56.) everyone will be happy always. Among things that will no longer exist in heaven, the Adventists cite work, hunger and death, as well as crimes, pain, tears, age, sickness, care, heat and cold.[89] In addition, like the Catholics here, the Adventists describe a comprehensive equality, which is expressed in the disappearance of differences with respect to gender, body size, age, skin colour, language, thoughts, actions and property. According to Naki (56.), everyone will be 'equal and like brothers', and no one will have children, wives or families of their own any more.[90] This comprehensive equality is also extended to nature, since, for Adventists as for Catholics, in heaven there are no mountains or valleys.[91] In comparison to the Catholics, the Adventists represent heaven even more clearly as a counter-prestation for the 'hard work' they perform. The words reproduced below, with which Pastor Koya concluded one of his sermons, stressed the desire not to alter the world, but to leave it. The more sombrely the world is described, the more attractive does heaven seem to be as a sort of 'anti-world':

> Jesus must come soon. Let us leave this place, where sickness… fear, cares, sorrow, sickness, tears, sexual offences and theft reign. We must leave this whole evil place and must quickly obtain this eternal life, in which there is no sickness, no trouble, no sorrow. There is no one who cries, goes hungry or becomes ill. Sickness of the eyes, of the teeth, of the limbs, all this does not exist. I wish to prepare people to obtain this life, I wish to leave this evil earth quickly.[92]

Since, for Adventists as much as for Catholics, their own form of Christianity appears as a contrast to the traditional culture, for them too the distancing from tradition goes along with a claim to a Christian identity. If, however, the Adventists carry out this distancing from tradition with greater rigidity, the rigidity of their assessment of themselves is also greater. Accordingly, in contrast to the Catholics, the Adventists affirm, even unofficially and in confidential conversations, that they are good Christians, that is, they respect all the rules, take part in community work, go to all services, pray regularly and have already achieved equality among their number.[93] Pastor Koya (46.) even claimed that there were neither quarrels nor fighting, nor any other bad customs. Obviously most members of the community are themselves convinced of this, since they collectively and spontaneously denied the rhetorical question Kevin posed during one Saturday service: 'In our church, can a man who drinks beer, hits another man and steals remain in this church?'[94] Accordingly, in Adventist thought the purity of the individual seems to extend to the whole community, which, like the individual, represents, as it were, the embodiment of God. So just as the individual seeks after purity, not through gradual change, but through the removal of impurity, so too the purity of the community as a whole is achieved through the removal of individual members who to some extent are thought of as impure. In one prayer, Pastor Koya expressed the wish that God may expel all those who cannot go to heaven from the Church of the Seventh-day Adventists because they are still thinking of some forbidden food or other, or still playing cards.[95] Here, Adventist villagers very frequently stress how difficult it is for them and how many privations it costs them, to follow all the prohibitions and commandments. In many sermons and interviews, it is remarked that, in Adventist Christianity, the Word of God is 'pleasant to hear' but 'difficult to follow'.[96] Obviously, therefore, the efforts with which one presses for obedience even gives rise to a certain pride. Finally, the Adventists share with the Catholics the idea that, as good Christians, they participate in the power of God. According to Muya (55.), only those who belong to the SDA community are led by God and, for example, are spared as individuals in attacks. According to Robert (83.), up until now no Adventist villager has fallen victim to an accident or illness. Kevin (45.) pointed out the power of prayer by saying that God fulfils every wish if you ask him Saturday after Saturday. Naki (58.) said that, if you pray, unlike the Catholics, you do not have any fear even on long journeys.

Adventists do not restrict themselves to describing themselves as good Christians officially as well as unofficially. They even see themselves as basically the only true Christians. Thus the rigidity of the Adventists' assessment of themselves leads to a claim to exclusivity, which is expressed in the statement that only baptised members of the SDA community can go to heaven. Adventists justify this claim to exclusivity through the history they ascribe to their church. According to Pastor Koya, originally the service was conducted by Jesus and his disciples on the Sabbath. Only in AD 528, under Satan's influence, did the King of Rome decree a 'Sunday law' (*sande lo*), ordering that the divine service be moved from the Sabbath to Sunday on pain of death. In the following 1,260 years – a number given in Revelation 12,6, according to Pastor Koya – a total of 52,000,000 Christians, that is, adherents of the Sabbath, have fallen victim to the *sande lo*; thus until 1798 no more services took place on the Sabbath.[97] Accordingly the Sabbath is the day of the divine service, prescribed by God himself and also kept by Jesus, whereas the move to Sunday is ultimately to be traced back to an error caused by Satan. In the Adventist view, therefore, it follows that the only church that fully corresponds to the will of God is the one that holds its divine service on the Sabbath, which means the Church of the Seventh-day Adventists alone. Accordingly, Adventist inhabitants of Pairundu informed me right in my first interviews with them that in Papua New Guinea there were altogether seven hundred different churches, of which, however, only the seven-hundredth – that is, their own – represented a 'Sabbath church' (*sabbat lotu*). All the others, by contrast, were arranged in the manner of the Catholics as 'Sunday churches' (*sande lotu*).[98] Naki assured me that basically there are only two sorts of churches, the church of God and the church of Satan – one Sabbath church and 699 Sunday churches.[99] The frequently used self-designation as a 'church of God' (*church bilong God*) gives expression to the conviction that only this church out of all of them fully corresponds to the will of God. In my view, the dualism that is typical of Adventist thought manifests itself in the idea that the existing churches worship either God or the Devil. The Adventist claim to exclusivity appears as the expression of a certainty of salvation, which assures the Adventists, relatively speaking, that they truly understand God's message and that

Adventist Christianity does not have any secrets that have been hidden up to now.[100] Unlike the Catholics, therefore, not even the 'ordinary' members of the Adventist community ever asked me – not even in confidential conversations – to tell them or to answer questions about when the end of the world would come, or what would happen in 2000.[101]

In comparing Catholic and Adventist ideas, some similarities emerge. In the first place, Catholics and Adventists agree in thinking that acceptance of their respective form of Christianity presupposes a prior distancing from tradition. According to the official emic view, the Catholic or Adventist Christianity respectively that has replaced the now obliterated traditional religion counts as a 'pathway to heaven'. This 'pathway' is understood as 'hard work' consisting of various elements. In both denominations, the goal of heaven is defined as negatively – that is, marked by the absence of everything that characterises life in this world – as the pathway, which is marked primarily by prohibitions and commandments. Together with the need for social withdrawal propagated especially by the Adventists, the requirement to obey prohibitions and commandments can be understood as a demand for passivity. Accordingly, when the Kome as a whole ascribe for themselves a passive role in representing their own past (Chapter 2), this could be put down to the influence of missionisation. The heaven that people aim for is unanimously described as a place of all-embracing equality by both Catholics and Adventists. Officially it is claimed that this equality has been realised in one's own community as much as has protection from sickness and misfortune, which comes from participation in God's power. The adherents of both denominations thus hope for a quick answer to the question whether they have carried out their 'hard work' successfully, for both believe that the Last Day of Judgement, as the day of decision between heaven and hell, between reward and punishment, is more or less imminent.

The differences between Catholic and Adventist beliefs are, on the whole, less substantial than gradual, since the Adventists in general are characterised by their comparatively greater rigidity. It is as if the Adventists take up Catholic beliefs and develop them further in the direction of intensifying them. Thus, for example, the Adventists surpass the Catholics in distancing themselves from tradition and in stressing obedience, since, unlike the Catholics, for them even a small breach of the rules holds out the danger of causing sickness and death, or preventing access to heaven.[102] Alongside this, Muya's comment, that God is as likely to let one into heaven for nothing as one is to obtain a harvest without planting, indicates the conviction that, to some extent, access to heaven is a counter-prestation for 'hard work'. If carrying out this work as a gift in conformity with all the prohibitions and commandments brings forth a counter-prestation, almost by compulsion – if, therefore, the desired reciprocity is to be enforced primarily by keeping to the rules – then this idea should be described as legalistic. I see a further expression of rigidity, finally, in the dualism according to which, for the members of the SDA community, the whole world appears to be realised, as it were, in the dichotomy between God and Satan, heaven and hell, so that, for example, a sole church of God is distinguished from all the churches of Satan. Such a clear evaporation of all ambivalences – also in the view of the individual – may create the impression that there were simple answers to all questions. In comparison with the Catholics, the rigidity of the Adventists, as expressed in the emphasis on obedience, legalism and dualism, leads to a comparatively greater convergence between official and unofficial views, between the positions of the representatives of the church leadership and 'ordinary' members of the community. This concerns not only the question whether traditional transcendent authorities and magical practices are still effective today, but also the interpretation of baptism, the expectation of the end of the world and people's own self-assessments.[103] Out of this greater convergence between the official and unofficial views on the Adventist side, there also arises a relatively marked certainty of salvation, as comes from Bible instruction, which the Adventists believe provides them with an all-embracing competence. The certainty of salvation finds its clearest expression in the claim to exclusiveness that is made by the Adventists in contrast to the Catholics and that goes along with the claim the Adventists make for themselves of an individual and collective purity. Taken together, the certainty of salvation and the claim to exclusiveness form the precondition for the frequently observed efforts, supported by representatives of the church leadership like Pastor Koya and Kevin, to persuade Catholics to switch community affiliation and convert.[104] This missionisation effort with respect to the other denomination comes exclusively from the Adventist side, not the Catholics. It has been part of the Adventist community in Pairundu since it was founded and, as its growth shows, has not been without success. Also in relation to myself, compared to the Catholics, the Adventists generally showed much greater interest in explaining their beliefs to me as such.

During my fieldwork, I was only able to discern serious changes in beliefs in sermons and interviews in the case of Coleman Makoa. On 30 June 1991, for the first time in a sermon, he said, to my surprise, that pigs were bad animals and one should not eat too much of their meat.[105] On 4 August 1991, also during a Sunday service, he claimed that after having read the Bible the priest had prohibited the enjoyment of beer, betel nuts and tobacco, as well as the consumption of birds, tree kangaroos and pigs. Then an excited discussion immediately broke out, during which Ari, among others, asked how people were to earn money without pigs. Already, the evening before the 4 August, Coleman Makoa had told me in an informal conversation that the new prohibitions had been decreed by the Pope with effect from 1992 and that in the future one might have to follow the 'SDA custom' (*pasin SDA*). These new views, which neither found any resonance nor have been able to influence the Catholic community discernibly, represent an attempt to move towards the SDA position in content – a move incidentally criticised by Kenneth (42.).

Cult practices

While the foregoing discussion of Catholic and Adventist beliefs is based primarily on official and unofficial statements that I collected in sermons, formal interviews and informal conversations, the following descriptions of Catholic and Adventist cult practices are based mainly on observations I was able to make during fieldwork.[106] The most important cult practices of the Catholics are held regularly on Sunday, since Jesus is also supposed to have risen on a Sunday. In addition, evening services take place irregularly on different days of the week.[107] Before the Sunday services, which mostly take place in the church building in Pairundu** (no. 25 in Map 3) between 10.00 and 14.00 and last about two hours, the catechist Coleman Makoa calls the congregation together by beating several times on the rim of a car wheel called a 'belo'.[108] The church is built in the traditional manner, as a rectangular building with a gabled roof, though in contrast to the old men's houses it does not stand on posts and has wickerwork walls (*blain*). The main door is located in the cross wall facing westwards and is decorated with a white wooden cross. The two cross walls have diamond-shaped, open windows under the roof. Inside the church stand two wooden boxes and a table covered with a cloth that serves as an altar. The community follows the service sitting on the floor, the men on the right facing the altar, the women on the left. The older children sit in the first rows, mostly separated according to gender, while small children and infants remain with their mothers. Usually individuals occupy the same places each time.

In discussing the Sunday services, I shall first describe how they should appear in the ideal case according to Kenneth (39.), that is, corresponding to the church regulations, and then go into the deviations that were actually observed. According to Kenneth, the Sunday service begins with the catechist standing in front of the altar and greeting the congregation, singing an opening hymn with them and crossing himself. Then he says a prayer and calls on the congregation to repent of the sins they have committed since the previous Sunday. Different prayers follow, which are spoken aloud by the congregation in chorus and then by the catechist alone. Then the catechist sits at the side and one of the *prayer lida* steps up to the altar, takes a Bible out of one of the wooden boxes and reads out a text from the Old Testament. Then he changes places with another *prayer lida*, who reads a passage from the letters in the New Testament.[109] When the *prayer lida* sits down again, the congregation sings a hymn and the catechist again goes up to the altar in order to read from the Gospel. In choosing any text, he must follow a church calendar distributed by the priest giving the passages in the Bible to be used for each Sunday. Another hymn sung by the congregation is followed by the catechist's sermon, in which he should refer especially to the word of the Gospel and, for example, deal with questions concerning how far the Old Testament prophets prepared Jesus' work and the possible parallels between the Bible and the congregation's own tradition. Usually the sermon mentions the basic ideas in the particular text from the Gospel and provides an illustrated parable and finally an explanation of the parable, as well as, often, the demands that arise out of it. The catechist can also take parables from a plan distributed by the priest, though he is not obliged to do so. After the sermon, the congregation sits still for a few moments until the catechist says two prayers with them out loud. Then he sits at the side again and the collection is made.[110] This ends to the accompaniment of a hymn sung by everyone. Then the catechist steps up in front of the altar, says a prayer and sits down at the side again. Now the *komunio lida* takes a plastic vessel from the second wooden box together with the *komunio* or wafers that the priest has blessed beforehand. The *komunio lida* holds these wafers aloft one after the other in order to distribute them to the individual members of the congregation, who slowly move past him. The consumption of the *komunio* is regarded as the re-enactment of the Last Supper as described in the Bible. When the *komunio lida* and all the other members of the congregation have resumed their places, the catechist stands up and says a prayer, first alone and then with the congregation. Finally, the congregation sings a hymn and the catechist ends the service by crossing himself again. Basically, all prayers, hymns and readings, as well as the sermon, are in Kewa.[111] Most prayers are said with heads bowed and eyes closed. The reading out of the different Bible passages is not preceded by any announcement of the lines, verse, book or letter being referred to. The congregation accompanies most hymns, whose choice and number are a matter for the catechist, with rhythmic handclapping.[112]

However, there are usually differences between this 'ideal type' as described by Kenneth and the actual events that can be observed on individual Sundays, so that, within particular boundaries, the Sunday service proves to be relatively variable.[113] Still before the opening hymn, Mayanu or Ari occasionally report on earlier meetings of the church committees of the region, and Coleman Makoa calls the names of the community members to check their attendance. At the end of the service, he sometimes announces the time and place of the community work for the coming week. Kenneth considered many of these deviations to be breaches of the rules on the part of Coleman Makoa. I could see, too, that the chosen Bible passages did not always correspond with what was laid down in the church calendar.[114] On the other hand, the fact that the number of hymns, prayers and Bible texts read out varies,[115] as does, therefore, the total length of services, is not seen as problematic. Some changes only found acceptance temporarily and were given up again later.

For example, this was the case with the guitar accompaniment that was provided for certain hymns, which rang out for a number of Sundays from 13 May 1991, but was then forgotten. Then some of the women began, at the beginning of June and again in mid-August, to decorate the floor of the church, the altar and the two wooden boxes with flowers.[116] The attempt by Ari and Mayanu from 4 August 1991 to take over disciplinary functions during services by positioning themselves on the side wall or the entry door with a stick, which they used to wake those who were sleeping and exhort those who were talking to keep quiet, did not last long either. However, other innovations were retained, for example, the use, from 13 May 1991, of Tok Pisin for some hymns and Bible texts, though without Coleman Makoa always translating them into Kewa afterwards. While in the following weeks use of Tok Pisin did recede somewhat, from October 1991 it became a fixed part of the Sunday service. Only the Gospel and the sermon remained strictly reserved for Kewa. In addition, from the end of October 1991, Coleman Makoa began to announce, or have someone else announce, the line, verse, book or letter of each Bible text before reading them out. According to Kenneth (42.), however, since such announcements tempt the congregation to flick through the pages of the Bible and prevent them from hearing the reading, they are forbidden in the context of divine services as much as the use of Tok Pisin, which older people would not understand.

On the whole, assessing the major cult practices of the Catholic inhabitants of Pairundu, it appears that most of the sermons that are based on prescribed passages in the Bible rarely address the immediate, day-to-day problems of village life. My impression is that interest in the Sunday service varies considerably. While I sometimes thought I detected an emotional participation in the case of many people in the congregation, especially during hymns that were accompanied by rhythmic handclapping, on other Sundays I had rather the feeling of being present at the unenthusiastic performance of a routine. Generally, a certain level of noise is always noticeable, since many members of the congregation converse with one another, children cry, and women wander round with their children or return to their places. Apparently, this does not prevent some people present from spending most of the time asleep, which the others usually greet with smiles. However, Sundays do have a special significance from the social point of view, since they bring a large part of the community together on a regular basis.[117] After the service especially, questions of general importance are frequently discussed in conversations that sometimes go on until sunset, for example court cases with other villages or the nomination of candidates for future elections. People like Amakoa and Ruben, who usually stay away from the church, do take part in such discussions. The members of the Catholic community usually mark Sundays – on which, in the general view, one should not carry out either house-building or garden work – by wearing cleaner and better clothes, which they would not otherwise use during the week. This

'Sunday best' consists of short-sleeved shirts and short trousers for men, though one can sometimes also see the traditional bark belt.

The evening services that took place sporadically on weekdays and were also called 'lotu' were gradually introduced by mid-May, stopped again for about two weeks, taken up again for about six weeks between the beginning of July and mid-August, stopped again and held once more during the second half of September.[118] However, Coleman Makoa participated in them as little as did most other Auro Kome. The readiness to conduct evening services generally increases at full moon and when stars can clearly be seen in the night sky. Given this readiness, the Rata Kome mostly meet under the leadership of Sayna either in Ari's house (no. 26 in Map 3) or in the church building, while the Alia Kome, under the leadership of Neambunu, assemble in the houses of either Alupa (no. 45) or Rekepea (no. 52). Sometimes Rata Kome and Alia Kome also meet in the church building, in which case Sayna or Neambunu beat the *belo*. In the church building a maximum of ten to fifteen participants, not separated by gender, sits in a circle, though otherwise not in any fixed order. A typical evening service begins with hymns and a prayer said by the leader. Then a Bible text is discussed, which the leader reads out as a whole and also in short sections, without identifying it precisely beforehand. Further hymns follow, plus prayers said by the leader and then by all participants together and a final hymn. The hymns, which are usually accompanied by rhythmic handclapping, are in Kewa, as are the readings and discussion. Like the Sunday services, the evening services also vary, though to a comparatively lesser extent. In any case, the number of hymns sung, the length of the discussion and thus the total length of the service are matters for the respective participants alone. In choosing the Bible texts for discussion, the leader relies on various methods. She can decide the text herself, she can follow a plan published by the church leadership prescribing a particular passage in the Bible for each day, or she can appoint someone to open the Bible without looking and pointing to a paragraph. However, the value of this practice is controversial. While Ripu thinks that the Bible provides answers to actual questions in this way, Kenneth said that one is certainly allowed to proceed like this, but not too often, at most twice a month, otherwise the Church's plan should be used. Sr Marie, on the other hand, admittedly talking about the Holy Spirit movement, rejected the practice of 'opening the Bible blind'. A further change occasionally made consists in laying the Bible in a circle of flowers. After an evening service conducted in Pairundu** on 6 June 1991, Sayna distributed the flowers that had been used, saying that they would cause dreams if laid next to the head at night. All in all, I had the impression that, in contrast to the Sunday services, only those who share a stronger motivation meet for evening services. Thus on these evenings a comparatively greater degree of emotional participation is evident, the overall noise level is less,[119] and usually no one sleeps. The discussions of the Bible passages that are read out are uncontroversial. Instead, the text that has just been heard is reformulated through a process of consensus, in order to support, for example, exhortations to follow all prohibitions and commandments better in the future. From time to time, an attempt is even made to refer texts to present-day conflicts in the village, so that in general, when compared to the Sunday services, a closer link is made between the cult practice and the concrete life situation. In general, men lead the discussion – especially Ripu in Pairundu** and Ata Francis in Porai – though women also express their views from time to time, as when, for example, they occasionally complain that they have not properly understood the text that has been read out. For this reason, on 27 May 1991 Yapanu and Puku demanded of Sayna that in future she should read the selected passages in the Bible in the daytime, in order to be able to explain them better in the evening. Unlike to the Sunday services, no special clothing is worn to the evening services.

The most important cult practices of the Adventists are held regularly on Saturday, the Sabbath, since, according to the Adventist view, God first rested on the Sabbath after creating the world and since the shifting of the divine service to Sundays allegedly does not correspond to His will. Other cult practices take place on different days of the week, in the mornings and evenings. The members of the SDA community hold their Sabbath services roughly between 9.00 and 13.00, with a total length of three hours, in the church in Pokaranda (no. 17 in Map 3). As with the Catholics, the congregation is summoned beforehand by beating a car wheel rim called a 'belo'.[120] The Adventists' church is also a rectangular building built at ground level with wickerwork walls and a gable roof, though in this case the corners of the roof have been rounded off. Unlike the Catholics, in the long side facing the forecourt are two small doors and two rectangular windows covered with wire mesh. The left-hand door leads to a table provided with a desk and serving as an altar, which stands in front of a wooden bench. Through this door come those who will assume the functions of the service. The congregation, by contrast, usually enters through the right-hand door, in order to seat themselves on the wooden benches that stand to the right and left of the middle aisle that leads to the altar. The left bench, facing the altar, is usually occupied by the men, the right by the women. As among the Catholics, the older children sit, separated according to gender, in the first few rows, while small children and infants remain with their mothers. In addition, with the Adventists too individuals usually occupy the same places from service to service. In contrast to the Catholics, however, the Adventists never decorate their church with flowers. The Sabbath service itself is rooted in the larger context of the Sabbath as a whole, which lasts from sunset on Friday to sunset on Saturday. During this period, any work, including the preparation of food, is forbidden. As a result, many Adventists make an earth oven before the evening service on Friday, so that they can feed themselves from the food that has been prepared up to Saturday evening.

Saturday morning usually begins with a full wash often lasting several hours. After the Sabbath service, people usually remain together during the afternoon until the evening service that ends the Sabbath. In this period, people sit in the church or on the forecourt, talking or practising new hymns. From time to time people also enquire about individuals who have repeatedly stayed away from services. More frequently, however, neighbouring villages are visited, as in the context of the communal work that takes place on other days, in order to bear witness and sing hymns. In contrast to the Catholics, therefore, the Adventists have, as it were, structurally rooted the element of missionisation that is based on their belief. In my view, the Sabbath has the same significance for Adventists as Sunday for the Catholics.

In the course of my fieldwork, individual Sabbath services did not differ from one another as much as the Catholic Sunday services. Therefore, instead of first discussing an 'ideal type' and then depicting the actual deviations that emerged, in what follows I shall describe as an example the cult practices I attended on 14 September 1991 and took notes at: Alex started by standing between the altar and the left-hand door facing the sitting congregation and by beginning to sing different hymns one after the other, which were then sung together. Alex either chose these hymns himself or called on all the men, or all the women, or all the visitors from a particular village, for example, to name the titles of their choice. The hymns ceased abruptly when Coleman Komea, Piu and Kandipia entered and sat down on the wooden bench at the back of the altar, facing the congregation. After a moment Piu and Kandipia got up, and Piu welcomed those present in Kewa, before listing and numbering consecutively the visitors from the different villages and lastly adding the inhabitants of Pairundu. Kandipia translated individual sections of the welcome speech into Tok Pisin. Then, like Coleman Komea, Piu and Kandipia knelt down and prayed, followed silently and with eyes closed by the seated congregation. As soon as the three kneelers resumed their places, the first 'special item' followed. This consisted of a group moving forward, mostly standing right next to the altar and singing a hymn in chorus, before sitting down again. The number of hymns presented in such 'special items' varies, as does the composition of the groups, but people are especially keen to see them when they come from another village. After the 'special item', Coleman Komea knelt again with the entire congregation and said a prayer out aloud with eyes closed. The first collection was then made. While the congregation sang a hymn with the title 'Let the toeas drop in', individuals stepped forward and placed money, their *tait*, on the altar. Then Robert and Don entered and Don presented the so-called *misin stori*, in other words he recounted some of the history of the SDA Church.[121] Robert translated this into Kewa. At the next point in the programme too, the book-keeping described as *kisim ripot*, Don spoke Tok Pisin and Robert Kewa. Don checked the attendance of the individual members of the congregation and asked, for example, how many people prayed regularly, bore witness in other villages, helped others or took part in community work. He recorded the answers in lists, which, it is said, are sent via Kagua, Ialibu and Mount Hagen to Australia and America. Following a further 'special item', everyone stood up and closed their eyes, and Kandipia said a prayer out loud in Tok Pisin.

With this, the first part of the Sabbath service came to an end, to be followed by Bible instruction, splitting the congregation up into groups of the baptised, the *klas baptais* and the *klas redi*. One group remained in the church, while the other two sat separately on the forecourt. Each group was instructed by a different person, who read from the Bible after a common prayer, asked questions about it, led the discussion of these questions and then led a prayer to end with.

The third part of the service again began with Alex starting to sing hymns, calling on the congregation to rise before many of them. When Robert came in and announced the community work for the coming week in a short speech, the hymns ceased immediately, only to be resumed after Robert's departure, until Don, Amos and Robert entered and took their seats on the wooden bench behind the altar. Whoever is going to give the sermon always sits in the middle. Then Don and Robert stood up and, as in the first part of the service, Robert gave a short welcome speech in Tok Pisin, which Don translated into Kewa. Then Don and Robert prayed silently together with Amos who was also standing up and with the congregation, before a 'special item' followed. Then Don knelt together with the congregation, in order to say a prayer out loud in Tok Pisin. As soon as everyone had resumed their places again, Robert administered the second collection accompanied by another 'special item' by going around and collecting the money. In comparison to the Catholics, the Adventist collection contains no goods in kind and in relation to the number of visitors seems more comprehensive, being done twice. Finally the sermon, as the last item in the programme, was preceded by a last 'special item'. The sermon, which was given by Amos standing at the desk in Kewa, was translated into Tok Pisin in sections by Don, who was also standing. After beginning the sermon, Amos said a prayer as a preparation for a longer quotation from the Bible, before continuing with his performance. In contrast to the Catholics, the Adventists only use the Tok Pisin Bible.[122] Moreover, those giving the sermons select which Bible passages to use themselves, always announcing or identifying them by giving the line, verse, book or letter. Such information runs through the whole sermon, so that altogether far more different Bible passages are referred to and also cited than among the Catholics. Instead of dealing with a single text, therefore, there is rather a combination of a great variety of different texts. Although SDA preachers are thus not tied to particular quotations and themes, for the most part they are no more likely to engage with the present-day problems of village life than are the Catholic preachers. Amos ended his performance with an appeal to the congregation to approve him, rise up and sing a hymn, before he said a prayer to conclude the service, in which the still standing congregation took part. Including the greetings and announcements, the *misin stori* and the *kisim ripot* as well as the sermon, basically most of the parts of the Saturday service are translated either from Tok Pisin into Kewa or vice versa. An exception are the prayers that are said in one or the other language, partly silently, partly out loud, partly standing, partly kneeling, partly sitting and with heads bowed and eyes closed. Unlike among the Catholics, hymns are sung without rhythmic handclapping or guitar accompaniment, as well as almost exclusively in Tok Pisin, while the men and the women sometimes sing verses alternately.

The Adventists number their Sabbath services consecutively, generally endowing the thirteenth Sabbath, which always brings a quarter to an end, with special significance. Any service held on this occasion continues until the sermon, as do all the others. However, the congregation then divides along gender lines into two groups, in which, accompanied by hymns, they wash one another's feet by putting them in already provided buckets of water and then drying them. Then the communion is distributed, consisting first of small pieces of biscuit, then of small glasses of wine, taken together respectively with closed eyes at the command of the pastor. Both the foot-washing and the taking of communion count as a re-enactment of the Biblical example of Jesus and thus also as a precondition for access to heaven. Thus only baptised members of the congregation, the *church memba*, may take part in foot-washing and communion.[123] The thirteenth Sabbath service usually took place in Kagua. I myself was able to attend such a service on 30 March 1991. Since Adventist communities from Sumbura and Kuali Lombo also participated, this was an important social event, which Adventists from Pairundu were already talking about weeks beforehand by happily pointing out to me that they would soon be going to Kagua for 'foot-washing'. On 17 August 1991, foot-washing and communion were conducted in the church building in Pairundu.[124]

In comparison with the Catholic Sunday service, a Sabbath service contains a greater number of different elements and different functions, which are always taken over by different people from one Saturday to another.[125] Within a relatively stable structure this produces a larger number and fluctuation of functionaries, which in turn leads to a greater degree of variety.[126] Among the functionaries whom the layman Kevin names, mostly before the start of the cult practices, are also young men and women. The women, for example, can take over greetings, announcements or the leading of prayers, though, in contrast to the men, they are not allowed to preach any more than they are among the Catholics.[127] The sermon was claimed by Kevin on most Saturdays, when, for example, Pastor Koya did not attend. My impression is that a relatively tight discipline prevailed at Sabbath services on the whole, indicated, for example, by the fact that no one sleeps and that there is less background noise relative to the number of participants. No one talks at the same time and if children cry, their mothers take them outside the church building either straightaway or after being warned by Robert or Muya. Alongside this are the efforts to obtain cleanliness, expressed in both the emphasis on washing the body before the service and the use of particularly clean and undamaged clothing on the Sabbath. Unlike among the Catholics, however, for men this clothing does not include the bark belt but long suit trousers and white long-sleeved shirts, sometimes combined with a necktie and for women long white dresses. Also, unlike the Catholics, head coverings are prohibited. The cleanliness of the body and of clothing corresponds to the inner individual and collective purity that the Adventists strive for or lay claim to.

Apart from the Sabbath services, evening services, announced by striking the *belo*, take place ideally every day, though in reality four or five times a week at most, but certainly on Wednesdays, Fridays and Saturdays, between about 17.00 and 18.00, for about thirty to forty-five minutes. In addition, thirty-minute morning services should be held daily between 7.30 and 9.00 in the church, though on average they are cancelled three or four times a week, whenever Kevin is visiting other villages. As with the Sabbath services, the individual participants always sit in the same places, both morning and evening, the men occupying the left-hand bench, the women the right-hand. A typical evening service consists of a series of communal hymns, communal prayers said first sitting and then kneeling, a sermon and a prayer said standing, followed finally by a hymn that is always sung standing.[128] The preacher, standing facing the congregation, can not only lead the prayers and hymns, but also translate from Kewa into Tok Pisin or vice versa. Sometimes, however, the sermon and its translation are delivered by two different people, who then both stand in front of the congregation. The sermon, which Kevin delegates to other members of the congregation from time to time but more usually preaches himself, is sometimes linked to a brochure obtained from Kagua called a *lesson buk*, each treating a particular part of the Bible for the period of a quarter,[129] and providing a specific passage in the Bible for each day of that quarter, together with questions and food for thought. In accordance with the information given by Pastor Koya (46.), however, to the effect that one does not have to keep to the *lesson buk* too closely, I could not see any connection between the sermon and the particular text at the evening services I attended. Adventist villagers accord a comparatively greater significance to the evening cult practices that take place on Wednesdays and Fridays and that are usually led by Kevin by washing the body beforehand, unlike at other evening services and wearing clothing that is otherwise only used on Saturdays. Moreover, numerous visitors from other villages usually arrive and are greeted with a special speech as on Saturday. Whereas the Friday evening service takes its relevance from the fact that it begins the Sabbath period, the Wednesday evening service is marked by the events that follow the sermon. After problems of general importance are mentioned and those present who feel themselves weighed down with trouble or sicknesses call out their names, the members of the congregation, separated according to gender, divide into pairs of two persons, kneel down, clasp hands and say their own prayers, more or less silently, with heads bowed and eyes closed, some in Tok Pisin and some in Kewa. In these prayers, they ask forgiveness for their own transgressions, for the solution of the problems mentioned and finally for help for those who have called out their names.

In contrast to the evening services, the briefer morning services are led only by Kevin. They consist of a series of prayers and hymns, between which Kevin briefly discusses a Bible verse, usually in Kewa. Here too he can fall back on the *lesson buk*, which lists a passage from the Bible for each day, the so-called 'moning was ves'. My observations suggest that individual evening and morning services do not vary very much from one another.[130] Moreover, in comparison with the Catholics, there is a much smaller difference between the evening services and the larger services that take place once a week. The Adventists' evening cult practices seem rather like a smaller version of the Sabbath service shortened by a few elements. Unlike the assemblies led by Sayna or Neambunu on the Catholic side, the SDA evening cult practices do not involve discussions, but rather listening to the sermons. However, these usually make hardly any more reference to the actual problems of village life than the sermons that can be heard on Saturdays.

For the members of the SDA community, an evangelism week, which took place from 30 June to 6 July 1991 in Pairundu and concluded with the baptism of some members of the community, was a singular event that far surpassed the ordinary cult practices in significance and was a topic of conversation weeks beforehand and afterwards, even among the Catholics.[131] For the Adventist inhabitants of Pairundu, carrying out this event – which consisted, among other things, of five morning and seven evening services altogether, as well as a Sabbath service – required building a shed and a meeting house consisting of wooden scaffolding covered with a plastic tarpaulin brought from Kagua (see cover photo). Alongside this, food was prepared for visitors from Kagua, Sumbura and Kuali Lombo. The evening services began between 19.00 and 19.30 with prayers and hymns, followed by the answering of questions, which were said to have been set in the daytime, even by Catholics. Then the sermon was given, usually by Pastor Koya, but also twice by District Director May from the Markham valley and once by Pastor Epawa from Erave. Among other things spoken of were signs of the end of the world, the significance of Jesus and the legitimation of the Sabbath.[132] Then, up to the end of the meeting between 22.00 and 22.30, video clips from Bible films of North American provenance were shown. For most of the inhabitants of Pairundu and its area – who, even when they have lamps, can rarely afford the kerosene for them – it was already a considerable change from their day-to-day lives and therefore a great attraction, for the meeting house to be artificially lit by a generator brought from Kagua. A still greater attraction, though, were certainly the video clips that were shown, which, in my judgement, led to about two hundred people coming to each of the first evenings of the evangelism week, some coming from Wasuma, Anapote, Rulupare, Yakoa, Pira, Yaware, Sumi or Sua/Yeibu and including numerous Catholics. Of the Kome, as well as the Big Men Yawa and Wala, among others the Catholics Sayna, Neambunu, Ata Francis and even Coleman Makoa attended, even though the Catholic church committee in Pairundu had spoken out against participation.[133] The attraction of the new soon seems to have evaporated, however, since the number of visitors clearly fell on the fourth evening.

After the flesh of a communally purchased cow had been cooked and eaten on 5 July (Figure 4.2), the evangelism week ended on 6 July with the Sabbath service and the ensuing baptisms. These took place in the river to the west of Pasereanda that is called 'Yassaweli', like part of Ropena and had previously been dammed by Robert. Most of the inhabitants of Pairundu were present, with some exceptions including Coleman Makoa and Ipapula, but including all the members of the Catholic church committee, as well as numerous visitors from Wasuma, Yakoa, Sumi, Anapote and Sua/Yeibu, so that in my estimate the total number of people present was about one hundred fifty. Those being baptised stood together in a double line on the bank of the Yassaweli, the Adventists sang and prayed, and Pastor Koya gave a speech in which he pointed out that only the baptism by immersion that was usual among the Adventists corresponded to the example of Christ. Then he entered the water along with Pastor May and Pastor Epawa, where, acting together, they baptised three novices at a time, by first saying prayers and then ducking them backwards until they were completely immersed (Figure 4.3). Afterwards the newly baptised arranged themselves in a line, to which those who also intended to convert to the Adventists were then supposed to attach themselves. This line was then inspected by all those present, including the Catholics, shaking hands with them. Although shortly after the baptism only the novices themselves were crying, somewhat later first most of the Adventists and then very many of the Catholics also burst into floods of tears. These included people like Ripu, Pogola, Yapanu and Ari, who, with Alex, counted one of the novices among their close family members, but also many that this did not apply to.[134]

The comparison of Catholic and Adventist cult practices shows that in both cases a weekday is chosen for large services and that these are marked by wearing especially clean and well-maintained clothing, as well as avoiding day-to-day work. This day is also endowed with considerable social significance, since it usually brings together most members of each community. All in all, the Adventists spend more time in their church building than the Catholics in theirs, since not only do

Figure 4.2 Communal meal concluding the Seventh-day Adventists' evangelism week (Rakepanda, 5 July 1991; photo: Holger Jebens).

they hold evening and morning services more frequently, their Sabbath service also lasts longer on average than a Catholic Sunday service. However, the Sabbath service, with its many individual elements, which rapidly follow one another and are interrupted by hymns and prayers, offers a relatively great degree of variation. In addition, the community has to rely on its own efforts in larger measure. It appoints numerous office-holders who themselves seek out hymns, stand for prayers and hymns, or kneel for prayers, which are less fixed among the Adventists than among the Catholics. Alongside this, the members of the congregation must themselves take part in the discussion of the

Figure 4.3 Seventh-day Adventists Coleman Komea, Don and Alex (clockwise) are baptised (between Pasereanda and Wapuanda, 6 July 1991; photo: Holger Jebens).

instruction, for which purpose some of them leave the church. At the end of the sermon, an appeal is usually made to them for their approval and for them to stand up and sing a hymn. Whereas, among the Catholics, it is always the same small circle of individuals that reads only a few preselected Bible passages, among the Adventists there is, as already described, a larger number and fluctuation of functionaries, who choose the many Bible passages used during their sermons at will. In my view, this is not only an indication of autonomy, but also of equality, since to some extent the variety of functionaries also includes young men and even women in part. The greater variety and involvement of the community, compared with the Catholic Sunday services, may make the Sabbath services much more entertaining for those taking part in them.

At the same time, however, the rigidity typical of the Adventists is expressed in their cult practices as much as in their beliefs. Thus, for example, even food preparation is forbidden on Saturdays and in general a comparatively greater discipline prevails in the church building. This discipline is based not least on the checks that are carried out through the regular *kisim ripot*, as well as on the relatively frequent visits of Pastor Koya, who comes to Pairundu much more frequently than Fr Matthias among the Catholics. Moreover, the larger number and fluctuation of functionaries necessarily leads to mutual supervision. To that extent it is not surprising that, in contrast to the procedures led by Coleman Makoa, the Adventist cult practices do not contain any parts that the representatives of the church leadership classify as being against the rules. Another indication of the rigidity of the Adventists, which simultaneously constitutes a further difference between themselves and the Catholics, may be considered the fact that Adventist cult practices remained basically unchanged during my fieldwork, whereas, in the case of the Catholic Sunday services, innovations were to be observed. These were supposedly introduced to increase their attractiveness and entertainment value, as with the temporary introduction of guitar music and flower decorations, but they also appear to have constituted attempts to come nearer to the Adventists in respect to the outward form of the cult practices. Among such adaptations, for example, that were attempted especially by Coleman Makoa were the use of Tok Pisin and the identification of the respective Bible passages to the congregation, as well as the announcement of the cult practices by striking the *belo* and the introduction of evening and morning services, both of which, according to Muya, were taken over directly from the Adventists.[135] These changes, which Robert (80.) commented on by saying that the Catholics would perhaps soon begin washing each other's feet in the church, were partly subjected to Kenneth's (42.) criticisms as much as were Coleman Makoa's corresponding attempts to approach more nearly to the Adventists in respect of the content of belief.

Relations between the two denominations

Having described the community structures, basic beliefs and cult practices of the two communities represented in Pairundu, I now describe the relationships of the adherents of the two denominations with one another. Instructive in this respect is how Adventists and Catholics judge one another. Here various conflicts must be taken into account. Sometimes the members of the two communities turn against each other, and sometimes they regard themselves as being commonly confronted by members of other clans.

In the context of the official view, the Adventists judge the Catholics relatively moderately. According to Pastor Koya, Jesus died not only for the Adventists, but also for the Catholics and Lutherans, whom He loves equally.[136] To my question whether the Catholics can go to heaven like the Adventists, Muya (55.) answered that he did not know, while Pastor Koya (46.) said that this was always possible for those who have not yet heard that one must hold the divine service on the Sabbath. In the context of the unofficially formulated view, on the other hand, the Adventist claim to exclusivity produces a much more negative judgement. If only the Church that holds its major cult practices on Saturdays is a Church of God, then all other Churches are necessarily not Churches of God and are even Churches of Satan. As Naki (56.) explained, for example, as a result Catholics are already excluded from access to heaven, among other things because they have offended against the fourth commandment, which requires the keeping of the Sabbath. This view is only rarely articulated, though in principle it is still shared by all Adventists. From the Adventist point of view, therefore, the difference between the official and unofficial positions in judging the Catholics is greater than in the case of the respective evaluations of the traditional culture, views of Christianity or assessments of one's own community. Since, for the Adventists, their Christian identity arises in the first instance from their following the appropriate prohibitions and commandments, the accusation made by Pastor Koya, among others, that the Catholics allow everything and prohibit nothing is especially serious to them.[137] According to Robert (81.), the Catholics – like Amakoa, for example, who married a second wife even after his baptism – are basically just continuing the life they were already living in the pre-colonial period.[138] When, however, following specific rules is especially required in order, as it were, to change from adherents of the traditional religion into Christians, then a lack of such rules means that this change has not yet taken place. Thus in accusing the Catholics of allowing everything and prohibiting nothing, the Adventists are implicitly claiming that the Catholics are not only not Christians, but in addition that they are still following the traditional religion. Precisely because the Catholics hold their major cult practices on a Sunday, that is, on the day of the sun, in the Adventist's view they are worshipping not God, but the sun or humans, since in the Adventist version it was originally a human who shifted the divine service from Saturday to Sunday.[139] In one sermon Pastor May declared: 'Heathens worship the sun, they worship stones, they worship cows, they worship many things, they worship crocodiles, they worship everything possible, that's heathens for you'.[140] Here, admittedly, Catholics are not directly mentioned by name, but nonetheless all the Adventists who had been listening might well agree that, by heathens who worship the sun and who by worshipping stones are still caught up in the traditional religion, only Catholics can be meant.[141] This assessment simultaneously justifies Adventist attempts to missionise. If, as heathens and adherents of the traditional religion, the Catholics are near to eternal damnation at the coming end of the world, then the Adventists are obliged to missionise them and persuade them to convert to Christianity, that is, Adventist Christianity, in order to give them an opportunity to escape the hell that threatens them and to enter heaven too.

The members of the SDA community certainly not only prophesy God's punishment for the Catholic villagers, they also believe that they will fall victims to the Catholics in future themselves. These views are linked with the idea of a 'Sunday Law' (*sande lo*) and in my judgement are shared by more or less all Adventists in Pairundu. Already on 1 March 1991, Alex (1.) pointed out to me that, according to a law decreed by Pope John Paul II, in this year or the next, only Sunday services would be allowed, so that all Adventists would soon be taken to court. On 9 April 1991, it was said that new banknotes were circulating with the Pope's face on them and that in 1994 the Catholics would kill all Adventists.[142] I only learned of these rumours from Alex. Otherwise, people were spreading them within the Adventist community only and on condition that they were not passed on to the Catholics. On 7 June 1991, however, Pastor Koya claimed publicly in a sermon that the Prime Ministers of 186 countries had either signed a law or would be decreeing one, according to which in future there would only be one world government, one currency and one Church, namely the Church of Sunday services. Whoever did not participate in these services, whoever therefore worked on Sundays, wandered about or played cards, would have to go to prison.[143] Moreover, Pastor Koya (46.), who described this law as a 'Sunday Law', claimed in an interview with me that, as would clearly be seen between 1992 and 1994, the Catholics were attempting to achieve world rule. Actually, as the statements of many of them emphasise, most Adventist villagers anticipate future persecution by the Catholics with, in part, the greatest fear. Pastor Koya announced that the Adventists would soon have to hide themselves in the bush, since the Catholics wanted to murder them out of anger over the numerous conversions.[144] To those attending a Sabbath service, Amos prophesised that their opponents would pour petrol over them and set them alight.[145] According to Muya (55.), God said that all his followers would be killed, thrown in prison, whipped, tied to cars and ripped apart. In the Adventist view, the *sande lo*, whether already approved or to be expected, would partly resume the earlier *sande lo*, to which 52,000,000 adherents of the Sabbath had already fallen victim.[146] However, this imminent martyrdom, which thus appears as a repetition of the history of the SDA Church, not only creates fear, it also strengthens the Adventist certainty of salvation since in the Adventist view the renewed *sande lo* is a sign of the coming end of the world and only those who have previously been subjected to persecution through the powers of the Devil will subsequently belong to the chosen who will go to heaven.[147]

It follows from the expectation of future persecution by the Catholics that in principle the Adventists – as Robert (80.), for example, said clearly –

regard all adherents of the Sunday services as their enemies. The requirement not to live too closely with Catholics or, from the point of view of the Adventists, non-Christians, which is fed by the efforts to achieve purity, corresponds to this view. To my question concerning his relationship with Coleman Makoa – with whom, after all, he shares the same father – Muya replied that he was not his brother; his brothers were rather the other Adventists.[148] However, the relationship of Adventists to Catholics does seem ambivalent, since, alongside the desire for separation, efforts are simultaneously being made to missionise the Catholic villagers and bring about their conversion.

While, on the Adventist side, in judging the other denomination the official and unofficial positions clearly differ from each other, on the Catholic side there is more agreement in this respect. People complain unanimously that the arrival of the Adventists has caused social conflicts and that, in the words of Coleman Makoa (30.), they 'damage the name of the Catholics'.[149] With Sr Marie (48.), Fr Dunstan and Fr Matthias (46.), leading representatives of the leadership of the Catholic Church, describe the Adventists as 'anti-Catholic'.[150] Fr Dunstan even calls them 'the biggest problem in the whole country' and claims that altogether they would create more problems than make positive contributions.[151] According to Fr Matthias (46.), they are less concerned with belief than with bringing as many people as possible over on to their side. Nonetheless, the Adventists' accusations fall largely on fertile ground, since, at least among the 'ordinary' members of the Catholic community, people partly believe themselves that they do not properly understand the Christian message and are not following the Christian prohibitions sufficiently. This may contribute to the fact that Catholics do not react to the criticisms made of them by denying the Adventists access to heaven in turn.[152] Instead they are attempting to strengthen their own beliefs through, for example, Coleman Makoa's claim that the Bible specifies Sundays for the divine service.[153] Coleman Makoa also sought to prevent people from making further conversions by stating that Jesus did not help those who followed other prophets and that He was already with the Catholic community anyway, so that He could not be found anywhere else.[154] Here, the other denomination is usually not mentioned by name any more than it is in most of the Adventists' sermons. In my view, when Fr Matthias came to Pairundu on the day of the SDA baptism, he was concerned in the first instance to counter the attractiveness of the Adventists by underlining the historical legitimacy of the Catholic Church and calling on the members of the community not to let themselves be impressed by the car, plastic tarpaulin, generator and video films that the Adventists had brought to Pairundu for their evangelism week. Many of the older Catholics told me that they had not converted to the Adventists in particular because the Catholic Church – already shortly after the start of their mission activities – had prophesied that at some point later many new denominations would surface and that one should then resist their temptations. This statement had come true and therefore people were following it. As the originators of these announcements – disputed, incidentally, by Fr Dunstan[155] – the Catholic villagers mention either the Chimbu catechists (16., 77.), Fr August,[156] or the first priests in general (7., 92.).

Compared to the effort of strengthening their own beliefs, Catholics invest less energy in criticising SDA-beliefs. Nevertheless, Ripu (77.) referred to the Adventists' efforts to attain purity when he said that they erred in assuming that they could throw out all troublemakers, remain on their own and thus go to heaven. Pogola (72.) found fault with the fact that, in their sermons, Adventist functionaries mentioned many different passages in the Bible, instead of treating only a few texts extensively. The Adventist baptism, mostly being in fact a second baptism, was often rejected by concluding that Jesus had only been baptised once and that ultimately one could not return to the womb after birth.[157] Moreover, the Catholics frequently mock the Adventists' certainty of salvation by asking members of the SDA community whether they had already been to heaven, since they knew the answers to all questions so well. Kenneth (40.) formulated a rather theological objection with the view that, unlike the Catholics, the Adventists still adhered to the old, not the new covenant with God: if they were truly Christians, they would follow the custom of Jesus and not the custom of Moses. A remark of Yali's, according to which the Adventists follow the Old Testament and not the New Testament like the Catholics, also points in this direction.[158] Finally, Kenneth (40.) accused the Adventists of making the Catholics afraid with the threat that they would have to go to hell in 2000 at the latest, in order to seduce them into conversion.[159] Characteristically, however, no one on the Catholic side blames the Adventists for rejecting the traditional culture comparatively more strongly. Of particular significance for the Catholics, on the other hand, is criticism of the Adventist ban on keeping pigs and the consequences of this ban. Ripu and Amakoa, among others, pointed out that without pigs the Adventists can barely afford the brideprice needed to marry and thus ultimately to guarantee the continuation of the clan by providing successors. Ruapo (16.) claimed that the Adventists are not in a position to make compensation payments, meaning that they cannot regulate conflicts themselves, but must push them on to their Catholic relatives, who must then bear the costs of the damages arising.

As the Catholics are generally reserved in their assessment of the Adventists, in principle they attempt to avoid open confrontations with them. According to Coleman Makoa (30.), the priests too, as prominent representatives of the church leadership, come out in favour of not answering the Adventists' accusations. Accordingly, in the Catholic view, Fr Dunstan kept out of a quarrel with the SDA Pastor Wilson (Chapter 3) and the members of the Catholic church committee also kept away from the SDA evangelism week. Thus, just as the Kome as a whole quickly gave up the resistance they had practised at the start of colonisation in the form of attacks and flight after their lack of effectiveness became clear, so also today the Catholic villagers seem to accept the presence of the Adventists after their attempts to prevent their establishment failed.[160] Clearly, here, the Catholics want the adherents of the two denominations to live together as closed groups that are completely separated from one another. Already, at the feast held for me at the beginning of my fieldwork (Introduction), the meat cooked in the earth oven was distributed to the three sub-clans of Auro Kome, Rata Kome and Rundu Kome, as well as the Mamarepa, but also to the SDA community, which was thus also treated as an autonomous sub-clan. When, on 23 September 1991, a discussion took place in front of Yapa's house (no. 33 in Map 3) on whether a pig should be slaughtered for my departure and when Adventists came by and followed the conversations with ironic comments, Alupa and Ari asked them, in a manner that was as sharp as it was loud, to go away again, since it was better they kept to themselves, just as the Catholic community wanted to keep to itself too. In my view, consciously or unconsciously, the Catholic villagers believe that, by separating the denominations, they might be able to prevent Adventists from future missionisation among the Catholics and from bringing more of them over on to their side.

Whether aimed at out of fear of further conversions, future persecution or a loss of purity, the separation of the denominations leads to a situation in which there are hardly any points of either contact or friction between the members of the two communities in day-to-day life. Neither the Catholics nor the Adventists attend each other's services, nor is there any mutual assistance in communal work. Certainly on various occasions minor quarrels arise over, for example, the question of which is the proper day for the major cult practices, but I have neither heard of nor myself seen any use of physical violence. Painting a picture of complete freedom from conflict, however, would mean over-evaluating the fact that Catholics and Adventists usually do not attack each other verbally in public directly. The general reserve was only broken by Coleman Makoa, who, at a Catholic Sunday service in Pairundu** that took place on 4 August 1991, suddenly interrupted his sermon with an emotional outburst in order to complain about a disturbance by Adventists sitting near the church building, which, however, had been noticed neither by myself nor, I believe, by those sitting near me:

> Now disappear, you SDA, ah... I hear a talk coming into the church... you come to mock us, ah [although many in the congregation called out to him that he should not leave the church building, he hurried to the door, looked outside and called outside, still entirely in Tok Pisin]... we don't come into [your] church... I will tell my, my people, they will kill you.[161]

Quarrels are more frequent and also certainly taken more seriously by the villagers, over Catholic parents trying to prevent their children from going over to the Adventists. For Ari, for example, as the 'founding father' of the

Catholic Church in Pairundu, it was particularly painful, so to say, to lose his son Alex (Figure 4.4) to the SDA community. As Alex (3.) told me, Ari had beaten him, refused him food and threatened to smash everything to pieces at the Adventist baptism. In an interview with me, Ari (16.) said that after this baptism Alex was no longer his son and that neither he nor Ripu nor Pogola, who had also criticised Alex's conversion to me, were prepared to support him with, for example, brideprice payments. Naki and Coleman Komea also reported the similarly futile attempts of their fathers to prevent them from switching denominations. On the other hand, Alupa had more success in getting his daughter Neambunu to give up participation in Adventist cult practices by threatening to deny her further access to his gardens. My impression is that such internal family conflicts took place especially in the period leading up to the Adventists' evangelism week and that afterwards they gradually receded into the background again. The resistance of Catholic parents to the conversion of their children is explained by the social consequences of this conversion. To begin with, given the limited possibilities to earn money in Pairundu, the obligatory prohibition on Adventists keeping pigs makes it almost impossible, as the Catholics critically remark, to afford compensation payments or the brideprice that is needed for marriage. Moreover, giving up pigs means giving up a means of accumulating property and increasing one's social prestige. The Adventist demand for withdrawal from society, which the members of the SDA community did comply with by hardly taking part in the discussions that preceded the election of a councillor in Pairundu**, fitted in with this.[162] In this sense, the Catholics are not wrong in assuming that they can no longer expect any support from their Adventist children or other relatives in quarrels or even fighting. The fact that the Adventists describe baptism as a death and accompany it with tears – an element of traditionally appropriate behaviour in cases of death – corresponds to the social consequences of SDA baptism. The Adventist interpretation is obviously shared by the Catholics, since they also broke out into tears at the SDA baptism. If, therefore, Catholic parents turn against the conversion of their children, they do so in order to prevent their children's 'social death' as well as the splitting up of families. According to Amakoa (16.), for example, Ari's attitude is traceable to the fear that, after his departure, only Ripu and Pogola will remain if Alex converts. According to Johannes, what was decisive for Ari was the fact that, as an Adventist, Alex will no longer be following his example at future pig-killing festivals. Some Catholics expressed their rejection of the Adventist baptism by explaining retrospectively why they had cried on this occasion. Ripu (78.) regretted no longer being able to fight together, play cards or slaughter pigs as in the past. Pogola (71.) referred to the promises that he, Ripu, Naki and Coleman Komea had once given one another to support one another in warfare, which were no longer valid.

My close living together with the villagers gave me the opportunity to make various observations, according to which, regardless of all the

Figure 4.4 Alex and his father's elder brother, Ipapula (Pairundu**, 4 September 1991; photo: Holger Jebens).

previous quarrels, internal family cooperation between Catholics and Adventists continued to take place even after the SDA baptism. For example, Muya shared a brideprice payment he had received for the marriage of a Raki Repa woman not only with Kevin, but also with Ata (I) and Coleman Makoa. When Alex had to stay in the health centre at Sumi for a few days because of an illness, he was visited there and provided with food by Yapanu, Ripu and Pogola, as well as Ari. To that extent, the claims of Ari and Muya that they no longer recognised Alex or Coleman Makoa as members of the family were not true from an etic perspective. The cooperation between Catholics and Adventists may even transcend the boundaries of individual families when the Kome as a whole see themselves as opposed to the representatives of other clans. This happened in the election for councillor, in which Coleman Makoa stood for the Kome,[163] Wane for the Akuna and Irianaya for the Ape. As I saw myself to some extent and as Pogola, among others, told me later,

practically all the Kome and Mamarepa, as well as all the members of the
SDA community in Pairundu, voted for Coleman Makoa.[164] Only when
people realised that Coleman Makoa was behind Wane and that Irianaya
would be elected did the remaining Kome and Mamarepa whose votes
had not yet been recorded vote for the existing office-holder Wane.
Although the latter was generally regarded as incompetent and
unsuccessful, he just won against Irianaya and claimed his office. If
Irianaya – who, as an Ape, counted among the Kome's traditional
enemies (Chapter 1) and who allegedly started the disparagement of the
Kome as 'opossums' (Chapter 1) – had become councillor, then, as
Pogola and Alex assured me, the Ape would certainly have mocked the
Kome even more in the future. Yet all the Adventists from Pairundu,
together with almost all the Catholic members of their clan or phratry,
voted for Coleman Makoa until the swing in favour of Wane. The only
Adventist living in Pairundu who voted not for Coleman Makoa but for
Wane was Don, originally an Akuna-Rola from Yakoa.[165]

As Catholics and Adventists are both striving for separation, albeit for
different reasons, the relationship between these denominations as a
whole appears to be one between two autonomous groups that are
demarcated from one another. Cooperation only exists between these
two groups in the case of conflicts with representatives of other clans.
However, serious quarrels are limited rather to individual families and to
the period of the Adventists' baptism, which, as a ritual act, obviously
also seals the splitting of traditional kinship groups in the eyes of both
Catholics and Adventists. From the Western point of view, the relationship
between the two denominations may generally seem to be surprisingly
peaceful and free of tension, especially given the Catholics'
condemnation of the Adventists for their attempts to bring about
conversions and the Adventists' denial of an identity as Christians to the
Catholics, whom they see as their future enemies. However, the
traditional pragmatism that is characteristic of the villagers, whereby
concrete action is more important than belief (Chapter 2), speaks against
any over-assessment of these ideas. In this sense, the opposition between
the members of the two communities is based less on their mutual
judgements of one another than on the fact that their major cult practices
take place on different days of the week. In the dichotomy that is
constructed by Adventists especially, between one Church of the Sabbath
and the many, in this view undifferentiated Sunday Churches, the
weekday of the major cult practices becomes a significant factor in the
creation of group identity. Accordingly, in the quarrel over whether one
should attend church on Saturday or Sunday, not only is the correct
performance of cult practices involved, but also, and especially, the
legitimacy of one's own denomination.[166] Regardless of the separation of
Catholics and Adventists, which culminates in the opposition between
Saturday and Sunday, kinship links still prove to be effective from time to
time, although this is officially disputed by both sides. Thus the opposition

between the denominations did not stop Ari from visiting Alex in the health centre, nor did it prevent Muya from sharing a brideprice payment with Coleman Makoa, among other things. In addition, the election for councillor revealed that clan solidarity remains stronger than community membership, even for the Adventists. Although, in the case of Coleman Makoa, it was a leading functionary of the Catholic church at the village level and a decisive opponent of the Adventists who was put up as a candidate, almost all the Adventist inhabitants of Pairundu voted for him, since, just like most other Kome, they wanted someone from their own clan to win against the Rulupare-Akuna Wane and the Ape Irianaya. Even Don, an Akuna-Rola, although he lived in Pairundu, supported his own clan by voting for Wane. Only when Irianaya seemed to be winning the election was Wane, despite his personal reputation, supported by the Kome, since his Rulupare-Akuna at least belonged to the Kome's traditional allies, whereas the Irianaya's Ape belonged to their enemies. This shows that the decisive consideration in voting was not community membership but clan membership. Accordingly, Kenneth (41.), for example, told me, supported by Alex, that if he ran for the Provincial Government, he would get the votes of all the Adventists because he belonged to 'the same group' (*lain*) as themselves.[167] The traditional principle of segmentary opposition thus retained its effectiveness even after the adoption first of Catholic, then of Adventist Christianity: in opposition to a member of another clan, one joins together with all those belonging to one's own clan. If the other clan belongs to one's enemies, then, it should be added, one unites with one's allied clans (Chapter 1).

The quantitative growth of the SDA community shows the increasing 'success' of the Adventists, even more than the relatively greater readiness in their ranks to take part in cult practices and communal work. The Catholics see this success as a threat, since the Adventists deny legitimacy to their Church; moreover, since the growth of the SDA community is frequently based on switching denominational affiliation, it takes place at the expense of the Catholic community. Because of this, it is not surprising that the Catholics have made various attempts to prevent still more people from converting out of their ranks in future. They strive for the separation of the two denominations, they conjure up a prophecy warning against conversion,[168] and Coleman Makoa tries not only to make Catholic services more entertaining and more attractive, but also to make adaptations vis-à-vis Adventist Christianity in terms of content and also formally. All these attempts, however, strike me as more or less hopeless, or at any rate as not very promising. In particular, the adaptations, both in content and formally, attempted by Coleman Makoa might rather be valued by the Adventist side as a confirmation of their own form of Christianity.

The increasing success of the Adventists is surprising, given the fact that the switch of denominational affiliation obviously brings disadvantages with it. Whoever decides upon conversion must, in comparison with the Catholic community, observe a stricter discipline and spend more time in both cult practices and communal work. In addition, as already described, giving up the keeping of pigs means de facto giving up marriage, giving up increasing one's social prestige and giving up a means of accumulating property. Moreover, another source of income is lost since, in contrast to Catholics, the Adventists may not sell food in the market on a Saturday. Alongside this, the withdrawal from society that the Adventist community requires excludes, with a few exceptions, the maintenance of exchange relationships, as well as various communal activities with Catholic families. Finally, one should not underestimate the fact that conversion requires giving up not only the enjoyment of tea, coffee, beer, betel nut and tobacco, but also the consumption of different types of meat. Altogether, therefore, from the etic point of view the judgement that the Adventists have of themselves, not without pride, can be confirmed, namely that within their denomination the appropriate rules are 'difficult to follow'. If, however, conversion requires such a large amount of effort and especially a large number of things that must be gone without, then the question why the younger inhabitants of the Pairundu area in particular are more and more willing to make this sacrifice themselves is posed all the more strongly.

Notes

1. Yawa goes to the service in Wasuma, Bele to the service in Anapote. Among those who generally stay away from the services are Ata (I), Amakoa, Ipapula, Pakua, Pisime, Renu, Ruben, Ruri and Walawe.
2. As with the census of the Kome as a whole, in explaining the composition of the Catholic and Adventist communities, I describe as 'men' and 'women' all members of the respective gender, regardless of age.
3. These individuals all belong to friendly groups. Mindu (Anapote), Naperasa (Anapote) and Ondasa (Sua/Yeibu) belong to the Mamarepa. Also to be noted are Councillor Wane (Rulupare, Akuna), Ralia (Yakoa, Akuna-Rola) and Kenneth (Wasuma, Wasuma).
4. Among these visitors, women are obviously in the majority, since, in the group of regular service-goers, they form a clearly greater proportion (56.14%) than the men (43.86%), though they have only a small predominance within the SDA community as a whole.
5. To these belonged, among others, Wasanu, Data and Nara.
6. Among the Adventists, the group of regular service-goers is composed of 56.14 percent women and 43.86 percent men. Among the Catholics, the corresponding figures are 64.47 percent women and 35.53 percent men.
7. Admittedly, of the Big Men only Ari has been baptised, but Yawa and Wala also consider themselves Catholics and take part in the Sunday services more or less regularly, although Yawa counts rather as a member of the Catholic community in Wasuma. As members of a sub-clan that is represented among the baptised Catholics to a particularly large degree, the Rata Kome as a whole possess the most pigs, with a value of up to 2,500 K each.
8. However, to the group of economically rising young men also belongs Serale, though he differs from Naki, Robert and Coleman Komea in that his economic position is due not to shops or coffee cultivation, but to pigs and accordingly he has not converted to the Adventists.

9. These are Mandali and Meriam among the *church memba*, Reponu among the *klas redi* and John Mandali, Kabu and Nanowa among the *klas baptais*. However, the persons named do not enjoy a high status within their respective groups and they do not represent them to the outside world.

10. From the etic point of view, it can be stated that the dioceses that are subject to each bishop are divided into deaneries, which themselves consist of several parishes. Pairundu belongs to Kagua Parish.

11. These visits took place on 6 July 1991 for three hours and from the afternoon of 24 September to the morning of 25 September 1991. In addition, Fr Dunstan, who was responsible for Pairundu from 1982 to 1986, led a Catholic service in Pairundu on one occasion in February, while he was holding an education course for several weeks in Kagua. Further contact with representatives of the church leadership arose during a visit by two Papua New Guinean Catholic sisters from 21 to 24 May 1991. On this occasion, Sr Marie also appeared briefly in Pairundu, on the 22 May.

12. As a rule the priest agrees with such suggestions, since, due to the lack of personnel, he is often not in a position to present a candidate himself.

13. Some catechists whom the priest believes to be particularly qualified, like Kenneth, also receive additional education at a catechist school in Erave (*katekis trening senta*).

14. From time to time, Kenneth, Kande and Ken have also read from the Bible.

15. Also, as Neambunu told me, she and Sayna were trained as assistant catechists in schooling occasionally carried out in Sumi, in order to be able to replace Coleman Makoa at a Sunday service if necessary. However, this never happened during my time in Pairundu.

16. All this was told to me by Kenneth (39.).

17. Kenneth said literally that Coleman Makoa wanted to become a 'man of talk' ('man bilong toktok').

18. This combination of praising services while criticising life-style was expressed unanimously by, among others, Ripu, Amakoa and Yapa.

19. Coleman Makoa voiced such complaints during the Catholic Sunday services that were held in Pairundu** on 15 June and 7 July 1991, as well as in a formal interview (30.), among other occasions. According to a letter from Fr Matthias (25 February 1992), Coleman Makoa had since given up his office. According to a letter from Alex (1 June 1992), he now occupies the catechist's post in a village in Pangia District, having been succeeded by Ken in Pairundu.

20. The term 'mama church' corresponds to the terms 'branch church' or 'company', which appear in a handbook published by the SDA church leadership (Robertson 1990: 86).

21. For example, Don said this in an address during the Saturday service in Rakepanda on 9 March 1991.

22. Kevin could not provide any further information on the higher levels of organisation that follow.

23. According to Robertson (1990: 44), these are the Central Pacific, Western Pacific, Trans-Australian and Trans-Tasman Union Missions.

24. Twelve divisions are not named by either Robertson (1990) or Seventh-day Adventists (1990).

25. 'Olsem Pope... wankain tasol'. Neil Wilson's name is also known in Pairundu to those who otherwise know little about the church structure. On this structure, see also Robertson (1990: 42–44).

26. 1–2 March 1991, 7–8 June 1991 and 16–17 August 1991.

27. This ordination included prayers and the laying on of hands.

28. Unlike the Catholics, the Adventists do not hand over these donations during the cult practices.

29. However, Robert (82.) claimed that previously the layman had received soap, clothing and 16 K monthly and still draws 10 K monthly. Pastor Koya (46.) also said that if anyone were to draw money regularly from the church leadership for his work as a layman, people would call him 'misinari'. However, the terms 'layman' and 'misinari'

do not appear in the literature published by the SDA Church, only the terms 'church leader' (Seventh-day Adventists 1990: 61) and 'church elder' (Seventh-day Adventists 1990: 57–61, Robertson 1990: 88–90), terms that correspond to the office of layman as exercised in Pairundu. At the same time Kevin confirmed that no one was appointed church elder in Pairundu.

30. In addition, other offices are mentioned in the literature published by the SDA Church leadership, such as 'church treasurer', 'personal ministries leader', 'Sabbath school officer' and 'adventurers' officer', though no one uses them in Pairundu (Robertson 1990: 100–109).

31. In theory, a so-called 'censure' (*sansa*) can be imposed on any office-holder (Robertson 1990: 117). This means that, for a fixed period, he can no longer exercise any church functions. The next sanction is the removal of his name from the list of the baptised, though this does not exclude the possibility of his being re-baptised (Robertson 1990: 119). Robert reported that Adventists frequently threaten one another with the imposition of a *sansa* and go to Kagua to make this happen. However, no such attempts were successful during my fieldwork.

32. Naki (56.) expressed himself like this, among others.

33. Robert (82.) expressed this especially.

34. As Robert (83.) told me, many Adventists also desire to travel once to the coast, in order to see the sea.

35. Nevertheless, it may rather be the personality of the two office-holders that contributes to the layman enjoying a relatively greater evaluation among his community.

36. 'Kain pasin bilong Setan na wok bilong Setan, em olgeta tok bilong God tasol i rausim na i no gat moa long hia, mipela i save bilipim tok bilong God tasol na olgeta kain samting God tasol i mekim, mipela save bilip olsem'.

37. (Chapter 2). Otmar even claimed that the *kalando* killed even more people today than in the pre-colonial period.

38. Only Kenneth claimed, with respect to Neambu, that injury is only possible if the person affected believes in it.

39. According to Serale (88.), it is anyway forbidden to sing, dance or decorate the body at, or to invite Ewa or Merepa to, a pig-killing festival.

40. 'Mipela i tu haps nau, olpela pasin bilong mipela i stap yet na pasin bilong ol wait i kam i stap na mipela i tu haps. Mipela i no pinisim olpela pasin yet, olgeta i stap yet na dispela wantaim mipela tanim tanim na mekim i kamap wanpela samting'.

41. Fr Matthias (50.) said literally: 'Who am I to stop this?'. Kenneth (42.), however, while speaking in favour of pig-killing ceremonies, also opposed one of their central elements by demanding that one should not use them to outdo other people.

42. The following explanations are based mainly on interviews with Coleman Makoa (30.), Ata Francis (23.) and Ripu (77.). While Coleman Makoa is an office-holder, Ata Francis and Ripu belong to the 'ordinary' members of the community, though, in their frequent visits to services and in their statements, they struck me as comparatively convinced Catholics.

43. Actually, however, the Catholics are very fond of playing cards, especially in the coffee-selling period, though not in the immediate vicinity of the church building.

44. Sermon during a Catholic service in Pairundu**, 10 February 1991.

45. Sermon during a Catholic service in Pairundu**, 4 August 1991.

46. None of the 'ordinary' members of the Catholic community reproduced the church leadership's version, according to which in baptism one dies along with one's sinful body and is buried with Jesus in order to accept the Holy Spirit and go into the church with Jesus (Smits 1981: 66). For many members of the community, the Christian names that the priest bestows at baptism play hardly any role in their day-to-day lives. These names are often recalled with difficulty in answer to direct questions.

47. 'Mipela lotu, mipela lotu. Jisas em i bin lotu na Jisas em i bin in dai long matmat na Jisas em i bin kirap bek long matmat na i go long heven na mipela laik bihainim dispela'. Ata Francis (23.) said, with reference to heaven: 'The whole time, afternoons,

nights, in the day time, we normally go to the service, we think only of this and thus we work so hard, and we do it' ('Mipela olgeta taim, apinun, nait, san, em mipela save lotu ya, tingting bilong dispela tasol mipela hatwok na mipela save mekim').

48. In some villages, four stars were mentioned, or just one.

49. However, in some cases, this also seems to have been the initial reaction in Germany, as acquaintances told me after my return.

50. During a Sunday service held on 4 June 1991, for example, a discussion developed in which various omens were mentioned which, in the general view, indicated the end of the world. According to Coleman Makoa, it no longer rained as much as it had in the past and in addition garden yields had all increased. Ari added that the sun and moon once rose in the direction of Yakoa and set in the direction of Sare, whereas now they rise in the direction of Kira and set in the direction of Wasuma. To the increase in garden yields mentioned by Coleman Makoa, in an interview Ripu added as further indications the formerly unusual breaches of the rule of clan exogamy committed by the Kome (Chapter 1) as well as the rumour that near Kagua a man had married his daughter.

51. 'Nain yias tasol i stap'. Catholic Sunday service in Pairundu**, 15 September 1991.

52. Coleman Makoa (30.) added sickness to the Biblically laid down but not yet occurring omens of the end of the world, while Ata Francis (23.) listed earthquakes, thunderstorms and famine.

53. Only Nosupinai (60.) concluded that everything would be white and clean. Equally unusual was Wala's reply (92.), that he did not know what heaven looked like.

54. 'Yumitupela i go i stap wantain God, em, yumitupela wanpela skin na wanpela tokples na wanpela tingting. Em dispela kain'.

55. 'Na marit nogat... Yu gat papamama tasol no gat papamama, olsem yu wanpela, yu wanpela independent man...'.

56. 'Dispela kain graun, em bai levelim olgeta na yumi stap long hia, yumi inap long lukluk i go daun long Mosbi o Amerika, Australia'.

57. 'Mipela i kam pas tru long tok bilong God' (15., cf. also 30.). The positive self-image of the Catholic villagers was confirmed to some extent by Fr Stanley Miltenberger, the first Catholic priest in the Kagua valley, who wrote to me concerning Kagua parish as a whole: 'It is considered as one of the best and most prosperous of our missions' (letter dated 28 May 1993).

58. 'Nau, em, mipela i stap olsem same man na same meri, pikinini tu olsem, na wanpela i no ken daunim wanpela... Yumi mas bihainim tok bilong Baibel na mipela i stap poroman, em gutpela'.

59. As Ari (15.) told me, the first missionaries said that, in cases of sickness, people should no longer 'do Rimbu' but pray and then the sickness will come to an end. According to Ari people tried this out, it worked and so they believe in it.

60. The officially disseminated view, that the Catholic Church is directly linked genealogically with Jesus himself, through the popes who have succeeded one another, corresponds to these informants' positive assessments of their own community. From this, it follows that the Pope and the bishops are deputies of Jesus as the founder of the Church, which is the origin of all the other churches and communities of believers that have formed by splitting off from it (cf. Smits 1981: 31).

61. Catholic evening service in Porai, 2 July 1991.

62. Catholic evening service in Porai, 29 May 1991.

63. All these meanings are contained in the Tok Pisin phrase, 'as i kamap olsem wanem'.

64. Sermon during an SDA evening service in Rakepanda, 4 July 1991, in the context of an SDA evangelism week.

65. According to Pastor Koya (46.) – and as for Kenneth – God also prohibits the central motif of *yawe*, namely 'the raising of one's own name', that is, increasing, as it were, one's own prestige at the expense of others. Naki, (57.) on the other hand, mainly criticised the fact that people spend time and money senselessly on *yawe*, which in my view corresponds to his reputation as a 'businessman'. In accordance with the Adventist condemnation of pig-killing festivals, on a visit to a *yawe* conducted in

Kamare (Figure 1.1), I saw no Adventists present apart from Naki, who only visited briefly, leaving before the beginning of the slaughtering to return to Pairundu.

66. Robert (83.) claimed this, among others.

67. While with respect to the *remo* and *kalando*, the Adventists largely share the same judgement, with respect to Yaki they do express different views. Many see Yaki as equivalent to *remo* and *kalando* in that they too, as Robert (83.) claimed, trace belief in his existence back to the influence of Satan, so that worshipping Yaki is like worshipping Satan. Others follow the view represented by the Catholics that, as Muya (55.) claimed, in invoking Yaki in the pre-colonial period, one was invoking God. As evidence for this, Kevin (45.) cited the fact that whatever one prayed Yaki for actually happened.

68. Sermon during an SDA evening service in Rakepanda, 4 July 1991, in the context of an SDA evangelism week.

69. 'Yumi no bihainim lo bilong God, dispela i gat pawa na yumi bihainim lo bilong God, mi tok, no gat pawa'.

70. Only Robert (83.) and Kevin thought that negative thoughts could still make one's own infants ill, though they had no effect on older children.

71. Like the Catholics, the Adventists speak comparatively rarely about the necessity to believe, to like others or to help others.

72. Coffee was mentioned by Pastor Koya during a Saturday service held in Rakepanda on 8 June 1991. However, although the Adventists themselves may not drink coffee, they are free to grow and sell it. Tobacco was mentioned by Muya (55.). Furthermore playing cards is also forbidden for Adventists.

73. This view was represented by Pastor Koya (46.), among others. Robert was the only Adventist I asked who followed the Catholics in thinking that one could also go to heaven without *lotu* if one followed all the rules.

74. I was assured of this by, among others, Muya (55.) and Robert (83.). Invoking James 2,10, Naki (57.) and Don (sermon during an SDA evening service in Rakepanda on 16 September 1991) claimed that someone who breaks even a single rule is as guilty as someone who breaks them all.

75. 'Yupela mas bihainim Baibel, Genesis to Revelation, yupela mas bihainim dispela, yupela i no ken lusim Baibel... Baibel bai tok wanem, yupela mas bihainim dispela, Baibel bai sevim yu'.

76. 'Ol friends, nau wanem samting bai kisim yumi i go long heven? Prea bilong yumi bai kisim yumi i go long heven, God bai kisim yumi long prea bilong yumi... Bihain long las de, em bai God bai sasim yumi long prea bilong yumi wanwan' (SDA evening service in Rakepanda, 7 August 1991).

77. Some tests preceded the examination held in Pairundu. During one Sabbath service held in Rakepanda on 2 February 1991, Pastor Koya asked the novices, among other things, how long they had been following the appropriate food rules already and how the ten commandments go. During the Sabbath service held in Rakepanda on 8 June 1991, he then asked the novices, for example, whether they would believe, whether they would *lotu* regularly, whether their clothes and bodies were always clean and whether they were not living too far from the SDA church building.

78. Unlike among Catholics, this official view, which is also found in SDA publications (Seventh-day Adventists 1988: 185, 1990: 27, Robertson 1990: 192f), is also articulated unofficially, that is, by 'ordinary' members of the community like Naki (57.).

79. 'Lusim olgeta samting na i stap olsem daiman'.

80. Sermon during an SDA evening service in Rakepanda, 6 August 1991.

81. 'Ol haidens, ol man we i no save prea, ol man we i no save stadi Baibel, ol man we i no gat Jisas long laip bilong ol...' (sermon during an SDA evening service in Rakepanda, 7 August 1991).

82. Thus Pastor Koya (46.) pointed out to me that problems, trouble and sickness only exist because Satan exists.

83. Pastor Koya (46.) expressed this view with special reference to the Book of Daniel and the Revelation in an interview with me, as well as in sermons that he gave at SDA evening

services held in Rakepanda on 1 July 1991 and 2 July 1991, during an evangelism week. The Adventist and Catholic villagers both count Sunday as the first day of the week.

84. Not only was this idea expressed similarly by Pastor Koya, Naki and Robert, it is also found in official SDA publications (Robertson 1990: 182f).

85. Among these signs, Naki (56.) included wars, shooting stars and a rise in family quarrels. Kevin (43.) cited a solar eclipse reported from Africa. In agreement with Robertson (1990: 181), Pastor Koya named famine, natural catastrophes, increases in crime, the increase in human knowledge and the fact that God's message had already been brought to all peoples on earth (sermon during the SDA evening service in Rakepanda on 30 June 1991, before the start of an SDA evangelism week). In addition, Robert (80.) considered the Holy Spirit movement that took place in Pairundu to be a harbinger of the Last Judgement.

86. Nevertheless, in harmony with the Adventist church leadership (Seventh-day Adventists 1988: 322, 1990: 31), Pastor Koya (46.) thought that the exact date of the end of the world had not yet been determined, though unlike the Catholics he did not refer to there being an individual *las de* only.

87. SDA evening service in Rakepanda, 1 July 1991, during an evangelism week.

88. On a roll of pictures sometimes used by Adventists in sermons is a picture of a man with two paths leading away from him into the distance. On one path stands an angel in a beckoning posture, on the other a devil. According to the corresponding message, the man must now decide in favour of one or the other possibility, since there are no crossroads or connections between the two paths.

89. Kevin listed crimes in a sermon in a SDA evening service in Rakepanda on 6 August 1991. Robert (80.) mentioned pain and tears. Pastor Koya (46.) named age. Naki (56.) mentioned sickness, care, heat and cold. The cleanliness Nosupinai noted for the Catholics resurfaced in a remark of Muya's (55.), according to which the necessity of washing the body would no longer exist. In addition, according to Muya everyone will live in his or her own house.

90. 'Olgeta bai kamap wanpela... olsem brata tasol'. Robert (80.) also referred to the disappearance of marriage.

91. Amos, for example, who comes from Wasuma, said this during a sermon at a Saturday service in Rakepanda on 14 September 1991.

92. Sermon during an SDA evening service in Rakepanda on 30 June 1991, before the start of an evangelism week.

93. Only Kandipia and Robert occasionally said that Adventists also fail to observe prohibitions and commandments. However, I heard such complaints much more frequently within the Catholic community.

94. 'Long church bilong yumi, wanpela man bilong dring bia, wanpela man i paitim narapela man, wanpela man i stil, inap long bai i stap long dispela church?' (Sabbath service in Rakepanda, 13 July 1991).

95. SDA evening service in Rakepanda, 16 August 1991.

96. This formula ('swit long harim... hat long bihainim') was used, among others, by Kevin during a Sabbath service in Rakepanda on 13 April 1991.

97. Pastor Koya's sermon during the SDA service in Rakepanda, 7 June 1991. He (46.) also told me the history of the *sande lo* in an interview. It is also described by Robertson (1990: 28ff.).

98. (52.). However, these ideas are not restricted to Pairundu, but were also expressed to me in chance conversations I had with Adventists elsewhere.

99. Accordingly, said Robert (83.), the Bible talks of a wide path and a narrow road, only the last of which leads to heaven. As, according to Robert, people now hear the pastors say and generally believe, the narrow road stands for one's own denomination, the wide one for the other 699 churches. In my view, in the eyes of the Adventists, the identification of one's own denomination with the narrow road refers not only to the limited membership in comparison with the total of all other churches, but also to the fact that, in their own view, it costs comparatively more privations and efforts to be an Adventist.

100. However, this is not to say at all that the Adventists anticipate the nearing end of the world with any less fear than the Catholics, since belonging to the 'right' church alone does not guarantee access to heaven. Instead, as already stated, even small errors can have the effect of excluding one from the group of the chosen at any time.

101. The only Adventist who expressed a certain scepticism of his own denomination in conversation with me was Robert (80.), the church deacon. He said that he did not understand how one could be planning to build an SDA school near Kagua when the *las de* was so imminent. Apart from that, he had heard the view that Adventist Christianity was as much a handed-down custom among the whites as pig-killing among the inhabitants of Papua New Guinea. In addition, Robert mentioned the thought that Adventist Christianity could be the Rimbu, Rombake or Opayo of the whites. Finally, according to Robert, a rumour was circulating that, because of a lack of money, the whites had sent the SDA Church to Papua New Guinea to cheat the locals out of theirs. However, Robert continued, as Pastor Koya had told the community, all these sceptical thoughts are ultimately to be traced back to Satan or to people who do not know enough about the Bible.

102. One intensification of Catholic beliefs is also that, as already described, Adventists talk more frequently about the *las de*, for example and they depict in more detail what will then happen and what life in heaven will look like afterwards.

103. When I claim that, among the Adventists, there is a comparatively greater congruence between the official and unofficial views, in principle this may also be due to the possibility that the Adventists never came to trust me, so that I never really gained access to their unofficial view. However, I believe this possibility can be ruled out, since, for example, Adventists told me of rumours that they were simultaneously keeping strictly secret from other non-Adventists.

104. For example, in a sermon he preached during a Sabbath service that took place in Rakepanda on 17 August 1991, Pastor Koya said that one's own community must grow and that Catholic relatives should be persuaded to join.

105. Catholic Sunday service in Pairundu**, 30 June 1991.

106. Altogether, I took minutes of twenty-four Catholic and thirty-two Adventist cult events. These minutes are based on the notes and tape recordings I made at these events. Depending on the individual case, I recorded either the whole event or only the sermon.

107. In addition, Coleman Makoa made attempts in June, the start of August and the second half of September to introduce a morning service for the young men, though without achieving any long-term response. Among the participants were, among others, Ata Francis, Ken, Pala, Yapi, Wabi, Ripu and Pogola. Finally, during the period of my fieldwork in Pairundu, some ad hoc services, as it were, took place, which I list here for the sake of completeness. On 13 March 1991, Kenneth gathered the community together at an evening service in the church at Pairundu**, at which he made a speech in which, as he told me later, he warned against joining the Adventists. From the evening of 21 May 1991 to the morning of 24 May 1991, two Papua New Guinean Catholic sisters stayed in Pairundu**, in order to lead services spread over the different days and give lectures, in which they called on the members of the community to think of their evil actions, desist from their sins and strengthen their beliefs. In addition, they suggested holding evening services every day in future. I felt that the sisters' efforts were less successful, since hardly any Auro Kome took part in their meetings and apart from Ari no Big Men. Also other men, like Ruapo, Nosope or Serale, failed to appear. On 6 July 1991, the Saturday of the SDA baptisms, Fr Matthias conducted a service in Pairundu**, in order, in the context of his service, to represent his view of the historical legitimation of the Catholic Church once more.

108. This car-wheel rim was hung up in Pairundu** first behind Amakoa's house (no. 29 in Map 3) and then near Ipapula's house (no. 31). Muya (54.) told me that Coleman Makoa had adopted this way of announcing services – which was not usual among

Catholics formerly – from the Adventists, among whom it had already been practised for a long time.

109. This is obligatory, whereas the Old Testament may be omitted.

110. In Pairundu, Ari and Mayanu, members of the church committee, went round the church for this purpose, during which time some women stepped up to the altar one after the other to place food on it, mostly sweet potatoes. This food later went to the catechist as part of the collection.

111. This is also true for the Ave Maria and the Lord's Prayer. The Ave Maria runs as follows in Kewa: 'Epe Maria, Gotena garasia nena kone wasupara suaaya. Gote ne raapu piruaaya. Naame ne kone ora epe kone wima, epe kone wima nena Iopara Yesu page. Sadu Maria, Gotena agi, naa koe winyalinuna betene pea. Abi go rabu ora komalima rabu page. Ora'. The Lord's Prayer runs as follows in Kewa: 'Nana Maiya, ne yapara piruale, nena bi naame epe kone wima. Nena epeau napara epena la. So yapara pimi, go sukama pimi, nimumi page nena agale waru pageme. Abi go yapi rabu, neme nana eda gianya. Naa rayona koeyounu maruba, naame nimuna koeyounu marubaema rupa, naame go koeyounu manda giaema. Gorupa nana koeyounu marubape. Remome naa koeyou mapealalo kogetea rabu, neme koeyou raoy maruba. Ora'.

112. According to Kenneth, the rhythmic handclapping has only been introduced in Pairundu since the Holy Spirit movement.

113. The following data come from the notes I took of nineteen of the Sunday services I attended.

114. This was the case, for example, on 13 May 1991, 7 July 1991 and 15 September 1991.

115. The number of Bible texts read out ranged from just one to a maximum of three.

116. The only reason given for this was 'to brighten things up'.

117. This is also true of the *wok sol* or community work – if many members of the community take part in it.

118. According to Muya (54.), no Catholic evening services had been held before Coleman Makoa's period of office.

119. Of course, this also has to do with the smaller circle of participants.

120. The Adventists' *belo* hangs in Pokaranda.

121. In doing this, he relied on a brochure distributed quarterly by the *mama church* in Kagua, which features a particular region each quarter, also under the title 'Misin Stori' and includes a text on the church's history in this region for each Saturday of this quarter. From April to June 1991 the South American Division was covered, from July to December 1991 the Trans-European Division.

122. Pastor Koya even tried now and then to read passages from the Bible in English and then translate them into Tok Pisin.

123. This is also stressed in official SDA sources (Seventh-day Adventists 1990: 80, Robertson 1990: 120f).

124. I was also able to attend this service, which, however, according to the rules, should already have taken place on 29 June 1991. The reason given for the delay was that Pastor Koya had had no time to come to Pairundu earlier.

125. The only exceptions are leading the hymns, for which Alex was permanently responsible, the *kisim ripot*, which Don was responsible for and the collection, which Robert took over.

126. Although, as already mentioned, on the whole the individual Saturday services differ from one another less than the individual Catholic Sunday services, my notes on twelve of the Sabbath services I attended show that the number of communal hymns, the 'special items', the prayers, the Bible texts read out and therefore the total length of the services do vary considerably. In addition, either at the start of the service or after the Bible instruction, the Adventists have occasionally introduced a so-called 'object lesson', a short dialogue scene or a pantomime performance, followed by an appeal. Thus, for example, on one occasion Alex placed a small piece of wood by the altar in order to illustrate his explanation that God is like a fire, which one must kindle. One

change, finally, that was only introduced after a SDA evangelism week at the beginning of June consisted in a choir taking up a position behind the altar, in order to provide background singing for the end of the sermon.

127. Kevin clearly indicated this during a Sabbath service on 20 July 1991. Amos described the fact that young men may also preach among Adventists as a sign of the imminence of the Last Judgement (sermon during Saturday service, 14 September 1991).

128. The description provided here is based on notes taken at twelve of the evening services I attended.

129. From April to June 1991 this was the Book of Hezekiel, from July to September 1991 the two letters of Paul to the Thessalonians.

130. One innovation consisted merely in Kevin hanging up, from August, a list naming those who were to preach at the evening and Sabbath services remaining in the quarter on the left-hand church door.

131. From Pairundu, Eya, Coleman Komea, Makirame, Naki, Alex, Papua, Simon and Don were baptised.

132. The sermons given on the different evenings were each oriented to Robertson's SDA Handbook, as follows: 30 June 1991: 'When will Jesus come back?' (1990: 273f); 1 July 1991: 'Jesus is coming again' (1990: 269f); 2 July 1991: 'What happens when someone dies?' (1990: 280f); 3 July 1991: 'God's Sabbath' (1990: 289f); 4 July 1991: 'The world's greatest need' (1990: 271f); and 5 July 1991: 'God's Prodigal Sons' (1990: 297ff.).

133. In fact, neither were the members of the church committee to be seen during the evening services nor, for example, Ripu, Ruapo, Yapa and Rekepea.

134. In the last category were, among others, Neambunu, Onakaya, Ken, Basupiai and Pandabame.

135. Catholic evening services were held especially frequently during the SDA evangelism week. Coleman Makoa directed the holding of morning services in particular towards the young men, a group that, on the whole, was most prepared to convert to the Adventists.

136. Sermon during an SDA evening service held in Rakepanda on 30 June 1991, at the start of the SDA evangelism week. Accordingly, Robertson warns people not to criticise other churches, whether at Bible instruction (1990: 159), when bearing witness (1990: 167) or at evangelism events (1990: 17).

137. According to Pastor Koya (46.), Catholics do this in order to attach as many people as possible to them.

138. However, Robert did not mention that, since his marriage, Amakoa has been excluded from taking communion and that he was hardly participating in the Sunday service any more. To the accusation of allowing everything, Adventists add the accusation of secrecy, meaning that the Catholics hide the appropriate prohibitions and commandments (46.), the Sabbath (44.) and the Book of Daniel, as well as Revelation, in the insufficiently translated Kewa Bible (sermon by Amos at a Sabbath service, Rakepanda, 14 September 1991).

139. Accordingly, in an informal conversation in my house, Alex accused those present, namely Johannes, Amakoa, Ripu and Ari, that they 'worshipped humans' ('lotu long man'). In a sermon (SDA service, Rakepanda, 9 February 1991), Kevin described the Sunday service as a 'false service' ('giaman lotu').

140. 'Pagan i save lotuim san, i save lotuim ston, i save lotuim cow, i save lotuim planti samting, i save lotuim pukpuk, i save lotuim olgeta samting, em i pagan' (SDA evening service in Rakepanda, 3 July 1991, in the context of the SDA evangelism week).

141. The Catholic inhabitants of Pairundu contradicted the ascription to the traditional religion when they declared that, at the time when Adventist mission activity started, they had already been baptised (Chapter 3).

142. Alex (2.) told me that the layman Peter had heard this during a visit to Mount Hagen.

143. SDA evening service on 7 June 1991 in Rakepanda.

144. Sermon during an SDA evening service in Rakepanda, 16 August 1991.

145. Sermon during a Sabbath service in Rakepanda, 14 September 1991.

146. Kevin, among others, said this in a sermon that he preached during an SDA evening service on 24 June 1991 in Rakepanda.
147. Naki and Robert (80.) said this, among others. In order to demonstrate the fact that the *sande lo* is also officially seen as a sign of the end of the world, I quote the points that Robertson (1990: 267) lists on a diagram under the entry 'Sunday Law' in his chapter entitled 'Last Day Events': '1. Under the guidance of Satan, the Papacy and America set up a world-wide religion (Image to the Beast). 2. A law is passed to force men to worship the Beast (Rev 13: 14). Whoever does not worship according to the law will be killed (Rev 13: 15). 4. Time for repentance ends with the Close of Probation (Rev 22: 11). 5. People will receive either the Mark of the Beast or the Seal of God. 6. The Seven Last Plagues fall, beginning a great time of trouble. (Dan 12: 1; Rev 12: 1; Jer 30: 5–7)'. On this, cf. also Seventh-day Adventists (1988: 167, 347).
148. This conversation took place in Tok Pisin as I was walking from Sumi to Pairundu together with Muya, Coleman Komea, Kandipia, Naki, Don, Kevin and Kenneth on 15 July 1991. Naki added to Muya's remark by claiming that in general the Adventists would not really see relatives who did not belong to the SDA community as relatives.
149. Coleman Makoa frequently used the Tok Pisin expression 'bagarapim nem'.
150. Fr Dunstan expressed himself thus in an undated letter I received in mid-June 1992.
151. The first statement was made in a conversation with Fr Dunstan (32.), the second one is expressed in an undated letter from Fr Dunstan (received mid-June 1992).
152. Thus Ata Francis (23.), Ripu (77.) and Kenneth (40.) answered my respective question by saying that they did not know whether Adventists could go to heaven. According to Smits (1981: 127), this is in principle possible for non-Catholics as well.
153. Sermon during Catholic Sunday service, Pairundu**, 14 July 1991 (cf. Smits 1981: 92f.).
154. Sermon during Catholic Sunday services, Pairundu**, 17 March 1991 and 30 June 1991.
155. Undated letter from Fr Dunstan (received mid-June 1992).
156. Fr August Rebel, the first priest to live permanently in Sumi, was named by Ata Francis (23.).
157. This conclusion was formulated to me not only in the Pairundu area, but also in Sumi and in the Sumbura area.
158. Yali said this in the context of a Catholic evening service that took place on 2 July 1991 in Porai. Kevin himself had accordingly expressed the view that the Old Testament had more power than the New Testament.
159. Ari (16.) also complained that the Adventists claimed that Catholics would go to hell.
160. Accordingly, before the start of the Catholic Sunday service on 7 July 1991, Ari held a speech with this effect: 'The Adventists and ourselves, we both pray to God. We got the Catholic Church earlier together with the government, and now all our children are going to the Adventists. We must wait and see whether this path is successful'.
161. 'Nau yupela SDA traim klia, ah... mi harim wanpela toktok i kam insait long church... yupela i kam tok bilas, ah... mipela i no kam long church... mi bai tokim ol, ol lain bilong mi long kilim yupela bai i dai'.
162. I observed such discussions in Pairundu**, among other times on 22 April 1991 and 12 May 1991. On 22 April, Coleman Komea and Naki expressed themselves briefly, only Robert talking at rather greater length and more loudly, though he was later criticised for this by the other members of the SDA community. On 12 May, Coleman Komea, Muya, Kandipia and Simon were present, without, however, speaking.
163. Alupa (8.) told me that, although most Kome were admittedly not in agreement with Coleman Makoa, they had still nominated him because he could read and write to some extent.
164. According to rumour, there were only the following exceptions: Yawa, Onakaya and Kandisi voted for Irianaya, because Yawa had received 10 K from Irianaya to do so. Ruben, Ruri and Andu voted for Wane, because Ruben hoped that Wane would support him later in the election for the village court magistrate.
165. Marcus (49.), who officiated as an assistant at the count, reported this to me.

166. This quarrel still struck me as abstruse at the start of my fieldwork, since after all the Western calculation of the days of the week had only been known since the mid-1950s in Pairundu.
167. Kenneth meant by this that, as a Wasuma, he came from a clan that had previously been counted among the allies of the Kome (Chapter 1).
168. I am not able to decide whether such a prophecy has actually been formulated.

PART II:
CHANGE AND CONTINUITY

5

Past and Future Changes

Conversion to the Adventists can only be understood as just one of several phases in the process of the adoption of Christianity. As a preparation for analysing this process and in order to understand particularly the desires that underlie it, I will examine the changes that the Kome hope will occur in connection with their concept of 'development'. Here, however, the hoped-for changes are connected with past changes that, from the emic point of view, occurred as a consequence of colonisation and missionisation.

Assessing past changes

To the extent that the Catholics and Adventists reject tradition, they tend to evaluate the changing of tradition positively. This becomes obvious especially with respect to, for example, traditional warfare and traditional religion. As, according to the various patrol reports, the indigenous population at first welcomed pacification and the possibility of returning to their home villages (Chapter 3), Ata (I) (25.) also stressed that it was possible henceforward to lay out gardens without having to be on one's guard against attacks from enemy groups and without being killed or driven from one's own houses and plantations. According to Robert (81.), moreover, today one receives and gives hospitality even to people whom one would earlier have killed or driven out because they did not belong to one's 'own group'. Even sitting peacefully together with me, an alien, according to Ripu (15.), was ultimately due to missionisation. Rekepea, finally, emphasised that, in contrast to the pre-colonial past, ceasing warfare permitted one to visit even remote villages without problems. Judged just as positively as pacification and finally contributing to the lifting of the traditional particularism, is the replacement of the traditional religion by Christianity, postulated by Catholics and Adventists, since along with the traditional religion the fear of ancestral spirits and of the stones that were used in the men's houses is also said to have gone.[1]

Muya (55.) said that today he could eat, without problems, many things that were prohibited formerly as causing death. According to the general view prevailing in Pairundu, the prohibition of traditional warfare, the traditional religion and especially traditional witchcraft techniques has led to an increase in the village's population, which is welcomed by the Kome.[2] From the etic point of view and as already described, supporting this growth, is the acceptance of non-agnatically linked persons and groups into the clan, as well as the lifting of the requirement to maintain exogamy between the Kome and the Mamarepa.[3]

The members of the two communities believe that distancing oneself from tradition is necessary in order to change, as it were, from membership of the traditional religion to membership of Christianity (Chapter 4). In this sense, generally one only strengthens one's own Christian identity when one judges the tradition negatively and its alteration positively. Idealising the consequences of colonisation and missionisation itself appears, therefore, to be a consequence of missionary influence. Accordingly, in one sermon, Coleman Makoa spoke of a transition from the pre-Christian darkness to the light that proceeded from the Word of God.[4] According to most villagers, the 'ending' of traditional warfare and of the traditional religion were only possible because the whites both wanted it and were able to bring it about, thanks to their superior power. In enumerating the different traditional cult practices, Ipapula (38.) said, with reference to Akera: 'This also killed us usually, but you whites came and helped us'.[5]

Alongside the positive evaluation, however, a negative evaluation of past changes is also articulated. Thus both Catholics and Adventists mention a process of biological degeneration starting with first contacts and being expressed especially in the gradual decline of people, pigs and garden harvests.[6] Bodily decay is also said to have speeded up, since men supposedly age more quickly nowadays than in the pre-colonial period.[7] The cause of this, especially for the Catholics, is not only the tendency for the traditional separation of the genders to be lifted – which, according to Ripu and Ruben, also leads to sickness – but also the damaging impact of Western goods. For example, the fact that Yapa allegedly looks as old as other men who were born long before him is – according to the general conviction, voiced even by himself – due to the fact that he eats rice all too often. As a reason for the general reduction in body size, Alupa (10.), Ipapula (34.) and Wapa mentioned the Western clothing with which the body was covered nowadays, instead of using the traditional arm rings and ribbons, among other things, or the body oil that people applied sometimes.[8] Wapa (93.) also gave a rather religious explanation by seeing the symptoms of decline and decay as an indication of the *las de*, while Muya (55.) supposed that they were an effect of Satan's as much as a punishment of God for people not following his commandments and prohibitions sufficiently. For the inhabitants of Pairundu, biological degeneration – which is also mentioned by the Huli and Wiru[9] – corresponds to a dissolution of the social order. This arises from the reduction in the separation of the genders mentioned above as much as from the already mentioned breaches of the rule of clan exogamy (Chapter 1). Moreover, in contrast to the pre-colonial period, today it is allegedly no longer normal for children to obey their parents or for the meat of a slaughtered tree kangaroo, for example, to be distributed to others, in order that one receives some in return on a later occasion.[10] The idea that the *kalando* – who, as it were, give punishment if one does not share food – are causing sickness and death as much today as before the coming of the whites can also be interpreted as a complaint about the increase in individualism and thus about social disintegration. An increase in witchcraft techniques would be fitting here, though this is only reported from other regions, not the Pairundu area.[11] For both Catholics and Adventists, the process of social disintegration first started with the beginning of colonisation and missionisation, only to enter a second phase with the attaining of independence in 1975. After this date, it is generally said, the whites, who gradually left, were increasingly replaced by businessmen and politicians from Papua New Guinea itself, which has led to an increase in fighting (21.), attacks, robberies, divorces (85.) and family quarrels,[12] as well as to price rises and a decline in the value of money (25.). Otmar (67.) claimed that judges today acquit thieves in return for bribes, instead of sentencing them to prison as in the colonial period. The second phase of the process of social disintegration also seems like the dissolution of social order, one which, however, no longer involves the pre-colonial period but the order introduced in the course of colonisation and missionisation. For the villagers, the dissolution of this order that was imported by the whites is due to the fact that the indigenous people who have succeeded the whites do not have comparable amounts of power available to them.[13]

Sevis: hoped-for changes

In discussing the emic concept of 'development', how Catholics and Adventists see the whites is especially important, since these are regarded as the bearers not only of past changes, but also of those that are hoped for in the future in connection with 'development'. It is not by chance that the emic picture of the whites is characterised above all by the power ascribed to them. From the start, the whites, as colonial officials and missionaries, could not be controlled by the indigenous population in any way, yet exercised control themselves by making sure their demands were implemented (Chapter 3). Only through their power did it seem possible for them to 'end' traditional warfare and the traditional religion, as well as simultaneously introducing a new order. The idea that the post-colonial withdrawal of the whites has led to the dissolution of the order they created corresponds to this notion.

Nevertheless, still today, the villagers regard the power of the whites – which is said to let cars drive and planes fly[14] – as inexhaustible, so that in general they are ascribed almost unlimited abilities, knowledge and wealth.[15] In many conversations I was assured that in Germany, as a land of the whites, 'all good things' were available in excess and all for nothing. Alex (6.) was convinced that – unlike in Papua New Guinea, where people had to work hard – the inhabitants of Germany only had to fill up pieces of paper and press buttons.[16] The members of the two denominations linked the power of the whites not least with the writing they introduced. After all, the first colonial officers had already insisted on listing the names of the villagers,[17] while the first missionaries mentioned a book that contained the Word of God. To that extent it is not surprising that considerable significance is placed on the Bible in both communities, though the Adventists place much more weight, comparatively speaking, on conformity to the written word.[18]

By initially believing whites to be immortal and identifying them as *nokerepa* or *remo* (Chapter 3), the villagers have ascribed what from the Western point of view is a supernatural quality to the power of the whites from the beginning. Seeing the foreign intruders as ancestral spirits simultaneously means comparing the unknown with the already known, because of a lack of handed-down models of explanation and action,[19] and thus to some extent integrating them in with the familiar. The convictions, expressed mostly by members of the older generation, that one assumes a white skin colour after death,[20] that the whites live under the earth – which is where the dead have been buried since missionisation – and that from there they come to Papua New Guinea with ships and aeroplanes through a hole, recalls the identification of the whites with the *remo* even today.[21]

According to the corresponding patrol reports, when it rapidly became clear, following the start of colonisation and missionisation, that any resistance in the form of fighting or flight was useless, members of the younger generation in particular greeted and supported the colonial officers. The offices that were bestowed by the colonial government also soon proved popular and the Catholic priests were asked to send catechists (Chapter 3). This clear change to a positive attitude to the whites soon led to their idealisation, which still determines their image. Accordingly the members of the two denominations similarly regard cleanliness and discipline as the most marked characteristics of the whites.[22] In connecting the whites with positively valued characteristics and modes of behaviour, the Catholics are outdone by the Adventists. Thus Kevin expressed the view that the whites would not lie, get drunk, play cards or, for example, quarrel in marriage.[23] The idealisation of the whites into a sort of model that, particularly among the Catholics, contrasts with one's own self-evaluation[24] was fed not least by the fact that it was the whites who brought Christianity to Papua New Guinea. This often leads to the conclusion that all whites are convinced

Christians. Ari (16.), for example, supposed that they had first completed the spread of Christianity in their own country before missionisation began. Kevin claimed that, without exception, the prophets of the Old Testament had also been *masta*.[25] In this sense, the idea that I must know everything about Christianity was plausible to the villagers.[26] To my assurance that not everybody went to church regularly in Germany, people reacted with astonishment, partly with shock and with the request that I did not tell anyone else this, lest they kept away from *lotu*. Since, in the emic picture of the whites, a positive evaluation predominates as a whole, criticisms are expressed quite rarely. For example, in the course of his argument with me, already mentioned (Introduction), Yawa said that he was no longer prepared these days to be kicked or ordered around by whites as when Papua New Guinea was still not independent. The complaint insistently expressed by Otmar (63.) and Wapa (93.), that colonial officers had not paid them enough money for their services as Village Constables, also refers to this period. Another accusation arises from the idea that in reality one's own ancestors had manufactured, for example, steel axes, bush knives, clothing, cars and tinned fish and then sent them to their descendants, that is to oneself, as the legitimate recipients before the whites deceitfully intercepted the arrival of these goods in order to compel the payment of purchase prices and thus enrich themselves. Among others, Nosupinai, Wapa (94.), Ata Francis, Kapu and Wala told me this with the explicit indication that they still believe it.[27] In addition, Wala (92.) assured me that he could tell by marks on bush knives that they had actually been manufactured by his father Rama and were therefore meant for him. The accusation of deceit corresponds to the conviction – held by some people according to Robert (88) – that the whites wanted to harm the locals. Despite the generally prevailing link between the whites and Christianity, only Ripu (77.) formulated a religiously grounded criticism by claiming that, on the Day of the Last Judgement, God's anger will first be directed against the whites, since they do not follow the Christian commandments properly. If, in the indigenous memory, the representatives of colonisation and missionisation first beat, kicked, imprisoned and in particular cases even shot the villagers (Chapter 3), it is quite surprising that, in comparison with the on the whole quite sporadically expressed criticisms, the positive evaluation of the whites generally predominates.[28] Possibly the mostly welcome consequences of colonisation and missionisation, which are, as it were, 'credited' to the whites, are seen as comparatively more serious, or perhaps from the etic point of view the attacks are legitimated through the superior power of the whites.

The power of the whites is generally seen as being necessary in order to bring about 'development', which both Catholics and Adventists understand as a change in their situation of relative marginality. This change, a hope for the future, is described by the Tok Pisin phrase 'kisim sevis', which can be translated literally as 'acquiring services'. However, the content of the meaning of *sevis* simultaneously embraces, among other things, Western food, medical provisions, roads, houses with corrugated roofs, schools, factories and coffee plantations.[29] Thus *sevis* also belongs to different ways of making money that are described as *bisnis*. The members of the two denominations view permanent settlement by a firm (*kampani*) or a white person as a good opportunity to acquire *sevis*. Thus it was often suggested to me – also in Anapote and Wasuma, as well as in other villages – that after my education I should settle down in the village and 'start a business'. Another possibility to acquire *sevis* in the emic view is to have a 'stronger', that is more powerful councillor arguing with the government and thus fulfilling the villagers' wishes. According to Alupa (9.), any such councillor must tell a representative of the government what is lacking in Pairundu, then this representative must repeat it at a meeting, then it must be written down on paper and then Pairundu would, for example, acquire roads and factories for nothing.[30] All in all, however, the Kome are convinced that they neither have a capable councillor, nor know how a *kampani* or a white can be persuaded to settle down among them. Thus Ari noted with regret: 'Here there is no way to get good government services'.[31] A *kampani* in Pairundu also promises an opportunity to pursue contract work in one's own village without, for example, having to visit the Western Highlands, where, according to Ata (I) (25.), many villagers have already disappeared or fallen victim to enemies and where a large part of one's wages necessarily goes on buying food.[32] According to Otmar (67.), with the money saved one could build a community school, charge school fees and later get support from children trained as doctors or priests. However, for the Catholics and Adventists, in the first instance the imagined contract work in Pairundu means making life easier, as well as, according to Pogola (72.), providing an opportunity to ride about in cars and eat tinned fish, tinned meat or rice. In contrast to most of my other informants, only Naki (58.) felt that he did not necessarily want to work for a *kampani* or a white in Pairundu and that he would rather like to learn how to make *bisnis*.[33]

In the villagers' hopes, the *kisim sevis* takes the form of the acquisition of Western goods. Certainly their use value should not be underestimated, as the comparison of steel tools with the traditional stone ones shows, but their symbolic value is nonetheless still more important. Western goods, which in part certainly found their way to Pairundu via the trade routes even before the first colonial officers appeared (Chapter 3), represent the superior power of the whites. Owning these goods therefore means partaking in the power of the whites and thus becoming 'like them'. In accordance with the traditional value of strength (Chapter 1), this would mean an increase in one's own status both inter- as well as intra-culturally and with respect to both the whites and other settlement communities.[34] At the same time, inter- and intra-cultural equality would be created, corresponding to the equally traditional value of equivalence (Chapter 1). In particular, members of the older generation laid a claim on these changes, as it were, by claiming that their ancestors had produced Western goods and sent these to them as their legitimate recipients.

Since at least the start of the 1970s, Catholics and Adventists have basically understood 'development' less as a process concerning one's own activities than as the passive receipt of what to some extent is given to them from 'the outside'.[35] Thus, for example, Ari and Luke (19.) asked me which government had given the whites reading and writing. While, in the context of the traditional religion, following established rules had promised protection, the curing of sickness or fertility (Chapter 2) and while, in the context of Adventist Christianity especially, among other things observing prohibitions and commandments should enable one to go to heaven (Chapter 4), people complain about the lack of instructions on how to come into possession of *sevis*. Accordingly, the inhabitants of Pairundu suspect another undisclosed secret behind the power of the whites or behind 'development', just as the Catholics do with respect to their form of Christianity (Chapter 4). This supposition obtains its plausibility from the fact that, even in the context of the traditional religion, power was fed by the secrecy surrounding particular knowledge (Chapter 2).

Concluding remarks

From the emic point of view, the changes – which on the one hand go back to the context of colonisation and missionisation and on the other hand are hoped for in the context of 'development' – show hardly any differences between the denominations. Catholics and Adventists ascribe themselves the same passive role with respect to both past and hoped-for changes, a role that they also adopt in their memories of the pre-colonial past. So, just as they claim to have been subject to the warlike attacks of enemy groups, the effects of transcendent authorities and magical practices in the pre-colonial period, without, for example, having had witchcraft techniques of their own (Chapter 2), so they assured me that previously they could not actively influence the consequences of colonisation, missionisation or the attaining of independence and that today they have no possibility for *kisim sevis*.

From the etic point of view, the villagers' passive self-portrait is true in so far as they did not themselves want, let alone bring about, either the arrival of the first colonial officers and missionaries, or, later, Papua New Guinea's independence and the partial withdrawal of the whites. Instead, as already described, a loss of autonomy arose out of the fact that the decline and increase in traditional social differences accompanied by colonisation and missionisation could at first not be controlled by the villagers, while for their part the whites, as representatives of a superior power, were able to enforce obedience at any time.[36] This loss of autonomy, which is certainly seen as threatening identity, is described by the members of both denominations as social degeneration, a process of disintegration expressed since the start of colonisation and missionisation among other things in a reduction in exchange activities and since the post-colonial withdrawal of the whites among other things in an increase in crime. The tendency towards the dissolution of social cohesion can also be attributed to the consequences of colonisation and missionisation from the etic point of view (Chapter 3). For the villagers, to the social degeneration corresponds a biological degeneration, which in their view, with the decay of the body, is to traced back to Western goods. On the whole, the claim of social and biological degeneration appears to me to be an emic criticism of the loss of social cohesion, as well as of strength, power and autonomy.[37] The idea that the rice that is obtained for money – which the purchaser usually consumes alone or in the narrowest family circle, without sharing it as one does with pig meat and regardless of all exchange relationships – leads to a speeding up of the ageing process is another reference to the emic connection between social and biological degeneration. Simultaneously, according to the traditional 'obligation to share' (Chapter 1), it is claimed here that the individual accumulation or consumption of property not only makes one ill, but that it is in itself already a symptom of illness.

If Catholics and Adventists wish to partake in the superior power of the whites through *kisim sevis* in order to create inter- and intra-cultural equality by increasing their own status, then the realisation of strength and equivalence as traditional values should win back or strengthen social integration, autonomy and identity. Thus in the context of 'development', the changes hoped for in the future would undo the past changes, that is, the consequences of colonisation and missionisation. Both the past changes and the changes hoped for are thus materialised similarly in the form of Western goods. They stand for the power of the whites or the threat emanating from them, as much as for the strengthening of one's own identity through the acquisition of *sevis*. In that sense, with respect to Western goods in the context of 'development', the villagers are making an attempt to acquire and put to use the essence of the threatening for the protection of the threatened. The same pattern is already found in the context of the traditional religion, where the various specialists always chose as a therapy Alamu-palaa Rimbu, Aga-palaa Rimbu, Salu Rimbu, Rombake, Akera or Opayo, according to whatever they believed had caused the particular illness (Chapter 2). All-embracing equality, finally, not only appears as a consequence of obtaining *sevis*, as already described, with the disappearance of personal distinctions, it also characterises the idea of heaven held by both denominations (Chapter 4). Consequently, the attempt to achieve possession of 'development' ultimately serves, if in a different way, the same goal as the attempt to enter heaven. In this sense, for the villagers *kisim sevis* is basically simply another 'pathway to heaven'.

Notes

1. On different occasions, including in Anapote and Yeibu, it was claimed that today, unlike in the pre-colonial period, touching these stones would no longer make you ill.
2. Among others, Yana (95.) and Makoa, who has since died – according to his son Muya (55.), his statement was made some years ago – expressed themselves in this fashion. According to Lederman (1982: 5), the Mendi are also convinced that there has been a growth in their population.
3. (Chapter 1). Accordingly, in 1958 a colonial officer estimated the number of Kome and Mamarepa together at only three hundred individuals (EPR 1958/59–5: 10).
4. Catholic Sunday service, Pairundu**, 14 July 1991.
5. 'Dispela samting tu i save kilim mipela, tasol yupela waitman i kam na helpim mipela'.
6. Wapa (93.), Alupa (10.), Makoa – according to his son Muya (55.) – and Ipapula (34.) spoke of such a decline. In contrast to all other informants, only Yana (95.) expressed the view that, although in general humans would shrink down the generations, they had not been any bigger in the past than, for example, Yawa or Wala today. The thesis of a shrinking of garden yields contradicts the view also expressed that garden yields were increasing as a harbinger of the Last Judgement (Chapter 4).
7. When, for example, with Ata (I) and Alupa, I visited Wapa, who was living in Sare, on 28 August 1991, Punda, who also lived there and was supposedly over sixty, claimed that Alupa already had white hair, even though he was not old enough to have any and that this would not have happened before the start of colonisation and missionisation.
8. Wapa (93.) explained the reduction in body size with reference to the fact that children were cleaner today than formerly and that they lived in towns in Western houses, with electricity and artificial light.
9. On the Huli, see Ballard (n.d.). According to J. Clark (1985: 211 n. 12, 1989a: 127f), the Wiru explain decline through the use of Western clothes. The Hua, who live in the Eastern Highlands, describe the 'feminisation' of the men since first contacts, caused by the giving up of purification rituals (Meigs 1984: 71).
10. Ipapula (38.) and Kenneth (42.) claimed this. The complaint about children not obeying anymore, however, is certainly not restricted to Papua New Guinea.
11. An association between an increase in witchcraft accusations and colonisation is described for the Kewa of Muli (Franklin and Franklin 1978: 471) and Mararoko (MacDonald 1991: 386–389), as well as the Mendi (Lederman 1981: 20), the inhabitants of the Nembi plateau (Crittenden 1987: 354) and, outside Southern Highlands Province, the Sibog, Madang Province (Kempf 1992: 86, n. 33) and the Wampar, Morobe Province (Fischer 1992: 172).
12. As already mentioned, Naki named an increase in family quarrels as a sign of the Last Judgement (Chapter 4.).
13. Among others, Alex (21.) gave this explanation during an interview with Ari. For the Adventists, Pastor Koya in particular mentioned a negative change in the religious context lasting from release into independence up to the present. In his view, since the 1980s people all over Papua New Guinea have been thinking only of natural resources and coffee cultivation and have forgotten religion. Thus people care only for the development of the country and their own progress, which amounts to neglecting the *lotu*. Pastor Koya linked this claim with the threat that all those who think in this way would be punished by Jesus when He returns (sermon during an SDA Sabbath service, 8 June 1991).
14. This statement was formulated on different occasions by numerous people, including, for example, Robert (83.).
15. On 2 July 1991, during a night-time walk near Porai, Ata Francis pointed to a star, which he claimed had not been there before and that it had very probably been manufactured by those who fly round in rockets. People also had a high estimation of my own abilities, believing that, if I stayed permanently in Pairundu, I would quickly ensure that roads, a

new health centre and a school were provided. As a white, I was even supposed to have love magic, a view voiced by Coleman Makoa, who asked me to give him some (Chapter 2).

16. On another occasion, Johannes told me that in general people think that all whites own a pistol and a car.

17. Thus at the start of my fieldwork, when I was collecting genealogies, I found myself perpetuating a historical continuity which the villagers were well aware of and which was at the same time unpleasant to me.

18. In answer to questions on Christianity, Catholics more often claim that they do not know exactly, because they cannot read or write.

19. One remark repeatedly made in corresponding interviews is that one's own parents and grandparents had not announced the later arrival of the whites beforehand.

20. Moreover, this idea was also expressed by Ata Francis as a young man. If the dead assume a white skin, then the thought that I was actually Wapi, Ari's dead brother, seemed plausible (Introduction). A white skin colour is also supposed to indicate the *kalando* (Chapter 2).

21. Wapa (94.) and Nosupiani (60.) claimed this to me. At the same time, Ripu (75.) and Alex (4.) told me that many other men would think the same.

22. Robert (83.) in particular emphasised that wherever the whites stayed it was cleaner. The impression given by the colonial officers may have played a role in the connection of the whites with discipline. Kevin pointed to what, in his view, is the typical strength of will of the whites in general by remarking that their heads were like stones, whereas those of the locals were like earth.

23. Kevin stressed this explicitly in a sermon at an SDA evening service that took place in Rakepanda on 6 August 1991. Earlier, his rhetorical question, whether the *masta* and *misis* would ever quarrel, had been collectively and immediately denied by the assembled congregation.

24. Here the claim made to me that, unlike the locals the whites would not lie, might also have been an only superficially encoded request to me to behave exactly as other whites in this respect.

25. The more power and competence people ascribe to the whites in general with respect to Christianity, the more significant becomes the 'victory' that, in the Adventists' view, they have achieved in their argument with Fr Dunstan (Chapter 3).

26. Ata Francis and Ripu, among others, expressed this supposition.

27. Nosupinai (60.) gave as evidence the fact that the whites come from under the earth, since, after all, the dead would also be buried under the earth. Kapu talked to me in an informal conversation that took place on 16 April 1991 in Porai in Tok Pisin. Alupa and Ruapo expressed similar views. Of my informants among the members of the younger generation, apart from Ata Francis only Robert (95.) was of the same view, while, at least outwardly, Alex, Naki, Ripu and Pogola laughed at this.

28. Not even the illness that spread more or less at the time the whites arrived (Chapter 3) was blamed on them.

29. Ruben (85.), among others, told me this in answer to my direct questions. This means that the term 'sevis' has the same meaning in Pairundu as the term 'gavman' ('government') has in Baluan, Manus Province, where, according to Otto (1992a: 271): 'In its widest meaning it may be identified with all aspects of modern development'.

30. It is not clear whether Alupa meant here the member of the Provincial Government elected by Aiya constituency or the member of the National Government elected by Kagua District. Nonetheless, it shows the power attributed to writing.

31. 'Long hia i no gat we long kisim gutpela sevis bilong ol gavman'.

32. Ata (I) also pointed out that if one stayed in Pairundu, one would no longer have to do the work of the Western Highlands' people.

33. In my view, in this remark Naki was again expressing his rather 'entrepreneurial spirit'. According to Burkins (1984: 246), people in the Muli region also justify their desire for a

kampani with reference to the opportunity to learn something about *bisnis* and be able to feed themselves other than from their own gardens in the distant future.

34. In my view, the intention to raise one's own prestige with respect to other settlement communities contributed to the desire of the Adventists for uniforms, just as much as to the Catholics' desire for a corrugated iron roof. However, the Adventist Robert (83.) also stressed how amazed the inhabitants of other villages would be if there was a house in Pairundu with a corrugated iron roof.

35. Already in the beginning of the 1970s, the colonial officer R.A. Cox wrote, concerning conversations he had had with 'several educated or advanced young men': '...it was obvious that they held the same attitude as the remainder of the peoples, i.e. "we want economic development, but have no ideas as to what form it will take. It does not particularly matter what it is so long as it does not require too much work and we don't have to think about it". In other words they are waiting for the Agricultural Officer to hand them Economic Development on a plate' (Kagua Patrol Report 1971/72–18).

36. In principle nothing in this is changed by the fact that, with contract work and cash crops, as well as with the offices bestowed by the colonial government, new methods of obtaining capital or increasing status came into existence, or that in the Pairundu area day-to-day life has changed less fundamentally, when compared to other villages that have been exposed to Western influences to a greater extent.

37. Cf. J. Clark (1989a), who, writing of the Wiru, interprets the idea of a shrinking of the body starting with first contacts as an indigenous description of the loss of autonomy.

6

Adopting Christianity

As already mentioned, the process of adopting Christianity consists of the start of Catholic missionisation, conversion to the Adventists and the Holy Spirit movement.[1] The individual phases certainly started in this order, though the villagers themselves did not pass through them in this order. Thus, no one joined the Holy Spirit movement as a baptised Adventist, though former participants in the Holy Spirit movement certainly converted to the Adventists. Moreover, the individual phases of the adoption should not be considered closed, since particular elements of the Holy Spirit movement have remained effective even since it ended, and villagers still undergo Adventist or Catholic baptism. In order to understand not only conversion to the Adventists, but also the whole adoption process, it is necessary to analyse the needs and beliefs that have been effective in every one of its phases and to do so from both the emic and the etic perspectives.

The beginning of Catholic missionisation

In accordance with the nowadays generally prevailing rejection of tradition, at least in the official view, the older Catholics claim that they obeyed the prohibitions of the first priests and catechists above all because they were already thoroughly weary of the traditional warfare and because they did not feel it right that the women could not consume pig meat in the cult houses. Accordingly, from the emic point of view, Catholic Christianity was adopted not despite the fact that this implied a distancing from the traditional culture in general and the traditional religion in particular, but precisely because of this. In addition, the adoption of Catholic Christianity is explained with reference to one's own fear, which is linked to various objects. Ari (15.) mentioned fear of the whites who had already been beating the villagers, putting them in prison and taking them to court when the first catechists appeared, also wearing Western clothing and speaking Tok Pisin. Thus people said to themselves:

'…these are the same sort of people. Let's go and really obey them, so that they don't beat us, so that they don't kill us… so that they don't take us to court'.[2] Walaya (63.), on the other hand, listed fear of the Last Judgement, which, as he remembered, had been prophesied by the Catholic priests and the Lutheran Pastor Imbrock.[3] According to Wala (92.), people feared especially their own dead rising up again at the end of the world. Ripu (15.) referred to the fear of hell. As he said, parents had used blows to force their children to go to Bible school because they believed: '…if we behave badly, we shall go into the fire… we must obey the Word of God and go to heaven…'.[4] Among the emic justifications for one's own obedience to the first priests and catechists, there is also the reference to the social pressure that arose from the fact that mission activities began later in the Pairundu area than in the neighbouring villages or, for example, the Ialibu and Kagua area. Pogola (72.) claimed that the villagers had burnt cult houses so that they would not be subject to the mockery of those among whom these new practices had already been introduced: 'All the people in this area, they have all given up these Rimbu and Rombake and replaced them with the Word of God and you want to be the only one to be able to retain these Rimbu and Rombake?'[5]

From the etic point of view too, the fear emphasised by the members of the Catholic community must have played an important role at the start of missionisation. Ultimately, as whites or as their representatives, the priests and catechists were in the first instance above all the agents of a superior power. Only gradually did the realisation become established that, as a group, the church functionaries were different from the representatives of the colonial government and had their own claims to make. From the etic point of view, I would ascribe as much significance to the fear of the whites as to the still detectable fear of the *las de*, whose alleged nearness strengthens still further the threat of hellfire. At the same time, however, at least according to Imbrock, the Kome received not only the promise of going to heaven if they obeyed, but also presents.[6] To attach oneself to the Christianity propagated by the whites or their representatives means imitating the whites. The efforts at such imitation are also expressed today in idealising the whites, as well as in the intention to obtain a corrugated iron roof for the church with the income from communal work. In my view, in imitating the whites in general and in accepting Catholic Christianity in particular, the inhabitants of the Pairundu area are making an attempt to partake in the power of the whites. The general conviction is that this power has the effect, among other things, of making prayers protect one against attacks by ancestral spirits and of curing illnesses. Thus prayers appear to some extent to be the functional equivalents of traditional cult practices or healing procedures, as a remark of Ari's (15.) makes clear: 'The missionaries have said, if anyone becomes ill, we should not kill a pig or do Rimbu, we should pray and then the illness will come to an end. We did that and it worked and we thought, it's true, that's really good'.

Accordingly, in the Catholic community the conviction prevails that the power linked to Christianity is concentrated especially in the main representatives of the church leadership. If it rains during a baptism and the priest raises his hand, so a Mamarepa assured me, the rain ceases immediately, so that one does know that one belongs to the right church.[7] The link between Christianity and power results, among other things, in social pressure, as Pogola noted. After the inhabitants of the surrounding settlement communities had already been entirely converted, the inhabitants of Pairundu and its area could not afford to remain the only village that was excluded from the new source of power. The need to imitate the whites goes along with the need to distance oneself from the traditional culture and religion. This distancing from tradition, which is a reason for conversion in the emic view, is on the one hand a precondition for partaking in the power of the whites and on the other hand is only made possible by the power of the whites. Ipapula (36.) said: 'Formerly we did Rimbu and Opayo and such things, that is all remo, but you gave us power and we have stopped doing that'.[8] Here, Catholic Christianity seems like a sort of liberation, as it were, from tradition. However, in the, at least today, officially propagated rejection of the traditional religion, for example, I see rather a consequence of missionisation, so that I hardly believe that the villagers had obeyed the first priests and catechists because of a desire they already had at that time to break with their own tradition.[9]

Although the start of Catholic mission activity went along with the distancing from tradition, from the etic point of view some parallels do emerge in respect of beliefs between the indigenous picture of Catholic Christianity on the one hand and tradition on the other.[10] This includes the fact that Christian prayers are obviously sometimes seen as a new form of the old cult practices or healing procedures. If, in the pre-colonial period, the world of the living and the world of the transcendent authorities, the secular and sacred spheres, were seen as closely interwoven (Chapter 2), for the members of the Catholic community today Christianity as a work consisting of various components embraces secular as well as sacred aspects. The idea that carrying out this work opens up access to heaven as a return (Chapter 4) recalls to some extent the traditional value of equivalence, according to which each prestation both includes and legitimises a counter-prestation (Chapter 1). The hope above all that Christian commandments and prohibitions will guarantee access to heaven is basically as legalistic as the expectation that traditional cult and magical practices lead almost necessarily to success, provided one observes the rules associated with them (Chapter 2). This legalism simultaneously promises protection, for the villagers basically consider human existence to be threatened. If, in the pre-colonial period, people believed that they were exposed to the attacks of bush or ancestral spirits and the use of witchcraft techniques (Chapter 2.4), in the context of Christianity too there is the threat of the impact of Satan and the possibility of forfeiting access to heaven through some transgressions.[11]

Altogether, the parallels that exist for the Catholics between their Christianity and the traditional religion in particular help to make plausible their obedience to the first priests and catechists, since they allowed Catholic Christianity to appear familiar. Basically, in my view, the readiness to accept and maintain something new increases to the extent that the new succeeds in being seen as related to what is already known. However, for this to happen, it is not necessary for the perceived parallels to become conscious too.

Conversion to the Adventists

After the start of Catholic missionisation, conversion to the Adventists forms the second phase in the process of the adoption of Christianity. In answering the question of the reasons for this conversion, many Catholics claim that the Adventists win adherents especially through the threat of hellfire. Here again is a reference to the fear that is already supposed to have explained one's own behaviour in relation to the first priests and catechists. According to Fr Dunstan, moreover, Adventist functionaries had also first spread the rumour that anyone who did not join them would go to prison (Chapter 3). In the first instance, however, the Catholics explain the increasing popularity of the SDA community by invoking materialist motives. As Alupa (7.), Pogola (72.) and Fr Matthias (46.), among others, told me, the Adventists succeed in drawing a lot of villagers over to their side by promising or giving them clothing and money. Kenneth (40.) referred to the comparatively high payments that functionaries in the SDA church and other new communities of belief would be able to receive. The hope of material advantage was also mentioned by Ripu (16.). In his view, it is young men especially who let themselves be attracted by the claim that, as an Adventist, if one marries an Adventist woman, one need only pay a modest brideprice, which, moreover, would be provided by all the members of the SDA community in common. At the same time, numerous Catholics assured me that, like the representatives of many other denominations, the Adventists had only come to Papua New Guinea in order to trick the locals out of their money.[12]

While most Catholic villagers traced changes in denominational affiliation more or less to the desire for individual enrichment, Coleman Makoa (30.) – who is not just the main representative of the Catholic Church leadership at village level, but also a determined opponent of the Adventists – interpreted conversion to them as a criticism of his own community. There, he stated in harmony with the Catholics' generally critical assessment of themselves, there are always defamations of character, lies and other bad customs going on, and in the first instance people are always thinking of possessing many pigs and pearlshells. The rarity with which members of the Catholic community wash themselves or their clothes before major cult practices reflects how little they have changed compared with the pre-colonial period. Things are different, however, with the Adventists:

> They all wash themselves really clean and put on shoes and socks and these good clothes and spectacles and other watches or such things. Their skin is particularly clean, and they all think... that God is with them – that's it – God isn't with us dirty people. Because of this thought, they [the Catholics] go, because they [the Adventists] show the true way of life.[13]

Accordingly, whoever changes denominations shares the Adventist idea that the cleanliness of the body and of one's clothes corresponds to an inner purity of the individual and of the SDA community as a whole. Alongside Coleman Makoa, Pogola (72.) and Alupa (7.) also referred to the attractiveness that comes from this cleanliness as much as from the Western clothing that is preferred among the Adventists. In addition, Alupa (7.) thought that young people in particular found great pleasure in the hymns that form an integral part of Adventist cult practices.

Given the way in which the members of the two denominations represented in Pairundu judge one another from time to time, it is not surprising that the Adventists themselves partly explain conversions to them differently than the Catholics do. Instead of materialist motives, for example, Robert (53.) and Naki (56.) cite theological motives by listing different Bible verses, according to which one should hold services on Saturday, not Sunday. The origin of the SDA community as a whole is said to lie in Muya's experience, already mentioned, of revelation.[14] Kevin cited the persuasiveness that Muya acquired through this experience as a reason for following him.[15] Many present-day Adventists assured me that they only decided to change denominations after Fr Dunstan was defeated in his argument with leading Adventist functionaries, that is, after Adventist Christianity had demonstrated, as it were, its superiority and its relatively greater power. In this sense, on the Adventist side too and in agreement with Coleman Makoa, conversion is ultimately explained as reflecting criticism of Catholicism. Accordingly, Naki (56.) said that when he was still a member of the Catholic community, the sermons had never spoken to him, so that he always fell asleep. Robert (77; 82.) reported that during Catholic services he had only thought about playing cards and that in general he did not follow the Christian commandments any more than other Catholics. How, in Robert's rhetorical question, could one ever attain the kingdom of God like that? According to Robert (53.; 77), criticism of Catholicism was concentrated especially on Ruben, who, even in his period of office as a catechist, was known for his inclination to quarrel and his seduction of many women, whereas under his predecessor Kenneth general satisfaction had prevailed.[16]

When Robert and Naki claim that they converted because the Bible prescribes keeping the Sabbath, from the etic point of view they are formulating a post facto rationalisation. This already reflects a longer period of influence by Adventist services and therefore might have arisen not before the decision was taken to join the Adventists, but afterwards.[17] A post facto rationalisation might also be effective in the reference to the argument with Fr Dunstan, which actually might also have taken place in the form in which the Catholics remember it. From the etic point of view, finally, the thesis offered on the Catholic side, that conversion is based on materialist motives, hardly seems plausible, especially since anyone joining the Adventists knows that he or she must give up potential sources of income by, among other things, no longer keeping pigs or working on Saturdays. My conviction is that changing denominations is rather based on a desire to imitate the whites. In the context of this imitation, the Adventists surpass the Catholics because of their greater rigidity in idealising the whites and making use of things that originally come from the world of the colonial officers and missionaries. Here belongs, for example, the preference for Western clothing, which is worn both in everyday life and for cult practices. Moreover, Western language (Tok Pisin) and Western furniture (wooden benches) also appear in the context of cult practices.[18] In addition, in contrast to the Catholics, the Adventists conceive heaven as a 'New Jerusalem', that is, as a city and thus as a space associated with a specifically Western way of life (Chapter 4). Cleanliness and discipline, which for the members of both denominations are typical characteristics of the whites, have a particular significance within the SDA community. The striving for discipline is expressed in the already mentioned rigidity, in *kisim ripot*, in mutual control by church functionaries and in Pastor Koya's frequent visits. Imitating the whites by adopting first Catholic, then Adventist Christianity is intended to help in obtaining access to the superior power of the whites. The claim to have joined the group which proved to be superior and therefore 'more powerful' in the argument with Fr Dunstan points especially to the Adventists' desire for power. Here the conviction of already having some of the power that is aimed at in the context of one's own community is shared with the Catholics. Thus some Adventists assured me that God fulfilled the wishes they expressed in prayers and that in particular they were protected from *remo*, *kalando*, magical practices and attacks. The Adventist claim to have obtained power can be accepted from the etic point of view, at least in the sense that the Adventists have achieved a comparatively greater degree of autonomy and equality through the larger number and fluctuation of functionaries. In addition the greater involvement of the community and the more rapid succession of separate, brief elements during services contribute to the fact that for the Adventists their cult practices appear to be more varied and entertaining (Chapter 4). On the other hand, the accusation of a lack of variety and entertainment is articulated in Naki's claim that he always fell asleep during Catholic services.

For the members of both denominations represented in Pairundu, imitating the whites requires and permits a distancing from the pre-colonial past in particular. The Adventists surpass the Catholics in this matter of distancing too, since, in comparison with Catholicism, Adventist Christianity presents itself as a clearer counter-model to the tradition. In addition, Adventist Christianity simultaneously seems to be a counter-model to Catholicism, since Naki and Robert claim that they had decided to convert among other things because of dissatisfaction with Catholic cult practices and since Coleman Makoa interprets this conversion as a criticism of his own community. The Adventists associate the Catholics with tradition, since they see them not as Christians, but as adherents of the traditional religion (Chapter 4). From this necessarily arises the idea that, as a Catholic, one cannot enter heaven on the coming *las de*. Thus I would agree with the Catholics when they assume that fear has contributed to the decision to convert. It is not for nothing that, in both interviews and services, the members of the SDA community emphasise strongly that the end of the world is imminent and that it is only by following all commandments and prohibitions, that is, by being an Adventist, that one can avoid hellfire. The criticism of Catholicism is particularly directed against the functionaries at village level, regardless of whether these are the first catechists to officiate in Pairundu, Ruben or Coleman Makoa, all of whom effectively represent the Catholic Church leadership as a whole, given the relatively rare visits of the priest.[19] In the case of Fr Jim, who was admittedly stationed in Sumi at the time the SDA community was established, but who never visited Pairundu personally, the criticism is also extended to the priest himself. Even Fr Matthias (46.) expressed the view to me that Fr Jim had not been 'as strong' as, for example, Fr Dunstan had been and that the Adventists had perhaps benefited from this. On the whole, therefore, I find it plausible from the etic point of view when members of both denominations say that dissatisfaction with Catholicism in general and its functionaries in particular increases the readiness to convert.[20]

In a historical and social situation in which the Kome generally complain of a process of social disintegration, first with reference to the pre-colonial past and then with respect to the order created by the colonial government, switching denominational affiliation promises membership in a firmly consolidated group. Essentially, external separation contributes to the integration of the Adventist community. This separation is expressed in the idea, which is typical of the Adventists and also addressed by Coleman Makoa, that it is dangerous to be too close to the Catholics. Thus, at least officially, conversion means the ending of all social relationships with non-Adventist relatives, that is, a 'social death', which, however, leads to membership in the SDA community, that is, in a way, to a 'social birth'. Accordingly, Muya claimed that, from now on, instead of, for example, Coleman Makoa, he would view every other Adventist as his brother (Chapter 4). Purity and separation, whether conscious or unconscious, had also already been aims in the context of the traditional religion. For example, purity should result from the prescription that no one who had had sexual relations beforehand was allowed to be present during a therapy for illnesses caused by Neambu or to visit Atasi's 'dream hut' (Chapter 2). The separation between functionaries and participants on the one hand and non-participants on the other arose with traditional cult and magical practices through the secrecy of specific knowledge (Chapter 2). Today, however, secrecy plays no role among the Adventists. Instead, one's own separation is justified rather by the expectation of the *sande lo* as a martyrdom projected into the future. The fact that one will fall victim to the Catholics shortly before the imminent end of the world means that one must already keep away from them while moving closer together within one's own community. At the same time, the expectation of the *sande lo* strengthens the Adventist claim to exclusivity, which also contributes to integration. Just as the Adventists will be the only ones to be persecuted by Satan before the Last Day of Judgement (and just as they are the only denomination represented in Papua New Guinea to conduct their major cult practices on Saturday instead of Sunday), so, according to their convictions, they will be the only ones to reach heaven.

Although, in comparison with Catholicism, Adventist Christianity is more clearly a counter-model to the traditional culture and traditional religion, among the Adventists too there are parallels between their understanding of their own version of Christianity and tradition.[21] Part of this is the close connection between what constitutes the secular and the sacred from the etic point of view. For the Adventists, components of the two spheres are combined to form the work that is to provide access to heaven as a counter-prestation. Here, as with the Catholics, the hope that one's own needs will be fulfilled is strengthened primarily by the, so to speak, traditionally justified expectation of reciprocity. Comparatively speaking, this expectation is more clearly expressed among the Adventists, in accordance with their rigidity. According to Muya, access to heaven is a consequence of attending divine services, among other things, just as harvests follow cultivation (Chapter 4). In the first instance, one guarantee of reciprocity for the members of the SDA community is to follow the prescriptions laid down in the Bible as in a sort of handbook of regulations. Here, in principle the same legalism is articulated that had already determined the relationship with the transcendent in the pre-colonial period as well as in Catholicism, though this legalism becomes intensified by the Adventist idea that the failure to observe even a single commandment prevents access to heaven (Chapter 4). As with the expectation of the *sande lo*, it follows that, for the Adventists, human existence is basically no less endangered than it is for the Catholics. In my view, the creation and maintenance of fear is also fed by the experience of a loss of autonomy resulting from colonisation and missionisation. A parallel with the traditional culture, which to some extent the Adventists have in greater measure than the Catholics, arises out of their separation from the outside. The pre-colonial separation of 'in-group' and 'out-group', which admittedly was sometimes lifted through the acceptance of non-agnates (Chapter 1), corresponds to the social antagonism between Adventists and non-Adventists, between the 'chosen' and the 'damned'. Today an overcoming of social antagonism could be seen in the efforts to persuade non-Adventists to convert. As for the Catholics earlier, for the Adventists too, the parallels between tradition and one's understanding of one's own version of Christianity contributes to the fact that this Christianity is considered and accepted as true.[22] From the etic point of view, comparatively speaking the parallels on the Adventist side seem even more clearly marked, because of the rigidity that prevails among the Adventists. This increases the certainty of salvation that allows them, in contrast to the Catholics, to avoid great doubt that they understand the Christian message properly and are following Jesus' example in the prescribed manner. However, analysing the parallels between tradition and one's understanding of one's own version of Christianity cannot explain the acceptance of all Christian beliefs. For example, the view expressed in both communities that the Last Day of Judgement is more or less imminent has, in my judgement, no model in the traditional religion.[23] The same goes for the conceptions of heaven and hell.

Finally, alongside the various parallels, a comparison between tradition and one's understanding of one's own version of Christianity also reveals contradictions. Among these in particular is the Adventist demand for withdrawal from society, which cannot be connected with the attempts that were significant in the traditional culture to demonstrate strength and acquire social influence. By wanting to be 'like the dead', members of the SDA community appear to have directed inwards the aggression which was traditionally linked with the value of strength and which, from the Western point of view, is generally ascribed to the inhabitants of the Highlands. Another contradiction arises from the moral dualism of the Adventists, which strictly separates heaven from hell, good from evil, God from Satan, without thereby allowing any ambivalences, tensions or transitions between the antagonistic categories. This creates the impression that there are simple answers to all questions, which certainly does give relief subjectively but which also opposes the pre-colonial world-view, according to which transcendent authorities like *remo* can both injure and help humans.[24] Moreover, people judged individual actions like, for example, deadly witchcraft techniques not according to established moral categories like the Adventists, but according to whether they had been used against a member of either one's own or an enemy group.[25] Altogether, the contradictions listed might strengthen the members of the SDA community in their conviction that, through conversion, they are distancing themselves from their tradition as well as, as it were, confronting the old with the wholly new.

The Holy Spirit movement

After the start of Catholic missionisation and after conversion to the Adventists, the third phase in the process of adopting Christianity, finally, is the Holy Spirit movement, which in Pairundu lasted from 1987 to 1989. In retrospect, this Holy Spirit movement is regarded positively only by some of its former participants. Yapanu (96.), for example, based a positive valuation on the claim that she had been inspired by the Holy Spirit. Ruben (85.), who, as a catechist, had read out Bible texts that had been chosen blind, but who claimed not to have come into contact with the Holy Spirit himself, stated that the Holy Spirit movement was 'something good', since within its framework one could cure illnesses and find stolen property.[26] According to Yapanu (27.), if the Holy Spirit movement had not been ended, it would have been possible to learn more not only about the past life of the ancestors, but also about future events. Accordingly, the women who participated had responded to the 'prohibition' of the Big Men by complaining that they were being deprived of a good form of divine service. Kenneth (39.), who had contributed substantially to the spread of the Holy Spirit movement after the end of his time as catechist, explained that those who participated in it were initially convinced that they had found the up till then unknown 'true core' of Christianity.[27] In addition, according to Kenneth, the possibility of bodily expression at the night-time assemblies, with handclapping, dancing and the shaking of limbs, met with a good response: 'Formerly we had read the Bible, but we did not convert what we heard into action and therefore we were happy about what was brought to us'.[28] I also heard indications of dissatisfaction with the usual forms of Christianity in other regions in which such phenomena were still spreading at the time of my fieldwork. In Pundia, some women complained that they were not sufficiently involved in the conduct of the traditional Sunday services, and in the Ialibu area these services were described as too boring.[29]

On the whole, however, among the Kome today rejection of the Holy Spirit movement predominates. In the case of Kenneth and Ata Francis, even former participants have joined the opponents, to whom otherwise belong non-baptised Big Men like Yawa and Rekepea, as well as Augustin as a former and Coleman Makoa as an officiating catechist. Augustin's view that this was 'a sort of sickness' ('wanpela kain sik') was shared by Kenneth, Ripu (39.) and Pogola (24.), among others. The mostly negative assessment of the Holy Spirit movement is indicated, for example, by the fact that Phillip (68.), who lived in Wasuma and who neither knew me nor knew what to make of me, said in front of many listeners that everywhere these meetings had long since ceased although he himself was still attending and even leading such meetings secretly in distant villages as Kenneth (39.) told me later. In rejecting the Holy Spirit movement, the Catholic villagers agree with the Adventists. According to Pastor Koya (46.), 'the good spirit' is no longer sent today, since, unlike the time of the

Apostles, God's message has already reached everyone. Thus it was only 'evil spirits' that could still be contacted at these cult practices. Other attempts at explanation specify a conscious decision by the participants rather than a sickness or the effect of evil spirits. Thus, according to the Big Men of Pairundu, the women in particular wanted to use the night-time meetings of the Holy Spirit movement in order to make arrangements for pre- or extra-marital sexual relations (Chapter 3). Augustin (27.) thought that individuals sought to increase their personal prestige (*apim nem*) through their involvement.

In contrast to the prevailing opinion at the village level, Holy Spirit movements are often seen rather positively in mission theology. Bus and Landu (1989: 174) describe such phenomena as 'strong and healthy, a genuine enrichment of the Church'.[30] Criticism here is often unspecific. Although Bus and Landu (1989: 174) speak of 'exotic excesses' occurring in the course of individual cult events, which have later been overcome, they do not say exactly what they mean by this. Many authors accuse participants of neglecting their daily work because of the night-time meetings.[31] According to Fr Dunstan (33.), the leading representatives of the Catholic Church leadership usually try to join the Holy Spirit movements in order to control them from the inside to some extent, that is, to moderate the emotions that are usually expressed within their context.[32] According to Sr Marie (48.), decisive rejection is directed only against prophesying, ascribing sins, attempting to expel evil spirits and the chance selection, with eyes closed, of the Bible passages that are to be discussed (cf. Chapter 4). Augustin's view, that participation in the Holy Spirit movement is mostly intended to raise one's own prestige, was only shared by Fr Don, who also claimed that participation was motivated just as much by the pursuit of variety and entertainment as by the feeling of not having enough standing and influence in one's own community.[33] All in all, however, the leading representatives of the Catholic Church leadership maintain a different position. Thus Kenneth (39.) and Augustin (27.), as former catechists, said that Fr Jim, the officiating priest at that time, had merely suggested shortening individual meetings, but otherwise waiting and submitting the Holy Spirit movement to a precise examination before possibly ending it. Accordingly, Fr Jim had finally urged the Catholic community to make an independent assessment and decision of its own.

The question whether a spirit – however it may be judged – really causes the Holy Spirit movement or not can only be decided on the basis of belief and therefore will not be discussed here. From the etic point of view, rather, it is the desire for power that motivates participation in the Holy Spirit movement. This power, sought after through direct contact with the Holy Spirit, becomes an object of concrete experience for participants in that it causes, in their view, handclapping, dancing and shaking of limbs, that is, those forms of corporeality and emotionality that, according to Kenneth, found a positive response generally.[34] In addition, the power of the Holy Spirit is supposed to bring about results that should seem familiar and plausible, since in the pre-colonial period these were the purpose of magical practices in particular. Thus people believed that the Holy Spirit could help them expose injurious thoughts and feelings, find hidden stolen property and cure sicknesses (Chapter 3). Accordingly, to some extent, the individual cult practices which make up the Holy Spirit movement are functional equivalents of the traditional procedures for divination and for curing illnesses. Wala (92.) therefore claimed that formerly the sick were cured after being brought into the house of Rimbu or Rombake and later they were cured after being visited by the adherents of the Holy Spirit movement.[35] The striving for the power of the Holy Spirit simultaneously includes the desire to raise one's status that was noted by Augustin and Fr Don. This raising of status appears to be realised as equality and autonomy in the case of the Holy Spirit movement, since, in principle, direct contact with the Holy Spirit is open to everyone. With respect to the relationship between the genders, the fact that women form the majority of participants can be taken as a sign of rising status, equality and autonomy (Chapter 3). With respect to the Catholic Church leadership, autonomy comes from the fact that – as Sr Marie criticises, in her view, not without reason – in choosing the Bible texts to be dealt with, one opens the Bible blind, instead of following the church calendar for Sunday services. When Kenneth speaks of a secret core in Christianity, in my judgement in principle he means nothing other than the power promised by direct contact with the Holy Spirit. The complaint that fundamentally, from the arrival of the first priests and catechists up to the present day, it has still not been possible to uncover the hidden core or partake of the striven-for power is in essence a criticism of Catholicism. Therefore, the dissatisfaction with Catholicism in general and with some of its representatives in particular, voiced in part by the members of the Catholic community themselves, has also made it much easier first to convert to the Adventists and then to participate in the Holy Spirit movement.

The ending of the Holy Spirit movement, which seems to have proceeded from the Big Men in particular, cannot be seen as final in many respects. Thus, for example, former participants claim that in principle they would be in a position to renew contact with the Holy Spirit at any time. Even more important, however, is the fact that numerous elements that originally only appeared with the introduction of the Holy Spirit movement still continue, above all in the Catholic evening services. Flowers are used for divinatory dreams, people sometimes consult the Bible blind, and women take over leading functions. In addition, in Sunday services too there is rhythmic handclapping accompanying hymns, as well as the sporadic use of flower decorations (Chapter 4). Here we are confronted, as it were, with present-day traces of the Holy Spirit movement, among which the possibility of divinatory dreams, together with the 'blind' opening of the Bible and the greater participation of women, represent an increase in equality and autonomy. Accordingly Kenneth (39.) assured me that today, through baptism, every member of the Catholic community has access to the Holy Spirit and thus in principle has the ability to heal the sick through the laying on of hands, whereas prior to the Holy Spirit movement, such healing could only be carried out by the catechists.

Alongside the Holy Spirit movement itself, the way in which it was ended does provide information concerning the desires of the villagers as a whole. While the Adventist functionaries condemn the various meetings unequivocally, Fr Jim ultimately demanded that his community came to an autonomous judgement and decision. However, Catholics dismissed the self-responsibility thus transferred on to them by converting Fr Jim's attitude into a decisive rejection that corresponded to the attitude of the Adventists.[36] Thus, the members of the Catholic community were able to claim that they were merely complying with their church leadership, without having to represent or be responsible for their own decision to bring things to an end themselves. Here it becomes clear that in principle the Catholics share with the Adventists the desire to be exonerated by submitting to authority, that is, by accepting simple statements and clear instructions for action that are issued by that authority. On the one hand, therefore, the adherents of the two denominations strive to win power and autonomy, while on the other they simultaneously wish to be released from the responsibility that goes along with an increase in autonomy.

Concluding remarks

A comparison of the desires and beliefs that are effective in the different phases of the adoption of Christianity explains not only the process of adoption as a whole, but also the 'success', that is, the increasing popularity, of the Adventists. Basically in my view, the adoption of Christianity serves people in moving closer to the whites and in distancing themselves from their traditional culture. In this respect, the Adventists seem to have greater success than the Catholics. Since the beginning of missionisation, for the villagers Christianity was essentially linked to the world of the whites and above all to their superior power.[37] Thus imitating the whites in general and the reception of Christianity in particular is motivated in the first instance by the desire to partake in the power of the whites. The hope to obtain power justifies, one after the other, the obedience to the first Catholic missionaries, the conversion to the Adventists and the introduction of the Holy Spirit movement. Accordingly, the adherents of both denominations understand the argument between Fr Dunstan and Adventist functionaries primarily as a struggle for power, and they share the view that is it sensible to attach oneself to the group of the victor.

Obtaining the power that is aimed for is supposed to permit one's own status to be raised by demonstrating one's strength, in order to create equivalence with respect to other locals as well as the whites, that is intra- as well as inter-culturally. This goal has already been reached in the idea of heaven that is held by both communities, in which equality prevails after the removal of all differences.[38] The two denominations represented in Pairundu thus form simultaneously not only two 'pathways to heaven' but also two 'pathways to equality'. Realising strength and equivalence as traditional values both intra- and inter-culturally means winning back one's lost autonomy, claiming one's own identity and controlling the fear of a loss of autonomy and of a threat to one's identity. In this sense, I would agree with the Catholics when they describe fear as one of the motives for the adoption, first of Catholic and then of Adventist Christianity. At the same time, however, I see here a contradiction between what the villagers are striving for and what in my view actually happens. On the one hand, the members of both denominations claim that their adoption of their particular form of Christianity has enabled them to distance themselves from tradition. On the other hand, my analysis shows that imitating the whites in general and the reception of Christianity in particular is ultimately supposed to serve the realisation of traditional values. In this sense, from the etic point of view, Catholics and Adventists are basically seeking to maintain the tradition in the very act of breaking with it. For the villagers, just like Western goods, the different forms of Christianity represent both the power of the whites and the threat to one's own identity that comes from it, as well as the hoped-for strengthening of this identity. Accordingly, the attempt to appropriate the essentials of the threat in order to protect the threatened in the context of the traditional religion and of the *kisim sevis* is repeated equally in the adoption of Christianity (Chapter 5).

From the emic point of view, people do actually manage to obtain power. Thus, people say, sicknesses are cured that, in the pre-colonial period, had been treated with traditional cult and magical practices. Admittedly here prayers said in common have taken the place of the old secret magical formulas, but nevertheless the saying of words retains great significance. Moreover, the power that is obtained includes protection for the villagers. The Catholics claim that the *remo* can no longer injure them, while the Adventists stress that they no longer fear *remo*, *kalando* or witchcraft. In addition, the increase in power is expressed in the increase of one's own status, for example when taking over a church office increases one's own prestige. Thus Sr Marie (48.) described the attempt to outdo others by wearing a badge indicating one's membership of a Church Committee and to regard the church of one's own village as 'one's own church' (*church bilong mi*). In Pairundu, such an attempt is best represented by Ari and Muya, who similarly enjoy a certain reputation for having contributed to the foundation of their own community, though they have also been criticised for boasting of their leading positions in their respective communities (Chapter 4). Finally, as already described, the cult practices of the Adventists, compared with those of the Catholics, represent a gaining of equality and autonomy, in particular for younger men and women. Altogether, therefore, although for some the desire for power is fulfilled in the different phases of the adoption of Christianity, this has mostly been restricted to the members of the same community or the participants in the Holy Spirit movement. Ultimately, therefore, this is rather a partial satisfaction of desires, a 'foretaste' of not yet attained but still sought after intra- and especially inter-cultural autonomy and equality. Many Catholics express the view that they still cannot sufficiently realise their goals by referring to the idea that their form of Christianity contains a not yet decoded secret (Chapter 4). Then the participants in the Holy Spirit movement saw the contents of this secret in their direct contact with the Holy Spirit. By representing a certain but admittedly not yet fully satisfying increase in power, equality and autonomy, the traces of the Holy Spirit movement in the Catholic evening services show that the needs that have led to the introduction of the Holy Spirit movement still retain their effectiveness now that the movement has been ended. In contrast to the Catholics, the Adventists deny that any secret exists, so that to some extent they are claiming that in principle they have already satisfied all their desires through their conversion.

The members of the two denominations represented in Pairundu believe that imitating the whites in general, like the adoption of Christianity in particular, requires above all a distancing from tradition. Whoever wants to become 'like the whites' can no longer be like his own ancestors. It is from this thought that the prohibitions and commandments acquire their significance, which in Catholic and especially Adventist Christianity are directed against the tradition. The rejection of the traditional culture and the traditional religion that is propagated by the Adventists corresponds to the position that, in the villagers' memory, was also maintained by the first priests and catechists. In this sense, with their distancing from tradition, Adventist children reproduce, so to speak, the behaviour that had already allegedly been demanded of their Catholic parents. However, while the members of the two denominations see their respective forms of Christianity similarly as a counter-image to tradition, the Adventists also see their form of Christianity as a counter-image to Catholicism, which they, as it were, include with tradition. Thus the Adventists integrate Catholicism in the idea of tradition, which, at least officially, is valued similarly negatively at village level. Nevertheless, from the etic point of view, above all it is parallels between the tradition and one's understanding of one's own version of Christianity that give rise to the impression of plausibility and truth for both Catholics and Adventists, consciously or not.[39] The differences between the tradition and the denomination-specific understanding of one's respective form of Christianity, on the other hand, may strengthen the members of the SDA community in particular in their view that they are distancing themselves from the traditional culture.[40]

If, in the different phases which make up the process of the adoption of Christianity, the same desires and beliefs are effective in principle and if the denominations represented in Pairundu – despite the obvious differences in their outward appearance – vary only gradually rather than substantially, then the villagers are not converting to the Adventists because they want something different or think differently than those who have not taken this step. In my judgement, the 'success' of the Adventists is based rather on their rigidity, which gives rise to a greater certainty of salvation by creating the impression that, in comparison to the Catholics, the Adventists have both imitated the whites and distanced themselves from the tradition in a more decisive and consistent manner. Thus the conviction arises that the desires which motivate the adoption of Christianity in all its phases could be satisfied rather within the SDA community. Certainly, in view of the traditional pragmatism, the significance of beliefs – compared to the significance of desires – should not be overestimated, but here too rigidity adds to the certainty of salvation. Thus, on the Adventist side, the parallels between the tradition and the denomination-specific understanding of Christianity prove to be more clearly marked, through which the plausibility and truth of one's own form of Christianity is increased, subjectively speaking. Although the Adventists therefore owe their popularity on the one hand to their decisive distancing from tradition, from the etic point of view it is precisely the parallels with the tradition that contribute to this popularity (cf. Jebens 1997). The connection between rigidity and the certainty of salvation can be clarified with the aid of the traditional principle of reciprocity. If Christianity is seen as a work consisting of various components for which, as in the case of a gift, access to heaven is expected as a counter-prestation, then the conviction that the acquisition of the counter-prestation is justified and at the same time probable is also increased with the size of the gift. Accordingly, the Adventists are basically strengthening their claim to access to heaven when they stress that the Adventist message is 'hard to follow' (Chapter 4), that one is subject to strict discipline in the SDA community, that potential sources of income are sacrificed when one gives up keeping pigs and working on Saturdays and that one must go without tobacco, betel nut and beer. In the Adventist view, none of this applies to the Catholics, who do not prohibit anything, but therefore do not go to heaven either – no counter-prestation without a prestation. If, in accordance with the principle of reciprocity, the extent of one's own efforts and deprivations increases the certainty of salvation, this suggests the thesis that many villagers do convert to the Adventists not despite, but precisely because of, the sacrifices that are linked with it. The 'escape' from the traditional social and economic obligations, culminating in the giving up of pig husbandry, might also have a liberating effect, especially for the sons of the Big Men, who are exposed to a particularly high degree to the general expectation that they should emulate the example of their fathers.

Through their certainty of salvation and their conviction that they are treading the correct path, as it were, the Adventists are strengthened in subjecting themselves to a moral dualism of precisely specified prohibitions and commandments. Certainly on the one hand the corresponding obedience in part contains considerable demands, but on the other hand it also leads subjectively to a reduction in fear and to exoneration. Here the ending of the Holy Spirit movement shows that in principle the Catholics also share the desire for such an exoneration. This is not surprising, given the general feeling of insecurity. The members of both denominations complain equally about the dissolution of the pre-colonial, colonial and now also post-colonial order. No one knows how to get possession of *sevis*. The Catholics see the Adventists questioning their identity as Christians, while for their part, for all their certainty of salvation, the Adventists fear being excluded from heaven by violating prohibitions.

The SDA community in Pairundu was founded against the resistance of a society that up until then had only been exposed to the influence of the representatives of the Catholic Church leadership. Moreover, given that the growth of the Adventist community tends to be based on conversions, that is, on a simultaneous reduction of the Catholic community, it becomes directly necessary to criticise the Catholics, to emphasise oneself over them and simultaneously to missionise them. As a precondition for this, the Adventists' certainty of salvation that is fed by their rigidity is to some extent a structural necessity, without which, in my judgement, the establishment of the SDA community would not have been possible. Finally, Adventist Christianity certainly also draws its attractiveness from the fact that, like the Holy Spirit movement, it can initially claim the attraction of the new for itself. Within the Catholic community, on the other hand, since the arrival of the first priests and catechists, that is, in the course of more than thirty years, the initial inspiration seems to have softened into a certain routinisation and 'tiredness'. Accordingly, at least implicitly, some villagers ascribe a comparatively greater entertainment value to the cult practices of Adventist Christianity and the Holy Spirit movement. From the etic point of view, certainly, the dissatisfaction with Catholicism in general and with some of its functionaries in particular is based above all on the fact that the adoption of Catholic Christianity has not led to the acquisition of power that was hoped for. Simultaneously I see this as an important factor that has contributed to the 'success' of the Adventists as well as to the rise of the Holy Spirit movement.

If the different phases of the adoption of Christianity are similar with regard to underlying desires and beliefs, then to some extent conversion to the Adventists can be interpreted structurally as a repetition of the start of Catholic missionisation. In their demand that people must 'give up everything' in order to become Christians and their linking of promises with threats, of heaven with hell, the Adventist functionaries are again taking up elements that – according to the 'ordinary' members of the

Catholic community, at least – had already been propagated by the first priests and catechists. In accordance with their rigidity, however, the Adventists are not only repeating the start of Catholic mission activities, they are also subjecting it to further development in the sense of intensifying or surpassing it. Thus, members of the SDA community, as Coleman Makoa also agrees, claim that they succeed in accomplishing a change where the Catholics have failed. All in all, therefore, at the start of their adoption of Christianity, villagers make an attempt, until some of them, disappointed with the results, proceed again with greater commitment and in a somewhat different form in the second phase of the adoption. Those who share the disappointment but do not take part in it then vary this same attempt once more in the third phase by participating in the Holy Spirit movement. The thesis that conversion to the Adventists repeats or intensifies the start of Catholic missionisation in a structurally similar manner would certainly be disputed by the members of the SDA community. In accordance with their claim to exclusivity, they see only themselves as 'proper' Christians, while denying a Christian identity to the Catholics. For the Adventists, therefore, causing the Catholics to convert means not resuming an earlier missionisation, but carrying out the first real Christianisation. From the etic point of view, conversely, the structural similarities between Catholic missionisation, conversion to the Adventists and the Holy Spirit movement suggest that the adoption of Catholicism both prepared and made easier the adoption of Adventist Christianity. The representatives of the Adventist Church leadership were able to build on ideas and patterns that had already been known for a long time. Seen in this way, the Adventist functionaries would have reason to thank their Catholic opponents for having smoothed their path for them.[41]

Notes

1. Obviously the individual phases only affect a part of the village population. Not everyone joined the Catholic community, not everyone changed over to the Adventists, and not everyone took part in the Holy Spirit movement.
2. '...emame lain na nogut ol bai paitim mipela, nogut ol bai kilim mipela, nogut ol i bai kotim mipela... yumi mas i go na harim gut tok'.
3. Imbrock himself, on the other hand, ascribes the corresponding threats exclusively to the Catholics (Chapter 3).
4. '...sapos mipela mekim pasin nogut, mipela bai i go long paia... mipela mas bihainim tok bilong God na i go long heven...'.
5. 'Olgeta man long dispela hap ol i bin lusim dispela Rimbu na Rombake na senisim tok bilong God na yu wanpela inap long holim dispela Rimbu na Rombake?'
6. (Chapter 3). However, the villagers themselves do not report having received presents from the whites.
7. '...mipela i holim trupela lotu...' (informal conversation with a Mamarepa from Sua/Yeibu, whose name is unknown to me, on 4 July 1991, in front of Yapa's house in Pairundu**). This implies a claim that the Church of the Seventh-day Adventists is not a *trupela lotu*, since the SDA evangelism week, during which it rained right the way

through, was taking place at the same time. During the SDA baptism itself, however, the sun shone, something the Adventists, for their part, referred to, not without satisfaction.

8. 'Bipo mipela Rimbu na Opayo na dispela kain, olgeta em i remo, tasol yupela givim pawa long mipela na mipela lusim i stap'.

9. Which thoughts were actually decisive at the time of contact with the first priests and catechists can no longer be reconstructed in detail with any certainty today.

10. In establishing such parallels, I am aware of the danger that the view of tradition may itself have already been coloured by Christian influence.

11. From the etic point of view, however, there is a difference as to whether one fears the punishment of breaches of the rules or whether one believes in moral categories, though in my view this difference is not seen in this way by the members of the community themselves.

12. Walaya (63.), Coleman Makoa (30.) and Alupa (7.) mentioned this. An unusual view that was not shared by other Catholics was that of Sr Marie (47.), who claimed that, like many other fundamentalist missions, the Adventists were supported by the CIA.

13. 'Ol waswas gut, klin gut na putim su na sokis na dispela gutpela klos na aiglas na ol arapela hanwas o samting olsem. Skin bilong ol i lait tumas na ol i ting olsem... God i stap wantaim – em nau – God i no stap wantaim mipela dirty lain. Dispela tingting, ol i go na, long wanem, ol i soim pasin tru'.

14. (Chapter 3). Incidentally, even Coleman Makoa and some other Catholics believed that this had actually occurred.

15. Kevin also said that it was normal traditionally to follow the example of one's older brother (Chapter 1).

16. This claim was implicitly confirmed by Kenneth (40.) himself, who on another occasion assured me that had he remained in office longer, no one would have left the Catholic community.

17. The question whether the service must 'actually' be conducted on the Sabbath or on Sunday can ultimately only be decided on the basis of belief and thus will not be examined here.

18. Muya had placed benches for sitting in his own house right at the start of the Adventist's mission activities, that is, even before the church had been built (Chapter 3), clearly because he believed that without them no proper service could be held.

19. As already mentioned, Pastor Koya appears more frequently in Pairundu than Fr Matthias. Because of the latter's relative rare visits, blessings and confessions often cannot be administered at Catholic Sunday services, since they can only be granted or taken by the priest (cf. MacDonald 1991: 55).

20. However, this not to say that functionaries in the SDA community like Peter, Robert or Muya (as the 'church founder') were not criticised (Chapter 4).

21. As with Catholicism, there is a danger that the view of tradition has been changed through Christian influence.

22. A purely external parallel between Catholicism, Adventist Christianity and tradition, in addition to what has already been described, can be seen in the fact that, in both church buildings today, men and women sit separately, just as the two groups of participants have formerly done during the Alamu-palaa Rimbu (Chapter 2). Alongside this, accepting food is still an element in religious practice, wafers in Catholic and Adventist Christianity having replaced the pig meat eaten and pig's blood drunk in connection with traditional cult and magical practices.

23. However, older informants like Alupa, Nokosi and Nosupinai (60.) reported, that according to their parents and grandparents, long before the coming of the whites, the clouds once fell from heaven and would do so again some time in the future. With the term 'Time of Darkness', a similar form of this idea has also been described for the Huli (Glasse 1963, Allen and Wood 1980), the Enga (Mai 1981) and numerous other language groups. According to Blong (1981, 1982, cf. Mai 1981), this is supposedly to be traced back to a fall of ash which happened between 1640 and 1800 even in the Highlands as a consequence of a volcanic eruption on Long Island, Madang Province. Unlike among

the Kome, on the other hand, a traditional view of the end of the world seems to exist among the Onabasalu living south of Mount Bosavi. According to Schiefflin (1991: 66), in the pre-colonial period they believed that, when a mythical figure returned, the events of creation would be undone and the world would be destroyed.

24. (Chapter 2). Accordingly, MacDonald (1991: 542, n. 140) writes, on the southern Kewa: 'Prior to the preaching of Christianity, the Kewa did not have a concept of a personified evil force which could be equated with the Christian concept of Satan'.

25. The use of the same deadly witchcraft techniques was condemned in the case of the 'in-group', but welcomed in the case of the 'out-group', since the well-being of the 'in-group' was viewed positively, that of the 'out-group' negatively. In this sense, in the pre-colonial period there only existed a moral dualism to the extent that the social dualism had a moral content.

26. Ruben said literally: 'prea grup, em samting tru'. This argument, which judges a cult practice by its concrete results ('it worked, so it was good'), seems like an expression of the traditionally widespread pragmatism.

27. Kenneth talked about the 'pasin tru bilong bihainim pasin Christianity'.

28. 'Bipo mipela i save ritim Baibel, tasol mipela i no save putim action long wanem samting mipela i harim olsem na mipela i amamas long dispela samting ol i kam mekim'.

29. The Lutheran Pastor Uland Spahlinger (89.) told me about the complaint of the women of Pundia after having talked with them (Chapter 3). People in the Ialibu area also referred to the Lutheran Church.

30. Ahrens (1986a: 143), in agreement with this, writes that there is a basic openness to Holy Spirit movements in both the Catholic and Lutheran Church leaderships.

31. See, among others, Teske (1983: 116).

32. Correspondingly, Fr Matthias (50.) described an attempt 'to minimise those emotion things'. Fr Brian (28.), who is responsible for the Ialibu area, expressed to me the view that the loss of self-control and of control in general could not be the work of the Holy Spirit.

33. Fr Don mentioned these reasons on 1 December 1990 in the Catholic mission station of Karia (Kagua), during a seminar he was holding for the catechists of the area. In a conversation with me alone (31.), after the conclusion of the corresponding period of instruction, he expressed to me his supposition – repeatedly and, in light of my amused and incredulous reaction, with emphasis – that the CIA was behind the Holy Spirit movement. As already described, Sr Marie also saw the CIA as supporting the Adventists.

34. Alongside this, expressions of corporeality and emotionality guarantee that degree of variety and entertainment which was often missed at traditional Catholic Sunday services and which therefore – to this extent the etic view agrees with Fr Don – offers an additional attraction for participation in the Holy Spirit movement.

35. Accordingly, although Wala, as one of the Big Men, was opposed to the Holy Spirit movement, he did not dispute its effectiveness.

36. On the other hand, though more rarely, I heard positive reinterpretations, as in the case of a comment by Alupa (7.), according to which the leading Catholic functionaries had said that people were doing something good and should continue it. This seems to me all the more remarkable because Alupa himself belongs to the opponents of the Holy Spirit movement in Pairundu.

37. From the emic point of view, there are other possible reasons for the links between Christianity and power. Like, for example, pearlshells, as a value object Christianity comes not from Pairundu and its area but from a very distant region. Water, which is traditionally linked with the transcendent sphere, since the *kalando* traditionally live either at or in rivers, also plays a role in Christian baptism (more clearly in the case of the immersion of the Adventists than the aspersion of the Catholics). Possibly, moreover, the desire Robert mentioned to travel once to the sea (Chapter 4) could be interpreted against the background of water's symbolic quality.

38. (Chapter 4). The fact that this is a matter of equality and not of the imitation of the whites for their own sake is indicated by the fact that Western elements do not have any special significance in either idea of heaven. Thus the following conclusion by J. Clark (1988: 51) cannot be applied to the situation in Pairundu: 'Being able to obtain luxury goods without money is a characteristic of Wiru perceptions of heaven… a place with a strong European overtone'.

39. A parallel of a rather formal nature that has not yet been mentioned is the fact that, in the pre-colonial period, cult practices like Aga-palaa Rimbu, Alamu-palaa Rimbu, Rombake, Akera and Opayo were each carried out within cycles (Chapter 2) and that in Christianity too cycles are created through the repetition of the church year. In addition, the Adventists stress every thirteenth Sabbath service through foot-washing and communion (Chapter 4).

40. A difference not yet mentioned is that baptism is practiced in both Catholic and Adventist Christianity, whereas the traditional religion seems to have had no initiation rites (Chapter 2). Here, possibly, the two forms of Christianity have closed a 'gap'.

41. However, the Catholic missionisation should not be seen as a precondition for conversion to the Adventists. In my judgement, even hypothetically, the representatives of the Adventist Church leadership would have converted many villagers to them even if they had arrived in Pairundu before the first priests and catechists.

7

The Influence of the Traditional Religion

In the two previous chapters, I have examined the changes that, in the emic view, go along with colonisation and missionisation, those that the Kome hope for in the context of 'development' (Chapter 5) and those that occur in connection with the adoption of Christianity (Chapter 6). From these changes the focus now turns to continuity, that is, to the present-day influence of the traditional religion. From the etic point of view, we shall see that the traditional religion has not been eradicated or replaced by Christianity to the extent that first appears or that the members of the two denominations claim, at least officially. The reason for this emerges out of the interaction between religious and social change. The socio-economic consequences of colonisation have entered into the process of the adoption of Christianity, which, for its part, does have effects in the socio-economic sense. Similarly, the traditional religion too had already included and constituted reality on the one hand, while also influencing it itself on the other (Chapter 2).

Tradition and Christianity

In Pairundu, on the levels of both beliefs and concrete actions, elements of Christianity and of tradition exist side by side in a dualistic way. As regular visitors to the Sunday services, the members of the Catholic community in particular reproduce the views of their church leadership, while at the same time they are also convinced of the existence of *remo* and *kalando*, as well as of the effectiveness of magical practices, which in part they continue to practice, in some cases in opposition to their church's leadership. This sort of dualism allows the villagers to orient their actions towards the tradition in some cases and towards Christianity in others. Thus as already described, Marcus attempted to cure his child's illness using very different means, one after another: Western medicine from the health centre in Sumi, prayers and the laying on of hands during a night-time Catholic service, the voicing of feelings and thoughts considered to be damaging (*autim tingting*) and finally drinking pig's blood in the course of a magical healing procedure (Chapter 2). The contradictions that go along with this, in so far as they are made conscious, can easily be retained on the level of belief, since, in accordance with the traditional pragmatism, the indigenous need for systematisation and coherence is not especially marked. Accordingly, it was already possible in the pre-colonial period to conduct different cult and magical practices alongside each other. Where concrete actions are mutually exclusive, however, tolerating contradictions is made more difficult. Thus, the Kome would not be able, for example, to retain a magical healing procedure if, because of traditional prescriptions, they could only carry it out at a time when present-day Christian cult practices take place.

Alongside this dualism, tradition also influences the understanding of Christianity. This leads to the emergence of the parallels already listed between tradition and one's understanding of one's own version of Christianity. In addition, the participants in the Holy Spirit movement to some extent transform their respective cult practices into functional equivalents of traditional procedures of divination and healing. Just as the villagers adopt Christianity in accordance with their traditional culture in general and their traditional religion in particular, so, right at the start of colonisation, they have interpreted the foreign according to the model of the familiar by identifying the first whites as ancestral spirits and by integrating them into their traditional world-view. In accordance with the significance bestowed on tradition in the adoption of Christianity, family membership determines the choice of denomination. The Rata Kome, who form the greatest number of baptised Catholics, mostly followed their Big Man, Ari, when he pushed decisively for the establishment of the Catholic Church. The Auro Kome, on the other hand, preferred to join Muya as one of their leading men and as the founder of the Adventist community.[1] Social pressures are also shown by the fact that married women always belong to the same denomination as their men. Although tradition influences the adoption and view of Christianity, the latter also influences the view of tradition. This is shown, among other things, by the attempt to explain elements of the traditional religion with reference to the Christian model. As mentioned before, Otmar, for example, explained that formerly, people only knew one Rimbu with several different types, just as now there is only one God but also Catholics, Lutherans and Adventists, among others (Chapter 2). Also, Otmar (64.) said that the bamboo flutes of the Alamu-palaa Rimbu would correspond to the present-day church bells. The influence of Christianity becomes even clearer when, at least officially, the villagers reject the tradition entirely as 'this whole remo thing' and claim that they welcomed the start of Catholic missionisation, because already they did not want to fight any more and because it had not been right to consume pig meat in the cult houses without the women. Another reinterpretation of tradition becomes manifest when the Catholic Church leadership attempts to equate the traditional authority Yaki with the Christian God as part of an effort at inculturation. To the extent that Christianity shapes the description and evaluation of the tradition, the present alters the representation of the past. I have already given various examples of how present-day interests decide how the memory of past events is constructed and applied. The Big Men draw up genealogies in order to claim land use rights for their own sub-clan (Chapter 1). The members of the two communities present in Pairundu impart the encounter between Fr Dunstan and the leading Adventist functionaries in a denomination-specific way, each justifying their own decision to join the Adventists or to decline to take this step (Chapter 3). Moreover, some Catholics reject conversion with reference to the claim, disputed by Fr Dunstan, that representatives of the Catholic Church leadership had already warned them, at the start of missionisation, against joining other denominations. Finally, Catholics and Adventists both seek to legitimate their own version of Christianity through their respective church histories (Chapter 4).

In the mutual influencing and the dualism of tradition and Christianity, I see a present-day impact of the traditional religion, which, in opposition to the statements of Catholics and Adventists, therefore cannot be described from the etic point of view as having been subjected or eradicated. Accordingly, the adoption of Christianity as a continuing, dynamic, ever-changing process of innovation is, in its different phases, not only fed by Western-type Christianity communicated through missionisation, but also by the traditional religion itself.

In the context of both denominations, differences arise between the official and unofficial levels, as well as between church officers and 'ordinary' members of the community. These differences seem to be relatively greater among the Catholics. This is presumably because the Adventists are visited more frequently by the chief representatives of their church leadership, which adds to a stricter control. Generally, from the etic point of view, the office-holders lean towards the Christianity communicated through missionisation, whereas the 'ordinary' members of the community, in particular among the Catholics, often correspond more to the traditional religion in their beliefs. Thus, the Catholic Church leadership represents the view that ancestral spirits do not stay among the living and that bush spirits do not exist, which, however, does not prevent the 'ordinary' members of the community from continuing to fear the injurious effects of the *remo* and *kalando*. Differences also emerge in memories of the start of Catholic missionisation. While Fr Dunstan and the former catechist Kenneth stress the cautious and lengthy approach undertaken by the first priests and catechists, Pogola describes the burning of cult houses (Chapter 3). The differences increase when the 'ordinary' members of the community reinterpret the views that the office-holders propagate, for example, with reference to the Holy Spirit movement or the traditional pig-killing festivals. As already described, in Pairundu people say that 'the priests and the sisters' would prohibit such events, while Fr Matthias himself assured me that he had nothing against them, and Kenneth thought that they could be carried out quietly, so long as people did not attempt to outdo others during them (Chapter 4). Differences that both denominations share refer to the date of the *las de*. Catholic and Adventist office-holders claim equally that they do not know this date, whereas at the village level the conviction generally prevails that the end of the world would come in 2000 at the latest. Other differences arise from the fact that, in answer to the question of the significance of baptism, the Catholic villagers do not reproduce the interpretation of their church leadership (Chapter 4) and that the Adventist villagers do not think themselves able to name the upper levels of their church organisation (Chapter 4). Although in their statements the Catholic office-holders differ from the 'ordinary' members of their community, they themselves do not form a homogenous group. This was shown formerly by the Chimbu catechists, who in practice could scarcely be controlled by the priests living at the mission stations when it came to the content of their sermons. Noteworthy at the present time is the position as an outsider of Coleman Makoa, whose qualifications are doubted by Fr Matthias and Sr Marie and whom Kenneth strongly criticises for one of his services, as well as for his shift in the direction of the Adventists.[2]

From the etic point of view, the difference between the 'ordinary' parishioners and the office-holders tends to correspond to the tension between the unofficial and official levels. However, office-holders too can sometimes voice views that are otherwise represented unofficially, while conversely the 'ordinary' members of the community sometimes appropriate official positions. Such official positions were expressed to me above all in formal interviews and in large meetings, especially at the start of my fieldwork, when people had not yet learned what to make of me. The unofficial level, on the other hand, was accessible to me rather in informal conversations in small contexts, though this only happened once a mutual relationship of trust had been created through my living together with the villagers and when it was clear that I was not a missionary. While official statements mostly correspond with the Christianity that is communicated through missionisation, the unofficial level – for which, following Vrijhoff and Waardenburg (1979) the term 'popular religion' can also be used – is somewhat closer to the traditional religion.[3] Thus, as already described, officially the Catholics situate the traditional magical practices and transcendent authorities in a sealed past, even though, unofficially, they continue to be granted effectiveness. On the one hand Pogola, for example, claimed that no one continued to use traditional methods of divination after being baptised, while on the other hand his own brother Ripu, also a member of the Catholic community, told me that he had visited Atasi's 'dream hut' (Chapter 2). If the differences between the positions of the office-holders and the 'ordinary' members of the community are, comparatively speaking, greater in the case of the Catholics, this is also true of the differences between the official and unofficial levels. On the Adventist side the greater degree of congruence leads to a greater certainty of salvation, so that, even when speaking in confidence, the members of the SDA community hardly ever express any doubts or self-criticism. Only with reference to the view of the other denomination is a clear difference to be noted among the Adventists between the official reserve and the unofficial opinion that the Catholics will not go to heaven. The Catholic villagers see things differently, articulating complaints about the Adventists' attempts to missionise in both informal conversations and formal interviews. On both sides, an identical tension between the official and the unofficial levels was only expressed when I asked about how the two communities lived together. Whereas Catholics and Adventists both claim officially that relationships of kinship between them have been broken off entirely, unofficially they do both admit that they share brideprice prestations with one another, visit one another in the health centre and vote for the same candidate at elections (Chapter 4).

Religious and social change

In what follows, I shall first go into the question of how the socio-economic consequences of colonisation enter into the process of religious innovation that I have already described, which is fed equally by the Christianity that is communicated through missionisation and the traditional religion. As I have already concluded, from the etic point of view – and as the villagers themselves note in their complaints about biological and social degeneration (Chapter 5) – the consequences of colonisation include the tendency for social cohesion to dissolve, the reduction in traditional power differences and the increase in individualism (Chapter 3).

A tendency towards the dissolution of social cohesion already arises from the fact that important values in the traditional culture are not strengthened by the Christianity that is communicated through missionisation to the same extent as they are by the traditional religion. Thus the traditional religion, with its cult and magical practices, offered various possibilities to demonstrate one's strength and enforced the maintenance of equivalence through the threat of witchcraft techniques or transcendent authorities. In contrast to this, taking over church offices only offers a relatively limited prospect to obtain prestige. The fear of the Last Judgement can also enforce the realisation of equivalence, but compared with the traditional conviction of the effectiveness of bush and ancestral spirits, the end of the world seems less imminent, despite the virulence of eschatological expectations. If social cohesion declines, so does separation from the outside, and the traditional particularism disappears, which in the pre-colonial period was expressed, among other things, in the idea that the impact of transcendent authorities was limited more or less to one's own settlement community. Moreover, one's own cult and magical practices were usually different from those of other groups, although naturally the adoption and further transmission of individual procedures sometimes produced similarities. Within Christianity, on the other hand, cult practices are supposed to resemble one another and it is said that there are no regional limits as far as the Christian God is concerned. When it comes to lifting the traditional particularism, the Catholics are surpassed by the Adventists, who, comparatively speaking, count more inhabitants of other villages in among the group of baptised, the community and visitors to Sabbath services. Even people from former enemy groups can be persuaded to convert (Chapter 4). The marked 'openness' of the Adventists – also expressed in the fact that from the start they were more interested in presenting their beliefs to me (Chapter 4) – is certainly based on the greater efforts they make, comparatively speaking, to increase their own community's numbers. At the same time, however, this 'openness' is linked with the rigid separation that is maintained from all non-Adventists (Chapter 4). In this sense, to some extent the traditional particularism has turned into a new particularism that is now justified solely in religious terms. The Adventists' withdrawal, their break with traditional culture and society, from which they seek to distance themselves strictly following their conversion as a sort of radical escape, almost seems like a consistent and extremely intensified continuation of the tendency towards the dissolution of social coherence.

The decline in the traditional differences of power is also reflected, as it were, in the process of the adoption of Christianity. Through the suppression of the external forms of the old religion, the traditional religious specialists, who are mostly identical with the Big Men, lose the possibility to acquire counter-prestations or increase their status in exchange for leading or passing on traditional cult and magical practices, whereas in the context of Christianity, it is younger and 'ordinary' men who, for the first time, are taking over the leading religious roles.[4] Compared to the Catholics, the Adventists are more successful in binding the young and 'ordinary' men to them, thanks to their larger number and fluctuation of functionaries. Even more than for men who lack status in the traditional system, the adoption of Christianity means an intra-cultural increase in power for the women. After basically being excluded from the different types of Rimbu as well as from Rombake, Akera and Opayo in the pre-colonial period and having to stay away even from empty cult houses,[5] today they are allowed not only to be present at Catholic and Adventist cult practices, but even to take over particular tasks – apart from preaching sermons.[6] The reduction of the traditional power gap between the genders, between the generations and between the Big Men and 'ordinary men' is to some extent being continued or intensified by Catholics and Adventists when they claim that 'everyone is equal' within their respective communities. Moreover, the tendency towards the dissolution of social cohesion, together with the decline in traditional power differences, basically leads to a process of individualisation, which is also expressed in the religious sphere. This applies especially to the Adventists, who place increasing value on the conclusion that, on the Last day of Judgement, people will only be judged and sent to heaven or hell for themselves and as individuals.[7]

If with the tendency towards the dissolution of social cohesion, the decline in traditional power differences and the increasing individualism, the socio-economic consequences of colonisation are effective within the adoption of Christianity, the experience of a changing social reality enters into the similarly changing religious world-view. Here, the Adventists manage to surpass the Catholics through their 'openness', their simultaneous withdrawal from the world, their integration of younger and 'ordinary' men and their emphasis on individualism. However, the consequences of colonisation are not only adopted or reflected, they are also continued in both denominations' ideas of heaven and to some extent 'thought through to the end'. For both Catholics and Adventists, people live in heaven without any social or economic ties or obligations, without differences in power and thus as individuals alongside one another.[8] By, on the one hand, adopting socio-economic changes, while on the other hand to some extent advancing and intensifying them in the form of religiously justified goals, in my view the members of both communities are making an effort to turn themselves from being the object into becoming the subject of the process of change, in order to win back their own autonomy. In addition, the respective ideas of heaven can be interpreted as criticisms of social reality. Accordingly, both the Catholic and the Adventists villagers are as tired of the existing differences in power as of the still prevalent kinship and economic obligations.[9]

On the one hand, the process of religious innovation, which is fed equally by the traditional religion and by the Christianity that is communicated through missionisation, adopts the socio-economic consequences of colonisation, but on the other hand it in itself also influences social reality. Thus, those who, in the pre-colonial period, only had a relatively modest reputation now seek to improve their position in the intra-cultural status structure by means of the adoption of Christianity. For example, the younger and 'ordinary' men strive for an intra-cultural increase in power by taking over church offices, while, in so doing, they are simultaneously turning against the traditional authorities, that is, the members of the older generation in general and the Big Men in particular. From the Catholic point of view, Coleman Makoa especially voiced criticism of the Big Men by appealing to them in many sermons to no longer think just about their own prestige, to retain only one wife in future and finally to get baptised. The Adventists, on the other hand, frequently claim that one need not listen to the Big Men, since they cannot get anyone into heaven.[10] The contrast between Big Men and 'ordinary' men, like the contrast between the generations, is articulated in denomination membership. While the Catholic community, with Yawa, Wala, Ari and Rekepea, has, so to speak, all the traditionally legitimised politically prominent figures and a relatively high average age, the Adventists exercise their attraction in the first instance on the sons of the Big Men and members of the younger generation as a whole.[11] Thus, the Adventists have a comparatively greater reservoir of potential members available to them, since most of the permanent inhabitants of Pairundu have not yet reached the age of twenty-five. Among the 'ordinary' men, it is accordingly mostly the younger men who want to assert themselves vis-à-vis the elders and the Big Men. In the course of the condemnation of the pre-colonial period that went along with colonisation and missionisation, the elders and the Big Men seem less and less to be in a position to suggest solutions to problems or give instructions for action that are appropriate for an altered social reality (cf. Chapter 1). As a consequence, the feeling of a loss of orientation and the desire for exoneration is marked especially among the young. The attempt to push Adventist Christianity in particular into the place, as it were, of the traditionally justified and recently weakened authorities is aimed at achieving this relief. Alongside this, in many cultures members of the younger generation certainly have the desire, in different ways, to confront the world of their parents and grandparents with something 'new'. In Pairundu, this desire is not only expressed in the conversion to the Adventists, since right at the start of colonisation, younger men were already the first to be prepared to attach themselves to the colonial officers.

The intention to assert oneself against the traditionally legitimised authorities often tends to go along with efforts to distance oneself from them and, as it were, to 'step out' of the traditional structure of social and economic ties. As already described, in the light of their conversion to the Adventists, this goes especially for the sons of Big Men, who are clearly more subject than others to the pressures of the expectation that, through increased efforts, they will become like their fathers and acquire a corresponding reputation.[12] Here, the distancing from the Big Men and the elders apparently becomes easier as their power seems to fade in the course of colonisation and missionisation. Many of the 'ordinary' and younger men believe that their attempt to 'escape' can only be achieved within the SDA community, since the Adventists propagate a radical break with tradition, whereas, in accordance with their efforts towards inculturation, the Catholic Church has basically entered a compromise with the traditionally legitimised authorities instead.[13] Even more than for the 'ordinary' and younger men, the adoption of Christianity implies an intra-cultural rise in status for the women, who, in contrast to the traditional religion, may now not only participate, but even take over certain functions.[14] Even the progressive reduction in the pre-colonial separation of the genders can be interpreted as a gain in prestige for the women, given that this separation strengthens the predominance of the men.[15] Their relative increase in status is even more evident in the context of the Holy Spirit movement, in which they formed the majority of the participants and generally played a leading role. To that extent, the ending of the Holy Spirit movement seems like an act of subjection, which, not accidentally according to Augustin, was mainly initiated by the Big Men and justified through the accusation that women wanted to 'outdo' them.[16] Since, for women in particular, the adoption of Christianity offers a possibility to gain intra-cultural power, it is not surprising that on the whole they constitute the greatest proportion of regular visitors to services and that, in the case of the SDA community as a whole, they are over-represented in comparison with their proportion in the village population. Accordingly, women regard Adventist Christianity as more attractive when compared with Catholicism.

Altogether it is obvious that the contrast between the denominations articulates tensions and conflicts in religious form arising out of the generally widespread desire to acquire power, equality and autonomy not only inter-culturally, that is in relation to the whites, but also intra-culturally, that is in relation to the Big Men, the members of the older generation or the men in general.[17] From the etic point of view, in comparison with the traditional religion, Catholicism does actually represent an increase in equality as much as Adventist Christianity and the Holy Spirit movement do in comparison with Catholicism. This is shown by the larger number and fluctuation of functionaries within the SDA community, the greater involvement of younger men and the possibility to choose Bible texts independently. With respect to the Holy Spirit movement, it should be noted that its participants assume that they are obtaining unrestricted access to the Holy Spirit as a source of power, that women play an important role in it and that here too the Bible texts that are going to be used can be selected independently of the church leadership.[18] To the extent that the process of religious innovation thus allows a partial realisation of power, equality and autonomy, it does change social reality. Whether it changes economic reality too cannot be decided at the present time, since up to now no significant relationship between, for example, denominational affiliation and the size of one's private property can be observed, even though Naki, the richest of the younger men, belongs to the SDA community. Because of their withdrawal from traditional kinship obligations, however, the accumulation of individual property may be comparatively easier for the Adventists,[19] and moreover, the money economy has become better established among them than among the Catholics, who in many respects are still restricted to the subsistence and exchange economies. On the other hand, through the prohibitions on keeping pigs and selling food on Saturdays, the Adventists are losing important sources of income and are moreover obliged to invest comparatively more labour and money on behalf of their community.

If the process of the adoption of Christianity incorporates the experience of changing living conditions on the one hand and itself has an effect on social reality on the other, then religious and social change are closely implicated and influence one another. From the etic point of view, the fact that, in principle, in the context of *lotu*, the same desires and beliefs are effective as in the context of *sevis* corresponds to this mutual influencing. As with the adoption first of Catholic and then of Adventist Christianity, with the adoption of 'development' and with obtaining *sevis*, the villagers also wish to participate in the power of the whites, in order to win back their autonomy and claim their identity in both inter- and intra-cultural relations through the realisation of strength and equivalence. If the fulfilment of this goal is already imagined in Catholic and Adventist ideas of heaven, then *kisim sevis* basically appears as another 'pathway to heaven' (Chapter 5). At the same time, for the members of both denominations, obtaining *sevis* presupposes the revealing of a secret as much as, at least for the Catholics, the completely successful adoption of Christianity. Even the transcendent authorities retain their significance. While, in the context of Christianity, people hope to find access to heaven through Jesus, in the context of 'development' people sometimes regard their own ancestors as the originators of Western wealth. Finally, the emic notions of *lotu* and *sevis* are each linked with the attempt to claim one's own identity as the threatened by appropriating the threatening, for the threatening power of the whites is represented by the different forms of Christianity to the same extent as it is by Western goods. Although both Catholic and Adventist villagers claim to have received *lotu* and *sevis* passively, from the etic point of view on the whole they make comparatively greater efforts in connection with *lotu*. In my view, this preference arises from the fact that since the beginning of colonisation and missionisation, people have come into contact far more frequently with representatives of the churches than with colonial officers or even traders and planters. Thus, instructions for action in the context of *lotu* were basically more easily accessible and, in the general situation of relative marginality, the impression must have arisen that, in comparison with *sevis*, the pathways of *lotu* were to be trodden with much greater success.[20]

Concluding remarks

The mutual influencing of religious and social change in the Pairundu area does not begin with the arrival of the whites. Even in the pre-colonial period, socio-economic processes of transformation passed over into religion and not without leaving traces. As Kohl (1988: 261), among others, emphasises, myths that are not fixed in writing are generally more likely to be accepted as traditional and therefore as 'true' the more they correspond to the external life world. Accordingly, in order to ensure acceptance, myths must react to changes in the external life world. This dependence of religious change on social change, which, following Schaeffler (1986: 243), can be described as a 'pressure to adapt', arises out of the fact that tribal religions in general represent not a separately demarcated area of culture, but an aspect of it that is thoroughly interwoven with other aspects in many different ways.[21] This interweaving continues today in the parallels between *lotu* and *sevis* and it has also certainly contributed to the fact that the Kome at first saw no difference between the colonial officers and the missionaries. If the different aspects of culture are closely linked with one another, if changes in one produces changes in another, then this also explains the variability of the traditional culture and, within it, the traditional religion.[22] With respect to Pairundu, the flexibility of social units can be seen as an expression of such variability as much as the basic readiness for experiment and innovation, that is, the importation of, for example, new styles of house-building, new elements in the pig-killing festival, or new cult and magical practices (Chapters 1, 2). These imported cult and magical practices were then replaced by the various forms of Christianity after the arrival of the first priests and catechists. In this sense, the adoption of Christianity in Pairundu marks not so much the intrusion of change into a formerly static system, but rather the beginning of a new period in a process of change that has already been going on for a long time.[23]

The villagers' traditional pragmatism corresponds to their readiness for innovation. The less the need for internal coherence, for freedom from contradiction and for systematisation, the more easily innovations can be integrated in principle, regardless of whether traditional cult and magical practices, different forms of Christianity or methods of *kisim sevis* are involved. As already described, the villagers' pragmatism thus explains the dualistic juxtaposition of elements of both tradition and Christianity, as well as the coexistence of the members of the two denominations. It is only because less significance is generally given to beliefs than to concrete actions that people can live relatively peacefully together, even though they deny each other's Christian identity or condemn each other's missionisation attempts. On the other hand, according to the primacy of action, there is an obvious separation arising out of the fact that the two communities each carry out their major cult practices on different days.

The fact that the traditional religion was not eradicated but still retains its influence today in, for example, the dualism of or mutual influencing between tradition and Christianity is explained by the dependence of religious change on social change, that is, the pressure to adapt to which the traditional religion is exposed. While on the one hand the socio-economic influences that have gone along with colonisation and missionisation certainly lead to a loss of autonomy and a threat to one's identity, on the other they have basically supplemented rather than replaced tradition, since, in accordance with the general situation of relative marginality, they prove to be relatively less serious when compared to other regions. Thus, in Pairundu, the subsistence economy continues to be the main source of food. Cooperation, co-residence and kinship continue to determine the coherence of society, and the Big Men have been able to preserve some of their power. If, therefore, the everyday life of the villagers corresponds to the pre-colonial period in many respects, social change has not led to a religious change that was so far-reaching as to have obliterated the identity of the traditional religion. Instead, socio-economic conditions have only changed to an extent that has allowed the traditional religion, thanks to its variability, to continue to exert its influence into the present, through, as it were, the adoption of new forms of expression. In my view, therefore, it is less a matter of the decline of the traditional religion than of its transformation and adaptation. Certainly this thesis cannot be applied to regions in which colonisation and missionisation have left more substantial traces. Even in Pairundu, however, there is an at least partial decline stemming from the fact that the religious knowledge of the old cult leaders, which is only handed down orally, is usually lost when they die. Already today, many of the elements of individual Rimbu cult practices are no longer known to most of the members of the younger generation. Although the contact with the Western world that has been communicated through missionaries and colonial officers has certainly contributed to a gradual change in awareness in Pairundu, it would seem an exaggeration to describe this as a process of secularisation, especially since secularisation is otherwise seen as a process in intellectual history in which religion becomes isolated as a separate cultural sphere with a tendency to turn into a private matter (Chapter 9). Certainly in Pairundu today people make the traditional religion as a whole an object of contemplation (and condemnation), whereas earlier they might have expressed themselves only in relation to individual parts of it, like particular cult or magical practices. On the other hand, the parallels between *lotu* and *sevis* in particular show that religion continues to be closely linked to other aspects of culture. In addition, the fact that the majority of permanent villagers belongs to one or the other denomination and regularly takes part in its services does suggest that religion in Pairundu cannot yet be regarded as a private matter.

The comparatively limited extent of socio-economic changes not only allows the traditional religion to adapt, it also influences the relationship between Catholics and Adventists. Had the process of social disintegration progressed considerably further in the wake of colonisation and missionisation, then kinship ties and obligations in specific contexts would not continue to be more important than denomination membership (Chapter 4) and conflicts between the members of the two communities would have gained that intensity that their judgements of one another would lead one to expect at first from the Western point of view. The thesis that the traditional religion has maintained its influence up to the present day through transformation and adaptation simultaneously provides information on the role of its carriers, that is, the people themselves. Just as the traditional religion can hardly be said to have declined because of the impact of a superior power, so too the villagers are not just the helpless victims of Western influence. Certainly Catholics and Adventists actually lost autonomy, yet they are not at all as passive as they themselves think they are when they are describing the pre-colonial period or the consequences of colonisation and missionisation. In my view, rather, having given up the attempt to seal themselves off from Western influences, members of both denominations are rapidly going over to actively adopting these influences, assimilating them and – in the context of *lotu* or, less intensively, *sevis* – deploying them in accordance with their own needs and beliefs, in order ultimately to win back their lost autonomy and claim their own identity.

Notes

1. The influence exerted by Ari and Muya is also shown in the fact that hardly any member of their respective sub-clans belongs to the opposite denomination. In this respect, Alex's conversion to the Adventists is naturally a painful exception for Ari.
2. (Chapter 4). Pastor Koya (46.) also noted differences within the Catholic Church leadership, when, in front of Coleman Makoa's house, he expressed the view to him that the statements of the priests were not always identical with those of the catechists, because the catechists did not learn everything from the priests. Here, Pastor Koya was simultaneously expressing the accusation of secrecy frequently made against the Catholics by the Adventists (Chapter 4).
3. However, this is not to say that the Western-type Christianity that is communicated through missionisation is itself uniform. The term 'popular religion' corresponds to the German term 'Volksreligion' (Ahrens 1978: 13).
4. Thus, already the Chimbu catechists preferred to train young men as catechists and in the years to follow, it also tended to be younger men who filled the church offices. Alongside this, however, there was also a certain personal continuity within the adoption of Christianity, since, in Ari and Otmar, the Catholic church committees of Pairundu and Anapote do have as members people who had led traditional cult practices in the pre-colonial period.
5. Instead, with reference to the traditional religion, only 'love magic' and 'fertility magic', participation in the Rimbu Eta and the consumption of pig meat after carrying out an Opayo were left to the women (Chapter 2).
6. Thus, among the Catholics, Mayanu belongs to the church committee, and Sayna and Neambunu lead evening services as *prayer lida*. Among the Adventists, Wareame occupies the office of church deaconess, and women can lead prayers, make announcements and issue greetings at services.
7. From my point of view, the emphasis on individuality cannot be reconciled with the Adventist demand for obedience or order in the community. The contrast between individuality and obedience thus counts as one of the contradictions that characterises the world-view of the Adventists, like the opposition between 'openness' and separation.
8. Accordingly Ripu emphatically pointed out that, as *wanpela independent man* in heaven, one would no longer have a wife or parents (Chapter 4).
9. Robert (80.) also voiced a criticism of the present when he justified his desire to go to heaven with the conclusion that, 'This world means tears, fighting and quarrelling' ('Dispela graun, em krai na pait na kros').
10. The attempt by participants of the Holy Spirit movement to drive out an 'evil spirit' from Yawa seems like another criticism of a Big Man (Chapter 3.2).

11. Overall, the generational conflict is also connected with the security problem, which is seen as overwhelming and which Papua New Guinea as a state also sees itself being subjected to today from the point of view of internal politics. Thus, Callick (1992) describes the younger generation, who usually cannot find work after their Western-oriented education and are thus often diverted into criminality, as a 'lost generation'.

12. In the case of Muya, fear might also have played a role in taking the decision to convert, since shortly before Usa – who, like him, was seen as a future Big Man and who also belonged to the Raki Repa (Auro Kome) – had allegedly been killed by other Kome through witchcraft (Chapter 3).

13. The Adventists accuse the Catholics of doing precisely this by allocating them to tradition.

14. The fact that women were excluded from the consumption of pig meat in the pre-colonial period is, according to a statement of Alex's (15.), the reason why they have especially welcomed 'God's Word' or 'words about God' (*tok bilong God*).

15. Nevertheless, gender separation is still maintained today in the seating arrangements during both Catholic and Adventist cult practices.

16. (Chapter 3). In this sense, the reinterpretation of the position that the church leadership adopted with respect to the Holy Spirit movement not only serves the desire for exoneration, it also helps to legitimise male dominance.

17. Moreover, the fact that the Catholics' present-day church building was erected not in Pasereanda, as at the start of the Catholic mission activities, but in Pairundu** can already be seen as an indication of intra-cultural conflict within the Catholic community itself.

18. In the inter-cultural situation, moreover, autonomy comes from the fact that, unlike Christianity, the Kome originally took over the Holy Spirit movement not from the whites, but from the inhabitants of neighbouring settlements. The same applies in principle to Adventist Christianity, which is admittedly closely linked with the whites, though, as already described, at least in Pairundu it is mainly traced back to the revelation experience of Muya and his encounter with Peter.

19. Certainly the 'obligation to share' also decreased in the course of colonisation and missionisation for the Catholics, though to a comparatively lesser extent. Thus, for the Catholics, unlike the Adventists, the idea of *daunim spet*, for example, which in a sense adds to such an obligation, still proves to be effective (Chapter 2). However, at least on the official level, members of both denominations do continue to represent the traditional egalitarian ethos (Chapter 1).

20. In addition, it sometimes even appears that the Adventists judge the attempt to acquire *sevis* negatively. Thus, Robert, for example, claimed occasionally but emphatically that those businessmen and company owners in particular who, even on the Sabbath, are thinking about work instead of the divine service will go to hell. Pastor Koya complained that, since the 1980s, the inhabitants of Papua New Guinea in general only concentrate on earning money and thus forget about religion (Chapter 5).

21. (Introduction). According to Schaeffler (1986: 243), a 'pressure to adapt' consists of the fact that from the variations of theoretical interpretations and practical adaptations of a religious tradition, future generations are accepting what fits best with changed social, political and cultural conditions. See also Jebens (1990b: 408–11).

22. This thesis is also held by Kohl (1988: 265), who points out that the 'the great degree of flexibility of autochthonous religion' is connected with the fact that, 'in relation to all other areas of culture, religion in non-literate societies has not yet become autonomous, but is rather closely bound up with the economic, social and political spheres'. On the changeable nature of Melanesian tribal religions as a whole, see also Stephen (1979), for whom altered states of consciousness, widespread in many of these religions, play an 'innovative role' in the acceptance of the new. Accordingly, such an 'innovative role' could be ascribed to direct contact with the Holy Spirit in the context of the Holy Spirit movement.

23. Nor does tradition seem at all rigid or unchangeable in the memories with which the villagers construct their own respectively different versions of the past.

PART III:
MISSIONISATION AND MODERNISATION

Now that, in the first two parts of the present work, I have described and analysed how the villagers deal with both Catholic and Adventist Christianity against the background of their traditional culture in general and their traditional religion in particular, the question arises whether Pairundu as a whole is a 'typical example' or a local special case. Examining this question involves placing Pairundu first in a regional and then in a theoretical context. Therefore, I shall deal first with the common features of missionisation throughout Papua New Guinea (Chapter 8), before addressing the phenomenon of fundamentalism (Chapter 9).

8

Missionisation in
Papua New Guinea

In presenting the common features of missionisation throughout Papua New Guinea, I shall describe, for both the mainline churches and the smaller denominations, the reasons that contribute to conversion for different authors and the relationship that, in their view, has developed between Christianity and tradition. The sources used here can only be seen as representative to a limited extent, since authors are mostly not interested in the acceptance of different forms of Christianity under the influence of tradition.

Mainline churches

Up to now, the acceptance of so-called mainline Christianity as transmitted by the larger churches has been treated first and foremost by mission theology. Frequently, however, this means that authors provide a history of the mission, which often has an apologetic character and is not specifically interested in the reasons for conversion or in taking up an emic point of view at all.[1] Another focus of mission-theological works is the effort to construct an indigenous Melanesian theology (Introduction). By contrast, it seems to me that Theodor Ahrens occupies a special position within mission theology.[2] In several articles based on his activities as a missionary in the region of Astrolabe Bay, Madang Province, from 1972 to 1975 and on several meetings with church office-holders from different areas (1977: 14), he addresses the indigenous concept of Christianity (1976), as well as the relationship between Christian communities and groups who are still attached to their traditional religion (1977, 1991). Also to be classified under mission theology is Mary MacDonald (1991), who is concerned with the relationship between tradition and Christianity with reference to the Kewa of the Mararoko region.[3]

If, with reference to present-day Papua New Guinea, religion is dealt with at all by anthropologists, it often involves the reconstruction of a reality that has yet to be influenced by colonisation or missionisation. This affects not only work that appeared before the Second World War, but also the results of research carried out in the 1950s and 1960s, as well as later attempts to provide an overview of the common features of Melanesian religions as a whole.[4] Many authors, who, conversely, are concerned with the present as they find it, subject both social practices and religious actions, ideas and world-views, to an often symbolic interpretation, though not explicitly describing the influence of Christianity.[5] Even Stephen (1979) leaves this influence disregarded, although she examines changes in traditional religion in the larger regional context, in which, in her view, altered states of consciousness play an essential role.[6] As a rule, anthropological engagement with the consequences of missionisation is restricted to short articles and only begins – apart from a few exceptions[7] – with the collection entitled *Mission, Church and Sect in Oceania*, edited by Boutilier, Hughes and Tiffany (1978). The texts assembled in this collection deal, among other things, with mission histories, changes in missionaries' attitudes and the relationship between missionaries and anthropologists (D. Hughes 1978, Forman 1978) in different areas. However, the authors (except for Counts 1978) concentrate more on the spread of Christianity by missionaries than on how local populations themselves receive Christianity. The indigenous adoption of Christianity moves centre stage following fieldwork in the second half of the 1970s by Michael French Smith (1980) and Miriam Kahn (1983). Kahn worked in Wamira, Milne Bay Province, Smith in Koragur, East Sepik Province, the latter examining in particular how villagers react to the changing attitudes of the Catholic Church leadership to tradition over time.[8]

The next important contribution to anthropological research on missionisation in Papua New Guinea in my view is the collection entitled *Christianity in Oceania* edited by John Barker (1990b), who complains about the lack of ethnographies showing how Christianity is actually experienced and practiced by the indigenous people themselves: '...few have attempted ethnographic appraisals of Christianity as it is currently experienced and practised in Pacific societies' (1990a: 1). Here, Barker is pleading for a shift in accent in favour of the emic point of view, which, with the exception of Kahn and Smith, has not received sufficient attention up to now. The effort to provide an emic perspective includes the attempt to describe the Christian beliefs that are expressed at village level after the end of actual missionisation and what the Christian services actually look like. In this way and also in contrast to previous work up to that point, 'local expressions of Christianity' should be taken seriously as 'phenomena in their own right' (Barker 1990a: 9). However, this demand is only partly fulfilled in the collection assembled by Barker, which, moreover, is mostly restricted to mainline Christianity. Only Chowning (1990) describes a situation in which different denominations compete with one another within the same settlement, without, however, asking the reasons for the coming into existence of these different denominations. In addition, the texts collected by Barker that concern Melanesia deal exclusively with coastal Papua New Guinea and the offshore islands. Thus, the Highlands of Papua New Guinea are not taken into account here any more than they are in the earlier collection of Boutilier et al. (1978). In this sense, J. Clark's dissertation (1985), already discussed, provides a certain exception.[9]

Explanations for the acceptance of mainline Christianity from the point of view of anthropology have usually been formulated in the context of interpreting cargo cults, though here too the indigenous perspective is usually not taken into account.[10] After authors initially saw cargo cults as a response to the disturbance of equilibrium in the traditional culture caused by colonisation and missionisation, a reaction to mental confusion, or a situation of socio-economic inequality, Lawrence in particular contributed to the further development of such interpretations.[11] In his main work, *Road Belong Cargo* (1964), following nearly thirty-four months of fieldwork altogether carried out between 1949 and 1958 among the Garia and Ngaing, present-day Madang Province, Lawrence analyses the cargo ideas and movements that circulated in the region between 1871 and 1950.[12] Ahrens (1977: 106, fn. 5) describes *Road Belong Cargo* as the 'best history of culture and the church for Madang District'. Alongside cargo cults, the Holy Spirit movements later offered another occasion for examining the reasons for conversion to the larger churches.

The acceptance of mainline Christianity seems to have taken place fairly quickly and without much resistance in most regions of present-day Papua New Guinea, once the decision to convert had been made. Most authors see as the decisive cause the desire of the indigenous people to acquire the wealth of the whites along with their religion.[13] This explanation, which, incidentally, was shared in part by colonial officers,[14] was first formulated especially by Lawrence. In his view (1954: 12f, 1956: 85f), the Garia saw the Christian God as the producer of Western goods, which he provided to the whites because they conducted the secret rituals needed for them in the context of Christianity.[15] In support of Lawrence, Ahrens (1976: 3, 1977: 21f, 1986b) and Kempf (1992: 75), among others, also claimed that the Christian God counted as the producer and therefore, as it were, the source of Western wealth. Accordingly, Christianity was regarded as the 'key to cargo', in Strelan's (1977: 113) words.[16] Certainly in Pairundu no cargo cults took place[17] that might correspond to the phenomena described by Lawrence, for example, though I was certainly able to find elements of a 'cargo world-view'. Thus, for example, Nosupinai (60.) answered the question whether the Kome believed they could acquire Western goods if they went to school and adopted Christianity by saying, 'We did think so'.[18] Basically, however, in my view the terms 'cargo', 'cargo cult' and 'cargo movement' are extraordinarily problematic, even though they recently returned more forcefully to the centre of anthropological interest, following an earlier 'boom' in the 1950s and 1960s.[19] For one thing, in part these terms are rejected by those they apply to as stigmatising,[20] while for another they are used for very different phenomena,[21] raising the question of whether they permit a uniform object to be recognised at all.[22] This has led, among other things, to neologisms like 'cargoism' (Ogan 1972: 172, Ploeg 1975: 198), 'cargo mentality' (Essai 1961: 55), '"cargo"-cult type of behaviour' (Firth 1955: 131) and 'cargo ideology'[23] or, as used above, 'cargo world-view'. More interesting, however, than the discussion of the coherence of the object and the justification of the respective terms, it seems to me, is the idea that 'cargo conceptions' provide information concerning the emic view of the whites and that to some extent one is here confronted with an 'indigenous ethnography', expressed partly in ritual form, of Western culture as embodied by, for example, colonial officers, missionaries and traders.[24]

The thesis that the indigenous people adopted mainline Christianity because of their desire for 'cargo' is only appropriate, in my view, if the meaning of 'cargo' is not reduced to Western goods as such. Here, Lawrence's point should be taken into account, namely that the indigenous people view 'cargo' as 'both the reason for, and the symbol of, European military and political supremacy' (1964: 233), so that owning 'cargo' means owning 'social and political equality or power' (1964: 232, cf. also 1971: 141). What emerges from this is that the acquisition of 'cargo' stands for the raising of one's own status, that is, for the realisation of strength and therefore also of equivalence or equality. On the other hand, this realisation of traditional values promises the strengthening or re-creation of one's own identity and autonomy (cf. Jebens 1990a: 111). In this sense, it is ultimately the same needs that account for both participation in cargo cults and the acceptance of Christianity in other parts of Papua New Guinea as in Pairundu.[25] Another common feature consists in the social consequences, that is, the effect of disintegration that arises from the separation of cargo cult participants from non-participants,[26] as much as of members from non-members of the community. In my view, the reason for this disintegration effect arises from the fact that efforts directed at acquiring strength and equivalence refer not just to the whites, but also to those who have a comparatively higher status within the same culture.[27] This is supported not least by the fact that a comparatively low intra-cultural status clearly represents a predisposition not only for participation in cargo cults, but also for the reception of Christianity in Pairundu and elsewhere.[28]

Alongside cargo cults, Holy Spirit movements, which can to some extent be seen as the successors of the former, are also linked with conversion to the larger churches. According to J. Clark, the direct contact with God or with the Holy Spirit that the Holy Spirit movements aim at strengthens the collective acceptance of Christianity.[29] At the same time, direct contact, which to some extent is seen as the source of power for the whites, is supposed to even out inequality in relation to them (J. Clark 1985: 361). In his description of a Holy Spirit movement in Pangia District, J. Clark bases himself primarily on material presented by Robin, for whom such movements arise because missionaries introduce 'cultural dislocation' (Robin 1982: 336f) by ending an old order and presenting a new one, thus creating, as with colonialism, a disturbance to the 'cultural equilibrium' and a 'vacuum' (Robin 1981a: 61). Robin (1981b: 162) regards 'hysteria' as an essential element of Holy Spirit movements, which he accordingly traces back to 'the presence of intense stress, introduced and developed through methods of intimidation, hellfire and brimstone evangelising, and techniques that produce heightened states of suggestibility'.[30] In this 'pathologisation' of Holy Spirit movements, which those villagers in Pairundu who describe such phenomena as 'a sort of illness' (Chapter 6) would certainly agree with, Robin is reproducing older interpretations that initially understood cargo cults as reactions to the disturbance of social equilibrium and to mental confusion. Other parallels, which are certainly grounded in the phenomena themselves, arise, among other things, from the underlying idea in both cases that ritual activities could create direct contact with a transcendent authority that is made possible through altered states of consciousness.[31] Ahrens's (1986a: 88) conclusion, that Holy Spirit movements indicate 'clear continuities with the older cargo cults', relates to such parallels.[32] In my judgement, the attempt to explain the acceptance of mainline Christianity through a Holy Spirit movement is not convincing, at any rate as far as Pairundu is concerned, where the Holy Spirit movement did not start with missionisation. If the introduction of a disturbance of equilibrium or a vacuum would be plausible at all, it would have to be this period, to which, according to Robin, the Holy Spirit movement would have been a response. Instead, as already described, in Pairundu the Holy Spirit movement only forms a later phase in the process of the adoption of Christianity, during which the same needs and ideas have basically been effective as in the other periods. Admittedly the literature recognises that Holy Spirit movements have a disintegrating effect by separating, as in Pairundu, participants from non-participants.[33] However, J. Clark and Robin, for example, overlook the fact that, as with cargo cults and the acceptance of Christianity, this is partly because those who, like women, younger and 'ordinary men', only have a relatively modest status within their own culture also want to obtain prestige within this same context.

If the acceptance of mainline Christianity was achieved similarly in other regions of Papua New Guinea and in Pairundu without great resistance and basically because of the same needs, then the question is raised whether other similarities exist with reference to the respective relationships between Christianity and tradition. To begin with, reports are actually available from other regions in which, as in Pairundu, there is a prevailing conviction that conversion presupposes a break with tradition, that is, that the needs linked to conversion can only be satisfied by first distancing oneself from tradition. According to J. Clark (1985: 178), among the Wiru too, Christian beliefs and traditional cults are opposed to one another and are therefore seen as incompatible. Kahn (1983: 107f) quotes an informant saying that people did not yet have any religion before the whites came and that they used to eat one another, whereas today, that is, following Christianisation, people have a religion and consume pigs.[34] In my view what is manifested in such statements is the cultural construction of a concept of tradition that is judged negatively and instrumentalised as a counter-image to a present that is thought of as Christian. The more negative the tradition, the greater the gap to be overcome by conversion and the more positive one's view of one's own belonging to Christianity.[35] In using the term 'construction', I would like to stress, following Linnekin (1992), that I am not seeing 'tradition' as something, so to speak, inherited unconsciously, as something received, but as a concept that people in the present equate with their life of the past and put to use for specific political ends.[36] Here what is interesting to me is how this happens, rather than whether this concept is identical with what an anthropologist may have described as 'traditional culture' had he carried out fieldwork before the start of colonisation or missionisation.[37] Thomas (1992a: 223) describes the process whereby, as in Pairundu and other regions of Papua New Guinea, tradition is transformed into a counter-image of the Christian present as 'the inversion of tradition'. Contact with another (for example, Western) culture leads to positive values being attributed to it and reversals of these values being linked to one's own self-image (Thomas 1992a: 216). In contrast to this, until now, research has tended to limit itself to the observation that the members of the different societies in Oceania value their constructions of 'tradition' positively in order to assert their own autonomy.[38] In relevant examples, which are often linked with the Tok Pisin term *kastom*[39] – and which, incidentally, mostly come from different island groups in Melanesia, only to a limited extent from the coastal region and not at all from the Highlands of Papua New Guinea – contact with an 'out-group', which is defined by another ethnic affiliation, if not a different skin colour, usually precedes the sketching of a concept of 'tradition'.

If, for indigenous peoples, the past is essentially and absolutely distinguished from the present – and if, in their view, contact with the whites leads to a fundamentally radical change, to the dawning of an entirely new time – then this appears to indicate an idea of history and change that Errington (1974: 257), following Gellner (1964), calls 'episodic'. Kahn (1983: 109), J. Clark (1988: 46) and MacDowell (1985, 1988) also note this idea, using the same term and referring to Errington. MacDowell (1988: 124) writes concerning the Bun: 'For them there is no gradual, cumulative, evolutionary change, change is always dramatic, total and complete. Discontinuity is a requirement of and for change'.[40] In my view, such an understanding of change and history may contribute to the conviction that conversion to Christianity presupposes an absolute break with tradition.[41]

However, the parallels between Pairundu and other regions of Papua New Guinea are not restricted to the fact that tradition is being deployed as a counter-image of the present in each case. Authors like Ahrens (1976: 13), Kahn (1983: 105) and J. Clark (1985: 175, 183, 371) also describe the dualistic juxtaposition of elements of tradition and Christianity by concluding that the indigenous people themselves sometimes retain traditional magical practices and transcendent authorities after being converted. According to MacDonald (1991: 215), for example, the inhabitants of Mararoko similarly use both the 'pathway of the ancestors' and the 'pathway of the Christians'.[42] Alongside this, Christianity influences tradition, that is, the indigenous picture of it.[43] This is expressed on the one hand in the negative evaluation of tradition and on the other hand – though etically this seems like a contradiction – in the attempt, in accordance with the striving for inculturation, to regard the traditional religion in particular as a prior form of Christianity and to identify the traditional transcendent authority Yaki with the Christian God.[44] At the same time, however, the indigenous picture of Christianity is influenced by tradition, which, according to J. Clark (1989b: 184), leads to Christianity taking over the functions of the pre-colonial cults: 'Christianity... operates within the traditional parameters of cult belief and has taken over the function and attributes of the cults and spirits that were formerly its expression'.[45] Another reinterpretation by the tradition implies the theses, represented by, for example, Kahn (1983: 97) and MacDonald (1991: 49), of a selective adoption of Christianity.[46] Alongside Christianity, this reinterpretation also affects other elements of the Western world, as is shown by the fact that, in the context of *lotu* and *sevis*, more or less identical beliefs and needs may be involved (Chapter 7). Accordingly, J. Clark (1988: 53) describes 'Christianity' and 'development' as two basically similar attempts to attain 'moral equivalence with Europeans', and MacDowell (1988: 121f) points out that in general the ideas and actions described for cargo cults can also come to the surface in the context of other activities.[47]

On the whole, therefore, the indications contained in the literature show that not only in Pairundu, but also in other regions of Papua New Guinea, there is a dualistic juxtaposition of, and mutual influence between, elements of tradition and Christianity, in which the continuing influence of the traditional religion, which is often denied by the indigenous people themselves, is made manifest. Thus, a religion emerges, which, as it were, is certainly fed in the same way by the traditional religion and the Christianity of Western type in a continuous process of transformation, yet is different from either.[48] This combining of tradition and Christianity – which is also noted by Lawrence in the case of cargo cults and by Robin in the case of Holy Spirit movements, among others – is more likely to occur where the indigenous people see similarities between tradition and Christianity.[49] In harmony with my thesis that such similarities give rise subjectively to an impression of plausibility and truth, for J. Clark and Robin they contribute to the success of Christianity in general.[50]

Kahn and Ahrens subject the relationship between Christianity and tradition to a further differentiation beyond what has already been described. In accordance with the difference to be noted in Pairundu between the official and unofficial levels, as well as between the statements of the church office-holders and of the 'ordinary' members of the community, Kahn distinguishes a 'surface layer', in respect of participation in church life and attending services, from an effective continuation underneath it of belief in traditional transcendent authorities and magical practices. Thus, she (1983: 97) cites an informant as follows: '… we have two layers. On the surface we act like Christians and go to church. But inside we are Wamirans. Our customs are strong and will not die'. The level of unofficially effective ideas and practices, for which, following Ahrens, I have used the term 'popular religion' (Chapter 7), should be distinguished from what Kahn calls the 'surface'. Ahrens (1976: 16) speaks of a 'basic form of religion', which arises in the indigenous people's attempt to tie the Christian message to their own cultural inheritance and which is overlain within the church by the 'superstructure', the 'special or organised form of religion'.[51] In place of this 'basic form of religion', the phrase 'christlich-nativistische Volksreligion' (Christian-nativistic popular religion) appears in a later article (Ahrens 1977: 70), according to which the office-holders are not aware of the relationship between 'Volksreligion' (popular religion) and 'Überbau' (superstructure).[52]

Smaller denominations

The general growth of the smaller denominations that often arrived after the larger churches is treated even more rarely by anthropology, let alone explained in terms of its causes, as is the adoption of mainline Christianity. Thus, in order to test whether the 'success' of the Adventists in Pairundu as a small community of belief represents a singular phenomenon or has analogues in other parts of Papua New Guinea, essentially one is forced to rely just on the works of S. Josephides (1982, 1990),[53] and the short articles by Schiefflin (1981a, 1981b) and Ballard (n.d.). Schiefflin asks why the Kaluli, who live north of Mount Bosavi, Southern Highlands Province, have accepted the evangelical Christianity transmitted by the Asian Pacific Christian Mission, the later Evangelical Church of Papua (ECP), without great resistance.[54] Ballard analyses the relationship between the Adventist announcement of the Last Judgement and the traditional ideas of a 'Time of Darkness' among the Huli, Southern Highlands Province. The Adventists are also mentioned by S. Josephides, who investigates conceptions of the past and of *bisnis* among the Boroi, Madang Province.[55] However, on the whole it becomes obvious that Schieffelin, Ballard and S. Josephides go as little into the living together of the members of the larger and smaller churches or the emerging conflicts as do authors who are mainly concerned with the acceptance of mainline Christianity.[56]

In so far as the smaller communities of belief are mentioned at all in the anthropological literature, it is to refer to their 'success', that is, their unbroken growth. In accounting for this 'success' with respect to the Adventists, S. Josephides (1990: 64) makes a connection with cargo cults by writing of the Boroi: 'It would hardly be surprising if people thought that they were taking part in some sort of cargo cult in becoming Seventh-day Adventists, for the Christian element is marked in cargo thought and Seventh-day Adventist doctrine is considerably closer than any other form of Christianity to cargo cultism' (cf. also S. Josephides 1982: 297). For S. Josephides, such closeness arises especially from the different promises directed at group members.[57] Thanks to its millenarian and messianic aspects, for Ross (1978: 196) Adventist belief is 'in effect a European-sponsored cargo cult'. Conversion to a smaller community of belief, like participation in cargo cults and the acceptance of mainline Christianity, is frequently explained with reference to the desire for wealth. For example, according to Schieffelin, for the Kaluli the ECP is a pathway to well-being (1981b: 153) and 'a centre of influence and power' (1981b: 155).[58] However, in my view, wealth and power stand for the realisation of traditional values and thus for the assertion of one's identity and the re-creation of one's autonomy no less than in the case of the mainline churches. The observation made in Pairundu, that the Adventists' 'success' is partly due to their criticism of the Catholics, is not articulated by other authors, though they too note a growing dissatisfaction with the larger churches. Thus, Ahrens (1986c: 255) notes 'the impression of a certain weariness... a certain staleness in Christian life'.[59] One expression of this dissatisfaction, this disappointment with the expectations originally linked to mainline Christianity, appears to be the accusation that the missionaries kept a secret from the indigenous people in the form of the knowledge they allegedly had of the origin of the 'cargo'.[60] Moreover, according to Smith (1980:44), the fact that, since the Second Vatican Council, within the Catholic Church leadership the overwhelming rejection of traditional culture has softened into a more differentiated attitude is seen as deceitful or two-faced.[61] Finally, some authors point out that conversion to the Adventists, for example, provides an opportunity to distance oneself from non-Adventists.[62] According to J. Clark (1985: 382f), one group of villagers tried to strengthen its autonomy with respect to another group by joining the Adventists, leaving the settlement and building a church of their own.[63] Accordingly, Thomas (1992a: 224) writes, with reference to Fiji: '... defection to Adventism... served as a powerful way for disaffected factions in particular villages to express their rejection of the rest of the community'.[64] This disintegrative effect – which the adoption of Adventist Christianity shares, for example, with cargo cults and Holy Spirit movements – supports the idea that the desire for an increase in status that is linked with conversion has an intra-cultural dimension elsewhere, as it has in Pairundu. Accordingly, it is first and foremost young men – that is, those who have relatively little prestige in the intra-cultural context – who belong to the converts, not only in Pairundu, but also, for example, among the Kaluli.[65]

As with mainline Christianity, in the case of the 'success' of the smaller communities of belief, the question also arises whether the common features between Pairundu and other parts of Papua New Guinea are restricted merely to the different reasons for conversion, or whether they extend to the respective relationships between Christianity and tradition. Generally speaking, authors ascribe a decisive rejection of the traditional culture, and especially of the traditional religion, to the smaller communities of belief. Using the example of the Adventists, S. Josephides describes in particular their attempt to represent the past and the present as completely contrary counter-images of one another (1990: 62), between which there is no continuity, since the past has been completely destroyed for the sake, as it were, of Adventist Christianity (1990: 64). Moreover, S. Josephides (1990: 60) assumes that the Adventists – as is certainly the case in Pairundu – also associate the Catholics with tradition, in harmony with their claim to exclusivity: '… there is even a possibility that Christianity is equated with Seventh-day Adventism and Catholicism with traditional religion'. As with the Adventist condemnation of the pre-colonial past, Schiefflin (1981a: 20) reports the attempt of the ECP pastors to suppress, for example, clothing, body decoration, music and dancing belonging to the traditional culture. Among others, Smith, S. Josephides and Thomas refer to the attraction of such a rejection of tradition.[66] As with the spreading of the larger churches, so, according to many authors, the 'success' of the smaller communities of belief is explained through parallels between the rejected tradition and the respective form of Christianity that, consciously or not, are effective for indigenous peoples. According to a statement by A. Strathern, as given to Ahrens (1986c: 235ff.), the growing numbers of Pentecostalists in the Mount Hagen area are continuing the practice, already current in the pre-colonial era, of using the discussion of social tensions to cure illnesses. Whereas Hogbin (1947) adds the stress on prohibitions in particular to the parallels between Christianity and tradition, Ballard (n.d.) and Schiefflin (1981b: 154ff.) see rather a correspondence between the concept of the Last Judgement and traditional ideas of the end of the world.[67] According to S. Josephides (1982: 18f), the Adventists are continuing the Boroi's traditional ideas by believing in the keeping of a secret as much as in the revelation of that secret in the form of the Last Judgement. Admittedly, the thesis developed for Pairundu, that the construction of such parallels creates an impression of plausibility and the certainty of salvation, is not put forward explicitly in the literature, but nevertheless May (1985a: 12), at least, notes the creation of a certainty of salvation, since he suggests that the communities he describes as fundamentalist offer 'a short cut to certainty, a no-questions-asked religion complete with instant – if alien – identity'.[68]

The situation in Pairundu

As far as can be seen, taken as a whole the anthropological literature on Melanesia contains no works in which the adoption of different forms of Christianity is examined using an approach from the anthropology of religion and based on stationary fieldwork. The authors who do consider the spread of the larger churches hardly mention the growth of smaller communities of belief,[69] and the authors who deal with the latter hardly mention conversion to the mainline churches. Moreover, as a rule they do not provide any information concerning which population groups tend to join the newer denominations and what conflicts arise from their doing so.[70] All this makes it more difficult to answer the question whether the reception first of Catholic and then of Adventist Christianity in Pairundu is a local special case or a representative example. Thus, the attempt to place Pairundu in a regional framework requires a reliance on sources which are centrally concerned with different themes. As a result, concrete descriptions of, for example, the form and content of Christian services and sermons are missing from such works as much as more precise information concerning how the data presented were communicated in each case, that is, for example, whether they came from interviews with church office-holders, 'ordinary' members of the community or 'outsiders'.[71] With J. Clark especially, it is to be regretted that he provides no precise information on the modalities of his fieldwork and that he characteristically does not, as a rule, mention his informants by name, nor even describe things like the positions they occupy within the society. This is all the more crucial, since it is almost always an open question with J. Clark whether his descriptions are based on his own observations or on the representations of the indigenous people.

Conversions that are explained with reference to the desire for 'cargo' – in the case of both the larger churches and the smaller communities of belief that are profiting from the growing dissatisfaction with mainline Christianity[72] – also occur in other parts of Papua New Guinea for the same reasons as in Pairundu, if the desire for 'cargo' is understood as an effort to acquire an increase in status, strength, equivalence and equality, or the assertion of identity and the re-establishment of autonomy. In this respect, fieldwork in Pairundu permits the recognition that this effort also demonstrates an intra-cultural dimension, that in the religious idiom, therefore, the genders are struggling over power as much as men of different ages and different prestige. I would expect that the same basically happens from time to time in other parts of Papua New Guinea too, although authors do not say so explicitly. But supporting this view is especially the disintegration effect noted in the case of cargo cults, Holy Spirit movements and changes in denominational affiliation, as well as the fact that it is first and foremost those who have only a comparatively modest status within their own cultures who participate in cargo cults and convert to the smaller communities of belief.[73] However, Pairundu corresponds to the broader regional context with respect not only to the reasons for conversion, but also the relationship between tradition and the particular view of Christianity. According to anthropological literature, indigenous peoples entirely believe that acceptance of the Christianity imparted by both the larger churches and the smaller communities of belief requires breaking with the pre-colonial past seen as a counter-image. At the same time, however, it is the parallels that are perceived, consciously or unconsciously, between the tradition and one's own form of Christianity that make this acceptance easier.[74] In addition, in other regions of Papua New Guinea, as in Pairundu, there is a dualistic juxtaposition as well as mutual influence of elements from the tradition and Christianity. In this way a religion is formed that differs similarly from both traditional religion and the Christianity of Western type transmitted through missionisation.

On the whole, this religion is only further differentiated by Kahn and by Ahrens. Kahn draws a distinction between, as it were, a 'Christian surface' and a 'traditional interior', in which, of course, it is scarcely possible to draw a precise boundary between 'shell' and 'core'.[75] From the emic point of view, at least, such a distinction also implies a negative judgement. Thus, in Pairundu, at any rate, both Catholics and Adventists would protest strongly if one were to describe them as 'superficial' Christians. It would perhaps be easier to agree with the distinction suggested by Ahrens, which in my view has not been appreciated sufficiently by anthropologists up to now, between 'popular religion' and 'superstructure'.[76] Admittedly Ahrens merely asserts the existence of this difference, without explaining its causes or illustrating it through examples by choosing a settlement community and presenting the appropriate beliefs.[77] Nevertheless, a distinction between 'popular religion' and 'official religion' can also be noted in Pairundu, where the 'popular religion' is linked with the traditional religion and the 'ordinary' members of the community, while the 'official religion' corresponds rather to the Christianity imparted through missionisation and the church office-holders.

Altogether, the indications given in the literature allow Pairundu to be seen as more or less representative with respect to the acceptance of different forms of Christianity, that is with respect to the reasons for conversion and the relationship between Christianity and tradition. However, if the reception of the Christianity imparted by the larger churches and the smaller communities of belief occurs basically because of the same needs and if in both cases conversion is seen similarly as a break with the tradition that nevertheless, from the etic point of view, profits from the perceived parallels with that tradition, then a connection emerges which other authors have not seen or at least not articulated: in other parts of Papua New Guinea, as in Pairundu, conversion to the mainline churches is, so to speak, repeated in a structurally similar form by conversion to the smaller communities of belief. In addition, the results of fieldwork in Pairundu lead some of the theses that have been put forward in the literature to be regarded with scepticism. This concerns primarily the role of the traditional religion, in so far as this can still be reconstructed today. In Pairundu, the initial impression that missionisation had eradicated traditional religion proves to be misleading. That is, adopting straightaway the claim formulated officially by church office-holders that, as 'convinced Christians', they no longer have anything to do with tradition would be to overestimate the changes connected with the reception of Christianity seen from the etic point of view. Experience in Pairundu rather allows the assumption that such an overestimate, an unchecked adoption of indigenous statements, is occurring precisely when, for example, in connection with an accusation of cultural destruction directed against the missionaries,[78] it is claimed that the traditional religion has declined or has been 'already eradicated by Christianity for decades'.[79] In my view, with respect to such theses, the question should be raised whether authors have actually grasped the 'popular religion' – which initially is not directly accessible – or considered the possibility that, despite outward appearances, the continuing influence of the traditional religion may be unfolding in the dualistic juxtaposition and mutual influence of elements from tradition and Christianity.

Notes

1. See, for example, Whiteman (1980) on the mission activities of the Anglican Church in the Solomon Islands. See also Garret (1982) on Protestant, Catholic and Anglican missionising throughout Oceania up to the turn of the twentieth century, as well as Delbos (1985) on the history of the Catholic Missionaries of the Sacred Heart (MSC) in present-day Papua New Guinea. A striking example of an apologetic treatment is Tomasetti (1976), who, after staying with the Lutheran community in Pare (Chimbu Province) from 1970 to 1971, admittedly describes, among other things, the indigenous view of Christianity and of the past and present, but does not acknowledge that this view has already been influenced by missionisation. Moreover, Tomasetti's (1976: 193) assessment that life has been 'enriched by Christian belief' seems at best simplistic. In contrast, the articles on the history of the Lutheran Church in Papua New Guinea edited by Wagner and Reiner (1986) offer a comparatively greater degree of self-criticism.
2. See Ahrens (1976). A large part of the data and reflections presented in this text are reproduced in later work (1977, 1986a, 1986b, cf. also 1991).
3. (Introduction). Hayward (1992) can also be mentioned in respect of mission theology, with reference to the Dani and therefore the western half of New Guinea. Having worked as a missionary for the Unevangelized Fields Mission from 1967 and 1987, he contrasts rather descriptively traditional ideas and practices, in order to give an account of how Christian practices and ideas are understood and accepted. However, he makes

no distinction between official and unofficial levels, presumably because of his missionary role.

4. See, for example, Williams (1928), Fortune (1935), Malinowski (1935) and Bateson (1936) as well as, for later publications, Strauss (1962), Nevermann (1968) and especially the influential collection edited by Lawrence and Meggitt under the title 'Gods, Ghosts and Men in Melanesia' (1965b). For overviews, see also Habel (1979), Stephen (1987) and Trompf (1991).

5. Schiefflin (1976). Keesing (1982) and Meigs (1984) as well as the collection of articles edited by Zelenietz and Lindenbaum (1981) and Herdt (1982) and Stephen (1987), who to some extent are concerned with religious phenomena in emulation of Lawrence and Meggitt (1965b).

6. On such states, see also Herdt and Stephen (1989).

7. See among others Hogbin (1947) on Busama, present-day Morobe Province, and on the Solomon Islands (1969), Dawn Ryan (1969) on the Toaripi, present-day Gulf Province, and Firth (1970) on Tikopia (Polynesia).

8. See also Senft (1992) for the Trobriand Islands, Milne Bay Province.

9. (Introduction). Also to be mentioned for the Highlands of Papua New Guinea is Dabrowski (1991), who, on the basis of fieldwork lasting from January 1981 to December 1992 in Rulna, Western Highlands Province, describes how Catholic Christianity (Societas Verbi Divinii) is being integrated into the traditional cosmology.

10. Cargo cults are religiously based social movements through which, following contact with white colonial officers, missionaries and traders, the inhabitants of Melanesia have attempted to explain and overcome the former's superiority of power by coming into possession of Western goods ('cargo'), which were often thought to emerge from secret rituals. On this, see the literature listed by Steinbauer (1971), as well as my own overview of the different approaches to interpretation (Jebens 1990a). Berndt (1952/53), A. Strathern (1971a), Meggitt (1973) and Gibbs (1977) give descriptions of cargo cults in the Highlands of Papua New Guinea.

11. Eckert (1940: 26) mentions an 'external disruption of the cultural equilibrium' (cf. Guiart 1951: 229). Williams (1976: 377) notes 'mental confusion' as a cause of the so-called 'Vailala madness' For the idea of socio-economic inequality causing cargo cults, see especially Worsley (1957), who first took up Bodrogi's (1951) theses and later influenced Mühlmann's (1961a, 1961b) interpretation among others.

12. Some of the ideas expressed in this work can also be found in Lawrence's earlier articles (1954, 1956).

13. See, among others, Counts (1978: 392), Whiteman (1980: 323, 327). Forman (1982: 89), Kahn (1983: 105), LeRoy (1985a: 33f) and MacDonald (1991: 218). Other causes cited are the fear of hell or of the announced end of the world, the desire to go to heaven (Hayward 1992: 214) and, at least in the initial phase of colonisation and missionisation, protection from the colonial government. Thus Guiart (1962: 136) writes: 'In the absence of any administrative structure to protect them, is it astonishing that the natives sought help and protection through conversion?'

14. J. Clark (1988: 48) quotes Pangia Patrol Report 13/72–3: 'There is no doubt that material gain, or the belief that it will ensue, is the major Christianising influence'.

15. Lawrence (1964: 73) describes this idea as the 'third Cargo Belief', spreading roughly from 1914 to 1933. The attempt of the indigenous people to enter into a proper relationship with the Christian God by obeying the missionaries in order to persuade Him to send 'cargo' to them too is for Lawrence (1964: 80) 'the first recognizable cargo cult in the southern Madang District'.

16. This is also claimed by Kulick and Stroud (1990: 301) for Catholicism around the lower Sepik. Cf. Smith (1980: 48f), who also supports Lawrence. Although the connection that Lawrence draws between cargo and Christianity has been widely adopted, nonetheless his work has encountered criticism basically along the lines that he sees the indigenous cosmology as 'finite and immutable' (Lawrence 1964: 225). Worsley (1973: 454f) sees here an exaggerated systematisation that makes it appear

incomprehensible how the indigenous people could have reacted to changes Accordingly, Gesch (1985: 306) concludes: 'Lawrence's cosmology and epistemology remain too static'.

17. Accordingly, colonial officers wrote 'There have been and are still no cargo cults in the region...' (KPR 1968/69–3) and 'The area is lucky in that it has no cargo cults or similar movements' (KPR 1971/72–18).

18. 'Mipela i gat dispela kain tingting'. However, because of the pointedness of the question and my own assessment of Nosupinai, I think he was saying on this occasion what he believed I wanted to hear. Other elements of a 'cargo world-view' in Pairundu were the idea that the power of the whites concealed a secret and that basically their own ancestors were the producers of Western goods, which the whites had illegally misappropriated (see, with further information on literature, Jebens 1990a: 54).

19. Thus, working groups on this theme have been founded at the First European Colloquium on Pacific Studies in Nijmegen (December 1992) and the Conference of the Deutsche Gesellschaft für Völkerkunde in Leipzig (October 1993). See also Trompf (1990), Lattas (1992) and Otto (1992c).

20. See Hermann (1992: 63) with respect to the Sor, who took part in some of the activities described by Lawrence.

21. Read (1958: 273, 292) has already noted this.

22. See in particular the article by MacDowell (1988), which has been influential in discussions of this matter.

23. Lawrence (1964: 269) claims, regarding this 'cargo ideology', that it 'virtually represents the native's whole way of life'. Here, the term 'ideology', literally 'the teaching of ideas', represents precisely that 'over-systematisation' for which Lawrence has been criticised and which, in my view, is also implied by the term 'cargoism'.

24. A thesis of Harding's (1967: 21) can also be interpreted in this sense, according to which 'cargoism' is 'nothing less that the Melanesian world view applied to the task of providing meaningful interpretation of European culture'. Wagner (1975: 31) later used the term 'reverse ethnography' and described 'cargo' as the Melanesian term for Western culture. For Wagner (1975: 34), therefore, 'cargo cult' is 'an interpretative counterpart of anthropology itself'. On this idea more recently, see Otto (1992b: 5).

25. Equality characterises the ideas of heaven held not only by Catholics and Adventists in Pairundu (Chapter 4), but also, according to J. Clark (1988: 54), by the Wiru and some Enga groups, Enga Province: 'For Tombena Enga (and Wiru) the millennium was not characterized as a time of unlimited access to cargo but as a world without exchange' (Feil 1983). However, cf. Chapter 6. A world without exchange means a world without differences, since each exchange presupposes differences between takers and givers. If one understands the strengthening or re-creation of one's own identity and autonomy as 'salvation' – and admittedly the content of the meaning of 'salvation' generally always depends on the values and ideals of each culture concerned (Jebens 1990a: 97f, Flasche 1993) – then cargo cults can actually be understood as 'Heilsbewegungen' (Jebens 1993) or, as is the case for mission theology (Steinbauer 1971, Schwarz 1980), as 'salvation movements'.

26. Cf. Dawn Ryan (1969: 112) and, for the later history of the ideas and phenomena described by Lawrence, Morauta (1972: 446).

27. J. Clark (1989a: 140) points out the intra-cultural rising of status for women by describing their participation in church life as limiting male control over the rituals and thus threatening 'male solidarity'.

28. With respect to the participants in cargo cults, see A. Strathern (1971b: 263) for the Mount Hagen area, Western Highlands Province, and Berndt (1952/53: 52) for the Kainantu area, Eastern Highlands Province. According to Ahrens (1976: 2), it was first and foremost those lineages that had 'sold' their land to a German trading company that attempted to use conversion to improve their status with respect to others who had not converted. According to Senft (1992: 5), the clans that occupied the lowest place in the traditional rank structure make up most of the church functionaries. LeRoy (1985a: 34,

1985b: xxiv) points out that women joined the churches and corresponding meetings in particularly large numbers.

29. Thus J. Clark (1985: 360) writes: '...possession by God or the Holy Ghost validated the group acceptance of Christianity and the discarding of the traditional cult system...'.

30. He adopts the same thesis elsewhere (1982: 334), almost word for word.

31. See Jebens (1990b: 406ff.) for an extensive comparison of Holy Spirit movements and cargo cults with reference to both ideas and needs.

32. Accordingly, a 'cargo aspect' (J. Clark 1988: 51) and 'elements of cargo thinking' (Robin 1981c: 59, 1982: 337) have been noted in Holy Spirit movements, while Ahrens (1986a: 72) classifies both Holy Spirit movements and cargo cults similarly as what he calls 'religiously motivated movements of protest, conformity and self-assertion'.

33. See, among others, Matiabe (1983: 149), Teske (1983: 120) and Ahrens (1986c: 257).

34. Ahrens (1976: 3, 1977: 45) also reports that a breach with tradition is the aim.

35. On this, cf. Errington (1974: 256) and Young (1977: 141).

36. Accordingly, Linnekin (1992: 251) writes: 'Cultural construction implies... that tradition is a selective representation of the past, fashioned in the present, responsive to contemporary priorities and agendas, and politically instrumental'.

37. Cf. Thomas (1992a: 220). The problem of authenticity, on the other hand, becomes central when, with Hobsbawm (1983: 1f), one speaks of 'invented traditions' that have only an 'artificial' continuity with the historical past. For a critique of Hobsbawm, see especially Jolly and Thomas (1992a: 242), who point out in particular that he is not using the term 'invention' in Wagner's (1975) sense.

38. See the collections edited by Keesing and Tonkinson (1982), Linnekin and Poyer (1990) and Jolly and Thomas (1992b). Linnekin (1990, 1992) offers corresponding overviews of the literature. Pokawin (1987: 30) accordingly writes, of traditional cultures in general: 'They have become a resource to use when we want to attack what we do not accept about the dominant influences today'.

39. This term derives from English 'custom'.

40. Following MacDowell, Kempf (1992) identifies a corresponding idea among the Sibog, Madang Province. Before MacDowell, and without referring to Gellner, Counts and Counts (1976: 304) had already written of the Kaliai, West New Britain Province: '...they foresee change, not as a process occurring by degree, but rather as a sudden qualitative transformation that alters fundamental relations'.

41. If moments of dramatic and total change stand at both the end and the beginning of individual periods of time, which repeat themselves more or less similarly, then the idea of 'episodic' change can be linked to the conviction that time proceeds not lineally, but in cycles (cf. Behrend 1983). That this is the case for the inhabitants of the Pairundu area seems to be supported by the fact that, in the context of their traditional religion, they have arranged Aga-palaa Rimbu, Alamu-palaa Rimbu, Rombake, Akera and Opayo in cycles, each of which can be ended or begun periodically through particular cult events (Chapter 2). Accordingly, MacDonald (1991: 180) found that pig-killing festivals also went in cycles. The stories of parents and grandparents should also be mentioned – though unlike the references to Nokerepa they are not linked to the coming of the whites (Chapter 3) – according to which long before the coming of the whites, the clouds fell from heaven and will do so again some time in the future (Chapter 9). Moreover, the respective baptisms and communions of the denominations represented in Pairundu seem to be repeating the Biblical example of Jesus and thus a primordial event, or to some extent a previous cycle. In addition, for the Adventists there is repetition in their idea of imminent persecution by the Catholics, in which, in their view, the *sande lo* described for the past is visualised and revived (Chapter 4). For the indigenous people, the Christian announcement of the imminent end of the world is perhaps a continuation of the tradition just mentioned of the clouds falling down, recalling, for them, the 'time of darkness' that has also been mentioned (Chapter 6). Against the background of an idea of the cyclical progression of time, the Last Judgement may be understood not as the final destruction, but as the conclusion of an old cycle and the start of a new one, in

which, as it were, renewed humans live in a renewed world. Thus the Last Judgement would be structurally comparable to some extent to a Rimbu Eta or a pig-killing festival. Even the acquisition of 'development' can be thought of in this way as the dawn of a new cycle. However, the idea of a cyclical progression of time was not expressed concretely in the conversations and interviews I recorded and is only revealed through an interpretation of, for example, the traditional cult practices, the pig-killing festivals and the emic view of baptism and communion. Admittedly, this involves the danger, to a particular degree, of constructing conclusive connections and coherences from an etic perspective, which, for the indigenous people, may be neither consciously present nor unconsciously influential. Because of this, I am merely representing the idea of a cyclical progression of time as a possibility, and a marginal one, without ascribing it to the inhabitants of the Pairundu area with certainty.

42. This dualistic juxtaposition of elements from Christianity and tradition, which is already indicated in the sub-title of Kahn's article 'Sunday Christians, Monday Sorcerers' (1983), is also described by, among others, Counts (1978: 376), Smith (1980: 43), Whiteman (1980: 593), with reference to the Kewa L. Josephides (1985a: 79) and Doetsch and Jentsch (1986: 573ff.).

43. Thus MacDonald (1991: 214) writes, of the inhabitants of Mararoko: 'They retell their stories and reinterpret their rituals to accommodate Christian postulates and Christian insights'.

44. (Chapters 3, 4). Accordingly, Smith (1990: 163f) says that the inhabitants of Koragur claim that, even before contact with the whites, they had heard of God and observed Christian values by behaving hospitably and generously towards one another. Toren (1988: 697, 712) reports a similar attitude with respect to the Fijian island of Gau, where the idea prevails that the missionaries had simply freed the already existing Christian core of the tradition by means of a few prohibitions. The identification of Yaki with the Christian God is also made by Apea (1985), who is not just a Catholic priest, but was also born a Kewa. He links the reinterpretation of the tradition with a rolling over of its negative aspects by, for example, describing the *remo* exclusively as positively valued 'personal guards and helpers' (1985: 226) and drawing parallels with the saints of the Catholic Church (1985: 234).

45. According to J. Clark, among these functions is contributing to social cohesion and continuity. Thus for Christianity today, as well as for traditional cults earlier, it can be said that 'it is emblematic of the group and assures its continuity through the ritual of the environment by propitiating spirits/God' (J. Clark 1985: 377, cf. 1989b: 178). With reference to Pentecostal Christianity, A. Stathern (1991: 52) also notes the taking over of elements of the tradition, though without identifying them: 'Pentecostal Christianity both denies indigenous cultures and provides scope for the essentials of these to be reborn in a new mold and with enhanced legitimacy'. In a similar vein, Ahrens (1976: 8), claims that 'the Christian message and Christian ethics are embraced by Melanesian thought forms' (cf. also Ahrens 1977: 70).

46. However, Kahn and MacDonald do not describe in detail the practices and beliefs imparted through missionisation. In my view, this would be essential in order to assess whether there really has been selection in the sense of a refusal or rejection of individual elements of Christianity. Apart from Kahn and MacDonald, such a selection is also noted by Counts (1978) and L. Josephides (1985a: 79), among others.

47. Elsewhere, J. Clark (1989a: 140) even claims that obtaining development may be expected as a reward for Christianity. 'Cargo cult elements' have been noted with reference to indigenous concepts of *bisnis*. See Errington (1974), Ploeg (1975: 203), B.J. Allen (1976: 188), Ahrens (1977: 57) and Bryant Allen (1990: 195f).

48. Accordingly, Hogbin (1947: 1) concluded already in 1947, if rather simplistically: 'Busama Christianity is a hodge-podge, some elements being derived from paganism and others stemming direct from the teachings of the missionaries'. See also Counts (1978: 375). Hayward (1992: 387) writes: '…the style of Christianity that is introduced is changed, and the culture that receives it is changed'. Cf. MacDonald (1991: 214): '… the style of Christianity which emerged is different from that of western cultures'.

49. Cf. Dawn Ryan (1969: 107): 'Like people everywhere, the Toaripi have emphasised those parts of the New Testament that fit best with their pre-existing beliefs and are most congenial to their current hopes and aspirations'. For Lawrence (1971: 139) cargo cults adopt elements of the Christianity taught by the missionaries, while at the same time he sees them as the expression of a 'cargo religion' obviously representing a sort of continuation of the traditional religion. Robin (1982: 339) sees in the Holy Spirit movements 'ritualized practices and behaviour illustrative of an interrelationship between indigenous belief and Christianity'.

50. See Robin (1982: 339): 'A final and major factor in the success of Christianity has been metaphysical similarity'. However, Robin only mentions very general similarities, namely contact with a 'spirit world', the drawing up of instructions for behaviour and the reference to the origins of humans. In the context of the traditional religion of the inhabitants of Pairundu, however, no reference to the origins of humanity can be recognised. Robin's thesis is cited approvingly by J. Clark (1985: 179), who then continues, though without any further explanation: 'The immediate appeal of Christianity was its similarity to facets of cult belief' (1985: 370, 1989b: 174). Accordingly, for A. Strathern (1991: 51) too the mutual influence of tradition and Christianity is promoted by their similarity, though he does not detail these similarities any more than J. Clark does: '... there are sufficient features of similarity between these two for some mutual reshaping to take place'.

51. As a synonym for 'basic form of religion', Ahrens (1976: 15), who generally does not demonstrate any great stringency in his use of terms, applies the description 'syncretistic folk religion'.

52. In addition, Ahrens (1986c, see also 1977: 13) sees both cargo cults and Holy Spirit movements as an expression of the 'popular religion'. Like Ahrens, May (1985b: xiii) distinguishes between a '"people's religion" [and] the "official religion" of the churches with the Western bias of their various structures and doctrines'. Referring to the mission theology of Brazil, Süss (1978: 26, 35) distinguishes between 'official Catholicism', 'popular Catholicism' and 'popular religiosity', which also includes elements of non-Christian origin. Ahrens's use of the adjective 'nativistic' creates the assumption that, for him, the 'popular religion' is influenced by tradition to some degree, since the term 'nativistic movement' goes back to Linton (1943: 230), who defines it as 'any conscious, organised attempt on the part of a society's members to revive or perpetuate selected aspects of its culture'.

53. S. Josephides's work is based on fieldwork that he carried out between August 1978 and September 1979 in some villages of the Boroi, Madang Province.

54. The Asia Pacific Christian Mission does not belong in this context in the sense that it was the first denomination to arrive in Kaluli. On the other hand, in my view its adherents entirely resemble the Seventh-day Adventists in their rigidity.

55. Ross (1978) also deals with the mission activities of the Adventists on Malaita, Solomon Islands. Further indications can be found in works that are mainly concerned with other themes (Hogbin 1947, J. Clark 1985, Thomas 1992b). From a mission theology perspective, finally, May (1985a) tries to explain the generally positive reaction of Melanesians to Christian fundamentalism. Since sources on the smaller communities of believers in general and the Adventists in particular are not all that exhaustive, I would also like to mention research by Ströbele-Gregor (1988, 1989), which admittedly refers to Bolivia, but which, based on a one-year field stay in an Adventist community, goes into the question of the consequences of Adventist mission activity as well as the reasons for conversion. One point of criticism, however, is that Ströbele-Gregor only reproduces the views represented by the SDA Church leadership, leaving unmentioned, for example, how the Adventists are judged by their unconverted relatives.

56. This goes for Ströbele-Gregor too.

57. 'Both Seventh-day Adventists and the cargo cult promise a better tomorrow both on earth and in heaven for giving up everything one has' (S. Josephides 1990: 65). At the same time, according to S. Josephides, the Boroi believe that Adventist Christianity will

help them turn away from tradition and towards *bisnis*, since the era of tradition has been eradicated by the era of *bisnis* (1982: 313f).

58. According to Ross (1978), the Adventists offer comparatively better medical care, a better education and the promise of economic growth, since as Protestants they practice investment rather than consumption. Certainly none of this applies to Pairundu, where only those who already have a certain 'property' – and that includes Catholics – tend to 'save' (Chapter 1). Referring to Bolivia, Ströbele-Gregor writes that Adventist Christianity offers a 'pathway to "civilization"', i.e., to social ascent' (1988: 278), in that the individual receives offers of education, can increase his prestige by taking over religious offices and tasks (1988: 281) and is enabled to legitimise it in a religious manner if he fails to fulfil traditionally justified expectations of generosity.

59. For Whiteman (1980: 650), Christianity in the Solomon Islands has lost a lot of its original dynamic, since people today, three or four generations after the start of mission activities, have been born into Christianity and no longer have to convert to it. May (1985a: 1f) describes a loss of meaning in the beliefs disseminated by the larger churches (and traditional ones) as giving rise to a 'vacuum', which conversely has helped bring about the growth of smaller communities of belief.

60. See Lawrence (1964: 88ff.), Ahrens (1976: 4f, 1977: 47ff.), Smith (1980: 49) and Kulick and Stroud (1990: 300) as well as Kahn (1983: 103, fn. 13), according to whom indigenous people complain that, although they have become Christians, the missionaries have not cared to ensure that they acquired cars, roads, televisions or money.

61. Certainly this accusation is not made in Pairundu by either Adventists or Catholics. In addition, S. Josephides (1982: 56) explains the conversion of the inhabitants of a Boroi village to the Adventists in terms of the fact that one representative of the SDA Church leadership would live in this village, but no leading Catholic Church officer, which has created dissatisfaction.

62. The idea of the Adventists in Pairundu, that after Adventist baptism one is 'like a dead person' (Chapter 4), corresponds to this distancing. Similar ideas are also propagated by the ECP, according to Schiefflin (1981a: 18): 'A Christian should be modest, quiet, never openly forceful or angry, he should "go like a sick man", as one pastor put it. Newly baptised Christians... will now (supposedly) never get angry or excited but maintain a calm, subdued, unassertive manner'.

63. This is the only point at which the SDA Church is mentioned in the whole of J. Clark's (1985) monograph.

64. Cf. Tiffany (1978: 452) for Western Samoa.

65. Schiefflin (1981b: 155). According to Ströbele-Gregor, the members of the SDA community she investigated in Creole society, where they are subject to 'racial discrimination' (1988: 281), have a marginal position (1988: 183). O. Lewis (1964: 82) claims, of a village located south of Mexico City in the late 1940s, that Adventist Protestantism speaks especially to those who could not obtain any advantage from social and political change.

66. As already mentioned, Smith (1980) describes how the renunciation of such a rejection of tradition is answered with disappointment. L. Josephides points out that inhabitants of the Sumbura region account for their moving over to the ECP by claiming that the Catholics would forbid too little of the traditional culture (letter dated 31 March1993). Thomas (1992a: 224, fn. 18), referring to Fiji, claims that more recent denominations acquire their attraction from the fact that they represent a rejection of the hierarchy of the chiefs.

67. Hogbin (1947: 21, fn. 26) writes: 'The stress on the taboos also furnishes a reason for the success of the Seventh-day Adventist Mission [*sic*], a never-ending source of amazement to many New Guinea residents. Giving up pork, certain kinds of fish, tobacco and Saturdays is a hardship, but this is the sort of demand which the pagan religions made...' In the case of Ballard and Schiefflin, however, it seems reasonable to ask if they have perhaps been misled by a Christian reinterpretation of tradition, when they claim that ideas of the end of the world already existed in the pre-Christian era. For

Ströbele-Gregor (1988: 284) too, acceptance of Adventist Christianity is explained by the fact that the Adventists are building on 'traditional social models and forms of thought'. She sees such links in sexual morality (1988: 175), explanations for sickness (1988: 177), the appearance of visions (1988: 156ff.) and in the fact that the relationship with God structurally resembles the relationship with the ancestors (1988: 154).

68. Accordingly, for Ströbele-Gregor, the Adventists impart a 'closed belief system' (1988: 227) and thus a 'feeling of security' (1988: 228) that promises 'freedom from fear, self-confidence, satisfaction and consistency' (1988: 213).

69. This concerns, for example, J. Clark, Ahrens, Kahn, MacDonald and also Lawrence.

70. This concerns, for example, Schiefflin, S. Josephides, Ballard and May.

71. This applies to different degrees to the works of MacDonald, Robin and Kahn, among others.

72. As already described, Ahrens, Kahn, Lawrence and Smith merely mention this dissatisfaction, without, however – in contrast to J. Clark, MacDonald, Robin or S. Josephides – linking it to the growth in the smaller communities of belief.

73. This applies equally to the participants in the Holy Spirit movement in Pairundu. In the case of other regions, however, authors do not specify these participants more precisely.

74. However, neither J. Clark nor Robin (nor Ströbele-Gregor) clearly say – apart from rather general statements – precisely what form the postulated parallels take. Schiefflin and Ballard describe such parallels with respect to the idea of the end of the world, though in doing so they are running the risk of incorporating a Christianised reinterpretation of the tradition.

75. If this difference really was expressed by an informant himself, as Kahn states, and if this informant was neither reproducing an alien view nor expressing what he thought was expected of him, then Neumann's (1992: 102ff.) criticism, that Kahn's differentiation derives from a Western perspective, does not apply.

76. The same is true of the dichotomy May (1985b: xiii) suggests between the 'official religion' and the 'people's religion'.

77. The recording of the appropriate data was presumably not possible for Ahrens, since a priori his role as a missionary may have closed off many avenues of information to him. Moreover, he was responsible for a large area, so that he presumably only knew a few inhabitants in each village. In my judgement, all of this also applies to Fr Matthias, although, as the chief representative of the church leadership, he did enjoy generally great respect in the Pairundu area.

78. For example, Schulze (1987) makes this accusation, especially in view of the sort of missionisation in Latin America that is described as evangelical and fundamentalist. See also the sweeping description of Paczensky (1991), which on the whole has something of a popular scientific character, without drawing regional boundaries.

79. Fischer (1992: 2, cf. Senft 1992: 17). Accordingly, Vicedom and Tischner (1943–48: 473) claim that the indigenous people had themselves produced 'the value judgement on their religion by turning to Christianity as united tribes with a rapidity and firmness that is rarely experienced in the mission field'. Schiefflin (1981b) also emphatically conveys the impression that the traditional religion had declined. One reason for this view may be the disappearance of the traditional ceremonies and exchange relationships that had been central to Schiefflin's interests during his first field trip in 1976.

9

Fundamentalism as a Response to Modernity

One theoretical framework for the example of Pairundu is obtained by relating the appearance there of the Seventh-day Adventists to the worldwide phenomenon of fundamentalism. To do this, however, it is first necessary to summarise the description and interpretation of this phenomenon in its essentials.

The problem of the concept

The phenomenon of fundamentalism seems to have acquired significance in all three major monotheistic world religions since the mid-1970s at the latest, whether in the form of orthodox movements in Israel, re-Islamisation movements or within North American Protestantism, in the form of the so-called 'moral majority'.[1] The term 'fundamentalism', on the other hand, which entered general awareness more forcefully at least when, in 1979, Khomeini took over political power in Iran, goes back originally to the twelve-volume series of writings entitled 'The Fundamentals: A Testimony to the Truth', published by North American Protestants between 1910 and 1915 with a print run of three million copies and distributed free. The principles laid down in this work deal with the divine inspiration and infallibility of the Bible, as well as 'elementary Christological teachings', that is, beliefs concerning the divinity of Jesus, His virgin birth, His sacrifice on the cross for the sins of others and His physically having risen from the dead and returned.[2] Only those who share these fundamentals of belief are said to be justified in claiming for themselves the status of 'true Christians'. Along with this determination of postulates that are regarded as generally binding, the propagation and defence of which is even demanded from the state,[3] goes the attempt to seal oneself off from scientific knowledge that contradicts the beliefs of the Bible by placing Biblical texts and ideas in a historical and critical perspective. At the same time, out of this separation must have come a feeling of security, which found a special response in North America at the start of the twentieth century, when a situation of social change generally predominated, characterised by economic depression, the change from an agricultural to an industrial state, the associated flight from the land and the sense of being threatened by immigrants (Odermatt 1991: 12).

Today, within Protestantism, the term 'fundamentalism' covers 'traditionally grown pietism, evangelism [and] new Pentecostalist-charismatic movements, right through to positions of Christian conservatism' (Küenzelen (1992: 4). The respective groups always invoke the fundamentals of belief laid down between 1910 and 1915, in particular the infallibility of the Bible.[4] In addition, according to Küenzelen, the idea often prevails that one's own community is chosen in opposition to a theological, ecclesiastical or secular adversary. In order to join this chosen community, it is usually considered necessary to subject oneself to baptism as an adult or to re-baptism, which is often understood as 'giving up one's life for Christ' (Küenzelen 1992: 5). Group membership that is sealed with such a baptism frequently manifests itself in outward forms, like clothing, hair-style or specific ways of behaving. According to Küenzelen (1992: 5f), other characteristics of Protestant fundamentalism consist in a marked expectation of the end of the world, which is viewed as a site of the struggle between God and Satan. Also to be added are the efforts to evangelise, that is, to increase the numbers of the chosen. At the same time, however, the term 'fundamentalism' is also applicable within Catholicism. Here, Ebertz (1992) distinguishes a Biblical, a traditionalistic and an institutionalistic patriarchal principle, meaning by the latter a position that is basically loyal to the Pope. Precisely just such an attitude is attested by Walf in his descriptions of groupings such as Opus Dei, Communione e Liberazione (1989: 251–254) and the adherents of charismatic movements of renewal (1989: 254ff.). Finally, Walf (1989: 258) speaks even of an 'official fundamentalism', since for him the impression is created that 'fundamentalist theoretical models of church and society have been given official legitimation in the Catholic Church for a long time'. Conversely, the traditionalism of the former Archbishop Marcel Lefebre (1905–1991) was directed against the Pope, if not the papacy itself, though nonetheless it is assigned to Catholicism and, within that context, to fundamentalism (Walf 1989: 249ff., Kepel 1991: 79–146). Basically, Lefebre sought to undo the changes that emerged from the Second Vatican Council, which he saw as a 'Protestantisation' of Catholicism.[5] Among these changes was in particular the reform of the liturgy, which, among other things, provided that the mass would henceforward be celebrated in the respective mother tongue. In opposition to this, Lefebre's fundamentalism retained the Latin of the so-called Tridentine Mass, which had been used up to then, having been introduced in 1570 by Pope Pius V, after the Council of Trient (1545–1563) (Walf 1989: 249, Ebertz 1992: 16).

Up to the present day, use of the term 'fundamentalism' has not been restricted to particular movements within Protestantism and Catholicism, but applied rather to non-Christian world religions – whether monotheistic (Judaism, Islam) or polytheistic (Hinduism) – as well as to phenomena that, at first sight, seem to have nothing to do with religion, such as fascism, Marxism, as well as generally dogmatic attitudes within ecology (Schütze 1992), 'green alternative politics', orthodox medicine and the so-called 'psychoscene'.[6] Given the differences between the various phenomena that are described respectively as 'fundamentalist', a generally recognised substantive definition is not possible. Instead, the impression is created that in principle one can name the content of anything 'fundamentalist', so long as it represents a certain degree of rigidity – though without defining it more precisely anywhere – and provided that it is linked to a claim of absolute validity, as well as to the renunciation of any discussion, openness, doubt or even humour.[7] However, the term 'fundamentalism' does not draw its problematic solely from the heterogeneity of its object: it has also been linked with connotations of 'illness' and evaluated negatively.[8] As a consequence, since the publication of the series of writings mentioned above – and the founding of the so-called 'World's Christian Fundamentals Association' in 1919 in the U.S.A. (Papenthin 1989: 33) – it has developed into a denotation of the other: 'Fundamentalists are always other people'.[9] Because of its negative evaluation and its growing significance worldwide in recent decades, 'fundamentalism' appears in many articles as a danger or a threat to be warned against and prevented.[10] This is especially true of Islamic fundamentalism.

Opposition to modernity

Although describing the phenomenon of 'fundamentalism' proves difficult because of the problematic that has been described, most authors agree in the interpretation that groups and movements that are characterised as 'fundamentalist' usually refer to modernity or seek to undo it in terms of its different aspects (Dubiel 1992: 750f). Modernity is usually understood as the 'process of continuing rationalisation, differentiation and autonomization' (Klinger 1992: 782) that started in Europe with the Enlightenment. According to Max Weber (1991: 250f), 'intellectual rationalisation through science and scientifically oriented technology' leads to the knowledge or belief 'that as a matter of principle there are no secret, unfathomable powers... that rather all things – in principle – can be mastered through calculation. However, this means demystifying the world'. Out of this arises a questioning of transcendent authorities, so that the 'structures of life and of social relationships laid down in religions' (Zinser 1992: 10), which are legitimated with reference to these authorities, are relativised, eradicated and robbed of their absolute validity, their collective commitment. At the same time, this feeds secularisation, which, as a central principle of modernity, basically contributes to religion losing its all-embracing significance for all areas of life, so that a separation between church and religion on the one hand and between state and society on the other, emerges. Thus religion develops alongside, for example, politics, economics and technology as a more or less separate domain of culture (Dubiel 1992: 755) and tends to become a private matter (Klinger 1992: 790, Zinser 1992: 15). The individual can and must construct meaning for and by himself, which gives rise to a pluralism of meanings and interpretations of the world.[11] For the individual, alongside the loss of previously valid models and structures, this leads to an increase in autonomy and freedom, though on the other hand it can also appear as a threat to one's identity, since the responsibility for one's own meaning also implies a greater burden.

Groups and movements that are described as 'fundamentalist' are now seeking to undo the process of modernity in its different aspects by linking particular ideas with transcendent origins and thus strengthening them religiously. Thus, it becomes possible to deny the historicity of different ideas in order to exclude them from any critical investigation, relativisation or questioning (Küenzelen 1992: 7). In accordance with this isolation from any aspect of Enlightenment thought, Meyer (1989a: 7) has described fundamentalism as a 'radical Counter-Enlightenment'. Finally, the selected and religiously justified principles that simultaneously justify a common assertion of exclusivity as a symbol of group identity are in principle supposed to be valid for all humanity and all areas of life. From this arises the abolition of the pluralism of meanings and of interpretations of the world in modernity, as well as the separation between church and religion on the one hand and state and society on the other, that is a part of secularisation (Kepel 1991: 271). At the same time, the reliance on fixed and absolutely valid principles has the effect of creating an identity after the loss of previously valid models and structures. As Küenzelen (1992: 8) stresses, with its closed world-view, its consciousness of being an elite, its rigid norms and its view of the present as an early stage in the coming of salvation, fundamentalism offers 'security in a new binding world-view, a "solid fortress" in the midst of plurality, relativisation and the dissolution of traditional certainties'.[12] In fundamentalist Christianity of both Protestant and Catholic persuasion, it is first and foremost to the Bible, as a religiously legitimised basis outside any historical change, that collective commitment in all areas of life is ascribed. According to the respective ideas, the text of the Bible was given directly by God, so that, being free from error and contradiction in all its parts, it is seen, as it were, as being beyond all criticism.[13]

Basically, according to Meyer (1989b: 22), fundamentalism can 'occur wherever contradictions between the promises and demands of modernity can no longer be tolerated'. This is most likely to be the case, as for example in North America at the beginning of the twentieth century, in a situation of economic crisis or social breakdown. It is characteristic of fundamentalist groups that they see the causes of the crises that give rise to them in a falling away of belief, a moving away from the foundations, rather than, for example, in problems of social structure. In this sense, a social problem is transformed into a moral one, which is then hoped to be solved through a return to belief or to one's alleged foundation.[14] This view exposes the representatives of fundamentalist missionisation in Latin America, for example, to the accusation that they are preventing indigenous populations from actually striving to improve their living conditions (see Rohr 1987, Schultze 1987). Since fundamentalism – whether through its isolation from Enlightenment thought or its abolition of pluralism and secularisation – seeks to undo the process of modernity, it is often seen as a counter-movement or even an escapist movement with respect to this process.[15] Dubiel (1992: 752) emphasises, certainly correctly, that such an interpretation ultimately assigns to fundamentalism the function of 'teaching modernity, which has fallen into crisis, its own inadequacy', so that 'fundamentalism [seems] like modernity's chance for self-perfection' (cf. Lau 1992). It would therefore be wrong, as Meyer (1989b: 22), Klinger (1992: 784) and Küenzelen (1992: 5) all stress, as well as Dubiel (1992: 753), to see fundamentalism as something entirely different from modernity. Rather, in that fundamentalism, in whatever way, refers to modernity, it moves on the latter's ground, it has modernity as a precondition, and to some extent it constitutes one of modernity's symptoms, even though the adherents of groups described as fundamentalist would presumably not agree.

From the heterogeneity of phenomena termed 'fundamentalist' it follows that the form in which the individual encounters modernity, as well as the foundation with which he opposes it, always depends on the concrete situational context. In the countries of the so-called Third World, for example, unlike in Europe or North America, modernity appears as something imported. Here, therefore, in the context of fundamentalist efforts as a counter-movement, an attempt may be made to strengthen one's own cultural tradition by confronting the representatives of the Euro-American world. Accordingly, Hemminger (1991: 10) regards fundamentalism in Asia as 'an attempt at politico-cultural self-assertion'. Generally, the phenomenon of fundamentalism cannot be linked a priori with a particular social stratum, a particular political tendency or, for example, a sweeping rejection of new technologies. In my view, the heterogeneity of what is described as 'fundamentalist' makes it sensible to restrict the term to those cases in which the different principles that are evoked are actually based on their being linked to a transcendent sphere. Conversely, I regard it as misleading to label dogmatic positions within ecology, 'green alternative politics', orthodox medicine or the so-called 'psychoscene' as fundamentalist too.

From the etic point of view, fundamentalist groups and movements are relatively easy to criticise. First, the choice of foundations used is basically arbitrary, even though, with reference to 'divine origins', the adherents of the respective groups and movements may dispute the idea that they themselves made such a choice. In addition, the alleged foundations may not be identical with actual historic reality – something they have in common with the construction of *kastom*. Lefebre, for example, kept to the Tridentine Mass, with its use of Latin, by invoking Jesus, even though Jesus Himself may have held the Last Supper in Aramaic and although Greek was the language of the mass in the Roman community until well into the fourth century AD (Schifferle 1991: 75). Finally, by offering 'security', fundamentalism frees the individual from the burden of oneself bearing insecurity, disorientation and threats to identity, as well as from taking the responsibility for finding meaning on his own. In order to be relieved in this way, however, the individual has to sacrifice his freedom and autonomy.

Many interpretations of fundamentalism are illustrated by particular currents in Islam, which Western authors frequently represent as a danger or a threat to warn against and to prevent. The foundation that the different forms of Islamic fundamentalism all similarly invoke relates to the first Islamic community that the Prophet Mohammed himself led in Medina between 622 and 623 AD, according to the corresponding tradition (Ghaussy 1989: 90). In this regard, Islamic fundamentalism is based on an effort 'to reconstruct the state, political, social, economic and moral ideals of the community of Medina as a backward-looking utopia' (Heine 1992: 24). Accordingly, the term 're-Islamisation' is particularly apt (Hummel 1991: 47). If the ideal of the community of Medina, opposing to a pluralism of meanings and of interpretations of the world, is supposed to be binding collectively for all aspects of life and if one desires to undo the introduction of secular legislation, schools and universities, or to reverse the expulsion of Islam from these spheres (B. Lewis 1992: 831f), then this is directed against the separation of society and religion, that is, against secularisation as a central principle of modernity. As a result, in its strivings for politico-cultural self-assertion, Islamic fundamentalism also tends to turn against the West, from which modernity was imported originally.[16] Accordingly, Heine (1992: 28) concludes for Iran: 'In Islam... Khomeini and his followers saw a possibility to defend and preserve the national and cultural identity of Islam from foreign infiltration from the west'. According to Kepel, in many states re-Islamisation movements are occurring at a time when post-independence generations have grown up and are articulating their dissatisfaction with those who took over power at the end of the colonial period. 'The successes of the Islamists are clearly a retribution for the political, economic and social failures of the elites that have ruled since independence' (Kepel 1991: 274). Zinser (1992: 10) points out that while most Moslems may well be objectively better off than before independence, subjectively they certainly feel deprived, especially when they compare their living standards with those of the elites or the whites. In any case, according to Zinser (1992: 10), dissatisfaction is fed by the fact that in many respects the expectations associated with independence have been disappointed. Accordingly, the example of Islam confirms the idea that, especially in situations of economic crisis, fundamentalist groups and movements are more likely to be articulated the greater the disparity between the hopes and actual consequences that are associated with modernity.

Although to some extent Islamic fundamentalism propagates a 'return' to the community of Medina, from the etic point of view, as Zinser (1992: 13) emphasises, there is actually 'an adoption of modern ideas of popular sovereignty and parliamentarianism... under the name of re-Islamisation [so that] under the name of re-Islamisation, modernisation' takes place. Thus, the example of Islamic fundamentalism supports two of the theses that have been developed in the interpretation of this phenomenon as a whole. What is put forward as a foundation may correspond as little to historical reality as the community of Medina really was characterised by popular sovereignty and parliamentarianism. Alongside this, it becomes clear that, although fundamentalism certainly turns itself against modernity, at the same time it not only shares in it, it also sometimes even advances it by introducing new ideas.

The situation in Pairundu

In comparing the phenomenon of 'fundamentalism' as described and interpreted in the literature with the ideas of the Adventists in Pairundu, some parallels are indicated. This applies especially to fundamentalist currents within North American Protestantism, from which the Church of the Seventh-day Adventists originally derives. Thus the Adventists believe equally, for example, in the principles laid down in the series of writings, 'The Fundamentals', mentioned earlier, of which Christological teachings, which make reference to the divinity of Christ, are as much a part as is belief in the inspiration, infallibility and freedom from contradiction of the Bible.[17] No less characteristic, moreover, of the Adventists in Pairundu are the features listed by Küenzelen. The members of the SDA community see themselves as belonging to a chosen group who must separate themselves from an external enemy (the Catholics) by sealing group membership through baptism as a 'giving up of one's life', as well as through outward manifestations (the emphasis on washing the body and on clean western clothing).[18] Alongside this, the Adventists also understand the world as a location of the conflict between God and the Devil, soon to become decided on the Last Day of Judgement. Finally, the Adventist inhabitants of the Pairundu area, like other fundamentalist Protestants, are trying to increase the size of their community through evangelisation. The parallels also extend to the fact that the Adventists, as Küenzelen describes for fundamentalist groups in North American Protestantism, provide an impression of security, with their closed world-view, their feeling of belonging to an elite group, their rigid norms and their expectations of salvation to come. Altogether, therefore, S. Josephides's (1990: 59) conclusion with respect to the Boroi also applies to the Pairundu area: 'The Seventh-day Adventists are fundamentalists...'[19]

On the other hand, it could be objected that – in, for example, their emphasis on Christological teachings and in contrast to the followers of fundamentalist groups in North America – the Adventists in Pairundu are relying not on their own foundations, but on those imported by the corresponding missionaries. However, this is only true on the emic level. From the etic point of view, there is certainly a strengthening of one's own foundations in that, as may be recalled, at least unconsciously, the Adventists are still guided by traditional needs and beliefs within the framework of their own denomination and in that the changes the Adventists are striving for and articulating in their idea of heaven are characterised by realising the values of the traditional culture. Parallels also emerge when comparing Adventist Christianity with Islamic fundamentalism. Basically, as with the rise of Islamic fundamentalism, the rise of the SDA community in Pairundu is a response to the disappointment of expectations that were originally linked with the importation of western modernity. In both cases, this response consists in an attempt – consciously on the part of fundamentalist Moslems and unconsciously on the part of the Adventists in Pairundu – to assert their own politico-cultural identity in opposition to the representatives of the imported modernity.

Admittedly, however, in doing so the Adventists and fundamentalist Moslems are moving in opposite directions, from both the emic and etic perspectives. On the emic level, fundamentalist Moslems turn against modernity and see their construction of tradition as positive. The Adventists, on the other hand, turn against their own construction of tradition and see modernity (their construction of the world of the whites) as positive. On the etic level, at least in Iran, fundamentalist Moslems are supporting the modernity they condemn by introducing new ideas. The Adventists, on the other hand, are strengthening the beliefs and values of the traditional culture that they condemn. The fundamentalist Moslems and Adventists differ diametrically with one another with respect to what they are aiming at, as much as in what they are attaining. A common feature between the two forms of fundamentalism merely consists of the fact that, in both cases, what from the etic point of view people are actually obtaining is the opposite of what from the emic point of view they are striving for.

Notes

1. The thesis of such a gain in meaning is already expressed by Kepel (1991) in the sub-title of his monograph, which can be translated as 'Radical Moslems, Christians and Jews on the advance'. On the 'moral majority', which is represented not least through so-called 'television evangelists' and which formed an essential part of the constituency of Ronald Reagan, see especially Papenthin (1989: 40), Kepel (1991: 19–24) and Küenzelen (1992: 3).

2. See Stöhr (1989: 238), Thiede (1991: 132), Dubiel (1992: 749) and Ebertz (1992, n. 3).
3. See Meyer (1989b: 13f), Küenzelen (1992: 5) and, on the origins of North American Protestant fundamentalism, Birnbaum (1989), Papenthin (1989) and Riesebrodt (1990).
4. Accordingly, May (1985a: 11) writes, concerning fundamentalism in Melanesia: 'Their basic affirmation, however, is rather that the Bible is absolutely and in its entirety without error...'
5. See Odermatt (1991: 21), Schifferle (1991: 93) and Ebertz (1992: 15).
6. Odermatt (1991). On Judaism, see Idalovichi (1989), Kepel (1991: 203–267) and Knochmalnik (1992). On Islam, see Ghaussy (1989: 91–96), Hummel (1991), Kepel (1991: 31–75), B. Lewis (1992: 824) and Heine (1992). On Hinduism, see Voll (1989) and Hummel (1991). Klinger (1992) examines fascism and fundamentalism in terms of their respective relationships with modernity. Heimann (1989) treats fundamentalist dispositions, elements and tendencies in Marxism.
7. Accordingly, Hemminger (1991: 5) writes: 'It looks as if each religion or world-view or even politics is called fundamentalist so long as it acts radical, intolerant, militant or conscious of power'.
8. Hummel (1991: 65) speaks, for example, of the 'bacillus of fundamentalism', and James Barr 1981: 30) describes fundamentalism as 'a pathological condition of Christianity' (see also James Barr 1981: 254).
9. Kallscheuer (1989: 66). See also Küenzelen (1992: 3).
10. Thus Meyer (1989a: 9) sees the goal of his edited volume as being 'to erect dams against the fundamentalist flood'.
11. Accordingly, Stephenson (1986: 296ff.) defines the process of secularisation as a change of consciousness.
12. See Odermatt (1991: 8): 'In its many shades, fundamentalism has to do with making safe a threatened identity or seeking to remake a lost identity'. Similarly, Hummel (1991: 64) writes: 'The dynamics of fundamentalist approaches arise from a situation that is experienced as endangering identity'.
13. See Löw (1989), Thiede (1991) and especially James Barr (1981: 70–127, 208–236), who places the Bible comprehension of Anglo-Saxon Protestant fundamentalism at the centre of his monograph.
14. The considerations presented here are based on an observation of Hartmut Zinser's (communication, 1993).
15. Meyer notes on the one hand a counter-movement, in that he describes fundamentalism as a 'global attack on the culture of modernity' (1989b: 20), while on the other hand, alluding to Kant's categorical imperative, he assumes an escapist movement: 'Fundamentalism is the self-caused escape from the demands of thinking for oneself, of taking responsibility for oneself, of being obliged to explain, as well as from the insecurity and openness of all claims to legitimacy, legitimations of rule and life forms – to which thought and life are irreversibly exposed by the Enlightenment and modernity – in the certainty and unity of self-elected, absolute foundations' (1989b: 18).
16. See Kepel (1991: 274), who describes Islamic fundamentalism as a protest against 'the heteronomous model of society imported from the west'.
17. Accordingly, James Barr (1981: 33) assigns the Adventist understanding of the Bible to fundamentalism.
18. Baptism may also appear to Adventists as a moment in episodic change, since, in the Adventist view, the 'new man' is produced not through a gradual process of change, but through the, as it were, sudden destruction of all his negative aspects (Chapter 4).
19. This attribution is also made by other authors. Keesing (1982: 232) numbers the Adventists among the different 'varieties of fundamentalism'. With respect to Bolivia, Ströbele-Gregor (1989: 75) counts them among the fundamentalist religious communities, and James Barr (1981: 24f) describes them as fundamentalists with respect to Anglo-Saxon Protestantism.

10

Concluding Remarks

How representative is Pairundu?

Judging from indications in sources in anthropology and mission theology, in general the Christianity imparted by the larger churches and smaller communities of belief spread as rapidly in other parts of Papua New Guinea as in Pairundu and with as little resistance. In addition, according to these sources Pairundu to some extent represents a 'normal case', a supra-regionally representative example, with regard to reasons for conversion and the relationship between Christianity and tradition. It is precisely in comparison with authors who concern themselves centrally with other themes, however, that stationary fieldwork involving systematic data collection based on mutual trust permits a more differentiated view of the needs and beliefs connected with the reception of Christianity. Catholics and Adventists both seek to participate in the power of the whites by adopting their different forms of Christianity, in order to increase their own status, demonstrate their own strength and create equivalence and equality. To the extent that this is also directed against the whites, it is in principle a form of resistance if the villagers no longer flee or refuse to obey, but instead ask for a catechist to be sent to them. Certainly alongside the whites, those of comparatively higher prestige within the culture, that is, the Big Men or other old men or men in general, appear as rivals in striving for increases in status, something that has often not been appreciated in other parts of Papua New Guinea. Through the realisation of strength and equivalence as traditional values, the desire is to turn oneself from an object into the subject of changes, both inter- and intra-culturally, in order to win back one's autonomy and strengthen one's own identity. While on the one hand, the threat to one's own identity results from the influences of the Western world, on the other the hand villagers regard the Catholic and Adventist forms of Christianity as characteristic of that world. Accordingly, from the etic point of view, what is threatened (one's own identity) is, in conversion, intended to be asserted by appropriating what is essential to the threat. For the members of both denominations, the reception of Christianity presupposes a break with tradition. Simultaneously, from the etic point of view, for Catholics and Adventists, it is precisely the parallels with tradition that contribute to the plausibility of their respective forms of Christianity. If, finally, conversion serves to realise strength and equivalence as traditional values, this goal also guides the distancing from tradition that comes before conversion. To that extent, from the etic point of view again, basically one seeks to preserve tradition by breaking with it.

The manner in which the members of the Catholic and Adventist communities instrumentalise their respective concepts of tradition, at first sight seems to constitute a locally particular formation – if authors have not simply overlooked a similar instrumentalisation in other regions. While sources on indigenous constructions of concepts of 'tradition' with the term 'kastom' merely cite examples from different island groups in Melanesia and the coastal regions of Papua New Guinea, which involve a positive view of one's own culture,[1] the Pairundu material confirms, for the first time in the Highlands, Thomas's (1992a: 216, 223) thesis that the notion of one's own tradition can also be rejected. According to Thomas, this occurs when the positive evaluation of the culture of the whites is reversed and linked with one's own view of oneself, that is, when the villagers arrive at a negative evaluation of their own culture from the positive evaluation of the foreign one. Accordingly, the members of both denominations in Pairundu sketch a negative construct of 'tradition' that they oppose to their respective forms of Christianity. In doing so, the Catholics regard traditional cult practices, the Adventists the keeping of pigs, as emblematic of the pre-colonial past.[2] Even in Thomas's article (1992a), however, as in other sources on *kastom*, the concept of a traditional culture of one's own is opposed to an 'out-group', which is defined if not by a different skin colour, then at least by a different ethnic affiliation. In Pairundu, on the other hand, constructions of 'tradition' feed the quarrels between the different denominations within the same village. Here, therefore, the 'out-group' not only has the same skin colour, it also belongs to the same clan. As already described, the Adventists turn the negatively valued concept of 'tradition' against the Catholics by incorporating the Catholics into this very concept. The Adventists claim that the Catholics are not Christians but still adherents of tradition who have not really changed, who have not 'given up everything', since they are still making use of traditional procedures for healing sickness and divination, still believe in the effectiveness of bush and ancestral spirits, still keep pigs and are still employing traditional clothing and body decoration. To this the Catholics can only respond with the sketch of a particular past event by reporting the announcements of the first Chimbu catechists and priests, who allegedly had predicted the appearance of new religious groups and warned people against leaving the Catholic community. From the Catholic point of view, these announcements, though disputed by Fr Dunstan, justify the decision to resist the Adventists' attempts to missionise.[3]

The reasons for the Adventists' 'success' must also correspond to the general context, that is, essentially they may not be different in principle from the causes of the growth of smaller communities of belief in other parts of Papua New Guinea, though many authors only hint at such causes or only name them in part. The example of Pairundu has the advantage that here both Catholic and Adventist mission activities took place in the same settlement and within a relatively short period of time. Such a situation is in no way exceptional for Papua New Guinea, though in most sources it has hardly been described, if at all. First it can be shown for Pairundu that conversion to the Adventists hardly differs structurally – that is, in respect of basic needs and beliefs – from acceptance of Catholicism or participation in the Holy Spirit movement. Instead, acceptance of Catholicism, conversion to the Adventists and the rise of the Holy Spirit movement in principle form similar phases succeeding one another and constituting together the process of adopting Christianity (Chapter 6). Thus, the growth in the SDA community is not based on the Adventists striving to achieve anything fundamentally different or to think differently from the Catholics or from participants in the Holy Spirit movement. Instead, in my view the Adventists simply believe that they can satisfy their needs better within Adventist Christianity than within Catholicism.[4] Accordingly, I see a reason for the 'success' of the Adventists in their comparatively greater certainty of salvation, which, however, to a large extent is due to their rigidity, which is expressed, for example, in their decisive distancing of themselves from tradition (the prohibition on keeping pigs) as well as in their clear imitation of the whites (the stress on Western dress and Tok Pisin). In addition, because of its rigidity, Adventist Christianity, with its legalism, its social dualism and its expectation of reciprocity, contains parallels with tradition, which, measured against Catholicism, are comparatively more marked. Such parallels increase the plausibility of one's own form of Christianity and thus simultaneously the certainty of salvation. Here, the expectation of reciprocity gives a good example: the greater the privations, efforts and burdens demanded by membership of the SDA community, the more likely and justified it appears that one will be allowed into heaven on the Last Day of Judgement as a counter-prestation, so to speak. However, if the parallels with tradition create plausibility, then from the etic point of view the Adventists owe their 'success' as much to their connection with tradition as to their emically articulated rejection of it. The certainty of salvation among Adventists that is fed by their rigidity allows their subjection of themselves to a rigid moral dualism, to a compulsory system of precisely determined prohibitions and prescriptions, to appear sensible to them. At the same time, this produces a feeling of anxiety reduction and security, which ultimately releases the Adventists both individually and collectively from having to draw up and take responsibility for their own strategies for action.

Finally, the fact that the different phases in the adoption of Christianity basically contain similar needs and beliefs implies that the acceptance of

Catholicism to some extent smoothed the path for Adventist missionisation, since – with the view of conversion as a move away from tradition, for example – the Adventists could rely on a known model. At the same time, however, Adventist Christianity represents itself as a critique of Catholicism that is still linked with the attraction of the new and that in particular profits from dissatisfaction with individual Catholic functionaries.[5] In addition, alongside the distancing from the Catholics, entry into the SDA community also represents a general 'exit' that is manifested in the break with the traditional culture in general and the traditional religion in particular, as much as in the withdrawal from the traditional networks of social and economic ties and obligations that goes along with conversion.[6] This withdrawal obviously appears especially relieving and therefore attractive to members of the younger generation and the sons of Big Men.[7]

Relative marginality and pragmatism

Certainly the manner in which the inhabitants of Pairundu have accepted the different forms of Christianity can in many ways be regarded as common and, to that extent, as representative, though on the other hand the example of Pairundu also shows some particular features. Among them in the first instance is the situation of relative marginality, since authors who make reference to the adoption of Christianity are usually writing about regions in which colonial and mission histories not only cover a relatively greater time span, but have also triggered comparatively more far-reaching changes. As far as Pairundu is concerned, the relatively short period of thirty years of mission activity could be seen as explaining the fact that there today a dualistic parallelism has emerged alongside the mutual influencing of elements from tradition and Christianity and that the traditional religion, whether partly subliminally or unconsciously, thus continues to exert an influence by transforming and adapting, instead of declining to a degree that corresponds to either first impressions or the claims of the villagers themselves.[8] In my judgement, however, the absence of decline or eradication is based less on the pure length of missionisation than on the fact that in Pairundu, corresponding to the situation of relative marginality, social, economic and political changes appear to be comparatively less marked. In favour of this view above all is the close link between religious and social change. With the tendency to dissolve social cohesion, the reduction in traditional power differences and the increase in individualisation, processes of socio-economic change are also occurring within the reception of Christianity, so that religion is adopting various factors that affect social reality, while at the same time it is also strengthening them itself. Religion therefore simultaneously reflects and causes social changes. Such causation of social change arises especially from the fact that the inhabitants of

Pairundu are struggling both inter- and intra-culturally over status in a religious idiom. In accordance with the close links between religious and social change, it is above all the relatively more limited extent of socio-economic change that is responsible for the traditional religion being transformed and adapted rather than eradicated. If socio-economic conditions should remain more or less stable in the years to come, then I would expect the traditional religion to continue to preserve its influence. Conversely, even after less than thirty years, the traditional religion would have declined, had socio-economic change proved to be more far-reaching.[9] If, however, the situation of relative marginality represents a prerequisite for the continuation of the traditional religion, then the suspicion might arise that, in regions in which such a situation does not exist, it is appropriate to note the eradication of the traditional religion. Nevertheless, I retain a basic scepticism regarding sweeping 'hypotheses of decline', since experience in Pairundu shows that what is generally accessible to the outsider may conceal a popular religion that is more strongly shaped by tradition, so that on this point the etic view differs from the emic view of those who, at least officially, regard themselves as adherents of a purely Western form of Christianity.[10]

The situation of relative marginality is ultimately also relevant to the question of how far the Adventists of Pairundu correspond to the worldwide phenomenon of fundamentalism. Although this phenomenon has usually not been discussed up to now with reference to societies in Oceania, the Adventists – despite the differences between themselves and, for example, fundamentalist Moslems – can be characterised as entirely fundamentalist, especially as, precisely like the adherents of other fundamentalist groups or movements, in principle they are responding to modernity. Admittedly in Pairundu, given the relatively limited extent of socio-economic change, the impact of modernity is only just beginning and is, so to speak, still in an 'embryonic state'. Certainly, changes are also taking place in Pairundu that may indicate what Smith (1980: 51) has called the development of a 'more secular viewpoint',[11] yet nevertheless in my judgement no secularisation can be discerned as yet in the sense that religion – in whatever form – becomes a demarcated domain of culture and thus tends to turn into a private matter. Consequently, the Adventists of Pairundu are responding rather to a modernity that is only beginning, is anticipated, is 'envisaged in the head', as it were – something that makes their form of fundamentalism particular. Here, therefore, to some extent awareness seems to be rushing ahead of social existence.

Also belonging to the particular features which are peculiar to the example of Pairundu, alongside the situation of relative marginality, is the villagers' pragmatism, which is expressed among other things in their basic readiness to accept and 'try out' innovations, without concerning themselves too much with questions of internal coherence, freedom from contradiction or systematisation. Even before colonisation and missionisation started, such variability was expressed in the flexibility of social units as well as in the adoption of new styles of house-building, new elements of pig-killing festivals and new cult and magical practices. Against the background of this pragmatic readiness to experiment with innovations, from the etic point of view the adoption of Christianity appears less as the sudden intrusion of change into a previously more or less static system, but as a continuation, in principle achieved without dramatic breaches, of a process of change that has already been going on for a long time. In my view, the living together of Catholics and Adventists impressively demonstrates the villagers' pragmatism as well. The manner in which the adherents of the two denominations talk about one another may at first indicate bitter enmity. The Adventists not only deny the Catholics an identity as Christians and access to heaven, in accordance with the concept of *sande lo* they also describe them as future murderers. The Catholics, on the other hand, accuse the Adventists of creating social conflicts through their attempts to missionise. Moreover, the fact that the adherents of both denominations both assure the outside world that they have nothing to do with one another and regard one another as rivals may give rise to the assumption that in day-to-day life there are frequently major conflicts, if not physical fights, between the members of the two communities. In the course of my fieldwork, however, I noticed that such fights were not only absent, but also that in some cases family or clan solidarity counted for more than denominational affiliation (Chapter 4). In my view, the astonishment that the almost peaceful coexistence of Catholics and Adventists may initially occasion in the Western observer is explained by the fact that, in the Western context, beliefs are regarded as at least as important as concrete actions when it comes to religion in particular. By contrast, the Kome of Pairundu grant concrete actions considerably more importance than what might be thought in their context, since these thoughts tend to count as a private matter of less importance for the group.[12] Accordingly, in interviews and informal statements, from the outset my conversational partners basically spoke more about their participation in cult practices than about their beliefs as regards both the traditional religion and Christianity.[13] In accordance with this 'primacy of action' as an aspect of their pragmatism, for the Kome in general, rather abstract contradictions and contrasts – as articulated in the relationship between the two denominations – are considerably easier to bear on the level of belief than in the context of social practice, for example.[14]

If a basic position of pragmatism is expressed in the readiness for innovation, the variability of traditional culture and traditional religion, the adoption of Christianity and the relatively peaceful coexistence of Catholics and Adventists, then the example of Pairundu seems to confirm the frequently stated view that, in comparison with the inhabitants of the coast, those of the Highlands are generally less religiously inclined and more strongly this-worldly, down-to-earth and 'secular'. This view can be traced back to Lawrence and Meggitt (1965a: 19), who, as early as 1965, noted a 'tendency towards secularism in the Highlands and towards religious thinking on the Seaboard' in the introduction to their collected volume, *Gods, Ghosts and Men in Melanesia*.[15] By this they mean that, for the inhabitants of the Highlands as for the Mae, Enga Province, success is exclusively based on secular techniques, while for people on the coast like the Ngaing, Madang Province, secular techniques are always linked with rituals. In addition, whereas a Big Man among the Mae owes his reputation solely to his own hard work and strength, among the Ngaing he also needs the support of transcendent beings (1965a: 18ff.). Against the possible tendency suggested by Lawrence and Meggitt, much discussed since, towards a dichotomy between a 'secular, pragmatic' orientation in the Highlands and a 'religious, other-worldly' attitude on the coast, examples have been cited of religiosity also being spread throughout the Highlands.[16] In addition, A. Strathern (1979/80: 173) sees cargo movements from the Mount Hagen area as an example of the fact that, there too, links are made between secular and ritual techniques: 'The Hagen case indicates both cargoism with pragmatism and, conversely, pragmatism with cargoism'. Accordingly, J. Clark (1988: 40) mentions that among the Wiru the indigenous idea of 'development' is linked with religious ideas and practices: '… development can have cult dimensions'. In a later article, Lawrence (1988) was moved by the criticisms of the dichotomy he and Meggitt had suggested, as well as the description of Holy Spirit movements in Southern Highlands Province that had since been published (Robin 1982), to grant the inhabitants of the Highlands greater religiosity and to apply the 'secular-religious' difference no longer between the Highlands and the coast, but within the Highlands as such: '…I now argue that differences between religiosity and secularism are most probably concentrated in the Highlands'.[17] With regard to the coast, however, Lawrence (1988: 20) sees confirmation for his view in the fact that, for him, religions there have a 'well-developed theological quality' consisting in the effort to ensure a 'satisfying interpretation of the modern world and a guide for action' through an 'elaborate mythology and exegesis of myths'. However, this does not apply to the religions of the Highlands, so that, according to Lawrence (1988: 22), the differences between the two main regions of New Guinea no longer consist in the relative degree of religiosity, but rather in the significance accorded to the respective myths and their internal coherence:

> Whereas both Seabord and Highlands peoples use myth to explain their cosmos and religious ritual to advance their aims, I find a strong characteristic of seabord religions in their stress on theology or exegesis… I see no strong evidence of this in the Highlands. The people there may experiment with ritual but appear not to be committed to it as an essential way of life.[18]

In my view, however, the suggested oppositions between the Highlands and the coast up to now basically suffer from the fact that authors have only carried out their own fieldwork in one of the two regions, creating the danger that data relating to the other region are in each case torn out of their context and thus distorted. In order to limit this danger in systematically comparing selected cultures of the Highlands and the coast, it would be desirable that the same author carries out similar research in both regions with respect to methods, questions raised and approach. In my case, this would entail examining the adoption of different forms of Christianity in a settlement on the coast against the background of the traditional religion. Unfortunately, no such comparative study exists at present. Certainly the pragmatism that prevails in Pairundu supports the idea that, in contrast to the 'religiously' oriented, 'other-worldly' inhabitants of the coast, those of the Highlands are generally more 'secular, this-worldly' inclined, though at the same time the Pairundu material also strengthens the criticism of this view. In Pairundu a Holy Spirit movement took place as well and the religious and secular domains cannot be sharply distinguished from one another – as J. Clark (1988) describes it for the Wiru – since in part the same ideas and expectations are linked with both the concept of 'development' and with one's own form of Christianity. Certainly the thesis later formulated by Lawrence, that the inhabitants of the Highlands lay comparatively less weight on the 'theological development' of their myths, also seems to be confirmed by the findings from Pairundu. Indeed, according to the information available to me, the inhabitants of Pairundu do not have all-embracing creation myths explaining the coming into existence of the world as a whole, nor were they concerned to create any internal coherence between the individual elements of their traditional religion (Chapter 2).

The particular features that characterise the example of Pairundu as a whole also include, finally – alongside the situation of relative marginality and prevailing pragmatism – the way in which missionisation is dealt with. Unlike in many of the other sources cited, in the case of Pairundu it becomes clear that the spread of Christianity need not necessarily be understood as the impact of a superior power that merely leaves to the villagers the role of passive recipients, of helpless and defenceless victims. Although this view has been widespread in the literature for a long time,[19] and although it also corresponds to the Catholics' and Adventists' own view of themselves, I hope I have been able to show in the preceding chapters that although the Kome do lose some autonomy in the course of colonisation and missionisation, they still seek actively to shape their own fate by adopting and deploying Western influences as a whole, including the different forms of Christianity, in accordance with their own needs and beliefs.[20]

Evaluations and future prospects

After concerning myself thoroughly with the Church of the Seventh-day Adventists as represented in Pairundu with respect to both the adoption of Christianity and the phenomenon of fundamentalism, it seems appropriate here to set out my basic assessment of this community of belief. Right at the start of my fieldwork, it occurred to me that, compared to the Catholics, the Adventists were both more punctual and more reliable when it came to keeping appointments. This made my work easier and was initially welcome to me. However, this feeling should not influence the reflections that follow, since it says less about the SDA community itself than about the fact that I was at first less successful in adjusting myself to the general management of time usual in Pairundu. Altogether, neither the consequences of colonisation and missionisation nor those of the conversion to the Adventists should be overestimated. Certainly the adoption of Christianity and thus also the conversion to the Adventists both entail the acceptance and strengthening of processes of socio-economic change, as well as an intra-cultural increase in power for women and young and 'ordinary' men. Yet this is fundamentally only a 'pre-taste' of the changes which are actually striven for and whose completion is similarly imagined by both Catholics and Adventists through their concept of 'development' and their idea of heaven. Just as the consequences of missionisation, the Catholics' accusation that the appearance of the Adventists caused social conflicts should also be relativised. While this accusation is actually justified to some extent, on the other hand social conflicts arising from processes of socio-economic change would certainly also be articulated in other ways if the Adventists had not appeared on the scene. The Adventists' claim that conversion to them brings with it a reduction in fear should be relativised as well. Certainly in opposition to the Catholics the members of the SDA community assure one, even unofficially, that they no longer fear ancestral or bush spirits and that they enjoy God's protection on long journeys.[21] However, from the etic point of view such a reduction in fear exists only seemingly, since, instead of fear being reduced, it is merely shifted on to other objects.[22] If, for the Adventists, human existence was exposed to the possible impact of the *remo* and *kalando* in the pre-colonial period, today the threats are attacks by the Devil and the danger of forfeiting access to heaven.[23]

The problem of fear reduction leads me to my central criticism of the Church of the Seventh-day Adventists. Not only does Adventist missionisation not remove fear from individuals, it even confirms them in feeling dependent on merciless, punishing powers. The Adventists' certainty of salvation, which promises safety and security, can basically only be obtained by adopting the corresponding world-view, which consists of strict rules and a rigid moral dualism and which, at the same time, in principle excludes any autonomous thought or action. To this extent, the members of the SDA community are paying dearly for their release from the demands of modernity – which are anyway only starting to have an impact on Pairundu – by relinquishing the freedom that this modernity might bring with it. Here, however, conversion to the Adventists ultimately includes an incapacity, a foregoing of this same autonomy, which people have precisely aimed for by adopting first Catholic and then in particular Adventist Christianity.

The question of how, in the coming years, the processes of transformation described in the foregoing chapters will develop further in principle can easily be answered: in essence, this depends initially on the changes that can be expected in socio-economic conditions. Certainly such changes could happen (Chapter 1), though they might not prove so far-reaching that the traditional religion will necessarily lose all influence. On the other hand, the decline of religious knowledge brought about by the death of the old men should not be underestimated any more than the significance of the Western type of school education, provided the Kome can acquire future access to it to a larger extent.

The question whether the Adventists will continue to have 'success' even in the future and increase their numbers is harder to answer. Here it would be desirable to undertake a comparison with an anthropological study examining, with reference to an already older Adventist community – for example, one that is influenced less by pre-colonial culture – how group size develops over many years, or how one solves the problem of not having pigs with which to pay the traditional brideprice. Unfortunately, there is no such study at present.[24] The fact that in Pairundu conversion to the Adventists only occurred a relatively short time ago may give rise to the supposition that the SDA community as a whole only represents a short-lived and temporary phenomenon. Against this is admittedly the fact that up to now the growth of the SDA community in Pairundu has stagnated as little as it has in other parts of Papua New Guinea. Moreover, at least in Pairundu, the Adventists have a comparatively large reservoir of potential new adherents, since people under twenty-five years of age and women in particular form a group of individuals who represent the majority of the permanent villagers. Even after any further increase in the number of members in the years to come, however, a point may come for the Adventists when they are forced to recognise that the real changes that go along with the switch of denominational affiliation are actually far from being identical with the changes aimed at and that therefore the needs that were the original reason for the conversion have basically not been satisfied or only seemingly so. Thus, just as the adoption of Adventist Christianity basically repeated the adoption of Catholicism in a sharper form, so, in my view and more sharply again, the experience of disappointment also must repeat itself. This disappointment will not necessarily produce a turning away from the SDA community, since, according to Festinger et al. (1964), the failure of a prophecy can indeed strengthen the belief in it as well as the attempt to convince others of it.[25] Similarly, the absence of the Western goods that had been announced did not necessarily compel cargo cult participants to revise their basic ideas. If, however, Adventist villagers leave their community, then I consider two reactions likely, which to some extent can be represented as ideal types.[26] First, the Adventists themselves could apply even externally what they would then be representing positively as their traditional culture or traditional religion.[27] However, although S. Josephides (1990: 65) regards such a 'return to tradition' as possible and although an appropriate example can be seen in Lawrence's description,[28] this strikes me as being extremely unlikely, since present-day Adventists have grown up with a rejection of tradition, propagated on different levels at least at the start of Catholic mission activity and since this rejection has to some extent been resumed and intensified during their 'second socialisation' within the SDA community. Secondly, after the Church of the Seventh-day Adventists, one might 'try out' one of the other denominations that are increasingly competing with one another throughout Papua New Guinea. This would correspond to the traditional readiness for innovation and to that extent be more likely than any return to the Catholics, who have already disappointed one's own expectations.[29]

For the Adventists the question of whether they should keep true to their community or leave it for one of the trends sketched out above will become a pressing one, once they find themselves in a situation in which, by comparing the changes they have sought with those that have actually occurred, they reflect whether the demands and privations linked with the acceptance of Adventist Christianity have really been 'worth it'. In my judgement, such a situation is to arise inevitably in the future – provided, of course, that the Last Day of Judgement will not take place.

Notes

1. Admittedly, these already cited sources (Chapter 8) refer entirely to regions with a much longer history of colonialism and missions than Pairundu.
2. This is not to say that there is no connection from the etic point of view between traditional cult practices and the keeping of pigs.
3. (Chapter 4). In referring to the drawing up of different genealogies to claim land-use rights (Chapter 1), the denomination-specific memory of the encounter between Fr Dunstan and leading Adventists (Chapter 3) and the handing down of different versions of church history (Chapter 4), I have already described other examples that show how, in Pairundu, different constructions of past events are used in the service of intra-cultural disputes.
4. In this respect, judging from the membership structure of the two denominations, it is in the first instance women and the younger and 'ordinary' men, who traditionally have rather modest levels of prestige, who appear to have assumed that conversion to Adventist Christianity would also bring with it an increase in intra-cultural status.
5. This same dissatisfaction also increases readiness to participate in the Holy Spirit movement.
6. An examination of the question whether the readiness for such an 'exit', for a splitting of traditional social groups by changing denominations, is basically more present in segmentary societies, as they are typical of the Papua New Guinea Highlands, than in other communities in Oceania must be reserved for future comparative studies.
7. Here the withdrawal or 'exit' and intra-cultural struggles for prestige need not contradict one another. If, among the Adventists, women, younger and 'ordinary' men and the sons of Big Men have, after 'exiting', increased their status within their new denomination in a way that was not available to them among the Catholics, this

simultaneously represents a gain in prestige in relation to men in general, older men and Big Men.

8. Basically, in differentiating transformation from decline, or change in form from change in content, the problem naturally arises of determining the point at which change turns into a loss of identity. Accordingly Colpe (1986: 6) raises the general question: 'When, therefore, do transformation and secularisation, for example, make such a quantum leap that the religion that has been transformed and secularised no longer exists?'

9. The reference to the situation of relative marginality and the close link between religious and social change could also provide an answer to the question posed by Keesing (1982: 2) in connection with the Kwaio, namely why the indigenous religion has preserved its effectiveness since the first contact with the whites 110 years ago. However, Keesing (1982: 240) does not choose this explanation but writes that tradition is a symbol of identity and autonomy in opposition to Christianity and Westernisation. In Pairundu, by contrast, it is precisely the transfer to Christianity that is intended to assert identity and autonomy. Since Keesing is basically more interested in the reasons for the continuation of the traditional culture and traditional religion than in the reasons for conversion, I do not discuss his work at length here. On the relationship between traditional religion and Christianity on the Solomon Islands, see also Burt (1994).

10. Thus, in my view a further differentiation is needed, when Josephides and Schiltz (1991b: 280), for example, conclude, concerning the southern Kewa: 'They embraced Christian missions enthusiastically, rapidly, and apparently, irrevocably'.

11. According to Smith, those who are adopting this viewpoint are above all the young and those who have more contact with the 'outside world'. In addition, according to Smith (1980: 50), traditional beliefs and Catholicism are disappearing partly in favour of a 'professed secular rationalism'. The advance of secularisation has been postulated for the whole of Melanesia following Worsley's (1957) thesis in connection with the interpretation of cargo cults. Thus, for example, Uplegger and Mühlmann (1961: 187) identify an 'increasing "secularisation"'.

12. In my judgement, the Kome's pragmatism does not necessarily mean that they also have to be materialistically inclined. Such materialism was ascribed to the inhabitants of the Highlands in general, especially in the course of interpretations of cargo cults, in which many authors have placed Western goods in the foreground, without taking sufficient account of their symbolic significance. A connection between pragmatism and materialism is also drawn by Lawrence and Meggitt (1965a: 18), who write, with reference to Melanesia as a whole that 'the prevailing attitude towards religion is essentially pragmatic and materialistic. Religion is a technology rather than a spiritual force for human salvation'.

13. For example, in discussions about Christianity, people did not start with depicting personal beliefs but with just reporting the days they went to church.

14. Naturally contrasts in the relationship between Catholics and Adventists are also effective in social practice, for example in the observance of different prescriptions and prohibitions, or the day of the most important cult practices for each. Yet these oppositions do not generally make themselves felt in a decisive way in day-to-day life apart from the weekend.

15. However, as their critics frequently overlook, Lawrence and Meggitt (1965a: 19f) write that the impression of this tendency might be based on the fact that anthropologists who work in the Highlands would be interested more in the relationship between belief, ritual and the social order (the 'social approach'), while their colleagues working in the coastal regions would rather be examining indigenous explanations for, and management of, the cosmos (the 'intellectualist approach'). Here, I am using the term 'coast' in the sense of Lawrence and Meggitt, who by 'Seabord' mean not only Island Melanesia and coastal New Guinea, but also, in relation to mainland New Guinea, those areas whose inhabitants have access to neither the coast nor the Central valleys of the Highlands.

16. See J. Hughes (1988) and Trompf (1991: 15). On the other hand, a rather general criticism is formulated by Herdt (1989: 17), who accuses Lawrence and Meggitt of having 'reduced great varieties into types'.

17. Lawrence (1988: 20). In this article, Lawrence also reports that the suggestion that the inhabitants of the Highlands can generally be 'more practical, more realistic, more secular-minded than the inhabitants of the seabord' (1988: 12) was first made by his wife, Fancy Lawrence (1988: 13).

18. In principle a limited requirement for 'theology' is also noted by A. Strathern (1979/80: 173), who writes, in his criticism of the dichotomy first formulated by Lawrence and Meggitt for the cargo movements of the Mount Hagen region: '... there was less of an attempt to build a systematic scheme of ideas (to "intellectualize" the cult in that sense'.

19. See Tiffany (1978: 305): 'There has been a tendency among anthropologists to view missionaries as an exogenous force unilaterally impinging upon passively recipient peoples'. May's (1985a) thesis that the phenomenon of fundamentalism is a response to a 'vacuum' (Chapter 8) corresponds as much to this tendency as do earlier attempts to explain cargo cults through the disruption of a cultural equilibrium or through spiritual confusion, both having been triggered by colonisation and missionisation (Chapter 8).

20. Thus in principle I agree with Whiteman, who consistently emphasises the active role of the indigenous people, especially with respect to the Solomon Islands (1980: 8f, 604, 613, 721), finally concluding that 'in the final analysis, it is the indigenes who make the choice to innovate through acceptance, modification or rejection of the missionaries' proposals' (1980: 741). Cf. the articles edited by Barker (1990b) and Dabrowski (1991: 502).

21. In addition, as already described, on the level of the official claims presented to the outside world, the Adventists share with the Catholics the view that they no longer fear war or witchcraft practices (Chapter 51).

22. To this extent, what goes for Pairundu is the opposite of what Ströbele-Gregor (1988: 137) writes, when she – in my view, unknowingly – reproduces the official view of the SDA church leadership: 'The Adventists do not live under the spell of fears or in a resigned manner, but awaiting Christ and reunion with the deceased'.

23. To be added here is the future persecution by the Catholics in the course of the announced *sande lo*. In any case, in the present as in the pre-colonial past, following established rules is in principle the only way to escape the dangers that threaten.

24. These questions might also be the subject of the research that I have already indicated would be desirable in comparing the Highlands and the coast. Certainly S. Josephides (1982, 1990) makes reference to an Adventist community that can look back over a twenty-five-year history, though without saying anything about either the development of the number of members nor how the members of the community marry.

25. As evidence for their thesis, Festinger et al. (1964: 12–22) mention various messianic movements, such as that led by William Miller, in which the failure of the world to end on the appointed day was simply met by postponing this date and by intensifying attempts to missionise.

26. Obviously mixed forms can also be envisaged.

27. Accordingly Wassmann (1992: 18) writes sweepingly, of Lutheran missionising in the Finisterre Range: 'If wealth and power do not appear in the expected or desired quantity, a distancing from the new and a return to the old is always a possibility'. In such a case, of course, it must be established that the ideas and practices then being propagated and assigned to tradition are clearly distinct from the etic point of view from what actually existed before the experience of colonisation and missionisation. Mühlmann (1961a: 11) had already concluded in this sense, that 'a cultural habitus that now only exists in the memory but is "revived" is no longer identical with itself'.

28. Lawrence (1964: 184) writes that after the disappointment with Christianity there was a so-called 'pagan revival', in which a cult leader demanded of the indigenous people that they should 'return to their pagan religious ceremonies so that the old ghosts and goddesses could be lured back to New Guinea to usher in a new period of prosperity'.

29. Nevertheless, there are examples of such a return in other parts of the world. In one case study, O. Lewis (1964) gives the story of a farmer living in a village south of Mexico City who, as a Catholic, converted to the Adventists in the second half of the 1940s, only to return to the Catholics later after quarrelling with a member of the Adventist community.

Glossary

For the most part, the transcription of the Neo-Melanesian Pidgin English (Tok Pisin) follows Mihailic's dictionary (1971), which is generally considered the standard work. Variations and anglicisms reflect the present-day usages of the inhabitants of Pairundu. Prenasals (buk/mbuk) and the vowels that are sometimes introduced between adjacent consonants (blu/bilu) are not indicated. There is a tendency sometimes to pronounce 'p' closer to 'f'.

Antap long maunten	On the mountain top
Apin nem	To increase one's name, one's prestige
Autim tingting	To voice anger or disgruntlement considered to be damaging
Belo	Church bell
Blain	Wickerwork panel woven of strips of bamboo
Bossboi	Village Constable
Bratalain	'Brother clan', agnatically related clan
Bus gaden	Bush garden
Church bilong God	The Church of God (Seventh-day Adventists' self-designation)
Church memba	Baptised member of the Adventist congregation
Daunim spet	To swallow saliva (frustration which arises from being neglected at a distribution of food and which is considered a cause of illness)
Giaman lotu	Wrong church service
Han church	'Sub church', local division of Seventh-day Adventist church
Hatwok	Hard work
Haus Kiap	Resthouse for colonial officers on patrol
Haus kuk	Cooking hut for colonial officers on patrol
Haus toilet	Toilet hut for colonial officers on patrol

Kaikai hariap	To eat quickly (to provide food often for as many people as possible)
Kampani	Economic enterprise
Kapul lain	Group of opossums (insulting term for 'hillbilly')
Kastom	Tradition
Kaukau gaden	Sweet potato garden
Kiap	Village court magistrate
Kisim ripot	Book-keeping (part of Adventist service)
Kisim sevis	To acquire 'services', to benefit from 'development'
Klas baptais	Candidates for baptism as Adventists
Klas redi	Regular attendees at Adventist services, who have not yet been baptised as Adventists nor been accepted as candidates for Adventist baptism
Komunio	Consecrated wafer in the Catholic Sunday service
Komunio lida	Eucharist minister
Kumu	Spinach-like leaf vegetable
Kunai	Swordgrass (*Miscanthus foridulus*)
Lain	Group
Las de	The Last Day of Judgment
Lesson buk	Primer (brochure used in the Adventist evening service)
Limbum	Palm leaf
Lotu	The Christian religion, church building, participation in services
Lotu long man	To worship people
Luluai	Village Constable
Mama church	'Main church', combination of several local divisions of Seventh-day Adventist church
Man bilong toktok	Man who knows how to talk (man of significance)
Man nogut	Bad man, bad person
Masalai	Bush spirit
Masta	Form of address and term for whites in general and white men in particular
Misin stori	Church history (part of Adventist service)
Misinari	Regularly paid *layman*
Misis	Form of address and term for white women
Moning was ves	Bible verses provided for Adventist morning services

Namel	In the middle
Nesenel memba	Member of the National Parliament
Pasin SDA	Adventist custom, way of life
Pitpit	*Saccharum edule*
Prayer lida	Prayer leader in the Catholic community
Prea grup	Prayer group
Provinsenel Memba	Member of the Provincial Government
Sabbat lotu	Church of Sabbath, of Saturday services
Sande lo	Sunday law
Sande lotu	Church of Sunday services
Sanguma	Witchcraft technique
Sansa	'Censure', time-limited prohibition on assuming posts in the Adventist Church
Singsing	Dancing event
Spirit nogut	Evil spirit
Taim bilong mani	Time of money
Taim bilong ren	'Time of the rains'
Taim bilong san	'Time of the sun'
Tait	Tenth of one's income, given by Adventists to their Church
Tambolo	Below
Tok bilong God	The word of God (Christianity)
Tok hait	Secret speech, a secret
Tok Pisin	Neo-Melanesian Pidgin English
Tokpait	War of words, quarrel
Trupela lotu	The right church
Wanpela kain sik	A type of illness
Wok sol	Community work

References

Interviews and informal conversations

1. Alex; 1 March 1991; Pairundu**, my house (map 3, no. 32); informal conversation; Tok Pisin; notes taken simultaneously
2. Alex; 9 April 1991; Pairundu**, my house (32); informal conversation; Tok Pisin; notes taken simultaneously
3. Alex; 21 April 1991; Pairundu**, my house (32); informal conversation; Tok Pisin; notes taken simultaneously
4. Alex; 22 April 1991; Pairundu**, my house (32); informal conversation; Pogola, Ripu, Yapa, one brother of Amakoa; Tok Pisin; notes taken afterwards
5. Alex; 31 May 1991; Pairundu**, my house (32); informal conversation; Tok Pisin; notes taken simultaneously
6. Alex; 20 September 1991; Pairundu**, my house (32); informal conversation; Luke, Ripu; Tok Pisin; notes taken afterwards
7. Alupa; 5 April 1991; Pokaranda, Alupa's house (46); formal interview; Ata Francis, Ata (I), Basupia, Coleman Makoa, Ken, Naname, Neambunu, other children of Alupa, young men from Yakoa; partly Tok Pisin, partly Kewa (translated by Ata Francis); partly recorded, partly notes taken simultaneously
8. Alupa; 4 May 1991; Pokaranda, Alupa's house (46); formal interview; Neambunu, Nokosi (left earlier), some small children; Kewa (translated by Neambunu); notes taken simultaneously
9. Alupa; 4 May 1991; Pokaranda, Alupa's house (46); informal conversation; Tok Pisin; notes taken afterwards
10. Alupa; 19 July 1991; Pokaranda, Alupa's house (46); formal interview; Neambunu, Pala, Pulueme, Kuta; Kewa (translated by Neambunu); notes taken simultaneously
11. Amakoa; 6 September 1991; Pairundu**, my house (32); informal conversation; Alex (sleeping), Kenneth; Tok Pisin; notes taken afterwards
12. Ari (Mamarepa); 9 September 1991; Yeibu, Ari's house; formal interview; one man not known to me, Ari's wife, some children; Kewa (translated by the young man); notes taken simultaneously
13. Ari; 4 March 1991; Pairundu**, my house (32); formal interview; Coleman Makoa, Naki; Kewa (translated by Naki); recorded entirely
14. Ari; 30 April 1991; Yampiri, Ari's house (26); formal interview; Alex, Amakoa, Disi, Geame, Loke, Nana, Pogola, Ripu, Ruapo, Wandonu; Kewa (translated by Alex); recorded entirely

15. Ari; 2 May 1991; Yampiri, Ari's house (26); formal interview; Alex, Disi, Loke, Pogola, Ripu, Ruapo, Wandonu, Yapa (left earlier), Yapanu, some children; Kewa (translated by Alex); recorded entirely

16. Ari; 7 May 1991; Yampiri, Ari's house (26); formal interview; Alex (came later, left earlier), Amakoa, Disi (came later), Johannes, Loke, Pogola, Ripu, Ruapo (sleeping), Wandonu; Kewa (translated by Alex, Amakoa, Ripu, Johannes); partly recorded, partly notes taken simultaneously

17. Ari; 15 July 1991; Yampiri, Ari's house (26); formal interview; Kuname, Luke, Loke, Pogola, Ruapo; Kewa (translated by Pogola); recorded entirely

18. Ari; 22 July 1991; Yampiri, Ari's house (26); formal interview; Kuname, Luke, Ruapo (sleeping), some children (sleeping); Kewa (translated by Luke, Kuname); partly recorded, partly notes taken simultaneously

19. Ari; 16 August 1991; Pairundu**, Ari's store (30); informal conversation; Luke; Kewa (translated by Luke); notes taken afterwards

20. Ari; 12 September 1991; began in Parundu**, Amakoa's house (28), continued in Yampiri, Ari's house (26); formal interview; Amakoa (left earlier), Coleman Komea (left earlier), Komborame (left earlier), Moses (came later), Nana (came later), Ondasa (left earlier), Ripu, Ruapo (came later), Sami (came later), Sayna (left earlier), Wara (left earlier), a visitor from Tambul (left earlier); Kewa (translated by Ripu); partly recorded, partly notes taken simultaneously

21. Ari; 19 September 1991; Pairundu**, my house (32); formal interview; Alex, Amakoa (came later), Rindinu, Ripu, Yawoa (came later); Kewa (translated by Ripu); recorded entirely

22. Ata Francis, Rekepea, Yali; 8 May 1991; Porai, Rekepea's house (52); informal conversation; Alupa (came later), Amakoa, Kapu (came later), Ken (came later), Kepe (came later), Marcus (came later), Nara (left earlier), Phillip (came later), Yawoa (came later), several people from Wasuma (came later), several women from Pairundu* and Ropena*; partly Tok Pisin, partly Kewa (translated by Ata Francis); partly recorded, partly notes taken simultaneously

23. Ata Francis; 24 May 1991; Porai, Rekepea's house (52); formal interview; Alex, Ken, Pala, Rekepea, Warea, Yali, some women and children; Tok Pisin; recorded entirely

24. Ata Francis; 2 June 1991; Yampiri, Ari's house (26); formal interview; Alupa (left earlier), Mindu (left earlier), Pogola (came later); Yapanu (left earlier); Tok Pisin; partly recorded, partly notes taken simultaneously

25. Ata (I); 18 August 1991; Pairianda, Ata (I)'s house (44); informal conversation; several children (came later); Tok Pisin; recorded entirely

26. Atasi; 17 May 1991; Wasuma, Atasi's house; formal interview; several men from Wasuma, Ata Francis, Yawa (came later); Kewa (translated by several men from Wasuma); recorded entirely

27. Augustin; 21 January 1991; Pairundu**, my house (32); formal interview; Alex, Yapanu; Tok Pisin; notes taken simultaneously

28. Fr Brian; 26 November 1990; Ialibu, Catholic mission station; informal conversation; English; notes taken simultaneously

29. Coleman Komea; 13 April 1991; Pasereanda, Naki's store; formal interview; Tok Pisin; notes taken simultaneously

30. Coleman Makoa; 14 August 1991; Pairundu**, Coleman Makoa's house (36); formal interview; Ata Francis (left earlier), Kapu (came later), Yawoa (came later); Tok Pisin; partly recorded, partly notes taken simultaneously

31. Fr Don; 1 December 1990; Karia, Catholic mission station; informal conversation; English; notes taken simultaneously

32. Fr Dunstan; 7 November 1990; Mendi, Catholic mission station; informal conversation; English; notes taken simultaneously

33. Fr Dunstan; 13 December 1990; Mendi, Catholic mission station; informal conversation; English; notes taken afterwards

34. Ipapula; 3 April 1991; Pairundu**, Ipapula's house (31); formal interview; Alex, Kata, Pandabame; Kewa (translated by Alex); notes taken simultaneously

35. Ipapula; 7 April 1991; Pairundu**, my house (32); informal conversation; Alex, Komborame; Kewa (translated by Alex); recorded entirely

36. Ipapula; 2 May 1991; Pairundu**, Ipapula's house (31); informal conversation; Alex; Kewa (translated by Alex); notes taken simultaneously

37. Ipapula; 5 June 1991; Pairundu**, Ipapula's house (31); formal interview; Alex, Ata (I) (came later, left earlier), Kata, Wara; Kewa (translated by Alex); partly recorded, partly notes taken simultaneously

38. Ipapula; 20 September 1991; near Rakianda, Pala's house (38); formal interview; Alex, Ondasa (came later), Pala (came later), Pandabame (came later), Pogola (came later); Kewa (translated by Alex); recorded entirely

39. Kenneth; 7 July 1991; Wasuma, Kenneth's house; formal interview; Ripu (came later, left earlier); Tok Pisin; recorded entirely

40. Kenneth; 19 August 1991; Pairundu**, my house (32); formal interview; Alex; Tok Pisin; recorded entirely

41. Kenneth; 19 August 1991; Pairundu**, my house (32); informal conversation; Alex; Tok Pisin; notes taken afterwards

42. Kenneth; 24 August 1991; Sumi, Catholic mission station; formal interview; Kenneth's wife and children (came later), Tok Pisin; partly recorded, partly notes taken simultaneously

43. Kevin; 9 April 1991; Rakepanda, SDA church building; formal interview; Coleman Komea (came later), Lombasu, Peter (came later), Simon (came later); Tok Pisin; notes taken simultaneously

44. Kevin; 26 May 1991; Rakepanda, SDA church building (17); informal conversation; Alex, Kandipia, Papua (left earlier), Robert (came later), Wareame (left earlier), one girl; Tok Pisin; notes taken simultaneously

45. Kevin; 30 August 1991; Walua, Muya's bush garden; formal interview; Tok Pisin; recorded entirely

46. Pastor Koya; 1 July 1991; Rakianda, Kalipoa's house (40); formal interview; Tok Pisin; recorded entirely

47. Sr Marie; 22 May 1991; road from Pairundu to Anapote; informal conversation; English; notes taken afterwards

48. Sr Marie; 14 June 1991; Karia, Catholic mission station; formal interview; English; recorded entirely

49. Marcus; 17 May 1991; Porai, Marcus's house; informal conversation; Kepe; Tok Pisin; notes taken afterwards

50. Fr Matthias; 12 June 1991; Karia, Catholic mission station; formal interview; English, Tok Pisin; recorded entirely

51. Mindu; 14 April 1991; Anapote, Mindu's house; formal interview; Amakoa, Wara, Mindu's wife and sons; Kewa (translated by Mindu's sons and Amakoa); recorded entirely

52. Muya; 9 February 1991; Pairundu**, my house (32); informal conversation; Alex, Kandipia, Peter; Tok Pisin; notes taken simultaneously

53. Muya; 13 March 1991; Rimbupiri, Muya's house; formal interview; Don, Coleman Komea, Kandipia, Kevin, Robert, several young men from Yakoa; partly Tok Pisin, partly Kewa (translated by Robert); partly recorded, partly notes taken simultaneously

54. Muya; 7 April 1991; Rakianda, Kalipoa's house (40); informal conversation; Tok Pisin; notes taken simultaneously

55. Muya; 8 September 1991; near Pokaranda, Muya's bush garden; formal interview; a child; Tok Pisin; recorded entirely

56. Naki; 15 May 1991; Pasereanda, Naki's store (3); formal interview; Tok Pisin; recorded entirely

57. Naki; 6 September 1991; near Pasereanda, Naki's garden; formal interview; Tok Pisin; recorded entirely

58. Naki; 17 September 1991; Pasereanda, Naki's store (3); formal interview; Eya, Yawa (came later), Yona, Yunes; Tok Pisin; notes taken simultaneously

59. Nosope; 1 April 1991; Yawireanda, Nosope's house (6); formal interview; Alex, Yawa (came later); Kewa (translated by Alex); notes taken simultaneously

60. Nosupinai; 16 September 1991; Pairundu**, Yapa's house (33); formal interview; Alex, Ari, Lombasu; Kewa (translated by Alex); recorded entirely

61. Ondasa; 14 March 1991; near Rakianda, Ondasa's house; formal interview; Alex, Kata, Puku, Wara; partly Tok Pisin, partly Kewa (translated by Alex); recorded entirely

62. Otmar; 8 June 1991; Anapote, Otmar's house; formal interview; Alex, Naperasa (came later), Yawoa (came later), Otmar's wife, several Mamarepa women (came later); Kewa (translated by Alex); recorded entirely

63. Otmar; 10 June 1991; Anapote, Otmar's house; formal interview; Alex (left earlier), Luke (came later), Walaya (came later), Yawoa (came later), Otmar's wife; Kewa (translated by Alex, Luke); recorded entirely

64. Otmar; 9 August 1991; Anapote, Otmar's house; formal interview; Alex, Ari (Mamarepa), Marambe (came later), some Mamarepa women (came later); Kewa (translated by Alex); recorded entirely

65. Otmar; 20 August 1991; Anapote, Otmar's house; formal interview; Alex, Otmar's wife, one Mamarepa boy (came later) and several Mamarepa girls; Kewa (translated by Alex); recorded entirely

66. Otmar; 2 September 1991; Anapote, Otmar's house; formal interview; Alex, Walaya (came later), Otmar's wife, one Mamarepa man; Kewa (translated by Alex); recorded entirely

67. Otmar; 13 September 1991; Anapote, Otmar's house; formal interview; Alex, two of Otmar's daughters; Kewa (translated by Alex); recorded entirely

68. Phillip; 8 May 1991; Porai, Rekepea's house (52); formal interview; Alupa, Amakoa, Ata Francis, Ira, Kapu, Ken, Kepe, Marcus, Pala, Rekepea, Yali, Yawoa, several people from Wasuma, several women from Pairundu* and Ropena*; Tok Pisin; notes taken simultaneously

69. Pogola; 3 April 1991; Pairundu**, my house (32); informal conversation; Alex (slept); Tok Pisin; notes taken afterwards

70. Pogola; 23 April 1991; Pairundu**, my house (32); informal conversation; Alex (slept); Tok Pisin; notes taken simultaneously

71. Pogola, Ripu, Ari; 16 June 1991; Pairundu**, my house (32); informal conversation; Alex, Yapa, one brother of Amakoa; Tok Pisin; notes taken afterwards

72. Pogola; 7 September 1991; Rakianda, Kalipoa's house; formal interview; Kalipoa (came later); Tok Pisin; recorded entirely

73. Rekepea; 5 February 1991; Porai, Rekepea's house; formal interview; Alex, some Alia Kome women and children; Kewa (translated by Alex); notes taken simultaneously

74. Rekepea, Ata Francis, Kandipia; 28 May 1991; Porai, Rekepea's house (52); informal conversation; Ken, Pala, Yali, several women and children; partly Tok Pisin, partly Kewa (translated by Ata Francis, Kandipia); notes taken simultaneously

75. Ripu; 6 February 1991; Pairundu**, my house (32); informal conversation; Ari, Ruapo, Yawa; Tok Pisin; notes taken afterwards

76. Ripu; 4 April 1991; Pairundu**, my house (32); formal interview; Ari; Tok Pisin

77. Ripu; 28 May 1991; near Rakianda, Pogola's bush garden; formal interview; Tok Pisin; recorded entirely

78. Ripu; 6 July 1991; Yassaweli; informal conversation; Tok Pisin; notes taken afterwards

79. Ripu; 1 September 1991; Pairundu**, my house (32); informal conversation; Tok Pisin; notes taken simultaneously

80. Robert; 27 May 1991; Ropena*, Robert's house (10); formal interview; Naki (came later), Ripu (came later), Wareame, Wasanu (came later), several young men; Tok Pisin; recorded entirely

81. Robert; 24 July 1991; Ropena*, Robert's house; informal conversation; Tok Pisin; notes taken simultaneously

82. Robert; 25 August 1991; Ropena*, Robert's house (10); formal interview; Wareame (left earlier), Wasanu (came later); Tok Pisin; recorded entirely

83. Robert; 19 September 1991; Ropena*, Kandipia's house; formal interview; Bele (left earlier), Pakua (left earlier), Rubi (left earlier), Warea (left earlier), several young men from Yakoa (came later, left earlier); Tok Pisin; recorded entirely

84. Ruben; 29 May 1991; Rimbupiri, Ruben's house (23); formal interview; Kata, Naranu; Tok Pisin; notes taken simultaneously

85. Ruben; 21 September 1991; Yawireanda, Wala's store (6); formal interview; Tok Pisin; recorded entirely

86. Serale; 15 March 1991; near Rakianda, Serale's house (41); formal interview; Alex, Onakapu, Pakua, Ripu, Walawe, some of Serale's children; partly Tok Pisin, partly Kewa (translated by Walawe); notes taken simultaneously

87. Serale; 29 May 1991; near Rakianda, Serale's house (41); formal interview; Alex, Bele Serale, Kone, Onakapu, Paulo, Wasanu, Nande; Tok Pisin; notes taken simultaneously

88. Serale; 18 June 1991; near Rakianda, Serale's house (41); informal conversation; Alex, Bele Serale, Onakapu, Paulo; partly Tok Pisin, partly Kewa (translated by Alex); recorded entirely

89. Pastor Tane; 22 November 1990; Pundia; informal conversation; Rev. Uhland Spahlinger, several people from Pundia; Tok Pisin; notes taken afterwards

90. Wala; 24 January 1991; Yawireanda, Wala's house (7); formal interview; Alex, Bele, Robert, several women and children most of them Rundu Kome; Kewa (translated by Robert); notes taken simultaneously

91. Wala; 21 August 1991; Yawireanda, Wala's house (7); formal interview; Robert, some Rundu Kome children (came later, left earlier); Kewa (translated by Robert); recorded entirely

92. Wala; 22 September 1991; Yawireanda, Wala's house (7); formal interview; Bele, Kalenda, Nosope, Robert, Ruben; Kewa (translated by Robert); recorded entirely
93. Wapa; 27 July 1991; Sare, Wapa's house; formal interview; Ata Francis, Coleman Makoa, Kalenda, Pundu (Kapiarepa), Ripu, Warea, several people most of them Kapiarepa; Kewa (translated by Coleman Makoa, Ripu); recorded entirely
94. Wapa; 28 August 1991; Sare, Wapa's house; informal conversation; Alupa, Ata (I), several family member of Wapa; Kewa (translated by Ata (I)); notes taken simultaneously
95. Yana; 8 August 1991; Yawireanda, Wala's store (6); formal interview; Diame (came later), Reranu (came later), Robert, Serale (left earlier), Wareame (came later); Kewa (translated by Robert); Kewa (translated by Robert); partly recorded, partly notes taken simultaneously
96. Yapanu; 12 September 1991; Yampiri, Yapanu's house (27); formal interview; Alex, Geame, Nana; Kewa (translated by Alex); recorded entirely
97. Yawa; 6 February 1991; Pairundu**, my house (32); formal interview; Alex, Amakoa, Ari, Ripu; Kewa (translated by Ripu); notes taken simultaneously
98. Yawa; 13 February 1991; Pasereanda, Yawa's house (4); informal conversation; Alex, Kalenda, several children (mostly Auro Kome); Kewa (translated by Alex); notes taken simultaneously

Patrol Reports

Erave Patrol Report 1958/59–5
Kagua Patrol Report 1956/7–57: 1
Kagua Patrol Report 1957/58–4
Kagua Patrol Report 1958/59–4
Kagua Patrol Report 1958/59–5
Kagua Patrol Report 1959/60–6: 2
Kagua Patrol Report 1959/60–8
Kagua Patrol Report 1960/61–8: 4
Kagua Patrol Report 1960/61–9: 5
Kagua Patrol Report 1960/61–11
Kagua Patrol Report 1960/61–no number
Kagua Patrol Report 1961/62–13: 1
Kagua Patrol Report 1962/63–7
Kagua Patrol Report 1962/63–18
Kagua Patrol Report 1963/64–18
Kagua Patrol Report 1963/64–19
Kagua Patrol Report 1965/66–1
Kagua Patrol Report 1968/69–3
Kagua Patrol Report 1969/70–7
Kagua Patrol Report 1971/72–18

Letters

Ari, Alex to Holger Jebens, 1 June 1992
Pastor Barnard, Len to Holger Jebens, 3 July 1992
Bergmann, Wilhelm to J. Kuder, 14 October 1958 (Archives of the Missionswerk
    der Evang.-Luth. Kirche in Bayern, Neuendettelsau)
Pastor Greive, Louis T. to Holger Jebens, 19 July 1992
Heidemann, G. to Holger Jebens, 25 May 1993
Fr Jones, Dunstan to Holger Jebens, 17 October 1992
Fr Jones, Dunstan to Holger Jebens, undated
Josephides, Lisette to Holger Jebens, 31 March 1993
Pastor Litster, Glynn to Holger Jebens, 10 May 1992
Fr Miltenberger, Stanley to Holger Jebens, 28 May 1993
Fr Olape, Matthias to Holger Jebens, 25 February 1992
Pastor Parker, Ed to Holger Jebens, 1 July 1992
Robin, Robert to Holger Jebens, 21 January 1989

Published and unpublished sources

Ahrens, Th. 1976, 'Christian Syncretism. A Study from the Southern Madang
    District of PNG', in *Eighth Orientation Course of the Melanesian Institute,* ed.
    Melanesian Institute, Goroka,1–22.
—— 1977, 'Kirche, Volkschristentum und Volksreligion in Melanesien', in
    Volkschristentum und Volksreligion im Pazifik, eds Th. Ahrens and W.J.
    Hollenweger (Perspektiven der Weltmission 4), Frankfurt/M., 11–80.
—— 1978, 'Melanesische und biblische Perspektiven in der Erfahrung von Macht',
    in *Theologische Beiträge aus Papua-Neuguinea,* ed. H. Bürkle, Erlangen, 13–60.
—— 1986a, 'Nativistischer Chiliasmus und thaumaturgische Heiliggeist-
    bewegungen in Melanesien als missionstheologisches und ökumenisches
    Problem', in *Unterwegs nach der verlorenen Heimat,* ed. Th. Ahrens
    (Erlanger Monographien aus Mission und Ökumene 4), Erlangen, 71–173.
—— 1986b, 'Kilibob, Manub und Christus. Eine Fallstudie transkultureller
    Theologie', in *Unterwegs nach der verlorenen Heimat,* ed. Th. Ahrens
    (Erlanger Monographien aus Mission und Ökumene 4), Erlangen, 11–70.
—— 1986c, 'Das verwandelte Herz: Ein Gespräch mit Andrew Strathern', in
    Unterwegs nach der verlorenen Heimat, ed. Th. Ahrens (Erlanger
    Monographien aus Mission und Ökumene 4), Erlangen, 229–62.
—— 1991, 'Zum Synkretismus melanesischer Volkskultur', in *Such-
    bewegungen,* ed. H.P. Siller, Darmstadt, 62–83.
Allen, B.J. 1976, 'Information Flow and Innovation Diffusion in the East Sepik
    District, Papua New Guinea' (Ph.D. diss., Australian National University).
Allen, Bryant 1990, 'The Importance of Being Equal: the Colonial and Post
    Colonial Experience in the Torricelli Foothills', in *Sepik Heritage: Tradition
    and Change in Papua New Guinea,* eds N. Lutkehaus, Ch. Kaufmann, W.
    Mitchell, D. Newton, L. Osmundsen and M. Schuster, Durham, 185–96.
Allen, Bryant and Frankel, S. 1991, 'Across the Tari Furoro', in *Like People You
    See in a Dream: First Contact in Six Papuan Societies,* eds E.L. Schiefflin and
    R. Crittenden, Stanford, 88–124.

Allen, Bryant and Wood, A.W. 1980, 'Legendary Volcanic Eruptions and the Huli, Papua New Guinea', *The Journal of the Polynesian Society* 89(3): 341–7.

Allen, M.R. 1967, *Male Cults and Secret Initiations in Melanesia*, Melbourne.

Apea, S. 1985, 'Footprints of God in Ialibu' in *Living Theology in Melanesia: a Reader,* ed. J.D. May (Point Series 8), Goroka, 218–55.

Arbuckle, G.A. 1983, 'Inculturation and Evangelisation: Realism or Romanticism?' in *Missionaries, Anthropologists and Cultural Change*, ed. D.L. Whiteman (Studies in Third World Societies 25), Williamsburg, 171–214.

Awesa, F.K. 1988, 'Brief Overview', in T. Puruno, *Provincial Brief for 10th Anniversary of Southern Highlands Provincial Government, 5–8th August, 1988*, Mendi, 1–7.

Ballard, C. n.d., 'The Fire Next Time: British Petroleum, the Book of Revelations and Huli Ritual', MS.

Barker, J. 1990a, 'Introduction: Ethnographic Perspectives on Christianity in Oceanic Societies', in *Christianity in Oceania: Ethnographic Perspectives*, ed. J. Barker (ASAO Monographs 12), Lanham, 1–24.

—— ed., 1990b, *Christianity in Oceania: Ethnographic Perspectives* (ASAO Monographs 12), Lanham.

Barr, James. 1981, *Fundamentalismus*, München, (English orig. 1977).

Barr, James and Trompf, G.W. 1983, 'Independent Churches and Recent Ecstatic Phenomena in Melanesia: A Survey of Materials', *Oceania* 54: 48–50.

Barr, John. 1983a, 'A Survey of Ecstatic Phenomena and "Holy Spirit Movements" in Melanesia', *Oceania* 54: 109–32.

—— 1983b, 'Spirit Movements in the Highlands United Church' in *Religious Movements in Melanesia Today*, vol. 2, ed. W. Flannery, Goroka, 144–53.

Bateson, G. 1965, *Naven: a Survey of the Problems Suggested by a Composite Picture of the Culture of a New Guinea Tribe Drawn from Three Points of View*, Stanford (orig. 1936).

Behrend, H. 1983, 'Die Zeit geht krumme Wege. Bei den Tugen in Ostafrika', *Kursbuch* 73: 97–103.

Beier, U. ed. 1977, *Kewa Stories from the Southern Highlands*, collected by S. Rambi and F. Nimi, Port Moresby.

Bergmann, W. n.d., 'Neue Gebiete' (W. Bergmann, Vierzig Jahre in Neuguinea 10), MS.

Berndt, R.M. 1952/53, 'A Cargo Movement in the Eastern Central Highlands of New Guinea', *Oceania* 23: 40–65, 137–58, 202–34.

—— 1965, 'The Kamano, Usurufa, Jate and Fore of the Eastern Highlands', in *Gods, Ghosts, and Men in Melanesia*, eds P. Lawrence and M. Meggitt, Melbourne, 78–104.

Birnbaum, N. 1989, 'Der protestantische Fundamentalismus in den USA', in *Fundamentalismus in der modernen Welt*, ed. Th. Meyer, Frankfurt/M., 121–54.

Biskup, P. 1970, *A Short Story of New Guinea*, Sydney.

Blaustein, A. and Flanz, G.H. eds 1985, *Constitutions of the Countries of the World*, New York.

Blong, R.J. 1981, 'Time of Darkness Legends and Volcanic Eruptions in Papua New Guinea', in *Oral Tradition in Melanesia*, eds D. Denoon and R. Lacey, Port Moresby, 131–50.

—— 1982, *The Time of Darkness: Local Legends and Volcanic Reality in Papua New Guinea*, Canberra.

Bodrogi, T. 1951, 'Colonization and Religious Movements in Melanesia', *Acta Ethnographica Academiae Hungaricae* 3: 259–92.

Boutilier, J.A., Hughes, D.T. and Tiffany, S.W. eds 1978, *Mission, Church and Sect in Oceania* (ASAO Monographs 6), Lanham.

Brown, P. 1982, 'Conflict in the New Guinea Highlands', *The Journal of Conflict Resolution* 26: 525–46.

Brunton, R. 1980, 'Misconstrued Order in Melanesian Religion', *Man* 15: 112–28.

Burkey, B. n.d., 'History of Mendi Diocese and Capuchin Mission Efforts in Papua New Guinea' MS.

Burkins, D. 1984, 'Waiting for "Company": Development on the Periphery of the Periphery in the Southern Highlands Province, Papua New Guinea' (Ph.D. diss., Temple University).

Burt, B. 1994, *Tradition and Christianity: the Colonial Transformation of a Solomon Islands Society* (Studies in Anthropology and History 10), Camberwell.

Bus, G. and Landu, M. 1989, 'Die Katholische Kirche' in *Papua-Neuguinea: Gesellschaft und Kirche,* eds H. Wagner, G. Fugman and H. Janssen (Erlanger Taschenbücher 93), Neuendettelsau, 161–78.

Callick, R. 1992, 'The Lost Generation: Tragedy That's Behind a Nation's Terrible Troubles Today', *Islands Business Pacific*, January: 41–5.

Chowning, A. 1990, 'God and Ghosts in Kove', in *Christianity in Oceania: Ethnographic Perspectives*, ed. J. Barker (ASAO Monographs 12), Lanham, 33–58.

Clark, J. 1982, 'Rusty Tractors and "Skin Kristens": a Report on Socio-economic Development in Pangia District, S.H.P.', field report no. 5, to be presented at a debriefing seminar to: Southern Highlands Research Committee, Department of Anthropology, U.P.N.G., Takuru, Pangia District, S.H.P., April.

——— 1985, 'From Cults to Christianity: Continuity and Change in Takuru' (Ph.D. diss., University of Adelaide).

——— 1988, 'KAUN and KOGONO: Cargo Cults and Development in Karavar and Pangia', *Oceania* 59(1): 40–57.

——— 1989a, 'The Incredible Shrinking Men: Male Ideology and Development in a Southern Highlands Society', in Culture and Development in Papua New Guinea, ed. C. Healey, *Canberra Anthropology* 12(1/2): 120–43.

——— 1989b, 'God, Ghosts and People: Christianity and Social Organization among Takuru Wiru', in *Family and Gender in the Pacific*, eds M. Jolly and M. Macintyre, Cambridge, 170–92.

——— 1992, 'Madness and Colonization: the Embodiment of Power in Pangia', in Alienating Mirrors: Christianity, Cargo Cults and Colonialism in Melanesia, ed. A. Lattas, *Oceania* 63(1): 15–26.

Clark, M.A. 1958, 'Jahresbericht Wabi Circuit', MS.

——— 1959, 'Jahresbericht Wabi Circuit', MS.

Colpe, C. 1986, 'Was bedeutet "Untergang einer Religion"?', in *Der Untergang von Religionen,* ed. H. Zinser, Berlin, 9–33.

Counts, D.A. 1978, 'Christianity in Kaliai: Response to Missionization in Northwest New Britain', in *Mission, Church and Sect in Oceania,* eds J. Boutilier, D.T. Hughes and S.W. Tiffany, Lanham, 355–94.

Counts, D.R. and Counts, D.A. 1976, 'Apprehension in the Backwaters', *Oceania* 46(4): 283–305.

Crittenden, R. 1987, 'Aspects of Economic Development on the Nembi Plateau, Papua New Guinea', *The Journal of the Polynesian Society* 96(3): 335–59.

—— and Schiefflin, E.L. 1991, 'The Back Door to the Purari', in *Like People You See in a Dream: First Contact in Six Papuan Societies*, eds E.L. Schiefflin and R. Crittenden, Stanford, 88–124.

Dabrowski, W.Z. 1991, 'A Line to Heaven: the Gamagai Religious Imagination' (Ph.D. diss., Australian National University).

Delbos, G. 1985, *The Mustard Seed: From a French Mission to a Papuan Church 1885–1985*, Port Moresby (French orig. 1984).

Doetsch, R. and Jentsch, Th. 1986, *Keman. Eine Siedlung im Hochland von Papua-Neuguinea*, Berlin.

Dubiel, H. 1992, 'Der Fundamentalismus der Moderne', *Merkur* 9/10: 747–62.

Ebertz, M.N. 1992, 'Wider die Relativierung der heiligen Ordnung: Fundamentalismen im Katholizismus', *Aus Politik und Zeitgeschichte*. Beilage zur Wochenzeitung 'Das Parlament' B 33: 11–22.

Eckert, G. 1940, 'Prophetentum und Kulturwandel in Melanesien', *Baessler Archiv* 23: 26–41.

Errington, F. 1974, 'Indigenous Ideas of Order, Time and Transition in a New Guinea Cargo Movement", *American Ethnologist* 1: 255–67.

Essai, B. 1961, *Papua and New Guinea: a Contemporary Survey*, Melbourne.

Feil, D.K. 1983, 'A World without Exchange: Millennia and the Tee Ceremonial System in Tombema-Enga Society (New Guinea)', *Anthropos* 78: 89–106.

Festinger, L., Riecken, H.W. and Schachter, St. 1964, *When Prophecy Fails: a Social and Psychological Study of a Modern Group that Predicted the Destruction of the World*, New York (orig. 1956).

Firth, R. 1955, 'The Theory of "Cargo" Cults: a Note on Tikopia', *Man* 55: 130–32.

—— 1970, *Rank and Religion in Tikopia: a Study in Polynesian Paganism and Conversion to Christianity*, London.

Fischer, H. 1992, *Weisse und Wilde. Erste Kontakte und Anfänge der Mission* (Materialien zur Kultur der Wampar, Papua New Guinea 1), Berlin.

Flannery, W. 1980, 'All Prophets: Revival Movements in the Catholic and Lutheran Churches in the Highlands', *Catalyst* 10(4): 229–57.

—— 1984, 'Mediation of the sacred', in *Religious Movements in Melanesia Today*, vol. 3, ed. W. Flannery, Goroka (Point Series 4), 117–57.

—— ed. 1983/84, *Religious Movements in Melanesia Today*, 3 vols (Point Series 2–4), Goroka.

Flasche, R. 1993, 'Heil', in *Handbuch religionswissenschaftlicher Grundbegriffe*, vol. 3, eds H. Cancik, B. Gladigow and K.-H. Kohl, Stuttgart, 66–74.

Forman, Ch.W. 1978, 'Foreign Missionaries in the Pacific Islands during the Twentieth Century', in *Mission, Church and Sect in Oceania*, eds J. Boutilier, D.T. Hughes and S.W. Tiffany (ASAO Monographs 6), Lanham, 35–63.

—— 1982, *The Island Churches of the Pacific: Emergence in the Twentieth Century* (American Society of Missiology Series 5), Maryknoll.

Fortune, R.F. 1935, *Manus Religion: an Ethnological Study of the Manus Natives of the Admirality Islands*, Nebraska.

Franklin, K.J. 1965, 'Kewa Social Organization', *Ethnology* 4: 408–20.

—— 1967, 'Names and Aliases in Kewa', *The Journal of the Polynesian Society* 76: 76–81.

—— 1971, *The Dialects of Kewa* (Pacific Linguistics Series B 10), Canberra.

—— 1989, 'Jack Hides' Visit to the Kewa Area', *The Journal of Pacific History* 24(1): 99–105.

—— and Franklin J. 1978, *A Kewa Dictionary* (Pacific Linguistics Series C 53), Canberra.

Fugmann, G. 1989, 'Melanesische Theologie', in *Papua-Neuguinea: Gesellschaft und Kirche. Ein ökumenisches Handbuch,* eds H. Wagner, G. Fugmann and H. Janssen (Erlanger Taschenbücher 93), Neuendettelsau, 229–46.

Garrett, J. 1982, *To Live among the Stars: Christian Origins in Oceania,* Genf.

Gellner, E. 1964, *Thought and Change,* London.

Gemeinschaft der Siebenten-Tags-Adventisten eds 1990, *Gelebter Glaube. Christsein Heute,* Hamburg.

Gesch, P. 1985, *Initiative and Initiation: a Cargo Cult-type Movement in the Sepik against Its Background in Traditional Village Religion* (Studia Instituti Anthropos 33), St. Augustin.

Ghaussy, G.A. 1989, 'Der islamische Fundamentalismus in der Gegenwart', in *Fundamentalismus in der modernen Welt,* ed. Th. Meyer, Frankfurt/M., 83–100.

Gibbs, P. 1977, 'The Cult from Lyeimi and the Ipili', *Oceania* 48(1): 1–25.

Gladigow, B. 1988a, 'Gegenstände und wissenschaftlicher Kontext von Religionswissenschaft', in *Handbuch religionswissenschaftlicher Grundbegriffe,* vol. 1, eds H. Cancik, B. Gladigow and M. Laubscher, Stuttgart, 26–40.

—— 1988b, 'Religionsgeschichte des Gegenstandes-Gegenstände der Religionsgeschichte', in *Religionswissenschaft. Eine Einführung,* ed. H. Zinser, Berlin, 6–37.

Glasse, R.M. 1963, 'Bingi at Tari', *The Journal of the Polynesian Society* 72(3): 270–71.

Guiart, J. 1951, '"Cargo Cults" and Political Evolution in Melanesia', *Mankind* 4(6): 227–29.

—— 1962, 'The Millenarian Aspect of Conversion to Christianity in the South Pacific', in Millennial Dreams in Action: Essays in Comparative Study, ed. S.L. Thrupp, *Comparative Studies in Society and History,* Supplement 2: 122–38.

Habel, N.C. ed. 1979, *Powers, Plumes and Piglets: Phenomena of Melanesian Religion,* Bedford Park.

Harding, Th. 1967, 'A History of Cargoism in Sio, North-East New Guinea', *Oceania* 38(1): 1–23.

Hayward, D.J. 1992, 'Christianity and the Traditional Beliefs of the Mulia Dani: an Ethnography of Religious Belief among the Western Dani of Irian Jaya' (Ph.D. diss., University of California).

Hecht, S. 1981, *Muruk and the Cross: Missions and Schools in the Southern Highlands* (Educational Research Unit Research Report 35), Port Moresby.

Heimann, M. 1989, 'Marxismus als Fundamentalismus?', in *Fundamentalismus in der modernen Welt,* ed. Th. Meyer, Frankfurt/M., 213–30.

Heine, P. 1992, 'Fundamentalisten und Islamisten. Zur Differenzierung der Re-Islamisierungsbewegungen', *Aus Politik und Zeitgeschichte. Beilage zur Wochenzeitung 'Das Parlament'* B 33: 23–30.

Hemminger, H. 1991, 'Fundamentalismus, ein vielschichtiger Begriff', in *Fundamentalismus in der verweltlichten Kultur,* ed. H. Hemminger, Stuttgart, 5–16.

Herdt, G. 1989, 'Self and Culture: Contexts of Religious Experience in Melanesia', in *The Religious Imagination in New Guinea,* eds G. Herdt and M. Stephen, New Brunswick, 15–40.

—— ed. 1982, *Rituals of Manhood: Male Initiation in Papua New Guinea*, Berkeley.

—— and Stephen, M. eds, 1989, *The Religious Imagination in New Guinea*, New Brunswick.

Hermann, E. 1992, 'The Yali Movement in Retrospect: Rewriting History, Re-defining "Cargo Cult"', in Alienating Mirrors: Christianity, Cargo Cults and Colonialism in Melanesia, ed. A. Lattas, *Oceania* 63(1): 55–71.

Hobsbawm, E. 1983, 'Introduction: Inventing Traditions' in *The Invention of Tradition*, eds E. Hobsbawm and T. Ranger, Cambridge, 1–14.

Hogbin, I.H. 1947, 'Native Christianity in a New Guinea village', *Oceania* 18(1): 1–35.

—— 1969, *Experiments in Civilization: the Effects of European Culture on a Native Community of the Solomon Islands*, London (orig. 1939).

Hughes, D.T. 1978, 'Mutual Biases of Anthropologists and Missionaries', in *Mission, Church and Sect in Oceania*, eds J. Boutilier, D.T. Hughes and S.W. Tiffany (ASAO Monographs 6), Lanham, 65–82.

Hughes, J. 1988, 'Ancestors, Tricksters and Demons: an Examination of Chimbu Interaction with the Invisible World', *Oceania* 59(1): 59–74.

Hummel, R. 1991, 'Fundamentalismus in Indien und im Islam', in *Fundamentalismus in der verweltlichten Kultur*, ed. H. Hemminger, Stuttgart, 17–65.

Idalovichi, I. 1989, 'Der jüdische Fundamentalismus in Israel', in *Fundamentalismus in der modernen Welt*, ed. Th. Meyer, Frankfurt/M., 101–20.

Imbrock, N. 1961, 'Jahresbericht Wabi Circuit', MS.

—— 1967, 'Jahresbericht Wabi Circuit', MS.

Jackson, J.E. 1990, '"I am a Fieldnote": Fieldnotes as a Symbol of Professional Identity', in *Fieldnotes: the Makings of Anthropology*, ed. R. Sanjek, Ithaca, 3–33.

Jebens, H. 1990a, *Eine Bewältigung der Kolonialerfahrung. Zur Interpretation von Cargo-Kulten im Nordosten von Neuguinea* (Mundus Reihe Ethnologie 35), Bonn.

—— 1990b, 'Cargo-Kulte und Holy Spirit Movements. Zur Veränderungs- und Widerstandsfähigkeit der traditionalen Religion im Hochland von Papua-Neuguinea', *Anthropos* 85: 403–13.

—— 1993, 'Heilsbewegung', in *Handbuch religionswissenschaftlicher Grundbegriffe*, vol. 3, eds H. Cancik, B. Gladigow and K.-H. Kohl, Stuttgart, 99–100.

—— 1997, 'Catholics, Seventh Day Adventists and the Impact of Tradition in Pairundu (Southern Highlands Province, Papua New Guinea)', in *Cultural Dynamics of Religious Change in Oceania*, eds T. Otto and A. Borsboom, Leiden, 33–43.

Jolly, M. and Thomas, N. 1992a, 'Introduction', in The Politics of Tradition in the Pacific, eds M. Jolly and N. Thomas, *Oceania* 62(4): 241–8.

—— eds, 1992b, The Politics of Tradition in the Pacific, *Oceania* 62(4).

Josephides, L. 1982, 'Kewa Stories and Songs', *Oral History* 10(2): iv-vi, 1–86.

—— 1983, 'Equal but Different?: the Ontology of Gender among Kewa', *Oceania* 53(3): 291–307.

—— 1985a, *The Production of Inequality: Gender and Exchange among the Kewa*, London.

—— 1985b, 'The Politics of Violence in Kewa Society (Southern Highlands)', in *Domestic Violence in Papua New Guinea*, ed. S. Toft (Law Reform Commission of Papua New Guinea Monographs 3), Pt. Moresby, 92–103.

—— 1985c, 'Bulldozers and Kings or Talk, Name, Group and Land: a Kewa Political Palindrome', in *Women in Politics in Papua New Guinea*, ed. M. O'Collins, Canberra, 6–18.

—— and Schiltz, M. 1991a, 'Through Kewa Country', in *Like People You See in a Dream: First Contact in Six Papuan Societies*, eds E.L. Schiefflin and R. Crittenden, Stanford, 198–224.

—— and Schiltz, M. 1991b, 'Kewa Aftermath', in *Like People You See in a Dream: First Contact in Six Papuan Societies*, eds E.L. Schiefflin and R. Crittenden, Stanford, 278–81.

Josephides, S. 1982, 'The Perception of the Past and the Notion of "Business" in a Seventh Day Adventist Village in Madang, New Guinea' (Ph.D. diss., University of London).

—— 1990, 'Seventh-day Adventism and the Boroi Image of the Past', in *Sepik Heritage: Tradition and Change in Papua New Guinea*, eds N. Lutkehaus, Ch. Kaufmann, W. Mitchell, D. Newton, L. Osmundsen and M. Schuster, Durham, 58–66.

Juillerat, B. 1980, 'Order or Disorder in Melanesian Religions?', *Man* 15(1): 372–74.

Kahn, M. 1983, 'Sunday Christians, Monday Sorcerers: Selective Adaptation to Missionization in Wamira', *The Journal of Pacific History* 18: 96–112.

Kallscheuer, O. 1989, 'Ökumene welcher Moderne? Fünf Nachfragen zur Marschrichtung im antifundamentalistischen Kampf', in *Fundamentalismus in der modernen Welt*, ed. Th. Meyer, Frankfurt/M., 62–80.

Kamale, K. 1982, 'Enemies, Red Men and Missionaries: Reflections on a Time of Change. As Told to Mary MacDonald', *Catalyst* 12: 192–95.

Keck, V. 1993, 'Talk about a Changing World: Young Yupno Men in Papua New Guinea Debate Their Future', *Canberra Anthropology* 16(2): 67–96.

Keesing, R.M. 1982, *Kwaio Religion: the Living and the Dead in a Solomon Island Society*, New York.

—— 1989, 'Some Problems in the Study of Oceanic Religion', MS.

Keesing, R.M. and Tonkinson, R. eds, 1982, 'Reinventing Traditional Culture: the Politics of Kastom in Island Melanesia', *Mankind* 14(4).

Kempf, W. 1992, '"The Second Coming of the Lord": Early Christianisation, Episodic Time, and the Cultural Construction of Continuity in Sibog', in *Alienating Mirrors: Christianity, Cargo Cults and Colonialism in Melanesia*, ed. A. Lattas, *Oceania* 63(1): 72–86.

Kepel, G. 1991, *Die Rache Gottes. Radikale Moslems, Christen und Juden auf dem Vormarsch*, München (orig. French).

Klinger, C. 1992, 'Faschismus: der deutsche Fundamentalismus', *Merkur* 9/10: 782–98.

Knochmalnik, D. 1992, 'Fundamentalismus und Judentum', *Aus Politik und Zeitgeschichte. Beilage zur Wochenzeitung 'Das Parlament'* B 33: 31–43.

Kohl, K.-H. 1986, 'Religiöser Partikularismus und kulturelle Transzendenz. Über den Untergang von Stammesreligionen in Indonesien', in *Der Untergang von Religionen*, ed. H. Zinser, Berlin, 193–220.

—— 1988, 'Ein verlorener Gegenstand? Zur Widerstandsfähigkeit authochthoner Religionen gegenüber dem Vordringen der Weltreligionen', in *Religionswissenschaft. Eine Einführung*, ed. H. Zinser, Berlin, 252–73.

Küenzelen, G. 1992, 'Feste Burgen: Protestantischer Fundamentalismus und die säkulare Kultur der Moderne', *Aus Politik und Zeitgeschichte*. Beilage zur Wochenzeitung 'Das Parlament' B 33: 3–10.

Kulick, D. and Stroud, Ch. 1990, 'Christianity, Cargo and Ideas of Self: Patterns of Literacy in a Papua New Guinean Village', *Man* 25: 286–303.

Lamnek, S. 1993, *Qualitative Sozialforschung, vol. 2: Methoden und Techniken*, München.

Lattas, A. ed. 1992, Alienating Mirrors: Christianity, Cargo Cults and Colonialism in Melanesia, *Oceania* 63(1).

Lau, J. 1992, 'Fundamentalismus: der häßliche Gegner der Moderne', *Merkur* 9/10: 910–16.

Laubscher, M. 1983, 'Religionsethnologie', in *Ethnologie. Eine Einführung*, ed. H. Fischer, Berlin, 231–56.

Lawrence, P. 1954, 'Cargo Cult and Religious Beliefs among the Garia', *International Archives of Ethnography* 47(1): 1–20.

—— 1956, 'Lutheran Mission Influence on Madang Societies', *Oceania* 27(2): 73–89.

—— 1964, *Road belong Cargo: a Study of the Cargo Movement in the Southern Madang District, New Guinea*, Manchester.

—— 1971, 'Statements about Religion: the Problem of Reliability', in *Anthropology in Oceania*, eds R. Hiatt and C. Jayawardena, Sydney, 139–54.

—— 1988, 'Twenty Years After: a Reconsideration of Papua New Guinea Seaboard and Highlands Religions', *Oceania* 59(1): 7–27.

—— and Meggitt, M.J. 1965a, 'Introduction', in *Gods, Ghosts and Men in Melanesia*, eds P. Lawrence and M.J. Meggitt, Melbourne, 1–26.

—— and Meggitt, M.J. eds, 1965b, *Gods, Ghosts and Men in Melanesia*, Melbourne.

Lederman, R. 1980, 'Who Speaks Here? Formality and the Politics of Gender in Mendi, Highland Papua New Guinea', *The Journal of the Polynesian Society* 89(4): 479–98.

—— 1981, 'Sorcery and Social Change in Mendi', *Social Analysis* 8:15–27.

—— 1982, 'Trends and Cycles in Mendi', *Bikmaus* 3: 5–14.

—— 1986a, *What Gifts Engender: Social Relations and Politics in Mendi, Highland Papua New Guinea*, Cambridge.

—— 1986b 'Changing times in Mendi: Notes towards Writing Highland New Guinea History', *Ethnohistory* 33(1): 1–30.

Lenturut, B. 1983, 'What the Charismatic Renewal Means for the Churches', in *Religious Movements in Melanesia Today*, vol. 2, ed. W. Flannery (Point Series 3), Goroka, 205–12.

LeRoy, J.D. 1975, 'Kewa Reciprocity: Co-operation and Exchange in a New Guinea Highland Culture' (Ph.D. diss., University of British Columbia).

—— 1979a, 'The Ceremonial Pig Kill of the South Kewa', *Oceania* 49(3): 179–209.

—— 1979b, 'Competitive Exchange in Kewa', *The Journal of the Polynesian Society* 88(1): 9–35.

—— 1981, 'Siblingship and Descent in Kewa Ancestries', *Mankind* 13(1): 25–36.

—— 1985a, *Fabricated World: an Interpretation of Kewa Tales*, Vancouver.

—— ed. 1985b, *Kewa Tales*. Vancouver.

Lewis, B. 1992, 'Der Traum von Koexistenz. Muslime, Christen und Juden', *Merkur* 9/10: 820–33.

Lewis, O. 1964, 'Seventh-day Adventism in a Mexican Village: a Study in Motivation and Culture Change', in *Process and Pattern in Culture: Essays in Honour of Julian H. Steward*, ed. R.A. Manners, Chicago, 63–83.

Linnekin, J. 1990, 'The Politics of Culture in the Pacific', in *Cultural Identity and Ethnicity in the Pacific*, eds J. Linnekin and L. Poyer, Honolulu, 149–73.

—— 1992, 'On the Theory and Politics of Cultural Construction in the Pacific', in The Politics of Tradition in the Pacific, eds M. Jolly and N. Thomas, *Oceania* 62(4): 249–63.

—— and Poyer, L. eds, 1990, *Cultural Identity and Ethnicity in the Pacific*, Honolulu.

Linton, R. 1943, 'Nativistic Movements', *American Anthropologist* 45: 230–40.

Löw, A. 1989, 'Fundamentalistischer und systematisch-theologischer Umgang mit biblischen Texten. Ein Vergleich', in *Religiöser Fundamentalismus*, eds C. Colpe and H. Papenthin (Dahlemer Hefte 10), Berlin, 123–29.

Lutzbetak, L.J. 1983, 'Prospects for a Better Understanding and Closer Cooperation between Anthropologists and Missionaries', in *Missionaries, Anthropologists and Cultural Change*, ed. D. Whiteman (Studies in Third World Societies 25), Williamsburg, 1–53.

MacDonald, M.N. 1984a, *Marriage and Family Life among the South Kewa* (Working Papers in Melanesian Marriage and Family Life 9), Goroka.

—— 1984b, 'Symbolism and Myth', in *An Introduction to Melanesian Religions*, ed. E. Mantovani, Goroka, 123–46.

—— 1984c, 'Magic, Medicine and Sorcery', in *An Introduction to Melanesian Religions*, ed. E. Mantovani, Goroka, 195–212.

—— 1984d, 'Melanesian Communities: Past and Present, *Point* 5: 213–30.

—— 1985, *Symbols of Life: an Interpretation of Magic*, Goroka.

—— 1991, *Mararoko: a Study in Melanesian Religion* (American University Studies Series 11. Anthropology and Sociology 43.), New York.

MacDowell, N. 1985, 'Past and Future: the Nature of Episodic Time in Bun', in *History and Ethnohistory in Papua New Guinea*, eds D. Gewertz and E. L. Schiefflin, Sydney, 26–39.

—— 1988, 'A Note on Cargo and Cultural Constructions of Change', *Pacific Studies* 11: 121–34.

Mai, P. 1981, 'The "Time of Darkness" or *Yuu Kuia*', in *Oral Tradition in Melanesia*, eds D. Denoon and R. Lacey, Port Moresby, 125–40.

Malinowski, B. 1935, *Coral Gardens and Their Magic: a Study of the Methods of Tilling the Soil and of Agricultural Rites in the Trobriand Islands*, 2 vols, London.

Matiabe, A. 1983, 'Revival Movements "Beyond the Ranges", Southern Highlands', in *Religious Movements in Melanesia Today*, vol. 2, ed. W. Flannery (Point Series 3), Goroka, 147–51.

—— 1987, 'General Perspective: a Call for Black Humanity to be Better Understood', in *The Gospel is not Western*, ed. G. Trompf, New York, 16–9.

May, J.D. 1985a, *Christian Fundamentalism and Melanesian Identity* (Occasional Papers of the Melanesian Institute 3), Goroka.

—— ed. 1985b, *Living Theology in Melanesia: a Reader*, Goroka.

Mayring, Ph. 1990, *Einführung in die qualitative Sozialforschung. Eine Anleitung zu qualitativem Denken*, München.

Meggitt, M.J. 1973, 'The Sun and the Shakers: a Millenarian Cult and Its Transformations in the New Guinea Highlands', *Oceania* 44(1): 1–37, 44(2): 109–26.

Meigs, A.S. 1984, *Food, Sex and Pollution: a New Guinea Religion*, New Brunswick.

Meyer, Th. 1989a, 'Einleitung', in *Fundamentalismus in der modernen Welt*, ed. Th. Meyer, Frankfurt/M., 7–9.

—— 1989b, 'Fundamentalismus. Die andere Dialektik der Aufklärung', in *Fundamentalismus in der modernen Welt*, ed. Th. Meyer, Frankfurt/M., 13–22.

Mihailic, F. 1971, *The Jacaranda Dictionary and Grammar of Melanesian Pidgin*, Pt. Moresby.

Mohr, H. 1993, 'Konversation/Apostasie', in *Handbuch religionswissenschaftlicher Grundbegriffe*, vol. 3, eds H. Cancik, B. Gladigow and K.-H. Kohl, Stuttgart, 436–45.

Morauta, L.P. 1972, 'The Politics of Cargo Cults in the Madang Area, *Man* 7(3): 430–47.

Mrossko, K.-D. 1986, 'Missionary Advance to the Highlands', in *The Lutheran Church in Papua New Guinea: the First Hundred Years 1886–1986*, eds H. Wagner and H. Reiner, Adelaide, 187–222.

Mühlmann, W.E. 1961a, *Chiliasmus und Nativismus. Studien zur Psychologie, Soziologie und historischen Kasuistik der Umsturzbewegungen*, Berlin.

—— 1961b, 'Das Mythologem von der verkehrten Welt', *Kölner Zeitschrift für Soziologie und Sozialpsychologie* 13(4): 614–24.

Narakobi, B. 1989, 'Melanesische Identität', in *Papua-Neuguinea: Gesellschaft und Kirche. Ein ökumenisches Handbuch,* eds H. Wagner, G. Fugmann and H. Janssen (Erlanger Taschenbücher 93), Neuendettelsau, 40–50.

Neumann, K. 1992, *Not the Way It Really Was: Constructing the Tolai Past* (Pacific Islands Monograph Series 10), Honolulu.

Nevermann, H. 1968, 'Die Religionen der Südsee', in *Die Religionen der Südsee und Australiens*, eds H. Nevermann, E.A. Worms and H. Petri (Die Religionen der Menschheit 5–2), Stuttgart, 1–123.

Odermatt, M. 1991, *Der Fundamentalismus. Ein Gott-eine Wahrheit-eine Moral? Psychologische Reflexionen*, Zürich.

Ogan, E. 1972, *Business and Cargo: Socio-economic Change among the Nasioi of Bougainville* (New Guinea Research Bulletin 44), Pt. Moresby.

Oosterwal, G. 1978, 'Introduction: Missionaries and Anthropologists', in *Mission, Church and Sect in Oceania*, eds J. Boutilier, D.T. Hughes and S.W. Tiffany (ASAO Monographs 6), Lanham, 31–4.

Opeba, W.J. 1987, 'Melanesian Cult Movements as Traditional Religious and Ritual Responses to Change', in *The Gospel is Not Western*, ed. G. Trompf, New York, 49–66.

Otto, T. 1992a, 'The Ways of Kastom: Tradition as Category and Practice in a Manus Village', in The Politics of Tradition in the Pacific, eds M. Jolly and N. Thomas, *Oceania* 62(4): 264–83.

—— 1992b, 'Introduction: Imagining Cargo Cults', in Imagining Cargo Cults, ed. T. Otto, *Canberra Anthropology* 15(2): 1–10.

—— ed. 1992c, Imagining Cargo Cults, *Canberra Anthropology* 15(2).

Paczensky, G.v. 1991, *Teurer Segen. Christliche Mission und Kolonialismus*, München.

Papenthin, H. 1989, 'Entstehung und Entwicklung des (klassischen) amerikanischen Fundamentalismus', in *Religiöser Fundamentalismus*, eds. C. Colpe and H. Papenthin (Dahlemer Hefte 10), Berlin, 13–52.

Patrick, A.N. 1987, 'Seventh-day Adventist History in the South Pacific: a Review of Sources', *The Journal of Religious History* 14(3): 307–26.

Pickering, W.S.F. ed. 1992, Anthropology and Missionaries: Some Case-studies, *The Journal of the Anthropological Society of Oxford* 23(2).

Ploeg, A. 1975, 'Wok Kako and Wok Bisnis', in *Explorations between Indigenous and Christian Traditions*, eds. W.E.A. van Beek and J.H. Scherer, The Hague, 190–212.

Pokawin, P.S. 1987, 'Interaction between indigenous and Christian Traditions', in *The Gospel is Not Western*, ed. G. Trompf, New York, 23–31.

Puruno, T. 1988, 'Brief History: Southern Highlands Province', in T. Puruno, *Provincial Brief for 10th Anniversary of Southern Highlands Provincial Government, 5–8th August, 1988*, Mendi, 1–25.

Quack, A. 1986, 'The Ambivalent Relationship between Mission and Anthropology: Criticism and Suggestions', *Verbum SVD* 27(3): 221–34.

Rath, G. 1989, *Papua-Neuguinea. Ein südpazifisches Entwicklungsland auf dem Weg in das Jahr 2000* (Mitteilungen des Instituts für Asienkunde Hamburg 178), Hamburg.

Read, K.E. 1955, 'Morality and the Concept of the Person among the Gahuku-Gama', *Oceania* 25(4): 233–82.

———— 1958, 'A "Cargo" Situation in the Markham Valley, New Guinea', *Southwestern Journal of Anthropology* 14: 273–94.

Renali, C. 1991, *The Roman Catholic Church's Participation in the Ecumenical Movement in Papua New Guinea: a Historical, Contextual, and Pastoral Perspective*, Rome.

Riesebrodt, M. 1990, *Fundamentalismus als patriarchalische Protestbewegung. Amerikanische Protestanten (1910–1928) und iranische Schiiten (1961–1979) im Vergleich*, Tübingen.

Robertson, D.E. (prepared by) 1990, *Church Leader's Manual: Island National Leadership Development, South Pacific Division, Seventh-day Adventist Church*, Victoria.

Robin, R.W. 1980, 'The Presence, Influence and Effects of Christian Missions on the People of the Southern Highlands Province, Papua New Guinea' (Ph.D. diss., University of Papua New Guinea).

———— 1981a, 'Revival Movement Hysteria in the Southern Highlands of Papua New Guinea', *Journal for the Scientific Study of Religion* 20(2): 150–63.

———— 1981b, 'The Role of Foreign Missions in an Independent Papua New Guinea', *Australian Outlook* 35(2): 138–51.

———— 1981c, 'An End of the World Revival at Erave, PNG', *Yagl-Ambu* 8(1): 52–66.

———— 1982, 'Revival Movements in the Southern Highlands Province of Papua New Guinea', *Oceania* 52: 320–43.

Rohr, E. 1987, '"Gott liebt uns ebenso wie die Weißen". Die sanften Verführer nutzen die Fehler der Herrschenden aus', *Die Zeit extra* 40, 25 September 1987, 49–52.

Ross, H.M. 1978, 'Competition for Beagu Souls: Mission Rivalry on Malaita, Solomon Islands', in *Mission, Church and Sect in Oceania*, eds. J. Boutilier, D.T. Hughes and S.W. Tiffany (ASAO Monographs 6), Lanham, 163–200.

Rudolph, W. 1964, '"Akkulturation" und Akkulturationsforschung', *Sociologus* 14(2): 97–113.

Ryan, D'Arcy 1955, 'Clan Organization in the Mendi Valley', *Oceania* 26(2): 79–90.

———— 1959, 'Clan Formation in the Mendi Valley', *Oceania* 29(4): 257–90.

Ryan, Dawn 1969, 'Christianity, Cargo Cults, and Politics among the Toaripi of Papua', *Oceania* 40(1): 99–118.

Schaeffler, R. 1986, 'Religionsimmanente Gründe für religionshistorische Krisen', in *Der Untergang von Religionen*, ed. H. Zinser, Berlin, 243–61.

Schiefflin, E.L. 1976, *The Sorrow of the Lonely and the Burning of the Dancers*, New York.

——— 1981a, 'The End of Traditional Music, Dance and Body Decoration in Bosavi, Papua New Guinea' in *The Plight of Periphal People in Papua New Guinea, Vol.1: the iInland Situation*, eds E.L. Schiefflin, G. Robert and J.G. Flanagan (Cultural Survival Occasional Paper 7), Port Moresby, 1–22 (orig. 1978).

——— 1981b, 'Evangelical Rhetoric and the Transformation of Traditional Culture in Papua New Guinea', *Comparative Studies in Society and History* 23: 150–56.

——— 1991, 'The Great Papuan Plateau' in *Like People You See in a Dream: First Contact in Six Papuan Societies*, eds E.L. Schiefflin and R. Crittenden, Stanford, 58–87.

——— and Crittenden R. eds 1991a, *Like People You See in a Dream: First Contact in Six Papuan Societies*, Stanford.

——— 1991b, 'Aftermath and Reflections', in E.L. Schiefflin and R. Crittenden, *Like People You See in a Dream: First Contact in Six Papuan Societies*, Stanford, 295–300.

——— 1991c, 'Appendix A: the Origins of the Story of Walali', in E.L. Schiefflin and R. Crittenden, *Like People You See in a Dream: First Contact in Six Papuan Societies,* Stanford, 295–300.

Schifferle, A. 1991, 'Katholischer Traditionalismus und Fundamentalismus', in *Fundamentalismus in der verweltlichten Kultur*, ed. H. Hemminger, Stuttgart, 66–96.

Schütze, Ch. 1992, 'Ökologischer Fundamentalismus?', *Merkur* 9/10: 799–808.

Schulze, H. 1987, *Menschenfischer-Seelenkäufer. Evangelikale und fundamentalistische Gruppen und ihr Wirken in der 3. Welt*, München.

Schwarz, B. 1980, 'Seeking to Understand Cargo as a Symbol, *Catalyst* 10(1): 14–27.

——— 1984, 'African Movements and Melanesian Movements', in *Religious Movements in Melanesia Today*, vol. 3, ed. W. Flannery (Point Series 4), Goroka, 14–28.

Senft, G. 1992, 'Magic, Missionaries, and Religion: Some Observations from the Trobriand Islands', MS.

Seventh-day Adventists eds, 1988, *Seventh-day Adventists Believe…a Biblical Exposition of 27 Fundamental Doctrines*, Washington.

——— 1990, *Seventh-day Adventist Church Manual: Issued by the General Conference of Seventh-day Adventists*, rev. edn, (no place).

Sillitoe, P. 1991, 'From the Waga Furari to the Wen', in E.L. Schiefflin and R. Crittenden, *Like People You See in a Dream: First Contact in Six Papuan Societies*, Stanford, 147–67.

Smith, M.F. 1980, 'From Heathen to Atheist: Changing Views of Catholicism in a Papua New Guinea Village', *Oceania* 51(1): 40–52.

——— 1990, 'Catholicism, Capitalist Incorporation, and Resistance in Kragur Village', in *Christianity in Oceania: Ethnographic Perspectives*, ed. J. Barker (ASAO Monographs 12), Lanham, 149–72.

Smits, K. 1981, *Askim na bekim: long bilip bilong Katolik Sios na ol narapela sios na lain bilipman*, Madang.
Stagl, J. 1971, *Der Geschlechtsantagonismus in Melanesien* (Acta Ethnologica et Linguistica 22. Series Oceania 4), Wien.
––––––– 1974, *Die Morphologie segmentärer Gesellschaften. Dargestellt am Beispiel des Hochlandes von Neuguinea* (Studia Ethnologica 48). Meisenheim am Glan.
Steinbauer, F. 1971, *Die Cargo-Kulte. Als religionsgeschichtliches und missionstheologisches Problem*. Erlangen.
Steley, D. 1988, 'A Note on Seventh-day Adventist Sources for the Pacific', *The Journal of Pacific History* 23(1): 102–5.
Stephen, M. 1979, 'Dreams of Change: the Innovative Role of Altered States of Consciousness in Traditional Melanesian Religion', *Oceania* 50(1): 3–22.
––––––– ed. 1987, *Sorcerer and Witch in Melanesia*, New Brunswick.
Stephenson, G. 1986, 'Säkularisierung als mögliche Form des Untergangs?' in *Der Untergang von Religionen*, ed. H. Zinser, Berlin, 295–308.
Stöhr, M. 1989, 'Fundamentalismus-protestantische Beobachtungen', in *Fundamentalismus in der modernen Welt*, ed. Th. Meyer, Frankfurt/M., 231–47.
Strathern, A. 1968, 'Sickness and Frustration: Variations in Two New Guinea Highlands Societies', *Mankind* 6(11): 545–51.
––––––– 1969, 'Finance and Production: Two Strategies in New Guinea Highlands Exchange Systems', *Oceania* 40(1): 42–67.
––––––– 1970, 'Male Initiation in New Guinea Highlands Societies', *Ethnology* 9(4): 373–79.
––––––– 1971a, *The Rope of Moka: Big-men and Ceremonial Exchange in Mount Hagen, New Guinea* (Cambridge Studies in Social Anthropology 4), Cambridge.
––––––– 1971b, 'Cargo and Inflation in Mount Hagen', *Oceania* 41(4): 255–65.
––––––– 1979/80, 'The Red Box Money-cult in Mount Hagen 1968–71', *Oceania* 50(2): 88–102, 50(3): 161–75.
––––––– 1982, 'Social Change in Mount Hagen and Pangia', *Bikmaus* 3(1): 90–100.
––––––– 1984, *A Line of Power*, London.
––––––– 1988, 'Conclusions: Looking at the Edge of the New Guinea Highlands from the Center', in *Mountain Papuans: Historical and Comparative Perspectives from New Guinea Fringe Highlands Societies*, ed. J.F. Weiner, Ann Arbor, 187–212.
––––––– 1991, 'Fertility and Salvation: the Conflict between Spirit Cult and Christian Sect in Mount Hagen', *Journal of Ritual Studies* 5(1): 51–64.
Strathern, M. 1972, *Women In Between*, London.
Strauss, H. 1962, *Die Mi-Kultur der Hagenbergstämme im östlichen Zentral-Neuguinea. Eine religionssoziologische Studie*. Unter Mitarbeit von Herbert Tischner (Monographien zur Völkerkunde 3), Hamburg.
Strelan, J. 1977, *Search for Salvation: Studies in the History and Theology of Cargo Cults*, Adelaide.
Ströbele-Gregor, J. 1988, *Dialektik der Gegenaufklärung. Zur Problematik fundamentalistischer und evangelikaler Missionierung bei den urbanen aymara in La Paz (Bolivien)* (Mundus Reihe Ethnologie 24), Bonn.
––––––– 1989, 'Ein schmaler Pfad zum besseren Leben? Zu Ursachen und Folgen des Missionierungserfolges fundamentalistischer und evangelikaler Religionsgemeinschaften in Bolivien', *Peripherie* 35: 57–79.

Süss, G.P. 1978, *Volkskatholizismus in Brasilien. Zur Typologie und Strategie gelebter Religiosität* (Gesellschaft und Theologie, Abt. Systematische Beiträge 24), München.

Sutlive, V.H. Jr. 1983, 'Anthropologists and Missionaries: Eternal Enemies or Colleagues in Disguise?', in *Missionaries, Anthropologists and Cultural Change*, ed. W. Flannery (Studies in Third World Societies 25), Williamsburg, 55–90.

Teske, G. 1983, 'The Holi Spirit Movement among Enga Lutherans (Kandep)', in *Religious Movements in Melanesia Today*, vol. 2, ed. W. Flannery (Point Series 3), Goroka, 113–24.

Thiede, W. 1991, 'Fundamentalistischer Bibelglaube im Licht reformatorischen Schriftverständnisses', in *Fundamentalismus in der verweltlichten Kultur*, ed. H. Hemminger, Stuttgart, 131–62.

Thomas, N. 1992a, 'The Inversion of Tradition', *American Ethnologist* 19(2): 213–32.

———— 1992b, 'Contrasts: Marriage and Identity in Western Fiji', in The Politics of Tradition in the Pacific, eds M. Jolly and N. Thomas, *Oceania* 62(4): 317–29.

Tiffany, S.W. 1978, 'The Politics of Denomination in Samoa', in *Mission, Church and Sect in Oceania*, eds. J. Boutilier, D.T. Hughes and S.W. Tiffany (ASAO Monographs 6), Lanham, 423–556.

Tomasetti, F. 1976, *Traditionen und Christentum im Chimbu-Gebiet Neuguineas. Beobachtungen in der lutherischen Gemeinde Pare* (Arbeiten aus dem Seminar für Völkerkunde der Johann Wolfgang Goethe-Universität Frankfurt/M. 6), Wiesbaden.

Toren, C. 1988, 'Making the Present, Revealing the Past: the Mutability and Continuity of Tradition as Process', *Man* 23(4): 696–717.

Triebel, J. ed. 1988, *Der Missionar als Forscher. Beiträge christlicher Missionare zur Erforschung fremder Kulturen und Religionen* (Missionswissenschaftliche Forschungen 21), Gütersloh.

Trompf, G.W. 1991, *Melanesian Religion*, Cambridge.

———— ed. 1987, *The Gospel is Not Western: Black Theologies from the Southwest Pacific*, New York.

———— ed. 1990, *Cargo Cults and Millenarian Movements: Transoceanic Comparisons of New Religious Movements* (Religion and Society 29), Berlin.

Tuza, E. 1984, 'Foreword', in *Religious Movements in Melanesia Today*, vol. 3, ed. W. Flannery (Point Series 4), Goroka, vi–ix.

Uplegger, H. and W.E. Mühlmann 1961, 'Die Cargo-Kulte in Neuguinea und Insel-Melanesien', in W.E. Mühlmann, *Chiliasmus und Nativismus. Studien zur Psychologie, Soziologie und historischen Kasuistik der Umsturzbewegungen*, Berlin, 165–89.

Vicedom, G.F. and Tischner, H. 1943–48, *Die Mbowamb. Die Kultur der Hagenberg-Stämme im östlichen Zentral-Neuguinea*, vol. 2 (Monographien zur Völkerkunde 1), Hamburg.

Vivelo, F.R. 1988, *Handbuch der Kulturanthropologie. Eine grundlegende Einführung*, München (English orig. 1978).

Voll, K. 1989, 'Fundamentalistische Tendenzen unter Hindus und Moslems in Indien', in *Fundamentalismus in der modernen Welt*, ed. Th. Meyer, Frankfurt/M., 155–92.

Vrijhoff, P.H. and Waardenburg, J. eds 1979, *Official and Popular Religion: Analysis of a Theme for Religious Studies* (Religion and Society 19), The Hague.

Wagner, Herwig and Reiner, H. eds 1986, *The Lutheran Church in Papua New Guinea: the First Hundred Years 1886–1986*, Adelaide.

Wagner, R. 1975, *The Invention of Culture*, Englewood Cliffs.

Walf, K. 1989, 'Fundamentalistische Strömungen in der Katholischen Kirche', in *Fundamentalismus in der modernen Welt*, ed. Th. Meyer, Frankfurt/M., 248–62.

Wassmann, J. 1992, 'Vorwort', in *Abschied von der Vergangenheit*, ed. J. Wassmann, Berlin, 7–22.

Weber, M. 1991, 'Wissenschaft als Beruf', in M. Weber, *Schriften zur Wissenschaftslehre*, ed. and intr. Michael Sukale, Stuttgart, 237–73 (orig. 1919).

Weeks, S.G. 1987, 'Introduction: Looking at the New Guinea Highlands from Its Edge', in *Mountain Papuans: Historical and Comparative Perspectives from New Guinea Fringe Highlands Societies*, ed. J.F. Weiner, Ann Arbor, 1–38.

Weiner, J.F. ed. 1988, *Mountain Papuans: Historical and Comparative Perspectives from New Guinea Fringe Highlands Societies*, Ann Arbor.

Whiteman, D.L. 1980, 'Melanesians and Missionaries: an Ethnohistorical Study of Socio-religious Change in the Southwest Pacific' (Ph.D. diss., Southern Illinois University).

———— ed. 1983, *Missionaries, Anthropologists and Cultural Change* (Studies in Third World Societies 25), Williamsburg.

Williams, F.E. 1928, *Orokaiva Magic*, London.

———— 1976, 'The Vailala Madness and the Destruction of Native Ceremonies in the Gulf Division', in *'The Vailala Madness' and Other Essays*, ed. E. Schwimmer, London, 331–84 (orig. 1923).

Worsley, P. 1957, *The Trumpet Shall Sound: a Study of 'Cargo' Cults in Melanesia*, London.

———— 1973, *Die Posaune wird erschallen. 'Cargo'-Kulte in Melanesien*, London (English orig. 1957).

Wurm, S.A. 1982, *Papuan Languages of Oceania* (Ars Linguistica 7), Tübingen.

Young, M.W. 1977, 'Doctor Bromilow and the Bwaidoka Wars', *The Journal of Pacific History* 12(3): 130–53.

Zelenietz, M. and Lindenbaum, S. eds 1981, Sorcery and Social Change in Melanesia, *Social Analysis* 8.

Zinser, H. 1984/85, 'Einführung in die Religionswissenschaft' MS.

———— 1988, 'Religionsphänomenologie', in *Handbuch religionswissenschaftlicher Grundbegriffe*, vol. 1, eds H. Cancik, B. Gladigow and M. Laubscher, Stuttgart, 436–45.

———— 1992, 'Einige Überlegungen zum Fundamenalismus' MS.

Zöllner, S. 1977, *Lebensbaum und Schweinekult. Die Religion der Jali im Bergland von Irian-Jaya (West-Neuguinea)*, Wuppertal.

Index